# CATEGORICALLY SPEAKING

## A
## REFERENCE WORK AND STUDY GUIDE
## FOR REALTIME WRITING

compiled by
Laurie Boucke

WHITE
BOUCKE
PUBLISHING
LAFAYETTE, COLORADO

First Published July 1996
Second Edition February 2006

Cover design by Rob Boucke
élan Mira and Stentura images courtesy of Stenograph, L.L.C.

ISBN-10: 1-888580-35-6
ISBN-13: 978-888580-35-8

**Printed in USA**

Library of Congress Cataloging-in-Publication Data

Boucke, Laurie.
    Categorically speaking : a reference work and study guide for realtime writing / compiled
    by Laurie Boucke.--2nd ed.
        p. cm.
    ISBN-13: 978-1-888580-35-8 (alk. paper)
    ISBN-10: 1-888580-35-6 (alk. paper)
    1. Computer-aided transcription systems.  2. Stenotypy.  I. Title.
    Z51.5.B68 2006
    635'.340285--dc22                                                    2005033298

PO BOX 400, LAFAYETTE, CO 80026, USA
www.white-boucke.com

# CATEGORICALLY SPEAKING

# CONTENTS

## PART 3: ALPHABETS & NUMBERS

## PART 4: A LEXICON OF WORD ASSOCIATIONS

# CATEGORICALLY SPEAKING

# INTRODUCTION

## GENERAL

*CATegorically Speaking* is a reference work and study guide designed to facilitate the learning of briefs, phrases and conflict resolution techniques for realtime writing. It contains briefs for alphabets, antonyms, blind/visually-impaired nomenclature, church/religious vocabulary, computer/internet terms, deaf/hearing-impaired nomenclature, homonyms, medical terms, numbers, Q&A and stenonymns. It also provides word compacting strategies, short-form prefix roots/foundations, short-form suffix roots/foundations and more.

This work can be used in conjunction with the *Brief Encounters* court-reporting dictionary which contains an extensive collection of realtime briefs and phrases. The two books complement each other in many ways. Both use a common philosophy to construct conflict-free briefs and phrases. (Note that this printing is conflict-free in conjunction with the fourth edition of *Brief Encounters*.) *CATegorically Speaking* presents guidelines for stylizing short-form outlines and features specialized vocabulary. It contains many single-syllable words that are outside the scope of *Brief Encounters*.

## GUIDE TO THIS REFERENCE WORK

- **Writing Conventions**
  A hyphen is used with vowelless entries to indicate the keyboard location of the consonant(s).
  > B– *("be")* indicates an initial consonant on the left side of the keyboard.
  > –RS *("remain silent")* indicates final consonants on the right side of the keyboard.
  > N–FRGS *("information")* indicates initial and final consonants.
  A slash (/) indicates stroke separation, e.g., BUNL/–G for *"bundling"* (avoids conflict with BUJ for *"budge"*).
  A variety of character combinations (some coined by the author) are used to provide easy-to-recognize-and-remember, conflict-free entries. Benefits of these outlines include their easy readability, instant recognition and association with the corresponding English.

- **Multicharacter Combinations**
  The following prefixes and word beginnings are included in this dictionary:
  > emb-, emp-, imb-, imm-, imp- = KB–, e.g., KBAK for *"impact."*
  > end-, ent-, ind-, int- = SPW–, e.g., SPWEFR for *"endeavor."*
  > sub-, cereb- = SB– (SPW–), e.g., SBORN (SPWORN) for

"*subordinate*" and SBRAL (SPWRAL) for "*cerebral.*"
z- = S*, e.g., ZIRP (S*IRP) for "*zipper.*"

TKPW– is normally written as initial G–, except when designating DB– e.g., DBAR for "*debar.*"

The following suffixes and word endings are included in this book:
-cal & -kle = –BLG, e.g., NURKL (NURBLG) for "*neurological*"
   and TAKL (TABLG) for "*tackle.*"
-ism = –FM, e.g., SEFM for "*sexism.*"
-mp = –FRP, e.g., HAMP (HAFRP) for "*hamper.*"
-nk = –FRPBG, e.g., FOENK (FOEFRPBG) for "*phone call.*"
-rv = –FRB, e.g., WREFRB for "*web server.*"
-tional = –LGS & –BLGS, e.g., FUNLGS for "*functional*" and
   RUXL (RUBLGS) for "*instructional.*"
-v = *F, e.g., SIVL (S*IFL) for "*civil.*"

–F is used for final "*s,*" e.g., SPLAEFD for "*displaced.*"
–FPLT is written as –FMT for words ending in "*ment,*" e.g.,
   SPLAEFMT for "*displacement.*"
–PL is normally written as final –M, except when more
   phonetically logical, e.g., PURPL for "*purple*" and BRUPL
   for "*abruptly.*"
*S is used for the suffix "*st,*" e.g., M*ES for "*domestic.*"
*T is used for the suffix "*th,*" e.g., WA*IT for "*one-eighth.*"

The asterisk is used as an apostrophe in some contractions, e.g., SH*ES for "*she's*" and W*ER for "*we're.*"

- **"Plural s" and "Final-s Sound"**
  A "plural s" and the "final-s sound" can be written three different ways: (–S, –Z and –F) in order to assist in the formation of briefs and to avoid conflicts. In this book, –F is often used for a "near-final-s," e.g., KPREFD for "*expressed*" and KAUFG for "*causing.*"

# CONFLICT RESOLUTION

The following techniques are employed to avoid conflicts.

- **Asterisk**
  When the same outline is used for two different words, an asterisk is used with one of the outlines. In general, the most frequently used word or phrase is written without an asterisk. Use OX for "*objection*" and O*X for "*ox.*"
  An asterisk is often used to render initial capital letters. Use HAOL for "*high school*" and HAO*L for "*High School.*"
  Where possible, alternative outlines are given for asterisked entries. Thus, KAENDZ and/or K*ENDZ can be used for "*contends.*"

- **Extra Vowels**
  An extra (nonphonetic) vowel may be added to an outline to avoid conflicts. Use KAENDZ for "*contends*" (avoids conflict with KENDZ for "*can he understand*").

- **Stenonyms**
  "Stenonyms" are steno outlines that have the same sound but are written differently (and usually represent different words). Use TWAIT for "*actuate*" and TWAET for "*activate.*"

- **Shadows**

  Although shadow-steno outlines are not featured in this book, it is important to remember that in many cases, shadows can successfully be incorporated into your dictionary. The problematic final –F can often include –R in additional entries. For example, to be sure you stroke *"evasiveness"* (VAIVNS, VAIFNS) correctly, make additional dictionary entries for the word (VAIVRNS and VAIFRNS). Use this philosophy with as many of your shadow-strokes as possible. Other common problem areas include:

  Initial DP–. Initial DP– (TKP–) can often include initial B– (making it TKPW– or G–). The word *"deponent"* can be written DPOENT, and if doesn't conflict with another entry, GOENT.

  Initial DM–. Initial DM– (TKPH–) is sometimes stroked as GL– (making it TKPWHR–). The word *"demise"* can be written DMAOIS, and if doesn't conflict with another entry, GLAOIS.

  Final –TSZ. Final –TSZ is sometimes stroked as –TSDZ. The word *"presidency"* can be written P–TSZ and P–TSDZ.

# TO STUDENTS . . .

This reference work does not represent any particular theory. The majority of entries can be used with most common steno theories.

Your writing style will change over the years. The best way to ensure that you do not create conflicts when changing your writing is to make new entries realtime. The beauty of realtime is that you know immediately if you have made an error or if a stroke you make has already been assigned to another word or phrase. Most schools provide realtime writing equipment and software for building your dictionary.

If you do not have access to realtime equipment, keep an updated list of your briefs to avoid creating conflicts.

Before adopting a brief for a particular word or phrase, you should be able to automatically and easily stroke the word/phrase in full. Then gradually incorporate briefs through repeated practice. Concentrate on a few at a time until you can use them without hesitation.

If some briefs cause you trouble, it is better to put them aside for later evaluation and incorporation.

# PART 1

# GRAMMATICAL ELEMENTS

general
comparatives
prefixes
suffixes
superlatives
the, them, these, those

# GRAMMATICAL ELEMENTS

## GENERAL

Part 1 of this book consists of a compilation of briefs and phrases by grammatical elements. It also provides information on the formation of briefs and phrases.

### CONSTRUCTION OF BRIEFS AND PHRASES

Common ways to form briefs and phrases are as follows:

- Compact or slur words and phrases into abbreviations. This is done by omitting letters, syllables and/or words. For example, use STREN for *"strengthen,"* SGLAIT for *"strangulate"* and RUR for *"refresh your recollection."*

- Use one (usually the first) syllable of a word only. For example, use SKWAOEM for *"squeamish"* and SKIRM for *"skirmish."* For words beginning with vowels, the first syllable is often dropped. Use GOE for *"ego."*

- Reverse one or more letters. Use TAEMT for *"attempt"* and SPET for *"upset."*

- Combine word compaction with reversing one or more letters. Use KLID for *"liquid"* and SPAOEV for *"perceive."*

- Insert a letter. Use PAEFRNS for *"appearance fee"* (PAERNS for *"appearance"* plus F for FAOE for *"fee")*.

- Eliminate a vowel. Use REPGS for "representation" and R–PGS for *"reputation."*

- Superimpose/overlap letters by using two letters which share a common key. Use NLEJ (TPHREJ) for *"negligently"* and JLAOIS (SKWHRAOIS) for *"generalize."*

- Interrupt/overlap letters. Use STRIKL (STRIBLG) for *"strictly"* and VBOND (SPWROND) for *"vagabond."*

- Combine word compaction with letter insertion. Include a final –L with STROUS (*"industrious"*) for STROULS (*"industriously"*).

- Omit the initial letter of certain high-frequency prefixes when there are not enough one-stroke outlines to accommodate a large number of words beginning with the same prefix. Use KBURS for *"reimburse"* and VULGS for *"revulsion."*

- Use related and/or rhyming words. For example, use DWEP for *"deadly weapon"* and SWEP or SDWEP for *"assault with a deadly weapon."*

- Transform acronyms into long forms by adding one letter. Use AOEJ for *"EKG"* and AOEJD for *"electrocardiogram."* Use SH– for *"SHHH"* and SH–D for *"Self Help for Hard of Hearing People."*

- Use foreign language association. Briefs can be based on foreign words with the same or even a different meaning. Use the outline KRAOEB for *"Caribbean"* (*"Caribe"* is Spanish for *"Caribbean"*).

- Use a W to replace a "u" sound (use SWAE for *"survey"*) or insert a W before a "u" sound (use DWAOUL for *"duel"*).

- Relate a pair or set of briefs by using an asterisk or by changing one significant letter. Use J–R for *"junior"* and J*R for *"Jr."* Use DHARD for *"deaf and hard of hearing"* and DHORD for *"deaf or hard of hearing."*

- Use short-form prefixes and suffixes whenever possible (see pages 1-8 to 1-71).

- For verb root outlines that end or conflict with an outline ending with a final –D, use a final –T to form the past tense. For *"paddle"* (PALD) use PALTD for *"paddled."* Use SUNTD for *"sunned"* since SUND is used for *"Sunday."*

- For verb root outlines that end with a final –D, use an initial D– to form the past tense. Use DWED for *"wedded"* (W*ED = *"we'd"*). Use DMELD for *"meddled"* (MELD = *"meddle"* and M*ELD = *"meld"*).

# COMPARATIVES

**as**

| | |
|---|---|
| as bad as | SBADS |
| as big as | SBIGS |
| as deep as | SDAOEPS |
| as difficult as | SD–LS |
| as far as | SFARS |
| as fast as | SFA*S |
| as good as | SGAODZ, SG–S |
| as great as | SGRAETS |
| as hard as | SHARDZ |
| as high as | SHAOIS |
| as large as | SLARJS |
| as little as | SLILS |
| as long as | SLONGS |
| as low as | SLOEZ |
| as many as | SM–S |
| as much as | S–FPS, SMUFPS |
| as near as | SNAERS |
| as small as | SMAULS |
| as smart as | SMARTS |
| as soon as | SAONS |
| as well as | SWELS |
| as wide as | SWAOIDZ |

**better**

| | |
|---|---|
| better than | BERN |
| better than the | BERNT |
| better than these | BERNZ |
| better than those | BERNS |

**bigger**

| | |
|---|---|
| bigger than | BIRNG |
| bigger than the | BIRNGT |
| bigger than these | BIRNGZ |
| bigger than those | BIRNGS |

**braver**

| | |
|---|---|
| braver than | BRAIVRN, BRAIFRN |
| braver than the | BRAIVRNT, BRAIFRNT |
| braver than these | BRAIVRNZ, BRAIFRNZ |
| braver than those | BRAIVRNS, BRAIFRNS |

**closer**

| | |
|---|---|
| closer than | KLOERN |
| closer than the | KLOERNT, KLOERNTS |
| closer than these | KLOERNZ |
| closer than those | KLOERNS |

**darker**

| | |
|---|---|
| darker than | DRARN |
| darker than the | DRARNT |
| darker than these | DRARNZ |
| darker than those | DRARNS |

**deeper**
deeper than .................................................................. DAOERN
deeper than the ........................................................... DAOERNT
deeper than these ....................................................... DAOERNZ
deeper than those ...................................................... DAOERNS

**different**
different than.................................................................... DIFRN
different than them .......................................................... DIFM
different than these .......................................... DIFRNZ, DIFRNDZ
different than those......................................................... DIFRNTS

**drier**
drier than ................................................................... DRAOIRN
drier than the ............................................................ DRAOIRNT
drier than these ........................................................ DRAOIRNZ
drier than those ........................................................ DRAOIRNS

**farther**
farther than .................................................................... FARN
farther than the .............................................................. FARNT
farther than these ........................................................... FARNZ
farther than those ........................................................... FARNS

**faster**
faster than ................................................................... FAFRN
faster than the ............................................................ FAFRNT
faster than them .......................................................... FAFRM
faster than these .......................................................... FAFRNZ
faster than those .......................................................... FAFRNS

**fewer**
fewer than ................................................................. FAOURN
fewer than the ........................................................... FAOURNT
fewer than these ....................................................... FAOURNZ
fewer than those ................................... FAOURNTS, FAO*URNS

**greater**
greater than .............................................................. GRAERNT
greater than the ....................................................... GRAERNTD
greater than these ..................................................... GRAERNZ
greater than those ..................................................... GRAERNTS

**greener**
greener than the ...................................................... GRAOERNT
greener than these ................................................... GRAOERNZ
greener than those ................................................... GRAOERNS

**higher**
higher than.................................................................. HAOIRN
higher than the .......................................................... HAO*IRNT
higher than them ........................................................ HAOIRM
higher than these ....................................................... HAOIRNZ
higher than those ....................................................... HAOIRNS

**hotter**
hotter than ................................................................... HAURN
hotter than the ............................................................. HAURNT
hotter than these .......................................................... HAURNZ
hotter than those ................................... HAURNTS, HA*URNS

**later**
later than ............................................................................................... LAIRNT
later than the ............................................................. LAERNT, LAIRNTD
later than these .................................................................................. LAIRNZ
later than those ................................................................................. LA*IRNS

**less**
less than *(exception)* ....................................................................... LEN

**louder**
louder than .............................................................. LOURN, LOURND
louder than the ...................................................... LOURNT, LOURNTD
louder than these ........................................................................... LOURNZ
louder than those ........................................................................... LOURNS

**lower**
lower than ........................................................................................... LOERN
lower than the ................................................................................ LOERNT
lower than these ............................................................................. LOERNZ
lower than those ............................................................................. LOERNS

**meaner**
meaner than ................................................................................. MAOERNT
meaner than the ....................................................................... MAOERNTD
meaner than these ........................................... MAO*ERNZ, MAO*ERNDZ
meaner than those ................................................................... MAOERNTS

**more**
more than ...................................................................................... MOERN
more than the ............................................................................... MOERNT
more than them ............................................................................. MOERM
more than these ............................................................................ MOERNZ
more than those ............................................................................ MOERNS

**newer**
newer than ............................................................................... NAO*URN
newer than the ......................................................................... NAOURNT
newer than them ...................................................................... NAOURM
newer than these ........................................................................ NAOURZ
newer than those ..................................................................... NAO*URS

**nicer**
nicer than ..................................................................................... NAOIRN
nicer than the ............................................................................. NAOIRNT
nicer than these ......................................................................... NAOIRNZ
nicer than those ......................................................................... NAOIRNS

**quieter**
quieter than ............................................................................... KWAOIRN
quieter than the ...................................................................... KWAOIRNT
quieter than these ................................................................... KWAOIRNZ
quieter than those ................................................................... KWAOIRNS

**sharper**
sharper than ................................................................................ SHAERN
sharper than the ........................................................................ SHAERNT
sharper than these ..................................................................... SHAERNZ
sharper than those ..................................................................... SHAERNS

**shorter**
    shorter than ...................................................................................... SHOERNT
    shorter than the ............................................................................. SHOERNTD
    shorter than these ........................................... SHOERNZ, SHOERNDZ
    shorter than those ......................................................................... SHOERNTS

**slicker**
    slicker than ............................................................................................ SLIRN
    slicker than the ................................................................................... SLIRNT
    slicker than these ............................................................................... SLIRNZ
    slicker than those .............................................................................. SLIRNS

**slower**
    slower than ....................................................................................... SLOERN
    slower than the ............................................................................... SLOERNT
    slower than these ........................................................................... SLOERNZ
    slower than those ........................................................................... SLOERNS

**smaller**
    smaller than .................................................................. SMAURN, SMAUNL
    smaller than the .................................................... SMAURNT, SMAUNLT
    smaller than these ...................................................................... SMAURNZ
    smaller than those ...................................................................... SMAURNS

**smarter**
    smarter than ................................................................ SMAERN, SMARNT
    smarter than the .................................................. SMAERNT, SMARNTD
    smarter than these .............................................. SMAERNZ, SMARNZ
    smarter than those .............................................. SMAERNS, SMARNTS

**smoother**
    smoother than ............................................................................... SMAORN
    smoother than the ....................................................................... SMAORNT
    smoother than these ................................................................... SMAORNZ
    smoother than those ................................................................... SMAORNS

**sooner**
    sooner than ..................................................................................... SAORNT
    sooner than the ............................................................................ SAORNTD
    sooner than these .......................................................................... SAORNZ
    sooner than those .......................................................................... SAORNS

**stronger**
    stronger than .................................................................................. STRORN
    stronger than the ........................................................................... STRORNT
    stronger than these ...................................................................... STRORNZ
    stronger than those ...................................................................... STRORNS

**sweeter**
    sweeter than ................................................... SWRAOEN, SWAOERNT
    sweeter than the ............................................ SWRAOENT, SWAOERNTD
    sweeter than these .......................................... SWRAOENZ, SWAOERNZ
    sweeter than those ............................. SWRAOENTS, SWRAOENS, SWAOERNTS

**taller**
    taller than ......................................................................................... TAURN
    taller than the ................................................................................. TAURNT
    taller than these ............................................................................. TAURNZ
    taller than those ............................................................................. TAURNS

**warmer**

| | |
|---|---|
| warmer than | WRARMT |
| warmer than the | WRARMTD |
| warmer than these | WRARMZ |
| warmer than those | WRARMS |

**whiter**

| | |
|---|---|
| whiter than | WHAOIRN |
| whiter than the | WHAOIRNT |
| whiter than them | WHAOIRM |
| whiter than these | WHAOIRNZ |
| whiter than those | WHAOIRNS |

**worse**

| | |
|---|---|
| worse than | WORNS |
| worse than the | WORNT |
| worse than these | WORNZ |
| worse than those | WORNTS |

# PREFIXES

This section contains a selected compilation of prefixes/word beginnings used to form briefs, along with examples of each type of prefix.

The writing of briefs and phrases starting with these prefixes is by no means limited to these lists. The lists are provided to facilitate and accelerate the learning process. To avoid the possible creation of conflicts, new briefs should ideally be formulated during realtime writing.

Multi-syllabic words can, of course, be written phonetically with two or more strokes if so desired, in which case the steno prefix would be different from the brief forms in this book. For example, the *"adv-"* prefix in brief form can be written as DW– or V–, but in full phonetic form, would begin with the stroke AD/. In this example, VANS and DWANS are used as short forms of AD/VANS for *"advance."*

## PREFIXES (by English)

**ab-** (B–)
| | |
|---|---|
| abandon | BAUN |
| abbreviate | BRAOEVT |
| aboard | BAORD |
| abolishment | BLOMT |
| abortion | BORGS |

**acc-** (K–)
| | |
|---|---|
| acclaim | KLAEM |
| accommodate | KOMT |
| accompaniment | KPOIMT, KOEMT |
| accurate | KRAT |
| accuse | KAOUS |

**acq-** (KW–)
| | |
|---|---|
| acquaint | KWAIN |
| acquiesce | KWAOEF |
| acquire | KWAOIR |
| acquit | KWI |

**ad-** (D–)
| | |
|---|---|
| adaptation | DAPGS |
| addiction | DIX |
| addition | DIGS |
| address | DRAES |
| adrenal | DRAOEN, DRAOENL |

**adv-** (DW–, V–)

DW–
| | |
|---|---|
| advent | DWENT |
| adventure | DWUR |
| adverb | DWERB |
| adverse | DWER, DWERZ |
| advocate | DWOEK |

**V–**

| | |
|---|---|
| advancement | VAMT |
| advantage | VANG |
| advice | VIS |
| advisable | VIBL |
| advocate | VOEK |

## af- (F–)

| | |
|---|---|
| affect | FAEK |
| affiliate | FILT |
| affirmative | FRIF |
| afford | FAURD |
| afraid | FRAID |

## ag- (G–)

| | |
|---|---|
| again | GEN |
| agglomerate | GLOMT |
| aggravation | GRAEVGS |
| aggressive | GREV |
| agree | GRE |

## al- (L–)

| | |
|---|---|
| alarm | LARM |
| alert | LAERT |
| alignment | LAOIMT |
| alike | LOIK |
| alive | LOIV |

## am- (M–)

| | |
|---|---|
| amazement | MAEFMT |
| amelioration | MAOELGS |
| America | MERK |
| among | MONG |
| amusement | MAOUFMT |

## an- (N–)

| | |
|---|---|
| announcement | NOUMT |
| annoy | NOI |
| annuity | NAOUT |
| anoint | NOINT |
| anybody | NIB |

## app- (P–)

| | |
|---|---|
| apparently | PAERNL |
| appearance | PAERNS, PAOERNS |
| applicable | PLIBL |
| approach | PROEFP |
| appropriation | PROEPGS |

## as- (S–)

| | |
|---|---|
| ascend | SAEND |
| ascertain | SAERN |
| ask | SK– |
| asphalt | SFAULT |
| aspirin | SPRIN |

**ass-** (S–)
| | |
|---|---|
| assault | SAULT |
| assessment | SAEFMT |
| assignment | SAOIMT |
| associate | SOERB |
| assumption | SUMGS |

**ast-** (ST–)
| | |
|---|---|
| astonish | STIRB |
| astound | STOUN |
| astrology | STROLG |
| astronomer | STRORM |
| astronomy | STROM |

**at-** (T–)
| | |
|---|---|
| athlete | TLAOET |
| Atlanta | TLAN |
| at last | TLA*S |
| atrocious | TROERB |
| atrophy | TROF |

**att-** (T–)
| | |
|---|---|
| attach | TAFP |
| attempt | TAEMT |
| attend | TAEND |
| attitude | TAOUD |
| attributable | TRIBL |

**av-** (W–)
| | |
|---|---|
| averse | WERS |
| aversion | WERGS |
| avert | WERT |
| avoid | WOI |
| avoidable | WOIBL |

**aw-** (W–)
| | |
|---|---|
| awake | WOIK |
| award | WAURD |
| aware | WAIR |
| awareness | WAIRNS |
| away | WA |

**be-** (B–)
| | |
|---|---|
| behalf | BAF |
| behavioral | BAIVRL, BAIFRL |
| behold | BHOLD, BHOL |
| bereave | BAOEV |
| betrayal | BRAEL |

**bel-** (BL–)
| | |
|---|---|
| belabor | BLAIB |
| belated | BLAITD |
| belittle | BLIL |
| belligerent | BLIJ |
| below | BLO |

## bi- (B–)

| | |
|---|---|
| biceps | BEPS |
| bifocal | BAOIFL |
| bifurcation | BIFGS |
| bilingual | BLINL |
| bipartisan | BAURN |

## cap- (KP–)

| | |
|---|---|
| capability | KPAIBLT |
| capital | KPAL |
| capitol | KPOL |
| capitulation | KPIFPGS |
| capriciously | KPRIRBL, KPRAOERBL |

## center- (SN–)

| | |
|---|---|
| center | SNER |
| center field | SNEFLD |
| center of | SNEF |
| center of attention | SNEFGS |
| centerpiece | SN*ERP, SNAOERP |

## co- (KW–)

| | |
|---|---|
| coagulation | KWAGS |
| coherent | KWERNT |
| cohesive | KWAOEV |
| cohort | KWORT |
| coincidental | KWINL |

## col- (KL–)

| | |
|---|---|
| collaborate | KLAB |
| collateral | KLARL |
| collective | KLEV |
| colorblind | KLORB, KLORND |
| columnist | KLUMT |

## com- (KM–)

| | |
|---|---|
| comedian | KMAOED |
| comet | KMET |
| compel | KMEL |

## comb- (KB–)

| | |
|---|---|
| combatively | KBAVL |
| combattant | KBANT |
| combination | KBAIGS |
| combustible | KBUBL |
| combustion | KBUGS |

## comm- (KM–)

| | |
|---|---|
| commander | KMARN, KMARND |
| commencement | KMEMT |
| commissioner | KMIRGS |
| commodity | KMOD |
| communique | KMAI |

---

## comp- (KP–)

| | |
|---|---|
| compensate | KPEN |
| completely | KPLEL |
| composure | KPOUR |
| comprehensible | KPRENL |
| computer | KPR– |

## con- (K–, SK–)

K–

| | |
|---|---|
| concurrently | KRUNL, KRURNL |
| concussion | KUNGS |
| condemn | KEM |
| condo | KOND |
| condominium | KMIM |

SK–

| | |
|---|---|
| conceal | SKAOEL |
| conceivable | SKAOEVL |
| conception | SKEPGS |
| concession | SKEGS |
| condescension | SKENGS |

## conf- (KW–)

| | |
|---|---|
| confide | KWAOI |
| confine | KWAOIN |
| confirmation | KWIRGS, KWIRMGS |
| conformation | KWORGS, KWORMGS |
| confound | KWOUN |

## cons- (K–, SK–)

K–

| | |
|---|---|
| conscientious | K–RBS |
| considerable | K–RL |
| considerate | K–RT |
| constitution | KAOGS |
| constructive | KRUV |

SK–

| | |
|---|---|
| consensual | SKENL |
| conservative | SKEFT |
| consistently | SKINL |
| consortium | SKOERB |
| consultation | SKULGS |

## cont- (T–)

| | |
|---|---|
| contagious | TAIJ |
| contain | TAIN |
| contaminant | TAMT |
| contingency | TIJS |
| contingent | TIJ |

## contr- (KR–, TR–)

KR–

| | |
|---|---|
| contradiction | KRIX |
| contrary | KRAIR |

contribution ................................................................ KRAOUX
contributory negligence ........................................ KRIJ
control .......................................................................... KROL

TR–
contrivance .............................................................. TRAOIVNS
contrive ...................................................................... TRAOIV
controversial ........................................................... TROVL
controversy .............................................................. TROV
controvertible ......................................................... TROVBL

## conv- (KW–)

convention ................................................................ KWENGS
converge .................................................................... KWERJ
conversion ............................................................... KWERGS
conviction .................................................................. KWIX
convulsion ................................................................ KWULGS

## corr- (K–, KR–)

K–
correlation ............................................................... KORLGS
correspondent ....................................................... KORNT
corridor .................................................................... KOERD

KR–
correct ...................................................................... KREK
correct me if I'm wrong ....................................... KRONG
corroborate ............................................................. KROB
corrosion .................................................................. KROEGS
corruption ................................................................ KRUPGS

## counter- (K–)

counteract ............................................................... KRAKT
counterclockwise .................................................. KOUNK
counterfeit .............................................................. KIFT
counteroffer ........................................................... KRAUFR
counterproductive ............................................... KPRUV

## de- (D–)

deadlock .................................................................. DLOK
dealership ............................................................... DLERP
deduction ................................................................ DUX
degradation ............................................................ DEGS
dental ....................................................................... DENL

## deb- (DB–)

debar ........................................................................ DBAR
debate ...................................................................... DB–T
debenture ............................................................... DBUR
debrief ...................................................................... DBAOEF
debris ....................................................................... DBRI

## dec- (D–, SD–)

D–
decease .................................................................... DAOES

---

decedent ......................................................................... DAOENT
deceive ............................................................................. DAOEV
decorate ........................................................................... DRAIT
decorum ........................................................................... DOERM

SD–
decease ........................................................................... SDAOES
deceive ............................................................................. SDAOEV
decently ........................................................................... SDAOENL
deception ......................................................................... SDEPGS
decide ............................................................................... SDI

**decl-** (DL–)
declarant ......................................................................... DLAIRNT
declassification ............................................................... DLAFGS
declassify ........................................................................ DLAF
declination ...................................................................... DLINGS
decline ............................................................................ DLAOIN

**def-** (DW–)
default ............................................................................. DWALT, DWAULT
defeat .............................................................................. DWAOET
defection ......................................................................... DWEX
deficient ........................................................................... DWIRBT
deformity ......................................................................... DWORMT

**del-** (DL–)
deletion ............................................................................ DLAOEGS
deliberate ........................................................................ DLIB
delineate .......................................................................... DLAET
delinquent ........................................................................ DLINT
delirious ........................................................................... DLIR, DLAOERS

**dem-** (DM–)
demented .......................................................................... DMENTD
demolish ........................................................................... DMORB
demotion .......................................................................... DMOEGS
demur ............................................................................... DMUR
demurrer ........................................................................... DMRUR

**dep-** (D–, DP–)

D–
departmentalize ............................................................... DAP
deposition ........................................................................ DEPGS
depravity .......................................................................... DRAVT
depress ............................................................................ D–P
deputy .............................................................................. DEP

DP–
depart .............................................................................. DPART
departure ......................................................................... DPAUR
deponent .......................................................................... DPOENT
deportation ...................................................................... DPORGS
depose ............................................................................. DPOES

**der-** (DR–)

    derail .................................................................... DRAIL
    derangement ......................................................... DRAEMT
    derision ................................................................. DRIGS
    derive .................................................................... DRIF, DRAOIV
    derogatory ............................................................ DROG

**des-** (D–, SD–)

    D–
    description ............................................................. DRIPGS
    desk ..................................................................... DEFK
    dessert .................................................................. DERT
    destitution ............................................................. DAOGS, DAOUGS

    SD–
    desertion ............................................................... SDERGS
    deserve ................................................................. SDEFRB
    design ................................................................... SDAOIN
    designation ............................................................ SDEGS
    desire ................................................................... SDIR, SDAOIR

**det-** (D–)

    detach .................................................................. DAFP
    detain ................................................................... DAIN
    detention .............................................................. DENGS
    deterioration ......................................................... DRAEGS
    determination ........................................................ DERGS

**dev-** (DW–)

    devaluation ............................................................ DWALGS
    development .......................................................... DWOMT
    deviate .................................................................. DWAIT
    devotion ............................................................... DWOEGS
    devour .................................................................. DWOUR

**dia-** (D–)

    diabetic ................................................................. DAOIBT
    diagnose ............................................................... D–G
    diagonal ................................................................ DAG
    diagram ................................................................ DRAM
    dialect .................................................................. DLEKT

**dil-** (DL–)

    dilapidation ........................................................... DLAPGS
    dilate .................................................................... DLAIT
    dilation ................................................................. DLAIGS
    dilemma ................................................................ DLEM
    dilute ................................................................... DLAOUT

**dis-** (S–, SD–)

    S–
    disagreement ........................................................ SGREMT
    disappearance ....................................................... SPAERNS
    disappointment ...................................................... SPOIMT

disapproval ........................................................................ SPROVL
disbarment ........................................................................ SBARMT

SD–
disability .......................................................... SDABLT, SDAIBLT
disaster ............................................................. SDAFT, SDA*S
disband .......................................................................... SBAND
disbursement ................................................................ SDBURMT
dissociate ..................................................................... SDOERB

**disc-** (SK–)
disclaimer ...................................................................... SKLAIRM
disclosure ...................................................................... SKLOUR
discount ........................................................................ SKOUNT
discouragement ............................................................. SKOURMT
discrepancy .................................................................... SKREP

**dism-** (SM–)
dismantle ....................................................................... SMANL
dismay .......................................................................... SMAI
dismember ...................................................................... SMEB
dismissal ....................................................................... SMIFL
dismount ........................................................................ SMOUNT

**disp-** (SDP–, SP–)
SDP–
dispel ........................................................................... SDPEL
dispensable ................................................................... SDPENL
dispersal ....................................................................... SDPERL
dispose ......................................................................... SDPOES
disposition ..................................................................... SDPOGS

SP–
disparity ........................................................................ SPAIRT
dispatch ........................................................................ SPAFP
disposition ..................................................................... SPOGS
disprove ........................................................................ SPROV
disputable ..................................................................... SPAOUBL

**distr-** (DR–, SDR–)
DR–
distraction ..................................................................... SDRAX
distribute ...................................................................... DRIB
distribution ...................................................... DRAOUGS, DRAOUX
district .............................................................. DRIK, DRIKT
district court .................................................................. DRORT

SDR–
distraction ..................................................................... SDRAX
distraught ..................................................................... SDRAUT
distress ............................................................. SDREF, SDRES
distressful ..................................................................... SDREFL
distrust .............................................................. SDRUF, SDRUFT

## div- (DW–)

| | |
|---|---|
| divergent | DWERNT |
| divestiture | DWAOUR |
| divide | DWI |
| divorce | DWORS |
| divulge | DWULG |

## emb- (KB–)

| | |
|---|---|
| embalm | KBAUM |
| embank | KBANG |
| embargo | KBARG |
| embarrass | KBAERS |
| embody | KBOD |

## emp- (KB–)

| | |
|---|---|
| emphasize | KBAOIS |
| emphatically | KBAFL, KBAFLT |
| empire | KBAOIR |
| employ | KBLOI |
| empowerment | KBAURMT |

## en- (N–)

| | |
|---|---|
| enable | NABL, NA*IBL |
| enact | NAKT |
| encompassment | NUMT |
| encourage | NURJ |
| enemy | NAOEM |

## end- (SPW–)

| | |
|---|---|
| endeavor | SPWEFR, SPWEVR |
| endorse | SPWORS, SPWOF |
| endowment | SPWOUMT |
| endure | SPWAOUR, SPWUR |

## ent- (SPW–)

| | |
|---|---|
| entail | SPWAIL |
| entangle | SPWANG |
| enter | SPWER |
| entertainment | SPWRAIMT |
| entice | SPWAOIS |

## esc-, esk- (SK–)

| | |
|---|---|
| escalate | SKLAIT |
| escape | SKAIP |
| escort | SKOERT |
| escrow | SKROE |
| Eskimo | SKWO |

## ex- (KP–)

| | |
|---|---|
| exacerbate | KPAEB |
| exaggerate | KPAJ |
| exalt | KPALT |
| exceed | KPAOED |
| excessive | KPEF |

## for- (F–)

| | |
|---|---|
| forbid | FORBD |
| forfeit | FOFT |
| for identification | FOID |
| forward | FARD |

## fore- (F–)

| | |
|---|---|
| foreclosure | FLOERK |
| forego | FOERG |
| forelady | FRAED |
| foreman | FRAM |
| foreperson | FOERP |

## imb- (KB–)

| | |
|---|---|
| imbalance | KBAL |
| imbed | KBED |
| imbibe | KBAOIB |
| imbue | KBAOU |

## imm- (KB–)

| | |
|---|---|
| immerse | KBERS |
| immigration | KBRAIGS |
| imminent | KBIMT |
| immolation | KBOELGS |
| immoral | KBORL |

## imp- (KB–)

| | |
|---|---|
| impact | KBAK |
| impairment | KBAIRMT |
| impale | KBAIL |
| impanel | KBANL |
| impartial | KBARBL |

## in- (N–)

| | |
|---|---|
| inability | NABLT |
| inaccurate | NAEK |
| inactivity | NAVT |
| in addition | NIGS |
| inadmissible | NIFL |

## inc- (SN–)

| | |
|---|---|
| incentive | SNEV |
| inception | SNEPGS |
| incest | SN*ES |
| incision | SNIGS |
| incited | SNAOITD |

## ind- (SPW–)

| | |
|---|---|
| indelible | SPWEBL |
| indeterminate | SPWERMT |
| indoctrinate | SPWOKT |
| inducement | SPWAOUMT, SPWAOUFMT |
| induction | SPWUX |

## ins- (SN–)

| | |
|---|---|
| insane | SNAIN |
| insect | SNEKT |
| insertion | SNERGS |
| inside | SNAOI |
| insignificant | SNIG |

## int- (SPW–)

| | |
|---|---|
| intangible | SPWANL |
| interaction | SPWRAX |
| interim | SPWRIM |
| intermittent | SPWRIMT, SPWR–MT |
| interrelate | SPWERLT |

## inv- (V–)

| | |
|---|---|
| invade | VAED |
| investor | VEFR |
| invite | VAOIT |
| invoice | VOI |
| involvement | VOFMT |

## kn- (N–)

| | |
|---|---|
| knead | NAED |
| knee | NAOE |
| kneel | NAOEL |
| knotted | NOTD |
| knowledge | NOJ |

## midw- (DW–)

| | |
|---|---|
| midway | DWAI |
| Midwest | DW*ES, DWEFT |
| Midwestern | DWERN |
| midwife | DWAOIF |

## misc- (SK–)

| | |
|---|---|
| miscarriage | SKAIRJ, SKAERJ |
| mischief | SKHIF |
| mischievous | SKHAOEV, SKHAOEVS |
| miscommunication | SKMUNGS |
| misconduct | SKUK |

## obl- (BL–)

| | |
|---|---|
| obligation | BLIGS |
| oblige | BLAOIJ |
| obliquely | BLAOEL |
| obliteration | BLAEGS |
| oblivion | BLIFN |

## out- (OU–, T–)

### OU–

| | |
|---|---|
| outbound | OUBD |
| outburst | OURB |
| outcome | OUK |
| outer | OURT |

outgoing ........................................................................... OUG

T–
outbound ........................................................................... TBOUN
outbreak ........................................................................... TBRAEK
outburst ........................................................................... TBURS, TB*URS,
T*URS
outlaw ........................................................................... TLAU
out loud ........................................................................... TLOUD

**over-** (V–)
overburden ........................................................................... VURD
overcharge ........................................................................... VAURJ, VA*RJ
overcome ........................................................................... VUM
overhead ........................................................................... VED
over-the-counter ........................................................................... VOURNT

**pre-** (PR–)
precaution ........................................................................... PRAUGS
precinct ........................................................................... PRINGT
precipitate ........................................................................... PRIP
preempt ........................................................................... PREMT
premature ........................................................................... PRAUR

**pri-** (PR–)
principal ........................................................................... PRAL
printout ........................................................................... PROUT
prioritize ........................................................................... PROIR
prison ........................................................................... PRIN, PRIZ
privileged ........................................................................... PRIVD

**pro-** (PR–)
probation ........................................................................... PRAIX
problem ........................................................................... PROB
proceed ........................................................................... PRAOED
procurement ........................................................................... PRAOURMT
product ........................................................................... PRUT

**re-** (R–)
recall ........................................................................... RAUL
receipt ........................................................................... RET
recharge ........................................................................... RARJ
reciprocation ........................................................................... RIRPGS
record ........................................................................... RORD

**sacr-** (SKR–)
sacral ........................................................................... SKRAL
sacrament ........................................................................... SKRAMT
sacred ........................................................................... SKRAID
sacrifice ........................................................................... SKRAOIF
sacrilege ........................................................................... SKREJ

**sal-** (SL–)
salad ........................................................................... SLAD
saleslady ........................................................................... SLAED

saliva ....................................................................... SLAOIV
salon ....................................................................... SLON
saloon ....................................................................... SLAON

## sed- (SD–)

sedan ....................................................................... SDAN
sedative ....................................................................... SDAEV
sedentary ....................................................................... SDAIR, SDAER
sedimentation ....................................................................... SD–MGS
seduction ....................................................................... SDUX

## self- (S–)

self-confidence ....................................................................... SK–FD
self-defense ....................................................................... SD–FS
self-employment ....................................................................... SPLOIMT
self-esteem ....................................................................... SFAOEM
self-explanatory ....................................................................... SPLARNT

## sen- (SN–)

senate ....................................................................... SNAT
senatorial ....................................................................... SNORL
senile ....................................................................... SNAOIL
sensible ....................................................................... SNIBL
sentence ....................................................................... SNENS

## seq- (SKW–)

sequel ....................................................................... SKWEL
sequence ....................................................................... SKW–NS, SKWUNS
sequestration ....................................................................... SKWERGS
sequoia ....................................................................... SKWOI

## some- (SM–)

somebody ....................................................................... SM–B
some more ....................................................................... SMOR
some of the ....................................................................... SM–FT
something else ....................................................................... SM–LG
somewhere else ....................................................................... SM–RL, SM–RS

## sub- (S–)

subdivision ....................................................................... SDWIGS
subliminal ....................................................................... SBLIM
submissive ....................................................................... SMIV
subordination ....................................................................... SBORNGS
subsequence ....................................................................... SKWENS

## summ- (SM–)

summarize ....................................................................... SMAOIS
summary judgment ....................................................................... SMUMT
summation ....................................................................... SMAIGS
summer ....................................................................... SMER
summon ....................................................................... SMON

## super- (SPR–)

superb ....................................................................... SPR–B
superimpose ....................................................................... SPROES

| | |
|---|---|
| supermarket | SPR–M |
| superstitious | SPRIRB |
| supervision | SPR–GS |

**suppl-** (SPL–)

| | |
|---|---|
| supplement | SPLEMT |
| supplication | SPLAEGS |
| supplier | SPLAOIR |
| supplying | SPLIG, SPLAOIG |

**surv-** (SW–)

| | |
|---|---|
| surveil | SWAIL |
| surveillance | SWAINS |
| survey | SWAE |
| survival | SWAOIVL |

**trans-** (TR–)

| | |
|---|---|
| transaction | TR–X |
| transcription | TRIPGS |
| transfer | TR–FR |
| transform | TR–FM |
| transfusion | TR–FGS, TRAOUFGS |

**tri-** (TR–)

| | |
|---|---|
| tribulation | TRIBLGS |
| tribute | TRAOUT |
| trillion | TR–L |
| triumphant | TRUFMT |
| trivial | TRIVL |

**un-** (N–, SN–)

N–

| | |
|---|---|
| unable | NAIBL |
| unbelievable | NEFBL |
| uncomfortable | N–FRBL, NUFRBL |
| uncover | NOVR |
| underground | N–RG |

SN–

| | |
|---|---|
| unacceptable | SNEBL |
| uncertain | SNERN |
| unsafe | SNAIF |
| unsatisfactory | SNAF |
| unstable | SNAIBL |

**up-** (P–)

| | |
|---|---|
| up and down | POUN |
| update | PAIT |
| uphold | POELD |
| upon | PON |
| uproar | PROER |

## PREFIXES (by steno)

**B–** (ab-, be-, bi-)

ab-
| | |
|---|---|
| abandon | BAUN |
| abbreviate | BRAOEVT |
| aboard | BAORD |
| abolishment | BLOMT |
| abortion | BORGS |

be-
| | |
|---|---|
| behalf | BAF |
| behavioral | BAIVRL, BAIFRL |
| behold | BHOLD, BHOL |
| bereave | BAOEV |
| betrayal | BRAEL |

bi-
| | |
|---|---|
| biceps | BEPS |
| bifocal | BAOIFL |
| bifurcation | BIFGS |
| bilingual | BLINL |
| bipartisan | BAURN |

**BL–** (bel-, obl-)

bel-
| | |
|---|---|
| belabor | BLAIB |
| belated | BLAITD |
| belittle | BLIL |
| belligerent | BLIJ |
| below | BLO |

obl-
| | |
|---|---|
| obligation | BLIGS |
| oblige | BLAOIJ |
| obliquely | BLAOEL |
| obliteration | BLAEGS |
| oblivion | BLIFN |

**D–** (ad-, de-, dec-, dep-, des-, det-, dia-)

ad-
| | |
|---|---|
| adaptation | DAPGS |
| addiction | DIX |
| addition | DIGS |
| address | DRAES |
| adrenal | DRAOEN, DRAOENL |

de-
| | |
|---|---|
| deadlock | DLOK |
| dealership | DLERP |
| deduction | DUX |
| degradation | DEGS |
| dental | DENL |

dec-
| | |
|---|---|
| decease | DAOES |

decedent .................................................................... DAOENT
deceive ...................................................................... DAOEV
decorate .................................................................... DRAIT
decorum .................................................................... DOERM

dep-
departmentalize ........................................................ DAP
deposition ................................................................. DEPGS
depravity ................................................................... DRAVT
depress ..................................................................... D–P
deputy ....................................................................... DEP

des-
description ................................................................ DRIPGS
desk .......................................................................... DEFK
dessert ...................................................................... DERT
destitution ................................................................. DAOGS, DAOUGS

det-
detach ....................................................................... DAFP
detain ........................................................................ DAIN
detention ................................................................... DENGS
deterioration .............................................................. DRAEGS
determination ............................................................ DERGS

dia-
diabetic ..................................................................... DAOIBT
diagnose ................................................................... D–G
diagonal .................................................................... DAG
diagram ..................................................................... DRAM
dialect ....................................................................... DLEKT

**DB–** (deb-)
debar ........................................................................ DBAR
debate ....................................................................... DB–T
debenture .................................................................. DBUR
debrief ...................................................................... DBAOEF
debris ....................................................................... DBRI

**DL–** (decl-, del-, dil-)

decl-
declarant ................................................................... DLAIRNT
declassification .......................................................... DLAFGS
declassify .................................................................. DLAF
declination ................................................................. DLINGS
decline ...................................................................... DLAOIN

del-
deletion ..................................................................... DLAOEGS
deliberate .................................................................. DLIB
delineate ................................................................... DLAET
delinquent ................................................................. DLINT
delirious .................................................................... DLIR, DLAOERS

dil-
dilapidation ............................................................... DLAPGS
dilate ........................................................................ DLAIT
dilation ...................................................................... DLAIGS

dilemma ............................................................................ DLEM
dilute .............................................................................. DLAOUT

## DM– (dem-)

demented .......................................................................... DMENTD
demolish .......................................................................... DMORB
demotion .......................................................................... DMOEGS
demur............................................................................... DMUR
demurrer .......................................................................... DMRUR

## DP– (dep-)

depart ............................................................................. DPART
departure .......................................................................... DPAUR
deponent ........................................................................... DPOENT
deportation ....................................................................... DPORGS
depose ............................................................................. DPOES

## DR– (der-, distr-)

### der-

derail ............................................................................. DRAIL
derangement ....................................................................... DRAEMT
derision ........................................................................... DRIGS
derive ............................................................................. DRIF, DRAOIV
derogatory ........................................................................ DROG

### distr-

detraction ........................................................................ DRAX
distribute ......................................................................... DRIB
distribution ...................................................................... DRAOUGS, DRAOUX
district ........................................................................... DRIK, DRIKT
district court .................................................................... DRORT

## DW– (adv-, def-, dev-, div-, midw-)

### adv-

advent ............................................................................. DWENT
adventure .......................................................................... DWUR
adverb ............................................................................. DWERB
adverse ............................................................................ DWER, DWERZ
advocate ........................................................................... DWOEK

### def-

default ............................................................................ DWALT, DWAULT
defeat ............................................................................. DWAOET
defection .......................................................................... DWEX
deficient .......................................................................... DWIRBT
deformity .......................................................................... DWORMT

### dev-

devaluation ....................................................................... DWALGS
development ........................................................................ DWOMT
deviate ............................................................................ DWAIT
devotion ........................................................................... DWOEGS
devour ............................................................................. DWOUR

### div-

divergent .......................................................................... DWERNT

divestiture .................................................................... DWAOUR
divide ............................................................................ DWI
divorce .......................................................................... DWORS
divulge .......................................................................... DWULG

midw-
midway ........................................................................... DWAI
Midwest .......................................................................... DW*ES, DWEFT
midwife .......................................................................... DWAOIF

## F– (af-, for-, fore-)

af-
affect ............................................................................. FAEK
affiliate .......................................................................... FILT
affirmative ...................................................................... FRIF
afford ............................................................................. FAURD
afraid ............................................................................. FRAID

for-
forbid ............................................................................. FORBD
forfeit ............................................................................ FOFT
for identification ............................................................. FOID
forward ........................................................................... FARD

fore-
foreclosure ..................................................................... FLOERK
forego ............................................................................ FOERG
forelady ......................................................................... FRAED
foreman .......................................................................... FRAM
foreperson ...................................................................... FOERP

## G– (ag-)

again ............................................................................. GEN
agglomerate ................................................................... GLOMT
aggravation .................................................................... GRAEVGS
aggressive ...................................................................... GREV
agree ............................................................................. GRE

## K– (acc-, con-, cons-, corr-, counter-)

acc-
acclaim .......................................................................... KLAEM
accommodate ................................................................. KOMT
accompaniment .............................................................. KPOIMT, KOEMT
accurate ......................................................................... KRAT
accuse ........................................................................... KAOUS

con-
concurrently ................................................................... KRUNL, KRURNL
concussion ..................................................................... KUNGS
condemn ........................................................................ KEM
condo ............................................................................ KOND
condominium .................................................................. KMIM

cons-
conscientious ................................................................. K–RBS
considerable ................................................................... K–RL
considerate ..................................................................... K–RT

constitution ............................................. KAOGS
constructive ............................................ KRUV

**corr-**
correlation .............................................. KORLGS
correspondent ....................................... KORNT
corridor .................................................. KOERD

**counter-**
counteract .............................................. KRAKT
counterclockwise .................................... KOUNK
counterfeit .............................................. KIFT
counteroffer ........................................... KRAUFR
counterproductive ................................... KPRUV

**KB–** (comb-, emb-, emp-, imb-, imm-, imp-)

**comb-**
combatively ............................................ KBAVL
combattant .............................................. KBANT
combination ............................................ KBAIGS
combustible ............................................ KBUBL
combustion ............................................. KBUGS

**emb-**
embalm ................................................... KBAUM
embank ................................................... KBANG
embargo .................................................. KBARG
embarrass ............................................... KBAERS
embody ................................................... KBOD

**emp-**
emphasize .............................................. KBAOIS
emphatically ........................................... KBAFL, KBAFLT
empire .................................................... KBAOIR
employ .................................................... KBLOI
empowerment .......................................... KBAURMT

**imb-**
imbalance ............................................... KBAL
imbed ..................................................... KBED
imbibe ..................................................... KBAOIB
imbue ..................................................... KBAOU

**imm-**
immerse .................................................. KBERS
immigration ............................................. KBRAIGS
imminent ................................................. KBIMT
immolation .............................................. KBOELGS
immoral ................................................... KBORL

**imp-**
impact .................................................... KBAK
impairment .............................................. KBAIRMT
impale .................................................... KBAIL
impanel ................................................... KBANL
impartial .................................................. KBARBL

## KL– (col-)

| | |
|---|---|
| collaborate | KLAB |
| collateral | KLARL |
| collective | KLEV |
| colorblind | KLORB, KLORND |
| columnist | KLUMT |

## KM– (com-, comm-)

com-

| | |
|---|---|
| comedian | KMAOED |
| comet | KMET |
| compel | KMEL |

comm-

| | |
|---|---|
| commander | KMARN, KMARND |
| commencement | KMEMT |
| commissioner | KMIRGS |
| commodity | KMOD |
| communique | KMAI |

## KP– (cap-, comp-, ex-)

cap-

| | |
|---|---|
| capability | KPAIBLT |
| capital | KPAL |
| capitol | KPOL |
| capitulation | KPIFPGS |
| capriciously | KPRIRBL, KPRAOERBL |

comp-

| | |
|---|---|
| compensate | KPEN |
| completely | KPLEL |
| composure | KPOUR |
| comprehensible | KPRENL |
| computer | KPR– |

ex-

| | |
|---|---|
| exacerbate | KPAEB |
| exaggerate | KPAJ |
| exalt | KPALT |
| exceed | KPAOED |
| excessive | KPEF |

## KR– (contr-, corr-)

contr-

| | |
|---|---|
| contradiction | KRIX |
| contrary | KRAIR |
| contribution | KRAOUX |
| contributory negligence | KRIJ |
| control | KROL |

corr-

| | |
|---|---|
| correct | KREK |
| correct me if I'm wrong | KRONG |
| corroborate | KROB |
| corrosion | KROEGS |
| corruption | KRUPGS |

## KW– (acq-, co-, conf-, conv-)

acq-
acquaint .......................................................................... KWAIN
acquiesce ..................................................................... KWAOEF
acquire ........................................................................ KWAOIR
acquit .................................................................................. KWI

co-
coagulation ................................................................... KWAGS
coherent ...................................................................... KWERNT
cohesive ...................................................................... KWAOEV
cohort ............................................................................ KWORT
coincidental .................................................................. KWINL

conf-
confide ............................................................................ KWAOI
confine ........................................................................ KWAOIN
confirmation ........................................... KWIRGS, KWIRMGS
conformation ........................................ KWORGS, KWORMGS
confound ...................................................................... KWOUN

conv-
convention .................................................................. KWENGS
converge ...................................................................... KWERJ
conversion ................................................................... KWERGS
conviction ........................................................................ KWIX
convulsion ................................................................... KWULGS

## L– (al-)

alarm ................................................................................ LARM
alert ................................................................................ LAERT
alignment ..................................................................... LAOIMT
alike .................................................................................. LOIK
alive ................................................................................. LOIV

## M– (am-)

amazement ................................................................. MAEFMT
amelioration .............................................................. MAOELGS
America ......................................................................... MERK
among ............................................................................ MONG
amusement ............................................................... MAOUFMT

## N– (an-, en-, in-, kn-, un-)

an-
announcement .............................................................. NOUMT
annoy ................................................................................ NOI
annuity ......................................................................... NAOUT
anoint ........................................................................... NOINT
anybody ............................................................................ NIB

en-
enable ................................................................ NABL, NA*IBL
enact ............................................................................. NAKT
encompassment ........................................................... NUMT
encourage ...................................................................... NURJ
enemy ......................................................................... NAOEM

in-
inability ................................................................ NABLT
inaccurate ............................................................ NAEK
inactivity .............................................................. NAVT
in addition ........................................................... NIGS
inadmissible ......................................................... NIFL

kn-
knead ................................................................... NAED
knee ..................................................................... NAOE
kneel .................................................................... NAOEL
knotted ................................................................. NOTD
knowledge ........................................................... NOJ

un-
unable .................................................................. NAIBL
unbelievable ......................................................... NEFBL
uncomfortable ...................................................... N–FRBL, NUFRBL
uncover ................................................................ NOVR
underground ........................................................ N–RG

## OU– (out-)

outbound .............................................................. OUBD
outburst ............................................................... OURB
outcome ............................................................... OUK
outer .................................................................... OURT
outgoing ............................................................... OUG

## P– (app-, up-)

app-
apparently ............................................................ PAERNL
appearance .......................................................... PAERNS, PAOERNS
applicable ............................................................ PLIBL
approach .............................................................. PROEFP
appropriation ........................................................ PROEPGS

up-
up and down ........................................................ POUN
update ................................................................. PAIT
uphold .................................................................. POELD
upon .................................................................... PON
uproar .................................................................. PROER

## PR– (pre-, pri-, pro-)

pre-
precaution ............................................................ PRAUGS
precinct ................................................................ PRINGT
precipitate ............................................................ PRIP
preempt ................................................................ PREMT
premature ............................................................ PRAUR

pri-
principal ............................................................... PRAL
printout ................................................................ PROUT
prioritize .............................................................. PROIR
prison .................................................................. PRIN, PRIZ

privileged ........................................................................ PRIVD

pro-
probation ...................................................................... PRAIX
problem ......................................................................... PROB
proceed ......................................................................... PRAOED
procurement ................................................................ PRAOURMT
product ......................................................................... PRUT

## R– (re-)

recall ............................................................................. RAUL
receipt ........................................................................... RET
recharge ....................................................................... RARJ
reciprocation ................................................................. RIRPGS
record ............................................................................ RORD

## S– (as-, ass-, dis-, self-, sub-)

as-
ascend .......................................................................... SAEND
ascertain ....................................................................... SAERN
ask ................................................................................. SK–
asphalt ........................................................................... SFAULT
aspirin ............................................................................ SPRIN

ass-
assault ........................................................................... SAULT
assessment .................................................................... SAEFMT
assignment .................................................................... SAOIMT
associate ....................................................................... SOERB
assumption .................................................................... SUMGS

dis-
disagreement ................................................................. SGREMT
disappearance ............................................................... SPAERNS
disappointment .............................................................. SPOIMT
disapproval .................................................................... SPROVL
disbarment .................................................................... SBARMT

self-
self-confidence .............................................................. SK–FD
self-defense ................................................................... SD–FS
self-employment ............................................................ SPLOIMT
self-esteem .................................................................... SFAOEM
self-explanatory ............................................................. SPLARNT

sub-
subdivision .................................................................... SDWIGS
subliminal ...................................................................... SBLIM
submissive ..................................................................... SMIV
subordination ................................................................. SBORNGS
subsequence ................................................................. SKWENS

## SD– (dec-, des-, dis-, sed-)

dec-
decease ......................................................................... SDAOES
deceive .......................................................................... SDAOEV
decently ......................................................................... SDAOENL

deception ............................................................... SDEPGS
decide ...................................................................... SDI

des-
desertion ............................................................... SDERGS
deserve ................................................................... SDEFRB
design ..................................................................... SDAOIN
designation ........................................................... SDEGS
desire ..................................................................... SDIR, SDAOIR

dis-
disability ............................................................... SDABLT, SDAIBLT
disaster ................................................................. SDAFT, SDA*S
disband .................................................................. SBAND
disbursement ........................................................ SDBURMT
dissociate ............................................................. SDOERB

sed-
sedan ..................................................................... SDAN
sedative ................................................................. SDAEV
sedentary .............................................................. SDAIR, SDAER
sedimentation ........................................................ SD–MGS
seduction ............................................................... SDUX

## SDP– (disp-)
dispel ..................................................................... SDPEL
dispensable ........................................................... SDPENL
dispersal ................................................................ SDPERL
dispose .................................................................. SDPOES
disposition ............................................................. SDPOGS

## SDR– (distr-)
distraction ............................................................. SDRAX
distraught .............................................................. SDRAUT
distress ................................................................. SDREF, SDRES
distressful ............................................................. SDREFL
distrust .................................................................. SDRUF, SDRUFT

## SK– (con-, cons-, disc-, esc-, esk-, misc-)

con-
conceal .................................................................. SKAOEL
conceivable ........................................................... SKAOEVL
conception ............................................................. SKEPGS
concession ............................................................ SKEGS
condescension ...................................................... SKENGS

cons-
consensual ............................................................ SKENL
conservative .......................................................... SKEFT
consistently ........................................................... SKINL
consortium ............................................................. SKOERB
consultation ........................................................... SKULGS

disc-
disclaimer .............................................................. SKLAIRM
disclosure .............................................................. SKLOUR
discount ................................................................. SKOUNT

discouragement .................................................. SKOURMT
discrepancy ........................................................ SKREP

esc-, esk-
escalate ............................................................. SKLAIT
escape ............................................................... SKAIP
escort ................................................................. SKOERT
escrow ............................................................... SKROE
Eskimo ............................................................... SKWO

misc-
miscarriage ....................................... SKAIRJ, SKAERJ
mischief ............................................................. SKHIF
mischievous ................................. SKHAOEV, SKHAOEVS
miscommunication .......................................... SKMUNGS
misconduct ......................................................... SKUK

## SKR– (sacr-)
sacral ................................................................. SKRAL
sacrament .......................................................... SKRAMT
sacred ................................................................ SKRAID
sacrifice .............................................................. SKRAOIF
sacrilege ............................................................. SKREJ

## SKW– (seq-)
sequel ................................................................ SKWEL
sequence ................................... SKW–NS, SKWUNS
sequestration ...................................................... SKWERGS
sequoia .............................................................. SKWOI

## SL– (sal-)
salad ................................................................. SLAD
saleslady ........................................................... SLAED
saliva ................................................................. SLAOIV
salon ................................................................. SLON
saloon ................................................................ SLAON

## SM– (dism-, some-, summ-)
dism-
dismantle ........................................................... SMANL
dismay ............................................................... SMAI
dismember .......................................................... SMEB
dismissal ............................................................ SMIFL
dismount ............................................................ SMOUNT

some-
somebody ........................................................... SM–B
some more .......................................................... SMOR
some of the ........................................................ SM–FT
something else .................................................... SM–LG
somewhere else ........................................ SM–RL, SM–RS

summ-
summarize .......................................................... SMAOIS
summary judgment .............................................. SMUMT
summation ......................................................... SMAIGS

summer ......................................................................... SMER
summon ........................................................................ SMON

**SN–** (center-, inc-, ins-, sen-, un-)

center-
center .......................................................................... SNER
center field ................................................................. SNEFLD
center of ..................................................................... SNEF
center of attention ..................................................... SNEFGS
centerpiece ................................................................ SN*ERP, SNAOERP

inc-
incentive .................................................................... SNEV
inception .................................................................... SNEPGS
incest ......................................................................... SN*ES
incision ...................................................................... SNIGS
incited ........................................................................ SNAOITD

ins-
insane ........................................................................ SNAIN
insect ......................................................................... SNEKT
insertion ..................................................................... SNERGS
inside ......................................................................... SNAOI
insignificant ............................................................... SNIG

sen-
senate ........................................................................ SNAT
senatorial ................................................................... SNORL
senile ......................................................................... SNAOIL
sensible ...................................................................... SNIBL
sentence .................................................................... SNENS

un-
unacceptable ............................................................. SNEBL
uncertain .................................................................... SNERN
unsafe ........................................................................ SNAIF
unsatisfactory ............................................................ SNAF
unstable ..................................................................... SNAIBL

**SP–** (disp-)
disparity ..................................................................... SPAIRT
dispatch ..................................................................... SPAFP
disposition .................................................................. SPOGS
disprove ..................................................................... SPROV
disputable .................................................................. SPAOUBL

**SPL–** (suppl-)
supplement ................................................................ SPLEMT
supplication ............................................................... SPLAEGS
supplier ...................................................................... SPLAOIR
supplying ................................................................... SPLIG, SPLAOIG

**SPR–** (super-)
superb ........................................................................ SPR–B
superimpose .............................................................. SPROES
supermarket ............................................................... SPR–M

superstitious ....................................................... SPRIRB
supervision ......................................................... SPR–GS

## SPW– (end-, ent-, ind-, int-)

end-
endeavor ......................................................... SPWEFR, SPWEVR
endorse ........................................................... SPWORS, SPWOF
endowment ....................................................... SPWOUMT
endure ............................................................ SPWAOUR, SPWUR

ent-
entail .............................................................. SPWAIL
entangle .......................................................... SPWANG
enter .............................................................. SPWER
entertainment .................................................... SPWRAIMT
entice ............................................................. SPWAOIS

ind-
indelible .......................................................... SPWEBL
indeterminate ..................................................... SPWERMT
indoctrinate ...................................................... SPWOKT
inducement ....................................................... SPWAOUMT,
                                                                   SPWAOUFMT
induction ......................................................... SPWUX

int-
intangible ......................................................... SPWANL
interaction ........................................................ SPWRAX
interim ............................................................ SPWRIM
intermittent ....................................................... SPWRIMT, SPWR–MT
interrelate ........................................................ SPWERLT

## ST– (ast-)

astonish .......................................................... STIRB
astound ........................................................... STOUN
astrology .......................................................... STROLG
astronomer ....................................................... STRORM
astronomy ........................................................ STROM

## SW– (surv-)

surveil ............................................................. SWAIL
survey ............................................................. SWAE
survival ........................................................... SWAOIVL

## T– (at-, att-, cont-, out-)

at-
athlete ............................................................ TLAOET
Atlanta ............................................................ TLAN
at last ............................................................ TLA*S
atrocious .......................................................... TROERB
atrophy ........................................................... TROF

att-
attach ............................................................. TAFP
attempt ........................................................... TAEMT
attend ............................................................ TAEND

attitude ................................................................................ TAOUD
attributable ...................................................................... TRIBL

cont-
contagious ........................................................................ TAIJ
contain ............................................................................... TAIN
contaminant ..................................................................... TAMT
contingency ...................................................................... TIJS
contingent ........................................................................ TIJ

out-
outbound .......................................................................... TBOUN
outbreak ........................................................................... TBRAEK
outburst ............................................................................ TBURS, TB*URS,
T*URS

outlaw ............................................................................... TLAU
out loud ............................................................................ TLOUD

**TR–** (contr-, trans-, tri-)

contr-
contrivance ...................................................................... TRAOIVNS
contrive ............................................................................. TRAOIV
controversial .................................................................... TROVL
controversy ...................................................................... TROV
controvertible .................................................................. TROVBL

trans-
transaction ....................................................................... TR–X
transcription ..................................................................... TRIPGS
transfer ............................................................................. TR–FR
transform .......................................................................... TR–FM
transfusion ....................................................................... TR–FGS, TRAOUFGS

tri-
tribulation ......................................................................... TRIBLGS
tribute ............................................................................... TRAOUT
trillion ............................................................................... TR–L
triumphant ........................................................................ TRUFMT
trivial ................................................................................ TRIVL

**V–** (adv-, inv-, over-)

adv-
advancement ................................................................... VAMT
advantage ......................................................................... VANG
advice ............................................................................... VIS
advisable ........................................................................... VIBL
advocate ........................................................................... VOEK

inv-
invade ............................................................................... VAED
investor ............................................................................. VEFR
invite ................................................................................. VAOIT
invoice .............................................................................. VOI
involvement ...................................................................... VOFMT

over-
overburden ....................................................................... VURD

overcharge ............................................................. VAURJ, VA*RJ
overcome ........................................................................ VUM
overhead ......................................................................... VED
over-the-counter ........................................................ VOURNT

## W– (av-, aw-)

av-
averse ......................................................................... WERS
aversion ...................................................................... WERGS
avert ............................................................................ WERT
avoid ............................................................................ WOI
avoidable ..................................................................... WOIBL

aw-
awake ......................................................................... WOIK
award .......................................................................... WAURD
aware ........................................................................... WAIR
awareness .................................................................... WAIRNS
away ............................................................................ WA

# SUFFIXES

This section contains a selected compilation of suffixes/word endings used to form briefs, along with examples of each type of suffix.

The writing of briefs and phrases ending with these suffixes is by no means limited to these lists. The lists are provided to facilitate and accelerate the learning process. To avoid the possible creation of conflicts, new briefs should ideally be formulated during realtime writing.

Multi-syllabic words can, of course, be written phonetically with two or more strokes if so desired, in which case the steno suffix would be different from the brief forms in this book. For example, the suffix *"-ciousness"* in brief form can be written as –NS or –RBS, but in full phonetic form would require two strokes such as SHOUS/NES or SHUS/–NS. Another advantage of a brief-form suffix is that it can be included within a one-stroke brief (use VIRBS for *"viciousness"*) whereas a full-form suffix must be added to a prefix or word root, thus creating more strokes (VI/SHOUS/NES).

## SUFFIXES (by English)

### -ability (–BLT)

| | |
|---|---|
| acceptability | SEBLT |
| agreeability | GREBLT |
| applicability | PLIBLT |
| availability | VAIBLT |
| capability | KPAIBLT, KAIBLT |

### -able (–BL,–NL)

–BL

| | |
|---|---|
| acceptable | SEBL |
| agreeable | GREBL |
| applicable | PLIBL |
| available | VAIBL |
| capable | KPAIBL |

–NL

| | |
|---|---|
| commendable | KMENL |
| compoundable | KPOUNL |
| containable | TAINL |
| dishonorable | SHONL |
| dispensable | SPENL, SDPENL |

### -ably (–BL)

| | |
|---|---|
| acceptably | SAOEBL |
| agreeably | GRAOEBL |
| capably | KPAEBL |
| comparably | KPAERBL |
| improbably | KBROEBL |

### -age (–J)

| | |
|---|---|
| marriage | MAERJ, MAIRJ |
| massage | MAUJ |
| outrage | TRAIJ |

postage .................................................................................................. POEJ
reportage ............................................................................................. RORJ

## -al (–L,–NL)

### –L
accidental ..................................................................................... SDENL
actual .............................................................................................. TWAL
additional ..................................................................................... DIRBL
beneficial ...................................................................................... BERBL
casual ........................................................................................... KARBL

### –NL
continental ..................................................................................... NENL
continual ........................................................................................ KONL
cynical .......................................................................................... SNINL
dental ............................................................................................. DENL
detrimental .................................................................................... DRINL

## -ally (–L)

accidentally ............................................................................... SDAENL
actually ....................................................................................... TWAEL
additionally ............................................................................. DAOERBL
casually ..................................................................................... KAERBL
vocationally .............................................................................. VOERBL

## -ance (–NS, –S)

### –NS
abundance .................................................................................. BAUNS
ambulance .................................................................................. BLANS
significance ................................................................................. SFANS
surveillance ............................................................................... SWAINS
tolerance ...................................................................................... TLANS

### –S
brilliance ....................................................................................... BRILS
cognizance ................................................................................... KOGS
enhance ........................................................................................ HANS
exorbitance ............................................................................... KPORBS
vigilance ........................................................................................... VIJS

## -ancy (–NSZ, –S, –Z)

### –NSZ
aberrancy ................................................................................ BRANSZ
compliancy ........................................................................... KPLAOINSZ
deviancy ............................................................................... DWAOENSZ
expectancy .............................................................................. KP–NSZ
flamboyancy ........................................................................... FLOINSZ

### –S
blatancy ....................................................................... BLAINS, BLAITS
constancy ................................................................................ SKAENZ
fancy ............................................................................................ FAENS
relevancy ................................................................................... RAEVS
truancy ..................................................................................... TRAOUNS

–Z

| | |
|---|---|
| brilliancy | BRILZ, BRILSZ |
| irrelevancy | IRZ |
| occupancy | OUPZ |
| redundancy | DRUNZ |
| vacancy | VAIKZ |

## -ant (–NT)

| | |
|---|---|
| abundant | BAUNT |
| ambulant | BLANT |
| significant | SFANT |
| tolerant | TLANT |
| variant | VAIRNT |

## -antly (–NL, –NLT)

–NL

| | |
|---|---|
| abundantly | BAUNL |
| adamantly | DMANL |
| compliantly | KPLAOINL |
| significantly | SFANL |
| tolerantly | TLANL |

–NLT

| | |
|---|---|
| compliantly | KPLAOINLT |
| defiantly | DWAOINLT |
| ignorantly | GORNLT |
| indignantly | SPWINLT |
| tolerantly | TLANLT |

## -arian (–RN)

| | |
|---|---|
| disciplinarian | SPLIRN |
| librarian | LAIRN |
| ovarian | OIVRN |
| veterinarian | VAIRN |

## -arily (–RL)

| | |
|---|---|
| contemporarily | KRAERL |
| customarily | KMAIRL, KMAERL |
| sedentarily | SDAIRL, SDAERL |
| summarily | SMAIRL |
| temporarily | TRAERL |

## -ary (–AER, –AIR)

| | |
|---|---|
| adversary | DWAIR |
| contemporary | KRAER |
| customary | KMAIR, KMAER |
| dictionary | DRAIR |
| disciplinary | SPLAIR |

## -ch (–FP)

| | |
|---|---|
| bench | BEFP |
| church | KHUFP |
| porch | POFP |
| torch | TOFP |
| trench | TREFP |

## -cher (–FRP)

| | |
|---|---|
| clincher | KLIFRP |
| moocher | MAOFRP |
| researcher | REFRP |
| stretcher | STREFRP |
| voucher | VOUFRP |

## -cial (–RB, –RBL)

### –RB

| | |
|---|---|
| facial | FAIRB |
| racial | RAIRB |
| special | SPERB |
| unofficial | NOIRB |

### –RBL

| | |
|---|---|
| beneficial | BERBL |
| facially | FAIRBL |
| glacial | GLAIRBL |
| judicial | JURBL |
| official | FIRBL |

## -cially (–RBL)

| | |
|---|---|
| especially | SPAOERBL |
| racially | RAIRBL |
| socially | SOERBL |
| specially | SPERBL |
| unofficially | NOIRBL |

## -cious (–RB)

| | |
|---|---|
| precocious | PROERB |
| salacious | SLAIRB |
| spacious | SPAIRB |
| suspicious | SPIRB |
| tenacious | TAERB |

## -ciously (–RBL)

| | |
|---|---|
| precociously | PROERBL |
| salaciously | SLAIRBL |
| spaciously | SPAIRBL |
| suspiciously | SPIRBL |
| tenaciously | TAERBL |

## -ciousness (–NS, –RBS)

### –NS

| | |
|---|---|
| atrociousness | TROERNS, TROENS |
| deliciousness | DLIRBS |
| precociousness | PROENS, PROERNS |
| spaciousness | SPAINS |

### –RBS

| | |
|---|---|
| audaciousness | DAIRBS |
| salaciousness | SLAIRBS |
| tenaciousness | TAERBS |
| viciousness | VIRBS |

---

## -dling (–LGD, –NLG)

### –LGD
bridling ............................................................................................ BRELGD
fielding ........................................................................................... FAOELGD
meddling .......................................................................................... MELGD
paddling ........................................................................................... PALGD
riddling ............................................................................................. RILGD

### –NLG
dwindling ........................................................................................ DWINLG
handling ........................................................................................... HANLG
kindling ............................................................................................. KINLG
swindling ......................................................................................... SWINLG

## -el (–L)
barrel ............................................................................................... BAERL
brothel ............................................................................................. BROFL
bushel .............................................................................................. BURBL
cancel ............................................................................................... KAEL
compel .............................................................................................. KMEL

## -en (–N, –NL, –NT)

### –N
broken .............................................................................................. BROEN
driven ................................................................................................ DRIN
even .................................................................................................. AOEN
fasten ............................................................................................... FAEFN
sweeten ........................................................................................... SWAOEN

### –NL
fallen ................................................................................................ FAUNL
stolen ............................................................................................... STOENL
swollen ............................................................................................ SWOENL

### –NT
beaten .............................................................................................. BAENT
brighten ........................................................................................... BRAOINT
eaten ................................................................................................ AOENT
flatten ............................................................................................... FLANT
lighten .............................................................................................. LAOINT

## -er (–R)
administer ......................................................................................... M–R
appraiser .......................................................................................... PRAER
borrower ........................................................................................... BROR
bother ............................................................................................... BOFR
fewer ................................................................................................ FAOUR

## -est (*ES)
best .................................................................................................. B*ES
blood test ......................................................................................... BL*ES
closest .............................................................................................. KLO*ES
contest ............................................................................................. K*ES
Midwest ............................................................................................ DW*ES

## -fer (–FR)

| | |
|---|---|
| infer | N–FR |
| offer | AUFR |
| prefer | PREFR |
| suffer | SUFR |
| transfer | TR–FR |

## -ful (–F, –FL)

### –F

| | |
|---|---|
| beautiful | BAOUF |
| careful | KAIF |
| delightful | DLAOIF |
| disgraceful | SGRAIF |
| truthful | TRUF |

### –FL

| | |
|---|---|
| forceful | FOFL |
| unlawful | NAUFL |
| willful | WIFL |
| wonderful | WUFL |
| wrongful | WROFL |

## -fully (–FL)

| | |
|---|---|
| beautifully | BAOUFL |
| carefully | KAIFL |
| delightfully | DLAOIFL |
| disgracefully | SGRAIFL |
| truthfully | TRUFL |

## -fulness (–FNS)

| | |
|---|---|
| doubtfulness | DOUFNS |
| neglectfulness | GLEFNS |
| playfulness | PLAIFNS |
| truthfulness | TRUFNS |
| usefulness | YAOUFNS |

## -general (–G, –GT)

### –G

| | |
|---|---|
| attorney general | TOERNG |
| consulate general | SKWULG |
| state attorney general | STOERNG |
| Surgeon General | SURNG |

### –GT

| | |
|---|---|
| consulate general | SKWULGT |
| lieutenant general | LAOUNGT |
| state attorney general | STOERNGT |

## -ial (–L, –NL, –RL)

### –L

| | |
|---|---|
| alluvial | LAOUVL |
| colloquial | KWAOEL |
| controversial | TROVL |
| industrial | STRIL |
| jovial | JOEVL |

### –NL

| | |
|---|---|
| cranial | KRAINL |
| credential | KRENL |
| denial | D–NL |
| differential | DIFRNL |
| torrential | TRENL |

### –RL

| | |
|---|---|
| aerial | A*ERL |
| arterial | AERL |
| bacterial | BARL, BAOERL |
| commercial | KMERL |
| imperial | KBAOERL |

## -ian (–GS)

| | |
|---|---|
| Asian | AIGS |
| beautician | BAOUGS |
| Belgian | BELGS |
| musician | MAOUGS |
| obstetrician | STREGS |

## -ibility (–BLT, –LT)

### –BLT

| | |
|---|---|
| audibility | AUBLT |
| compatibility | KPABLT |
| possibility | POBLT |
| susceptibility | STIBLT |
| visibility | VIFBLT |

### –LT

| | |
|---|---|
| admissibility | MIFLT |
| comprehensibility | KPRENLT |
| defensibility | D–FLT, DWENLT |
| inadmissibility | NIFLT |
| tangibility | TANLT |

## -ible (–BL, –L, –NL)

### –BL

| | |
|---|---|
| audible | AUBL |
| collectible | KLIBL |
| combustible | KBUBL |
| compatible | KPABL |
| visible | VIFBL |

### –L

| | |
|---|---|
| admissible | MIFL |
| comprehensible | KPRENL |
| defensible | D–FL, DWENL |
| discernible | DERNL |
| inadmissible | NIFL |

### –NL

| | |
|---|---|
| comprehensible | KPRENL |
| discernible | DERNL |
| intangible | SPWANL |

irresponsible ........................................................................... RONL
tangible ..................................................................................... TANL

## -ibly (–BL, –L)

### –BL

audibly ................................................................................ AOEBL
indelibly ....................................................................... SPWAOEBL
plausibly ........................................................................... PLAUBL
possibly ............................................................................... POEBL
sensibly ........................................................................... SNAOEBL

### –L

defensibly ......................................................................... DWAOENL
intangibly ......................................................................... SPWAENL
ostensibly ........................................................................ STAOENL
responsibly ......................................................................... SPONL
tangibly ............................................................................ TAOENL

## -ily (–L)

bodily ...................................................................................... BOL
daily ...................................................................................... DAIL
dissatisfactorily ................................................................ SDAEFL
drearily ............................................................................. DRERL
heavily ................................................................................ HEVL

## -ing (–G, –GD, –GT)

### –G

parenting ............................................................................. PARNG
paroling ............................................................................ PROELG
participating ....................................................................... PARPG
quietening ......................................................................... KWAENG
reasoning ............................................................................. R–NG

### –GD

adjudicating ......................................................................... JUGD
amending ............................................................................. AMGD
powdering .......................................................................... PAUGD
pretending ........................................................................ PRENGD
providing .......................................................................... VAOIGD

### –GT

activating .......................................................................... TWAEGT
profiting ............................................................................ PROFGT
reiterating ........................................................................... RIGT
relating ............................................................................... RELGT
simulating ......................................................................... SMAIGT

## -ings (–GS)

belongings ......................................................................... BLONGS
billings ............................................................................... BILGS
happenings ......................................................................... HAPGS
listings ............................................................................... L–FGS
proceedings ...................................................................... PRAOEGS

---

## -ish (–RB)

accomplish ............................................................................ PLIRB
British .................................................................................. BRIRB
childish ............................................................................... KHAOIRB
distinguish .......................................................................... DWIRB
flourish ............................................................................... FLOURB

## -ishment (–MT)

establishment ...................................................................... BLIMT
garnishment ........................................................................ GAMT
impoverishment .................................................... KBOVMT, KBOFMT
nourishment ........................................................................ NOURMT
punishment ......................................................................... PUMT

## -ism (–FM)

absolutism .......................................................................... SLUFM
sexism ............................................................................... SEFM
snobbism ............................................................................ SNOFM
socialism ............................................................................ SOEFM
terrorism ............................................................................. TRIFM

## -ist (–FT, *IS)

### –FT
chauvinist ........................................................................... SHOEFT
sexist ................................................................................. SEFT
socialist .............................................................................. SOEFT
supremacist ........................................................................ SPREFT
terrorist .............................................................................. TRIFT

### *IS
economist ........................................................................... KM*IS
exist ................................................................................... KP*IS
guitarist .............................................................................. G*IS
hoist ................................................................................... HO*IS
insist .................................................................................. SN*IS

## -ity (–T)

annuity ............................................................................... NAOUT
ingenuity ............................................................................. JAOUNT
legality ............................................................................... LELT
locality ................................................................................ LOLT
masculinity .......................................................................... SKLINT

## -ive (–F, –V)

### –F
active ................................................................................. TIF
affirmative .......................................................................... FRIF
conclusive ........................................................................... KLAOUF
decorative ........................................................................... DRAIF
derive ................................................................................. DRIF

### –V
abusive ............................................................................... BAOUV
accumulative ....................................................................... KAOUV
active ................................................................................. TIV

administrative ................................................................................ MIV
cohesive ................................................................................ KWAOEV

## -ively (–FL, –VL)

### –FL
actively ................................................................................ TIFL
affirmatively ................................................................................ FRIFL
conclusively ................................................................................ KLAOUFL
decoratively ................................................................................ DRAIFL
elusively ................................................................................ LAOUFL

### –VL
abusively ................................................................................ BAOUVL
accumulatively ................................................................................ KAOUVL
actively ................................................................................ TIVL
administratively ................................................................................ MIVL
cohesively ................................................................................ KWAOEVL

## -iveness (–FNS, –VNS)

### –FNS
activeness ................................................................................ TIFNS
conclusiveness ................................................................................ KLAOUFNS
decorativeness ................................................................................ DRAIFNS
elusiveness ................................................................................ LAOUFNS
evasiveness ................................................................................ VAIFNS

### –VNS
abusiveness ................................................................................ BAOUVNS
activeness ................................................................................ TIVNS
cohesiveness ................................................................................ KWAOEVNS
combativeness ................................................................................ KBAVNS
creativeness ................................................................................ KRIVNS

## -ket (–KT)

basket ................................................................................ BAFKT
bracket ................................................................................ BRAKT
bucket ................................................................................ BUKT
docket ................................................................................ DOKT
jacket ................................................................................ JAKT

## -lding (–LGD)

beholding ................................................................................ BHOLGD
building ................................................................................ BILGD
holding ................................................................................ HOLGD
scaffolding ................................................................................ SKAFLGD
withholding ................................................................................ WHOELGD

## -le (–NL)

bindle ................................................................................ BINL
bundle ................................................................................ BUNL
dangle ................................................................................ DANL
dismantle ................................................................................ SMANL
dwindle ................................................................................ DWINL

## -less (–L, –LS)

### –L
| | |
|---|---|
| fearless | FAOERL |
| lawless | LAUL |
| lifeless | LAOIFL |
| nevertheless | NEFRL |
| nonetheless | NUNL |

### –LS
| | |
|---|---|
| doubtless | DOULS |
| humorless | HAOURLS |
| merciless | MERLS |
| thoughtless | THOULS |
| useless | YAOULS |

## -lessness (–NS)
| | |
|---|---|
| flawlessness | FLAUNS |
| lawlessness | LAUNS |
| thoughtlessness | THAUNS |

## -ling (–NLG)
| | |
|---|---|
| dismantling | SMANLG |
| impaneling | KBANLG |
| sprinkling | SPRINLG |

## -ly (–L)
| | |
|---|---|
| absolutely | SLUL |
| abusively | BAOUVL |
| intuitively | SPWAOUVL |
| lively | LAOIVL |
| tolerantly | TLANL |

## -ment (–MT)
| | |
|---|---|
| agreement | GREMT |
| statement | STAIMT |
| torment | TORMT |
| tournament | TOURMT |
| treatment | TREMT, TRAOEMT |

## -mental (–NL)
| | |
|---|---|
| detrimental | DRINL |
| environmental | VIRNL |
| experimental | SPERNL |
| fundamental | FENL |
| supplemental | SPLENL |

## -mentally (–NL)
| | |
|---|---|
| environmentally | VAOERNL |
| fundamentally | FAOENL |
| mentally | MOINL |
| sentimentally | SMAOENL |
| supplementally | SPLAENL, SPLAOENL |

## -mp ( –MP, –M)

### –MP
| | |
|---|---|
| lamp | LAMP |
| stomp | STOMP |
| summer camp | SMAMP |
| swamp | SWAMP |
| temp | TEMP |

### –M
| | |
|---|---|
| jump | JUM |
| stamp | STAM |
| swamp | SWAUM |
| temp | T*EM |

## -mpt (–MT)

| | |
|---|---|
| attempt | TAEMT |
| contempt | KEMT |
| exempt | KPEMT |
| preempt | PREMT |
| tempt | TEMT |

## -ness (–NS, –S)

### –NS
| | |
|---|---|
| absoluteness | SLUNS |
| abusiveness | BAOUVNS |
| awareness | WAIRNS |
| permissiveness | PIVNS |
| pervasiveness | PAIVNS |

### –S
| | |
|---|---|
| audaciousness | DAIRBS |
| facetiousness | FAERBS |
| gruesomeness | GRAOUMS |
| imperviousness | KBEFRBS |
| viciousness | VIRBS |

## -nk (–NG, –NK)

### –NG
| | |
|---|---|
| blank | BLANG |
| blink | BLING |
| bunk | BUNG |
| drink | DRING |
| embank | KBANG |

### –NK
| | |
|---|---|
| bank | BANK |
| blink | BLINK |
| debunk | DBUNK |
| drink | DRINK |
| shrink | SHRINK |

## -ologist (–OELT, –OLT)

| | |
|---|---|
| anesthesiologist | OELT, THOELT |
| anthropologist | POLT |
| astrologist | STROLT |

| | |
|---|---|
| sociologist | SOLT |
| zoologist | ZAOLT |

## -ology (–OELG, –OLG)

| | |
|---|---|
| anesthesiology | OELG, THOELG |
| anthropology | POLG |
| astrology | STROLG |
| sociology | SOLG |
| zoology | ZAOLG |

## -or (–R)

| | |
|---|---|
| chiropractor | KAOIR |
| conveyor | KWAIR |
| creator | KRIR |
| disfavor | SFAIVR |
| executor | SKOR |

## -ory (–OIR)

| | |
|---|---|
| category | KOIR |
| gory | GOIR |
| repertory | TWOIR |
| savory | SWOIR |
| supervisory | SPROIR |

## -ous (–JS)

| | |
|---|---|
| disadvantageous | SAJS |
| gorgeous | GORJS |
| indigenous | SDPWIJS |
| prestigious | PRAOEJS |
| sacrilegious | SKLIJS, SKLEJS |

## -out (–T)

| | |
|---|---|
| blowout | BLOUT |
| check out | KHOUT |
| in and out | NOUT |
| look out | LOUT |
| printout | PROUT |

## -over (–OEVR, –OVR)

| | |
|---|---|
| carryover | KROEVR |
| discover | SKOVR |
| pull over | PLOVR |
| recover | ROVR |
| turn over | TWOVR |

## -ple (–P, –PL)

### –P

| | |
|---|---|
| disciple | SDIP |
| grapple | GRAP |
| quintuple | KWUP |
| scruple | SKRAOUP |

### –PL

| | |
|---|---|
| couple | KUPL |
| people | PAOEPL |

purple ........................................................................................ PURPL
quadruple ............................................................................. DRAOUPL
scruple ................................................................................ SKRAOUPL

# -s (–FS, –S, –Z)

### –FS
biases ....................................................................................... BAOIFS
invests ......................................................................................... VEFS
involves ....................................................................................... VOFS
legalizes ..................................................................................... LOIFS
modifies ..................................................................................... MOFS

### –S
balloons ................................................................................ BLAONS
behaves .................................................................................. BAIVS
belittles ..................................................................................... BLILS
blueprints ............................................................................. BLAOUPS
colleges ................................................................................... KLEJS

### –Z
abducts ................................................................................... DBUKZ
belongs ................................................................................. BLONGZ
bombards .............................................................................. BORMDZ
borders ................................................................................ BROERDZ
bounds ................................................................ BOUNZ, BOUNDZ

# -ship (–P)

friendship ..................................................................................... FRIP
governorship ............................................................................. GORP
membership ................................................................................. MEP
ownership .................................................................................... OERP
partnership .................................................................................... PIP

# -sion (–GS)

abrasion ................................................................................ BRAEGS
aggression .............................................................................. GREGS
decision .................................................................................. SDIGS
delusion ...............................................................................DLAOUGS
explosion ............................................................................... SPLOEGS

# -sk (–FK)

bask ......................................................................................... BAFK
desk ......................................................................................... DEFK
disk .......................................................................................... DIFK
mask ........................................................................................ MAFK
task ......................................................................................... TAFK

# -some (–M)

bothersome ............................................................................ BOFRM
fearsome ................................................................................ FAOERM
gruesome ............................................................................... GRAOUM
quarrelsome ........................................................................... KWARM
twosome ................................................................................ TWOM

## -st (–FT, *S)

### –FT
| | |
|---|---|
| closest | KLOEFT |
| congest | GEFT |
| dust | DUFT |
| manifest | MEFT |
| Midwest | DWEFT |

### *S *(with vowel)*
| | |
|---|---|
| at last | TLA*S |
| contest | K*ES |
| economist | KM*IS |
| southeast | SAO*ES |
| west coast | WO*ES |

## -th (–T, *T)

### –T
| | |
|---|---|
| bequeath | KWAOET |
| billionth | B–LT |
| breech birth | BRAOEFPT |
| commonwealth | KWELT |
| eleventh | LEVNT |

### *T *(with vowel)*
| | |
|---|---|
| beneath | NAO*ET |
| bequeath | KWAO*ET |
| psychopath | SKPA*T |
| sabbath | SBA*T |
| thousandth | THO*UT |

## -tial (–L, –RB)

### –L
| | |
|---|---|
| circumferential | SFRENL, SK–FRNL |
| circumstantial | S–RBL |
| credential | KRENL |
| substantial | STANL |
| torrential | TRENL |

### –RB
| | |
|---|---|
| essential | SERB |
| initial | NIRB |
| partial | PARB |

## -tially (–L)
| | |
|---|---|
| impartially | KBAERBL |
| initially | NIRBL |
| partially | PARBL |
| sequentially | SKWAOENL |
| substantially | STAENL |

## -tient (–RB, –RBT)

### –RB
| | |
|---|---|
| inpatient | NAIRB |
| outpatient | TAIRB |

patient ............................................................................ PAIRB
quotient .......................................................................... KWOERB

–RBT

impatient ........................................................................ KBAIRBT
inpatient ......................................................................... NAIRBT
outpatient ....................................................................... TAIRBT
patient ............................................................................ PAIRBT
quotient .......................................................................... KWOERBT

## -tion (–GS, –JS, –X)

–GS

application ...................................................................... PLIGS
aviation .......................................................................... AIVGS
competition ..................................................................... KPEGS
creation .......................................................................... KRIGS
variation ......................................................................... VAIRGS

–JS

imagination ..................................................................... MAJS
incrimination ................................................................... KRIJS
origination ...................................................................... AURJS
refrigeration .................................................................... FRAIJS
regurgitation ................................................................... GURJS

–X

extraction ....................................................................... STRAX
fraction ........................................................................... FRAX
implication ...................................................................... KBLIX
induction ......................................................................... SPWUX
inhibition ........................................................................ BIX

## -tional (–L)

dysfunctional .................................................................. SFUNL
emotional ....................................................................... MORBL
intentional ...................................................................... SPWENL
national .......................................................................... NARBL
sensational ..................................................................... SENL, SAERBL

## -tionally (–L)

additionally ..................................................................... DAOERBL
emotionally ..................................................................... MOERBL
intentionally .................................................................... SPWLENL
nationally ....................................................................... NAERBL
nutritionally .................................................................... TRAOENL

## -tious (–RB)

ambitious ........................................................................ BIRB
cautious .......................................................................... KAURB
expeditious ................................. KPERB, SP*ERB, SPAO*ERB
facetious ......................................................................... FAERB
precautious ..................................................................... PRAURB

## -tiously (–RBL)

ambitiously ...................................................................... BIRBL
cautiously ....................................................................... KAURBL

facetiously ............................................................................................ FAERBL
precautiously ..................................................................................... PRAURBL
repetitiously ............................................................................................... TIRBL

## -tiousness (–S)

cautiousness .......................................................................................... KAURBS
facetiousness ........................................................................ FAERBS, FAERNS
precautiousness ............................................................... PRAURBS, PRAUNS
repetitiousness ........................................................................................ TIRNS

## -tory (–RT)

circulatory ................................................................................................ SLORT
congratulatory ................................................................... GLAIRT, GLORT
declaratory .............................................................................................. DLORT
defamatory ............................................................................................. DWORT
exploratory ............................................................................................ SPLOERT

## -ture (–UR)

adventure ............................................................................................... DWUR
capture ..................................................................................................... KPUR
debenture ................................................................................................ DBUR
departure ................................................................................................ DPAUR
infrastructure ............................................................................................ FRUR

## -ty (–T)

loyalty ........................................................................................................ LOILT
notoriety ................................................................................................ NAOIRT
penalty ...................................................................................................... PENLT
plenty ....................................................................................................... PLENT
poverty ..................................................................................................... POVRT

## -ver (–VR)

achiever ............................................................................................. KHAOEVR
braver ................................................................................................... BRAIVR
clever ....................................................................................................... KLEVR
forever ..................................................................................................... FREVR
maneuver .............................................................................................. MAOUVR

## -vor (–VR)

disfavor .................................................................................................. SFAIVR
endeavor ............................................................................................... SPWEVR
sexual favor ........................................................................................... SWAIVR
survivor ................................................................................................ SWAOIVR

## -x (–X)

administratrix .......................................................................................... MRIX
appendix .................................................................................................. PAEX
complex .................................................................................................. KPLEX
index ........................................................................................................... N–X
suffix ......................................................................................................... SFIX

## SUFFIXES (by steno)

### –AER, –AIR (-ary)

| | |
|---|---|
| adversary | DWAIR |
| contemporary | KRAER |
| customary | KMAIR, KMAER |
| dictionary | DRAIR |
| disciplinary | SPLAIR |

### –BL (-able, -ably, -ible, -ibly)

-able

| | |
|---|---|
| acceptable | SEBL |
| agreeable | GREBL |
| applicable | PLIBL |
| available | VAIBL |
| capable | KPAIBL |

-ably

| | |
|---|---|
| acceptably | SAOEBL |
| agreeably | GRAOEBL |
| capably | KPAEBL |
| comparably | KPAERBL |
| improbably | KBROEBL |

-ible

| | |
|---|---|
| audible | AUBL |
| collectible | KLIBL |
| combustible | KBUBL |
| compatible | KPABL |
| visible | VIFBL |

-ibly

| | |
|---|---|
| audibly | AOEBL |
| indelibly | SPWAOEBL |
| plausibly | PLAUBL |
| possibly | POEBL |
| sensibly | SNAOEBL |

### –BLT (-ability, -ibility)

-ability

| | |
|---|---|
| acceptability | SEBLT |
| agreeability | GREBLT |
| applicability | PLIBLT |
| availability | VAIBLT |
| capability | KPAIBLT, KAIBLT |

-ibility

| | |
|---|---|
| audibility | AUBLT |
| compatibility | KPABLT |
| possibility | POBLT |
| susceptibility | STIBLT |
| visibility | VIFBLT |

### *ES (-est)

| | |
|---|---|
| best | B*ES |

| | |
|---|---|
| blood test | BL*ES |
| closest | KLO*ES |
| contest | K*ES |
| Midwest | DW*ES |

## −F (-ful, -ive)

**-ful**

| | |
|---|---|
| beautiful | BAOUF |
| careful | KAIF |
| delightful | DLAOIF |
| disgraceful | SGRAIF |
| truthful | TRUF |

**-ive**

| | |
|---|---|
| active | TIF |
| affirmative | FRIF |
| conclusive | KLAOUF |
| decorative | DRAIF |
| derive | DRIF |

## −FK (-sk)

| | |
|---|---|
| bask | BAFK |
| desk | DEFK |
| disk | DIFK |
| mask | MAFK |
| task | TAFK |

## −FL (-ful, -fully, -ively)

**-ful**

| | |
|---|---|
| forceful | FOFL |
| unlawful | NAUFL |
| willful | WIFL |
| wonderful | WUFL |
| wrongful | WROFL |

**-fully**

| | |
|---|---|
| beautifully | BAOUFL |
| carefully | KAIFL |
| delightfully | DLAOIFL |
| disgracefully | SGRAIFL |
| truthfully | TRUFL |

**-ively**

| | |
|---|---|
| actively | TIFL |
| affirmatively | FRIFL |
| conclusively | KLAOUFL |
| decoratively | DRAIFL |
| elusively | LAOUFL |

## −FM (-ism)

| | |
|---|---|
| absolutism | SLUFM |
| sexism | SEFM |
| snobbism | SNOFM |
| socialism | SOEFM |
| terrorism | TRIFM |

---

## —FNS (-fulness, -iveness)

-fulness
doubtfulness ........................................................................... DOUFNS
neglectfulness .......................................................................... GLEFNS
playfulness ............................................................................... PLAIFNS
truthfulness .............................................................................. TRUFNS
usefulness ............................................................................... YAOUFNS

-iveness
activeness ................................................................................ TIFNS
conclusiveness ......................................................................... KLAOUFNS
decorativeness ......................................................................... DRAIFNS
elusiveness .............................................................................. LAOUFNS
evasiveness ............................................................................. VAIFNS

## —FP (-ch)

bench ...................................................................................... BEFP
church ..................................................................................... KHUFP
porch ...................................................................................... POFP
torch ....................................................................................... TOFP
trench ..................................................................................... TREFP

## —FR (-fer)

infer ........................................................................................ N–FR
offer ........................................................................................ AUFR
prefer ...................................................................................... PREFR
suffer ...................................................................................... SUFR
transfer ................................................................................... TR–FR

## —FRP (-cher, -mp)

-cher
clincher ................................................................................... KLIFRP
moocher .................................................................................. MAOFRP
researcher .............................................................................. REFRP
stretcher ................................................................................. STREFRP
voucher ................................................................................... VOUFRP

-mp
lamp ....................................................................................... LAMP
stomp ..................................................................................... STOMP
summer camp .......................................................................... SMAMP
swamp .................................................................................... SWAMP
temp ....................................................................................... TEMP

## —FS (-s)

biases ..................................................................................... BAOIFS
invests .................................................................................... VEFS
involves ................................................................................... VOFS
legalizes ................................................................................. LOIFS
modifies .................................................................................. MOFS

## —FT (-ist, -st)

-ist
chauvinist ................................................................................ SHOEFT
sexist ..................................................................................... SEFT

socialist ............................................................................. SOEFT
supremacist ...................................................................... SPREFT
terrorist .................................................................................. TRIFT

-st
closest ............................................................................... KLOEFT
congest ................................................................................. GEFT
dust ....................................................................................... DUFT
manifest ................................................................................ MEFT
Midwest ............................................................................... DWEFT

# –G (-general, -ing)

-general
attorney general ............................................................... TOERNG
consulate general ............................................................ SKWULG
state attorney general ...................................................... STOERNG
Surgeon General ................................................................ SURNG

-ing
parenting .............................................................................. PARNG
paroling .............................................................................. PROELG
participating ........................................................................ PARPG
quietening ......................................................................... KWAENG
reasoning ............................................................................. R–NG

# –GD (-ing)

adjudicating .......................................................................... JUGD
amending .............................................................................. AMGD
burdening ............................................................................ BURGD
pardoning ............................................................................ PARGD
pretending ......................................................................... PRENGD

# –GS (-ian, -ings, -sion, -tion)

-ian
Asian ...................................................................................... AIGS
beautician ......................................................................... BAOUGS
Belgian ................................................................................. BELGS
musician ........................................................................... MAOUGS
obstetrician ........................................................................ STREGS

-ings
belongings ......................................................................... BLONGS
billings ................................................................................. BILGS
happenings .......................................................................... HAPGS
listings ................................................................................ L–FGS
proceedings ..................................................................... PRAOEGS

-sion
abrasion ............................................................................ BRAEGS
aggression .......................................................................... GREGS
decision .............................................................................. SDIGS
delusion ........................................................................... DLAOUGS
explosion .......................................................................... SPLOEGS

-tion
application ............................................................................ PLIGS
aviation ............................................................................... AIVGS

competition ............................................................................. KPEGS
creation .................................................................................. KRIGS
variation ................................................................................ VAIRGS

## –GT (-general, -ing)

-general
consulate general ............................................................. SKWULGT
lieutenant general ............................................................ LAOUNGT
state attorney general ...................................................... STOERNGT

-ing
accelerating ....................................................................... SLERGT
accounting ........................................................................... K–GT
parenting ............................................................................ PARNGT
quitting ............................................................................... KWIGT
reconnoitering .................................................................... NOIRGT

## *IS (-ist)

economist ........................................................................... KM*IS
exist .................................................................................... KP*IS
guitarist ................................................................................ G*IS
hoist ................................................................................... HO*IS
insist ................................................................................... SN*IS

## –J (-age)

marriage ................................................................... MAERJ, MAIRJ
massage ............................................................................. MAUJ
outrage ................................................................................ TRAIJ
postage ............................................................................... POEJ
reportage ............................................................................ RORJ

## –JS (-ous, -tion)

-ous
disadvantageous ................................................................ SAJS
gorgeous ............................................................................ GORJS
indigenous ........................................................................ SDPWIJS
prestigious ....................................................................... PRAOEJS
sacrilegious ........................................................... SKLIJS, SKLEJS

-tion
imagination .......................................................................... MAJS
incrimination ...................................................................... KRIJS
origination .......................................................................... AURJS
refrigeration ....................................................................... FRAIJS
regurgitation ...................................................................... GURJS

## –KT (-ket)

basket ................................................................................ BAFKT
bracket ............................................................................... BRAKT
bucket ................................................................................. BUKT
docket ................................................................................. DOKT
jacket .................................................................................. JAKT

**–L** (-al, -ally, -el, -ial, -ible, -ibly, -ily, -less, -ly, -tial,
-tially, -tional, -tionally)

### -al
| | |
|---|---|
| accidental | SDENL |
| actual | TWAL |
| additional | DIRBL |
| beneficial | BERBL |
| casual | KARBL |

### -ally
| | |
|---|---|
| accidentally | SDAENL |
| actually | TWAEL |
| additionally | DAOERBL |
| casually | KAERBL |
| vocationally | VOERBL |

### -el
| | |
|---|---|
| barrel | BAERL |
| brothel | BROFL |
| bushel | BURBL |
| cancel | KAEL |
| compel | KMEL |

### -ial
| | |
|---|---|
| alluvial | LAOUVL |
| colloquial | KWAOEL |
| controversial | TROVL |
| industrial | STRIL |
| jovial | JOEVL |

### -ible
| | |
|---|---|
| admissible | MIFL |
| comprehensible | KPRENL |
| defensible | D–FL, DWENL |
| discernible | DERNL |
| inadmissible | NIFL |

### -ibly
| | |
|---|---|
| defensibly | DWAOENL |
| intangibly | SPWAENL |
| ostensibly | STAOENL |
| responsibly | SPONL |
| tangibly | TAOENL |

### -ily
| | |
|---|---|
| bodily | BOL |
| daily | DAIL |
| dissatisfactorily | SDAEFL |
| drearily | DRERL |
| heavily | HEVL |

### -less
| | |
|---|---|
| fearless | FAOERL |
| lawless | LAUL |
| lifeless | LAOIFL |
| nevertheless | NEFRL |
| nonetheless | NUNL |

**-ly**
absolutely ............................................................................................. SLUL
abusively ........................................................................................... BAOUVL
intuitively ....................................................................................... SPWAOUVL
lively ................................................................................................ LAOIVL
tolerantly ........................................................................................... TLANL

**-tial**
circumferential ......................................................... SFRENL, SK–FRNL
circumstantial ................................................................................... S–RBL
credential ...................................................................................... KRENL
substantial ..................................................................................... STANL
torrential .......................................................................................... TRENL

**-tially**
impartially ..................................................................................... KBAERBL
initially ............................................................................................. NIRBL
partially ............................................................................................ PARBL
sequentially ................................................................................. SKWAOENL
substantially .................................................................................. STAENL

**-tional**
dysfunctional ................................................................................. SFUNL
emotional .......................................................................................... MORBL
intentional ....................................................................................... SPWENL
national ............................................................................................. NARBL
sensational .......................................................................... SENL, SAERBL

**-tionally**
additionally ................................................................................... DAOERBL
emotionally ....................................................................................... MOERBL
intentionally ................................................................................... SPWLENL
nationally ........................................................................................ NAERBL
nutritionally .................................................................................. TRAOENL

# –LGD (-dling, -lding)

**-dling**
bridling .............................................................................................. BRELGD
meddling ............................................................................................ MELGD
paddling ............................................................................................ PALGD
riddling ............................................................................................. RILGD

**-lding**
beholding ........................................................................................... BHOLGD
building ............................................................................................. BILGD
holding .............................................................................................. HOLGD
scaffolding ...................................................................................... SKAFLGD
withholding ....................................................................................... WHOELGD

# –LS (-less)

doubtless ......................................................................................... DOULS
humorless ......................................................................................... HAOURLS
merciless ........................................................................................... MERLS
thoughtless ...................................................................................... THOULS
useless ............................................................................................. YAOULS

---

## –LT (-ibility)

admissibility ............................................................................ MIFLT
comprehensibility ................................................................ KPRENLT
defensibility ............................................................. D–FLT, DWENLT
inadmissibility ............................................................................ NIFLT
tangibility ................................................................................ TANLT

## –M (-mp, -some)

-mp
jump ........................................................................................ JUM
stamp ................................................................................... STAM
swamp ............................................................................... SWAUM
temp ..................................................................................... T*EM

-some
bothersome ........................................................................ BOFRM
fearsome ........................................................................... FAOERM
gruesome ......................................................................... GRAOUM
quarrelsome ...................................................................... KWARM
twosome ............................................................................. TWOM

## –MT (-ishment, -ment, -mpt)

-ishment
establishment ..................................................................... BLIMT
garnishment ......................................................................... GAMT
impoverishment ....................................................... KBOVMT, KBOFMT
nourishment ...................................................................... NOURMT
punishment ........................................................................ PUMT

-ment
agreement ......................................................................... GREMT
statement ......................................................................... STAIMT
torment ............................................................................. TORMT
tournament ...................................................................... TOURMT
treatment ............................................................. TREMT, TRAOEMT

-mpt
attempt ............................................................................. TAEMT
contempt ............................................................................ KEMT
exempt .............................................................................. KPEMT
preempt ........................................................................... PREMT
tempt ................................................................................. TEMT

## –N (-en)

broken ............................................................................... BROEN
driven .................................................................................. DRIN
even ................................................................................... AOEN
fasten ................................................................................ FAEFN
sweeten .......................................................................... SWAOEN

## –NG (-nk)

blank ................................................................................. BLANG
blink .................................................................................. BLING
bunk .................................................................................. BUNG
drink .................................................................................. DRING
embank ............................................................................. KBANG

## —NK (-nk)

bank ............................................................................... BANK
blink ............................................................................. BLINK
debunk ......................................................................... DBUNK
drink ............................................................................. DRINK
shrink .......................................................................... SHRINK

## —NL (-able, -al, -antly, -en, -ial, -ible, -le, -mental, -mentally)

### -able

commendable ................................................................ KMENL
compoundable .............................................................. KPOUNL
containable ................................................................... TAINL
dishonorable ................................................................ SHONL
dispensable ................................................... SPENL, SDPENL

### -al

continental ..................................................................... NENL
continual ....................................................................... KONL
cynical .......................................................................... SNINL
dental ........................................................................... DENL
detrimental .................................................................... DRINL

### -antly

abundantly ..................................................................... BAUNL
adamantly ..................................................................... DMANL
compliantly .................................................................. KPLAOINL
significantly ................................................................... SFANL
tolerantly ...................................................................... TLANL

### -en

fallen ............................................................................ FAUNL
stolen ........................................................................... STOENL
swollen ......................................................................... SWOENL

### -ial

cranial .......................................................................... KRAINL
credential ...................................................................... KRENL
denial ........................................................................... D–NL
differential .................................................................... DIFRNL
torrential ....................................................................... TRENL

### -ible

comprehensible ............................................................ KPRENL
discernible ................................................................... DERNL
intangible ..................................................................... SPWANL
irresponsible ................................................................ RONL
tangible ........................................................................ TANL

### -le

bindle ........................................................................... BINL
bundle .......................................................................... BUNL
dangle .......................................................................... DANL
dismantle ...................................................................... SMANL
dwindle ......................................................................... DWINL

### -mental

detrimental .................................................................... DRINL
environmental ................................................................ VIRNL

          © 2006 White-Boucke Publishing

experimental ........................................................................ SPERNL
fundamental ............................................................................. FENL
supplemental ..................................................................... SPLENL

-mentally
environmentally ............................................................. VAOERNL
fundamentally ................................................................. FAOENL
mentally ............................................................................. MOINL
sentimentally ................................................................ SMAOENL
supplementally ............................................... SPLAENL, SPLAOENL

# –NLG (-dling, -ling)

-dling
dwindling ......................................................................... DWINLG
handling ........................................................................... HANLG
kindling ............................................................................. KINLG
swindling .......................................................................... SWINLG

-ling
dismantling ...................................................................... SMANLG
impaneling ....................................................................... KBANLG
sprinkling ......................................................................... SPRINLG

# –NLT (-antly)

compliantly ................................................................... KPLAOINLT
defiantly ....................................................................... DWAOINLT
ignorantly ........................................................................ GORNLT
indignantly ...................................................................... SPWINLT
tolerantly ......................................................................... TLANLT

# –NS (-ance, -ciousness, -lessness, -ness)

-ance
abundance ........................................................................ BAUNS
ambulance .......................................................................... BLANS
significance ........................................................................ SFANS
surveillance ...................................................................... SWAINS
tolerance ............................................................................ TLANS

-ciousness
atrociousness ........................................... TROERNS, TROENS
capriciousness ............................................ KPRINS, KPRAOENS
precociousness ............................................. PROENS, PROERNS
spaciousness ................................................................... SPAINS

-lessness
flawlessness ..................................................................... FLAUNS
lawlessness ...................................................................... LAUNS
thoughtlessness .............................................................. THAUNS

-ness
absoluteness .................................................................... SLUNS
abusiveness .................................................................. BAOUVNS
awareness ....................................................................... WAIRNS
permissiveness ................................................................ PIVNS
pervasiveness ................................................................. PAIVNS

## –NSZ (-ancy)

| | |
|---|---|
| aberrancy | BRANSZ |
| compliancy | KPLAOINSZ |
| deviancy | DWAOENSZ |
| expectancy | KP–NSZ |
| flamboyancy | FLOINSZ |

## –NT (-ant, -en)

### -ant

| | |
|---|---|
| abundant | BAUNT |
| ambulant | BLANT |
| significant | SFANT |
| tolerant | TLANT |
| variant | VAIRNT |

### -en

| | |
|---|---|
| beaten | BAENT |
| brighten | BRAOINT |
| eaten | AOENT |
| flatten | FLANT |
| lighten | LAOINT |

## –OELG, –OLG (-ology)

| | |
|---|---|
| anesthesiology | OELG, THOELG |
| anthropology | POLG |
| astrology | STROLG |
| sociology | SOLG |
| zoology | ZAOLG |

## –OELT, –OLT (-ologist)

| | |
|---|---|
| anesthesiologist | OELT, THOELT |
| anthropologist | POLT |
| astrologist | STROLT |
| sociologist | SOLT |
| zoologist | ZAOLT |

## –OEVR, –OVR (-over)

| | |
|---|---|
| carryover | KROEVR |
| discover | SKOVR |
| pull over | PLOVR |
| recover | ROVR |
| turn over | TWOVR |

## –OIR (-ory)

| | |
|---|---|
| category | KOIR |
| gory | GOIR |
| repertory | TWOIR |
| savory | SWOIR |
| supervisory | SPROIR |

## –P (-ple, -ship)

### -ple

| | |
|---|---|
| disciple | SDIP |
| grapple | GRAP |

| | |
|---|---|
| quintuple | KWUP |
| scruple | SKRAOUP |

**-ship**

| | |
|---|---|
| friendship | FRIP |
| governorship | GORP |
| membership | MEP |
| ownership | OERP |
| partnership | PIP |

# −PL (-ple)

| | |
|---|---|
| couple | KUPL |
| people | PAOEPL |
| purple | PURPL |
| quadruple | DRAOUPL |
| scruple | SKRAOUPL |

# −R (-er, -or)

**-er**

| | |
|---|---|
| administer | M–R |
| appraiser | PRAER |
| borrower | BROR |
| bother | BOFR |
| fewer | FAOUR |

**-or**

| | |
|---|---|
| chiropractor | KAOIR |
| conveyor | KWAIR |
| creator | KRIR |
| disfavor | SFAIVR |
| executor | SKOR |

# −RB (-cial, -cious, -ish, -tial, -tient, -tious)

**-cial**

| | |
|---|---|
| facial | FAIRB |
| racial | RAIRB |
| special | SPERB |
| unofficial | NOIRB |

**-cious**

| | |
|---|---|
| precocious | PROERB |
| spacious | SPAIRB |
| specious | SPAOERB |
| suspicious | SPIRB |
| tenacious | TAERB |

**-ish**

| | |
|---|---|
| accomplish | PLIRB |
| British | BRIRB |
| childish | KHAOIRB |
| distinguish | DWIRB |
| flourish | FLOURB |

**-tial**

| | |
|---|---|
| essential | SERB |
| initial | NIRB |
| partial | PARB |

-tient
inpatient ............................................................................................. NAIRB
outpatient .......................................................................................... TAIRB
patient ................................................................................................ PAIRB
quotient ......................................................................................... KWOERB

-tious
ambitious ............................................................................................. BIRB
cautious ............................................................................................ KAURB
expeditious ................................................. KPERB, SP*ERB, SPAO*ERB
facetious ........................................................................................... FAERB
precautious ...................................................................................... PRAURB

## —RBL (-cial, -cially, -ciously, -tiously)

-cial
beneficial .......................................................................................... BERBL
facially ............................................................................................ FAIRBL
glacial ........................................................................................... GLAIRBL
judicial ............................................................................................. JURBL
official .............................................................................................. FIRBL

-cially
especially ................................................................................... SPAOERBL
racially .......................................................................................... RAIRBL
socially ........................................................................................... SOERBL
specially ......................................................................................... SPERBL
unofficially ....................................................................................... NOIRBL

-ciously
precociously .............................................................................. PROERBL
salaciously .................................................................................... SLAIRBL
spaciously ..................................................................................... SPAIRBL
suspiciously ..................................................................................... SPIRBL
tenaciously ................................................................................... TAERBL

-tiously
ambitiously ....................................................................................... BIRBL
cautiously ...................................................................................... KAURBL
facetiously ...................................................................................... FAERBL
precautiously ............................................................................... PRAURBL
repetitiously .................................................................................... TIRBL

## —RBS (-ciousness)

audaciousness ............................................................................... DAIRBS
deliciousness ................................................................................. DLIRBS
salaciousness ................................................................................. SLAIRBS
tenaciousness ............................................................................... TAERBS
viciousness ....................................................................................... VIRBS

## —RBT (-tient)

impatient ........................................................................................ KBAIRBT
inpatient ........................................................................................... NAIRBT
outpatient ........................................................................................ TAIRBT
patient ............................................................................................. PAIRBT
quotient ........................................................................................ KWOERBT

## −RL (-arily, -ial)

### -arily
| | |
|---|---|
| contemporarily | KRAERL |
| customarily | KMAIRL, KMAERL |
| sedentarily | SDAIRL, SDAERL |
| summarily | SMAIRL |
| temporarily | TRAERL |

### -ial
| | |
|---|---|
| aerial | A*ERL |
| arterial | AERL |
| bacterial | BARL, BAOERL |
| commercial | KMERL |
| imperial | KBAOERL |

## −RN (-arian)
| | |
|---|---|
| disciplinarian | SPLIRN |
| librarian | LAIRN |
| ovarian | OIVRN |
| veterinarian | VAIRN |

## −RT (-tory)
| | |
|---|---|
| circulatory | SLORT |
| congratulatory | GLAIRT, GLORT |
| declaratory | DLORT |
| defamatory | DWORT |
| exploratory | SPLOERT |

## −S (-ance, -ancy, -ness, -s, -tiousness)

### -ance
| | |
|---|---|
| brilliance | BRILS |
| cognizance | KOGS |
| enhance | HANS |
| exorbitance | KPORBS |
| vigilance | VIJS |

### -ancy
| | |
|---|---|
| blatancy | BLAINS, BLAITS |
| constancy | SKAENZ |
| fancy | FAENS |
| relevancy | RAEVS |
| truancy | TRAOUNS |

### -ness
| | |
|---|---|
| audaciousness | DAIRBS |
| facetiousness | FAERBS |
| gruesomeness | GRAOUMS |
| imperviousness | KBEFRBS |
| viciousness | VIRBS |

### -s
| | |
|---|---|
| balloons | BLAONS |
| behaves | BAIVS |
| belittles | BLILS |
| blueprints | BLAOUPS |
| colleges | KLEJS |

-tiousness
cautiousness ........................................................................................... KAURBS
facetiousness ........................................................................... FAERBS, FAERNS
precautiousness ................................................................... PRAURBS, PRAUNS
repetitiousness ......................................................................................... TIRNS

## *S (-st) *(with vowel)*

at last ....................................................................................................... TLA*S
contest ........................................................................................................ K*ES
economist ................................................................................................ KM*IS
southeast ................................................................................................ SAO*ES
west coast ............................................................................................... WO*ES

## –SZ (-ancy)

compliancy ....................................................................................... KPLAOINSZ
deviancy ......................................................................................... DWAOENSZ
expectancy ......................................................................................... KP–NSZ
flamboyancy ....................................................................................... FLOINSZ
jubilancy ......................................................................................... JAOUBLSZ

## –T (-ity, -out, -th, -ty)

-ity
annuity ................................................................................................ NAOUT
ingenuity ........................................................................................... JAOUNT
legality .................................................................................................. LELT
locality .................................................................................................. LOLT
masculinity ......................................................................................... SKLINT

-out
blowout ............................................................................................... BLOUT
check out ........................................................................................... KHOUT
in and out ............................................................................................. NOUT
look out ............................................................................................... LOUT
printout .............................................................................................. PROUT

-th
bequeath ........................................................................................... KWAOET
billionth ................................................................................................ B–LT
breech birth ................................................................................... BRAOEFPT
commonwealth ..................................................................................... KWELT
eleventh .............................................................................................. LEVNT

-ty
loyalty ................................................................................................. LOILT
notoriety ............................................................................................ NAOIRT
penalty ................................................................................................ PENLT
plenty ................................................................................................. PLENT
poverty ............................................................................................... POVRT

## *T (-th) *(with vowel)*

beneath ............................................................................................. NAO*ET
bequeath ......................................................................................... KWAO*ET
psychopath ......................................................................................... SKPA*T
sabbath ............................................................................................... SBA*T
thousandth .......................................................................................... THO*UT

## –UR (-ture)

| | |
|---|---|
| adventure | DWUR |
| capture | KPUR |
| debenture | DBUR |
| departure | DPAUR |
| infrastructure | FRUR |

## –V (-ive)

| | |
|---|---|
| abusive | BAOUV |
| accumulative | KAOUV |
| active | TIV |
| administrative | MIV |
| cohesive | KWAOEV |

## –VL (-ively)

| | |
|---|---|
| abusively | BAOUVL |
| accumulatively | KAOUVL |
| actively | TIVL |
| administratively | MIVL |
| cohesively | KWAOEVL |

## –VNS (-iveness)

| | |
|---|---|
| abusiveness | BAOUVNS |
| activeness | TIVNS |
| cohesiveness | KWAOEVNS |
| combativeness | KBAVNS |
| creativeness | KRIVNS |

## –VR (-ver, -vor)

-ver

| | |
|---|---|
| achiever | KHAOEVR |
| braver | BRAIVR |
| clever | KLEVR |
| forever | FREVR |
| maneuver | MAOUVR |

-vor

| | |
|---|---|
| disfavor | SFAIVR |
| endeavor | SPWEVR |
| sexual favor | SWAIVR |
| survivor | SWAOIVR |

## –X (-tion, -x)

-tion

| | |
|---|---|
| extraction | STRAX |
| fraction | FRAX |
| implication | KBLIX |
| induction | SPWUX |
| inhibition | BIX |

-x

| | |
|---|---|
| administratrix | MRIX |
| appendix | PAEX |
| complex | KPLEX |

## –Z (-ancy, -s)

-ancy

-s

# SUPERLATIVES

## –S, –Z

| | |
|---|---|
| brightest | BRAOITS |
| brownest | BROUNS |
| cheapest | KHAEPS |
| earliest | ERLS |
| latest | LAITS |
| longest | LONGS |
| loudest | LOUDZ |
| nearest | NERS |
| smallest | SMALS, SMAELS |
| strongest | STRONGS |
| tallest | TAULS |
| youngest | YUNGS |

## *S

| | |
|---|---|
| biggest | B*IGS |
| busiest | B*IS |
| closest | KLO*ES |
| farthest | FA*ERS |
| greatest | GRA*ETS |
| soonest | SAO*NS |
| whitest | WHAO*ITS |

## –T

| | |
|---|---|
| closest | KLOEFT |
| soonest | SAOFT |
| yellowest | YOELT |

# THE, THEM, THESE, THOSE

## A

| | |
|---|---|
| aboard the | BAORTD |
| aboard these | BAORDZ |
| aboard those | BAORTS |
| about half of the | BHAFT |
| about half of them | BHAFM |
| about half of these | BHAFZ |
| about half of those | BHAFS |
| about the | –BT |
| about these | –BZ |
| about those | –BS |
| above the | BOVT |
| above them | BOVM |
| above these | BOVZ |
| above those | BOVS |
| according to the | KRORGT |
| according to them | KRORM |
| according to these | KORGZ |
| according to those | KORGS |
| across the | KROFT |
| across them | KROFM |
| across these | KROFZ |
| across those | KROFTS, KRO*FS |
| after all the | AFRLT |
| after all these | AFRLZ |
| after all those | AFRLS |
| after the | AFT |
| after them | AFM |
| after these | AFZ |
| after those | AFS |
| ahead of the | HAIFT, HAEFT |
| ahead of them | HAIFM, HAEFM |
| ahead of these | HAIFZ, HAEFZ |
| ahead of those | HAIFS, HAEFS |
| all of the | AUFLT |
| all of them | AUFM |
| all of these | AUFLZ |
| all of those | AUFLS |
| all the | AULT |
| all these | AULZ |
| all those | AULS |
| along the | LAONGT |
| along these | LAONGZ |
| along those | LAONGS |
| a lot of the | LAOFT |
| a lot of them | LAOFM |
| a lot of these | LAOFZ |
| a lot of those | LAOFS |

although the ............................................................................... AOLT
although these ........................................................................... AOLZ
although those ........................................................................... AOLS

among the ............................................................................... MONGT
among these ............................................................................. MONGZ
among those ............................................................................. MONGS

any of them .............................................................................. NIFM
any of these ............................................................................. NIFZ
any of those ............................................................................. NIFS

around the ............................................................................... ARNT
around these ............................................................................. ARNZ
around those ............................................................................. ARNS

**B**

back of them ............................................................................. BAFM
back of these ............................................................................ BAFZ
back of those ............................................................................ BAFS

because of the .......................................................................... BAUFT
because of them ........................................................................ BAUFM
because of these ....................................................................... BAUFZ
because of those ....................................................................... BAUFS

before the ................................................................................ B–FRT
before them .............................................................................. B–FRM
before these ............................................................................. B–FRZ
before those ............................................................................. B–FRS

behalf of the ............................................................................. BAFT
behalf of them ........................................................................... B–FM
behalf of these .......................................................................... B–FZ

behind the ............................................................................... BINTD
behind these ............................................................................. BINDZ
behind those ............................................................................. BINTS

be the ..................................................................................... B–T
be those .................................................................................. B–S

better than the .......................................................................... BERNT
better than these ....................................................................... BERNZ
better than those ...................................................................... BERNS

between the .............................................................................. TWAOENT
between them ............................................................................ TWAOEM
between these ........................................................................... TWAOENZ
between those ........................................................................... TWAOENS

beyond the scope of the ............................................................ YOEFPT
beyond the scope of these .......................................................... YOEFPZ
beyond the scope of those .......................................................... YOEFPS

billion of these .......................................................................... B–LZ

both of the ............................................................................... BOEFT
both of them ............................................................................. BOEFM
both of these ............................................................................ BOEFZ
both of those ............................................................................ BOEFS

braver than the ................................................................ BRAIVRNT, BRAIFRNT
braver than these ........................................................... BRAIVRNZ, BRAIFRNZ
braver than those ........................................................... BRAIVRNS, BRAIFRNS

by means of the ............................................................................... BIMT
by means of these ........................................................................... BIMZ
by means of those ........................................................................... BIMS

by reason of the ............................................................................. BIRNT
by reason of these .......................................................................... BIRNZ
by reason of those .......................................................................... BIRNS

by virtue of the ............................................................................... BIFRT
by virtue of them ............................................................................ BIFRM
by virtue of these ........................................................................... BIFRZ
by virtue of those ........................................................................... BIFRS

## C

cause of the .................................................................................. KAUFT
cause of them ............................................................................... KAUFM
cause of these .............................................................................. KAUFZ

center of the ................................................................................. SNEFT
center of them ............................................................................... SNEFM
center of these .............................................................................. SNEFZ

clean up the ............................................................................... KLAOEPT
clean up these ............................................................................ KLAOEPZ

clear up the .............................................................................. KLAOERPT
clear up these ........................................................................... KLAOERPZ

close by the ................................................................................ KLOEBT
close by these ............................................................................. KLOEBZ
close by those ............................................................................. KLOEBS

could be the ................................................................................ KOUBT
could be these ............................................................................. KOUBZ
could be those ............................................................................. KOUBS

## D

darker than the ............................................................................ DRARNT
darker than these ......................................................................... DRARNZ
darker than those ......................................................................... DRARNS

day of the ..................................................................................... DAIFT
day of these .................................................................................. DAIFZ

deeper than the ......................................................................... DAOERNT
deeper than these ...................................................................... DAOERNZ
deeper than those ...................................................................... DAOERNS

degree of the ............................................................................... DREFT
degree of these ............................................................................ DREFZ

different than the ......................................................................... DIFRNT
different than them .......................................................................... DIFM
different than these ........................................................... DIFRNZ, DIFRNDZ
different than those ..................................................................... DIFRNTS

drier than the .................................................................. DRAOIRNT
drier than these ............................................................... DRAOIRNZ
drier than those ............................................................... DRAOIRNS

during the ........................................................... DRURG, DURGT
during these ......................................................................... DURZ
during those ........................................................................ DURS

## E

each of the ................................................. AOEFT, AOEFPT, YAOEFPT
each of them ............................................... AOEFM, YAOEFPL
each of these ............................................. AOEFZ, AOEFPZ, YAOEFPZ
each of those ............................................. AOEFPS, YAOEFPS

eight of the ............................................................................ AIFT
eight of them ........................................................................ AIFM
eight of these ........................................................................ AIFZ
eight of those ........................................................................ AIFS

eighty of the .......................................................................... YIFT
eighty of them ....................................................................... YIFM
eighty of these ...................................................................... YIFZ
eighty of those ...................................................................... YIFS

either of them ....................................................................... EFM
either of these ....................................................................... EFZ
either of those ....................................................................... EFS

enough of the ...................................................................... NUFT
enough of them ................................................................... N*UFM
enough of these ................................................................... NUFZ
enough of those ................................................................... NUFS

every one of these ........................................................... EFRNZ

except the ......................................................................... KPEPT
except them ....................................................................... KPEM
except these ...................................................................... KPEPZ
except those ............................................. KPEPTS, KP*EPS

exclusive of the ................................................................ SKLUFT
exclusive of them .............................................................. SKLUFM
exclusive of these ............................................................. SKLUFZ
exclusive of those ............................................................. SKLUFS

## F

farther than the .................................................................. FARNT
farther than these ............................................................. FARNZ
farther than those ............................................................. FARNS

faster than the .................................................................. FAFRNT
faster than them ............................................................... FAFRM
faster than these .............................................................. FAFRNZ
faster than those .............................................................. FAFRNS

feature of the ................................................................... FAOEFPT
feature of them ................................................................. FAOEFM
feature of these ................................................................ FAOEFPZ

fewer than the .................................................................................. FAOURNT
fewer than these ............................................................................ FAOURNZ
fewer than those ................................................. FAOURNTS, FAO*URNS

few of the ....................................................................................... FAOUFT
few of them .................................................................................. FAOUFM
few of these .................................................................................. FAOUFZ
few of those ................................................................................... FAOUFS

five of the ........................................................................................ FAOIFT
five of them ................................................................................... FAOIFM
five of these ................................................................ FAOIFZ, FAOIVZ
five of those ................................................................................... FAOIVS

forty of the ...................................................................................... FRIFT
forty of them ................................................................................... FRIFM
forty of these ................................................................................. FRIFZ
forty of those .................................................................................. FRIFS

four of the ....................................................................................... FOUFT
four of them ................................................................................... FOUFM
four of these .................................................................................. FOUFZ
four of those ................................................................................... FOUFS

from the ........................................................................................... FR–T
from them ....................................................................................... FR–M
from these ....................................................................................... FR–Z
from those ....................................................................................... FR–S

front of the ...................................................................................... FROFT
front of them .................................................................................. FROFM
front of these ................................................................................. FROFZ
front of those ................................................................................. FROFS

**G**

give up the ..................................................................................... GUPT
give up these ................................................................................. GUPZ

greater than the ......................................................................... GRAERNTD
greater than these ...................................................................... GRAERNZ
greater than those ...................................................................... GRAERNTS

greener than the ......................................................................... GRAOERNT
greener than these ...................................................................... GRAOERNZ
greener than those ...................................................................... GRAOERNS

**H**

half of the ....................................................................................... HAFT
half of them .................................................................................... HAFM
half of these ................................................................................... HAFZ
half of those ................................................................................... HAFS

have the ............................................................................................ V–T
have these ...................................................................................... V–TSZ
have those ....................................................................................... V–TS

higher than the ............................................................................. HAO*IRNT
higher than them .......................................................................... HAOIRM
higher than these .......................................................................... HAOIRNZ
higher than those .......................................................................... HAOIRNS

hotter than the .................................................................................... HAURNT
hotter than these ................................................................................ HAURNZ
hotter than those .................................................... HAURNTS, HA*URNS

how about the ...................................................................................... HOUBT
how about these ................................................................................... HOUBZ
how about those ................................................................................... HOUBS

how can the ......................................................................................... HOUKT
how can these ...................................................................................... HOUKZ
how can those ...................................................................................... HOUKS

how many of the .............................................................................. HOUFMT
how many of them ............................................................................... HOUFM
how many of these ............................................................................HOUFMZ
how many of those .............................................................................HOUFMS

how much of the ............................................................................... HOUFPT

how much these .................................................................................HOUFPZ
how much those .................................................................................HOUFPS

hundred of the .......................................................................................HUFT
hundred of them ................................................................................... HUFM
hundred of these ................................................................................... HUFZ

**I**

in and out of the...................................................................................... NOUFT
in and out of these.................................................................................. NOUFZ
in and out of those ............................................................................... NOUFTS

including the ......................................................................................... KLUGT
including these ...................................................................................... KLUGZ
including those .................................................................................... KLUGTS

in each of the ...................................................................................... NAOEFPT
in each of them ................................................................................. NAOEFM
in each of these ................................................................................ NAOEFPZ
in each of those ................................................................................ NAOEFPS

inside of the ........................................................................................ SNAOIFT
inside of them ..................................................................................... SNAOIFM
inside of these .................................................................................... SNAOIFZ
inside of those .................................................................................... SNAOIFS

inside the ............................................................................................ SNAOIT
inside them ......................................................................................... SNAOIM
inside these ......................................................................................... SNAOIZ
inside those ........................................................................................ SNAOIS

in spite of the ...................................................................................... SPAOIFT
in spite of them ................................................................................... SPAOIFM
in spite of these .................................................................................. SPAOIFZ
in spite of those .................................................................................. SPAOIFS

instead of the ....................................................................................... STEFT
instead of them ................................................................................... STEFM
instead of these ................................................................................... STEFZ
instead of those ................................................................................... STEFS

| | |
|---|---|
| in terms of the | NERMT |
| in terms of these | NERMZ |
| in terms of those | NERMS |
| in the | N–T |
| in them | NEM |
| in these | NEZ |
| in those | NOS, NOZ |
| into the | NAOT |
| into them | NAOM |
| into these | NAOZ |
| in view of the | VAOFT |
| in view of them | VAOFM |
| in view of these | VAOFZ |
| in view of those | VAOFS |

## L

| | |
|---|---|
| later than the | LAERNT, LAIRNTD |
| later than these | LAIRNZ |
| law of the | LAUFT |
| law of these | LAUFZ |
| law of those | LAUFS |
| lieu of the | LAOUFT |
| lieu of them | LAOUFM |
| lieu of these | LAOUFZ |
| lieu of those | LAOUFS |
| light of the | LAOIFT |
| light of these | LAOIFZ |
| light of those | LAOIFS |
| lots of them | LOFM |
| lots of these | LOFZ |
| lots of those | LOEFS |
| louder than the | LOURNT, LOURNTD |
| louder than these | LOURNZ |
| louder than those | LOURNS |
| lower than the | LOERNT |
| lower than these | LOERNZ |
| lower than those | LOERNS |

## M

| | |
|---|---|
| many of the | M–VT |
| many of them | M–VM |
| many of these | M–FZ, M–VZ |
| many of those | M–FS, M–VS |
| meaner than the | MAOERNTD |
| meaner than these | MAO*ERNZ, MAO*ERNDZ |
| meaner than those | MAOERNTS |
| middle of the | MIFLTD |
| middle of them | MIFM |
| middle of these | MIFLZ |
| middle of those | MIFLS |

| | |
|---|---|
| more than the | MOERNT |
| more than them | MOERM |
| more than these | MOERNZ |
| more than those | MOERNS |
| most of the | MOEFT |
| most of them | MOEFM |
| most of these | MOEFZ |
| most of those | MOEFS |
| motion of the | MOFT |
| motion of these | MOFZ |
| much of the | MUFPT |
| much of these | MUFPZ |
| much of those | MUFPS |

**N**

| | |
|---|---|
| nature of the | NAIFPT |
| nature of them | NAIFM |
| nature of these | NAIFPZ |
| nature of those | NAIFPS |
| near the | NAOERT |
| near them | NAOERM |
| near these | NAOERZ |
| near those | NAOERTS |
| newer than the | NAOURNT |
| newer than them | NAOURM |
| newer than these | NAOURZ |
| newer than those | NAO*URS |
| nicer than the | NAOIRNT |
| nicer than these | NAOIRNZ |
| nicer than those | NAOIRNS |
| nine of the | NAOIFT |
| nine of them | NAOIFM |
| nine of these | NAOIFZ |
| nine of those | NAOIFS |
| none of the | NUNT |
| none of them | NUFM |
| none of these | NUNZ |
| none of those | NUNS |

**O**

| | |
|---|---|
| off the | AUFT |
| off these | AUFZ |
| off those | AUFS |
| of the | OFT |
| of them | OFM |
| of these | OFZ |
| of those | OFTS, O*FS |
| on and off the | NAUFT |
| on and off them | NAUFM |
| on and off these | NAUFZ |
| on and off those | NAUFS |

on behalf of the ........................................................................... BAOFT
on behalf of them........................................................................ BAOFM
on behalf of these ...................................................................... BAOFZ
on behalf of those ...................................................................... BAOFS

one-half of the .......................................................................... WAFT
one-half of them ......................................................................... WAFM
one-half of these........................................................................ WAFZ
one-half of those ........................................................................ WAFS

one of the................................................................................ WUFT
one of them .............................................................................. WUFM
one of these ............................................................................. WUFZ
one of those ............................................................................. WUFS

only the ................................................................................. ONLT
only these ............................................................................... ONLZ
only those ............................................................................... ONLS

on the ................................................................................... ONT
on these ................................................................................. ONZ
on those ................................................................................. ONS

onto the ................................................................................. AONTD
onto these ............................................................................... AONTSZ
onto those ............................................................................... AONTS

or the ................................................................................... ORT
or them .................................................................................. ORM
or these ................................................................................. ORZ
or those ................................................................................. ORS

out of the................................................................................ OUFT
out of them .............................................................................. OUFM
out of these ............................................................................. OUFZ
out of those ............................................................................. OUFS

outside of the ........................................................................... OUFTD
outside of these ......................................................................... OUFDZ
outside of those ......................................................................... OUFTS

**P**

part of the ............................................................................... PAFRT
part of them ............................................................................. PAFM
part of these ............................................................................ PAFRZ

plenty of the ............................................................................ PLEFT
plenty of them ........................................................................... PLEFM
plenty of these .......................................................................... PLEFZ

**Q**

quieter than the .......................................................................... KWAOIRNT
quieter than these........................................................................ KWAOIRNZ
quieter than those ....................................................................... KWAOIRNS

quite a few of the ....................................................................... KWAOIFTD
quite a few of them ...................................................................... KWAOIFM
quite a few of these ..................................................................... KWAOIFZ
quite a few of those ..................................................................... KWAOIFS

## S

| | |
|---|---|
| scope of the | SKOEFPT |
| scope of them | SKOEFPL |
| scope of these | SKOEFPZ |
| scope of those | SKOEFPS |
| seventy of the | SFIFT |
| seventy of them | SFIFM |
| seventy of these | SFIFZ |
| seventy of those | SFIFS |
| several of the | SEVRLTD |
| several of them | SEVRM |
| several of these | SEVRLZ |
| several of those | SEVRLS |
| sharper than the | SHAERNT |
| sharper than these | SHAERNZ |
| sharper than those | SHAERNS |
| shorter than the | SHOERNTD |
| shorter than these | SHOERNZ, SHOERNDZ |
| shorter than those | SHOERNTS |
| side of the | SAOIFT |
| side of them | SAOIFM |
| slicker than the | SLIRNT |
| slicker than these | SLIRNZ |
| slicker than those | SLIRNS |
| slower than the | SLOERNT |
| slower than them | SLOERM |
| slower than these | SLOERNZ |
| slower than those | SLOERNS |
| smaller than the | SMAURNT, SMAUNLT |
| smaller than these | SMAURNZ, SMAUNLZ |
| smaller than those | SMAURNS, SMAUNLS |
| smarter than the | SMAERNT, SMARNTD |
| smarter than these | SMAERNZ, SMARNZ |
| smarter than those | SMAERNS, SMARNTS |
| smoother than the | SMAORNT |
| smoother than these | SMAORNZ |
| smoother than those | SMAORNS |
| some of the | SM–FT |
| some of them | SM–FM |
| some of these | SM–FZ |
| some of those | SM–FS |
| sooner than the | SAORNTD |
| sooner than these | SAORNZ |
| sooner than those | SAORNS |
| speak about the | SPEBT |
| speak about them | SPEFM |
| speak about these | SPEBZ |
| speak about those | SPEBS |

speed of the .................................................................................. SPAOEFT
speed of them ............................................................................... SPAOEFM
speed of these ............................................................................. SPAOEFZ
speed of those ............................................................................. SPAOEFS

state of the ................................................................................... STAIFT
state of them ................................................................................ STAIFM
state of these ............................................................................... STAIFZ
state of those ............................................................................... STAIFS

stronger than the ......................................................................... STRORNT
stronger than these ..................................................................... STRORNZ
stronger than those ..................................................................... STRORNS

such as the .................................................................................. SUFPT
such as these ............................................................................... SUFPZ

sweeter than the ........................................................ SWRAOENT, SWAOERNTD
sweeter than these ..................................................... SWRAOENZ, SWAOERNZ
sweeter than those ........................... SWRAOENS, SWRAOENTS, SWAOERNTS

# T

talk about the ............................................................................... TAUBT
talk about these ........................................................................... TAUBZ
talk about those ........................................................................... TAUBS

taller than the ............................................................................... TAURNT
taller than these ........................................................................... TAURNZ
taller than those ........................................................................... TAURNS

than the ........................................................................................ THANT
than these .................................................................................... THANZ
than those .................................................................................... THANS

thirty of them ................................................................................ THRIFM
thirty of these ............................................................................... THRIFZ
thirty of those ............................................................................... THRIFS

thousand of the ............................................................................ THOUFT
thousand of them .......................................................................... THOUFM
thousand of these ......................................................................... THOUFZ
thousand of those ......................................................................... THOUFS

three of the .................................................................................. THREFT
three of them ................................................................................ THREFM
three of these ............................................................................... THREFZ
three of those ............................................................................... THREFS

through the ................................................................................... THRUT
through them ................................................................................ THRUM
through these ............................................................................... THRUZ
through those ............................................................................... THRUS

toward the .................................................................................... TWARTD
toward them .................................................................................. TWARM
toward these ................................................................................ TWARZ
toward those ................................................................................ TWARS

twenty of the ................................................................................ TWIFT
twenty of them .............................................................................. TWIFM
twenty of these ............................................................................. TWIFZ
twenty of those ............................................................................. TWIFS

| | |
|---|---|
| two of the | TWOFT |
| two of them | TWOFM |
| two of these | TWOFZ |
| two of those | TWOFS |
| type of the | TAOIFPT |
| type of these | TAOIFPZ |

**U**

| | |
|---|---|
| under the | N–RT |
| under these | N–RZ |
| under those | N–RS |
| until the | N–LT |
| until these | N–LZ |
| until those | N*LS |
| upon the | PONT |
| upon these | PONZ |
| upon those | PONS |
| up or down the | POURNT |
| up or down these | POURNZ |
| up or down those | POURNS |

**V**

| | |
|---|---|
| value of the | VAFT |
| value of these | VAFZ |
| value of those | VAFS |
| view of the | VAOUFT |
| view of them | VAOUFM |
| view of these | VAOUFZ |
| view of those | VAOUFS |

**W**

| | |
|---|---|
| warmer than the | WRARMTD |
| warmer than these | WRARMZ |
| warmer than those | WRARMS |
| whether the | WHR–T |
| whether these | WHR–Z |
| whether those | WHR–S |
| which of them | WIFM |
| which of these | WIFZ |
| which of those | WIFS |
| while the | WHAOILT |
| while these | WHAOILZ |
| while those | WHAOILS |
| whiter than the | WHAOIRNT |
| whiter than them | WHAOIRM |
| whiter than these | WHAOIRNZ |
| whiter than those | WHAOIRNS |
| whom the | WHAOMT |
| whom these | WHOMZ, WHAOMZ |
| whom those | WHAOMS |

| | |
|---|---|
| within the | W–NT |
| within these | W–NZ |
| within those | W–NTS |
| | |
| without the | WOUTD |
| without these | WOUTSZ |
| without those | WOUTS |
| | |
| with regard to these | WRARZ |
| with regard to those | WRARS |
| | |
| worse than the | WORNT |
| worse than these | WORNZ |
| worse than those | WORNTS |
| | |
| would be the | WOUBT |
| would be these | WOUBZ |
| would be those | WOUBS |
| | |
| would have the | WOUFT |
| would have them | WOUFM |
| would have these | WOUFZ |
| would have those | WOUFS |

# PART 2

**2**

# TOPIC CATEGORIES

general
blind & visually impaired
church and religion
compass points, etc.
computer / internet
court examinations
days & months
deaf & hearing impaired
family members
geographic data
medical
-ologist & -ology
q&a shortcuts
speaker identification
united states & territories
units of measure

# TOPIC CATEGORIES

## GENERAL

Part 2 is devoted to categorical listings by topic. Some topics are general while others are designed for specific types of reporting jobs. The majority of entries are logical "one strokers" designed for easy learning.

The medical terminology is conflict-free with respect to the book **Medical Briefs** or its CD-ROM version entitled **Medically Briefed**. Some of the other specialized terminology may require a case dictionary to avoid conflicts.

For more ideas for the general vocabulary briefs, refer to the book **Brief Encounters** or its CD-ROM version entitled **Briefs Encountered**.

## NOTE

This part includes specialized terms frequently used in blind/visually-impaired, deaf/hearing-impaired and deaf-blind communities. It is strongly advised that stenographers/reporters working in these areas familiarize themselves with the inherent protocol of the "cultures" in order to avoid alienating or offending those involved. This includes sign language interpreters and oral interpreters who will be present in many situations. A good working relationship between reporters and interpreters is beneficial to all parties.

# BLIND & VISUALLY IMPAIRED

**A**

| | |
|---|---|
| access | KRES, KREF |
| accessibility | KREFBLT |
| accessible | KREFBL |
| acuity | KWAO*UT |
| adapt | DAPT |
| adaptive | DAVPT |
| adaptive aid | DAVPTD |
| ALDA | ALD |
| American Association of the Deaf-Blind | MERNGS |
| American Council of the Blind | MERNG |
| American Foundation for the Blind | MEFRN |
| American Sign Language | MERNL |
| Americans with Disabilities Act | MERND |
| ASL | ALS |
| Association of Late-Deafened Adults | ALD/ALD |
| astigmatic | SNIKT, SGIK |
| astigmatism | SNIFM, SGIFM |
| audio-described TV programs | AOUPT |
| audiologist | AULD |
| audiology | AULG |

**B**

| | |
|---|---|
| blind | BLAOIN |
| blindly | BLAOINL, BLAOINLD |
| blindness | BLAOINS |
| blood sugar | BLUG |
| blood sugar level | BLULG |
| braille | BRAIL |
| brailler | BRAIRL |

**C**

| | |
|---|---|
| cataract | KAKT |
| cataract implant | KLANT |
| cataract implant lens surgery | KLENZ |
| CCTV | KR–VT |
| central vision | STRAVL |
| closed circuit | KLOEKT |
| closed-circuit television | KROEVT, KLOEVKT |
| closed-circuit TV | KLOEVK |
| CMV | KM–V |
| CMV retinitis | KM–VR |
| congenital | K–JT |
| congenitally | KEJT |
| conjunctiva | JIV |
| conjunctivitis | JIVT |
| cornea | KR–N |
| corneal | KR–NL |
| corneal transplant | KR–NT |
| corneal transplantation | KR–NGS |
| corrective lens | KR–VL |

**BLIND & VISUALLY IMPAIRED**

corrective lenses ........................................................................................... KR–VLS
cross eye ........................................................................................................ KROI
crystalline ................................................................................................ STLAOEN

**D**

deaf .............................................................................................................. DAEF
deaf-blind ...................................................................................... DAEFB, DEFB
deaf-blindness ....................................................................... DAEFBS, DEFBS
degenerate ................................................................................................ JAIRT
degeneration ........................................................................................... JAIRGS
degenerative ............................................................................................... JAIV
detached retina ..................................................................................... DRAENT
diabetes ................................................................................................. DAOIB
diabetes mellitus ..................................................................................... DMEL
diabetic ................................................................................................. DAOIBT
diabetic retinopathy ................................................................................ DO*PT
diameter .............................................................................................. DAOIRMT
dog guide ................................................................................................. DOGD
double vision .......................................................................... DOUBLGS, DUVGS

**E**

eye care ...................................................................................................... AOIK
eye care specialist ................................................................................... AOIKT
eye doctor ................................................................................................ AOIRD
eye examination ....................................................................................... AOIGS

**F**

fingerspell .................................................................................................. SFEL
fingerspelling ........................................................................................... SFELG
floater ..................................................................................................... FLOERT

**G**

glaucoma ................................................................................................ GLAUK
Guide Dog ................................................................................................ GAUG
Guiding Eyes ....................................................................................... GAOIGDZ

**H**

hearing-sighted ..................................................................................... HAERTD
Helen Keller .............................................................................................. HELG
Helen Keller National Center ................................................................. HELGS
Helen Keller National Center for Deaf-Blind Youth and Adults ...................... HELGD
HKNC ...................................................................................................... H–KZ

**I**

impaired vision ....................................................................................... KBIGS
intacs ................................................................................................... SPWAX
intraocular ......................................................................................... SPWROK
iris ......................................................................................................... AOIRZ
isolate .................................................................................................... ZOELT
isolation ........................................................................... ZOELGS, SOELGS

**K**

keratic .................................................................................................... KERKT
keratotomy ............................................................................................. K*ERT

## L

| | |
|---|---|
| large print | LIRNT |
| LASEK | LAEFK |
| laser | LAIRZ |
| laser-assisted in situ keratomileusis | LAEFKS, LAEFK/LAEFK |
| laser epithelial keratomileusis | LAIFKS, LAIFK/LAIFK |
| lasering | LAIRGZ |
| laser surgery | LURG |
| laser vision | LAIRGS |
| laser vision center | L–VK |
| laser vision correction | LAIRX |
| LASIK | LAIFK |
| Leader Dogs | LERGDZ |
| legal blindness | LEBS |
| legally blind | LEBD, LELD |
| lens | LENS |
| lipreading by vibration | LIRPGS |
| loss of vision | LOVGS |
| low vision | LOEVGS |
| low vision aid | LOEVD |

## M

| | |
|---|---|
| macula | MOUL |
| macula degeneration | MOULGS |
| macular degeneration | MOURLGS |
| magnification | MAFGS |
| maternal rubella | MOUB |
| mobility | MOEBLT |
| myopia | MAOP |
| myopic | MAOPG, MAOPK |

## N

| | |
|---|---|
| National Association for Visually Handicapped | NIVGS |
| National Captioning Institute | NAPGS |
| National Family Association for Deaf-Blind | NAEFM |
| National Federation of the Blind | N–FB |
| National Training Team | NARBT |
| nearsighted | NAOERTD |
| nearsightedness | NAOERTDZ, NAOERTSDZ |
| NTT | N*T |
| nystagmus | N*IS |

## O

| | |
|---|---|
| OCR | O*RK |
| OCR scanner | O*RKZ, SKAORN |
| ocular | AUK |
| ocular disorder | AURKD |
| ophthalmological | MOFLT |
| ophthalmologist | MOLT |
| ophthalmology | MOLG |
| optic | TAUPT |
| optical | TA*UL |
| optical aid | TAID |
| optical character recognition | TAULGS, ORPGS, O*RGS |

optician ........................ A*UPGS, OPGTS
optic nerve ........................ AUN
optometrist ........................ TOMT
optometry ........................ TROMT

## P

peripheral ........................ PRIF
peripherally ........................ PRIFL
peripheral vision ........................ PRIFGS
photo-refractive keratectomy ........................ FRAV, P–RK/P–RK
prescription ........................ PRIPGS
PRK ........................ P*RK
prosthetic ........................ PRO*T
prosthetic eye ........................ PRAO*IT
protrusion ........................ PRAOUGS
psyche ........................ SKPAOE
pupil ........................ PAOUP

## R

radial keratotomy ........................ R–KT, R*K/R*K
radius ........................ RUS
redness ........................ R–NZ
refract ........................ FRAEK
refraction ........................ FRAEX
refractive ........................ FRAEVK
rehab ........................ RAB
rehabilitation ........................ RABLGS
relay ........................ LAE
relay agent ........................ LAEJ
retina ........................ RAENT
retinal detachment ........................ RAENTD
retinitis ........................ RAOINTS
retinitis pigmentosa ........................ RAOIPTS
retinopathy ........................ RO*PT
RK ........................ R*K
rubella ........................ ROUB

## S

scanner ........................ SKARN
sclera ........................ SKLER
scleritis ........................ SKLAOIT, SKLAOITS
Seeing Eye dog ........................ SDAUG
silence ........................ SLENS
silent ........................ SLENT
spectacle ........................ SPAEKT
stigmatism ........................ SMIFM

## T

TAC ........................ TA*K
tactile ........................ TWOIL, TWAO*IL
tactual ........................ TWUL
Tadoma ........................ DO*EM
Tellatouch ........................ TLUFP
20/ *( vision rating )* ........................ TWARB

**U**

**V**

# CHURCH & RELIGION

**A**

| | |
|---|---|
| Aaron | A*IRN |
| abomination | BOMGS |
| Abraham | BRAUM |
| Abram | BR–M |
| abstinence | STIBS |
| acclamation | KLAEMGS |
| Adam | DYAM |
| adoration | DOERGS |
| adore | DOER |
| adulterous | DROULTS |
| adultery | DRULT |
| advent | DWENT |
| aglow | GLOU |
| alabaster | BRAFT, BRA*S |
| Alexandria | KPRIND |
| alleluia | LOUL |
| almightiness | LOIMTS |
| almighty | LOIMT |
| Almighty Father | LOIFMT |
| Almighty God | LOIMTD, LOIMG |
| alms | A*MS |
| altar | A*LT, AURLT |
| amen | A*IM |
| ancestor | STR– |
| angel | JANL |
| angelic | JEKL |
| angelical | JAEKL |
| angelically | JLEKL, JLAEKL |
| annunciation | NAUNGS |
| anoint | NOINT |
| apocalypse | PLOIPS |
| apocalyptic | PLOIPT |
| apocalyptical | PLAOIL |
| Apostle | PAOFL |
| apostle | PAOFLT |
| apostlehood | POFLD, PAOFLD, PAOFLTD |
| Apostles | PAOFLS |
| apostles | POFLS, PAOFLTS |
| archangel | JARNL |
| Archangel | JAENL, JAERNL |
| aromatic | RAURMT |
| ascension | SAENGS, SKAENGS |
| Asia | AIZ |
| asunder | SURND |
| atheism | A*EFM |
| atheist | A*ET |
| atonement | TO*ENT |
| awe | A*U |
| awesome | A*UZ |

## B

| | |
|---|---|
| Babylon | BLON |
| baptism | BIFM |
| Baptist | BIPT |
| Baptist Church | BIFPT |
| baptize | BAPT |
| baptizer | BARPT |
| Barabbas | BRAB |
| Bartholomew | BARMT |
| beast | BAO*ES |
| beatific | BAEFT, BAEFKT |
| beatifically | BAEFL |
| beatification | BAEFGS |
| beatify | BAOEFT |
| beauty | BAOUT |
| befriend | BRIF |
| beget | B–GT |
| begot | BO*GT |
| begotten | BOEGT, BAOEG |
| begotten son | BOEGTS, BAOEGS |
| beloved | BLOVD |
| bestow | STWOE |
| Bethlehem | BL*ET |
| betroth | TRO*T |
| betrothal | TRO*LT |
| Bible | BAOIBL |
| Bible school | BAOL |
| biblical | BIBL |
| biblically | BLAOEBL |
| bishop | BHOP, BORB |
| blasphemous | FOUM, FOUMS |
| blasphemy | FAOEM |
| bless | BLEF, BLES |
| blessed | BLEFD |
| blesses | BLEFS, BLESZ |
| blessing | BLEFG |
| blest | BLEFT |
| body | BOD |
| bounteous | BOUNZ |
| bread | BRAED |
| breath | BR*ET |
| brimstone | BROEMT |
| Buddha | BHUD, BAO*D |
| Buddhism | BHUFM, BAO*FM |
| Buddhist | BHUFT, BAO*FT |
| bulwark | BLAURK |
| buried | BRUD |
| bury | BRU |

## C

| | |
|---|---|
| Cabala | KBA*L, KBLAL |
| calvary | KRAVL |
| canonization | KAOIGS |
| canonize | KAOIS |

| | |
|---|---|
| canonized | KAOIFD |
| canonizer | KAOIFRZ |
| canonizes | KAOISZ, KAOIFZ |
| canonizing | KAOIFG |
| Catholic | KA*LT |
| Catholicism | KLAFM |
| celebrate | SBRAIT |
| celebration | SBRAIGS |
| celestial | SLES |
| centurion | SNAOURN |
| Chanukah | KHAUNK |
| chariot | KHOT |
| charitable | KHAIRBL |
| charitableness | KHAIRBLS |
| charitably | KHAOERBL |
| charity | KHAIRT |
| choir | KHOIR, KWOIR |
| Christ | KRAO*IS |
| christen | KRIFN |
| christened | KRIFND |
| christening | KRIFNG |
| christens | KRIFNS |
| Christian | KRIN |
| Christianity | KRINT, KRIFNT |
| Christmas | KROIM |
| Christmas Eve | KRAOEV, KROIVM |
| Christmas tree | KROIMT |
| Christopher | KRIFR |
| church | KHUFP |
| churchgoing | KHOEFPG |
| Church of Jesus Christ of Latter-day Saints | KHAINTS |
| churchyard | KH–RD |
| cloven | KLOEVN |
| command | KMAN |
| commander | KMARND, KMARN |
| commandment | KMANT, KMAMT |
| commemorate | KMEM |
| commemorating | KMEMG |
| commemoration | KMEMGS, KMEJ |
| commemorative | KMEV, KMEVT |
| communal | KMAOUNL, KMUNL |
| communally | KMAOENL |
| communion | KMAOUNGS, KMOUN, KMOIN |
| community | KMUNT, KMAOUNT |
| compassion | KPARB, KPAGS |
| compassionate | KPARBT, KPAGT |
| compassionately | KPAERBLT |
| conceive | SKAOEV |
| conceived | SKAOEVD |
| conception | SKEPGS |
| confess | FES |
| confessed | FEFD |
| confession | FEGS |
| confessional | FELGS |

confirm ................................................................................................ KWIRM
confirmation .............................................. KWIRGS, KWIRMGS, KWIRJ
congregate .......................................................................................... KRAEG
congregation .................................................................................... KRAEGS
conquer ............................................................................................... KWUR
conquerable ...................................................................................... KWURBL
conqueror ............................................................... KWR*UR, KWOER
conscience ......................................................................................... K–RB
consent ................................................................................................ SKENT
consenting adult ............................................................................... SKENGTD
consequence ..................................................................................... KWENS
consequent ........................................................................................ KWENT
consequently ..................................................................................... KWENL
contemplate ....................................................................................... KPLAIT
contemplation ................................................................................... KPLAIGS
contemplative ................................................................................... KPLAIV
contemplatively ................................................................................ KPLAIVL
contemplativeness ........................................................................... KPLAIVNS
Corinth ................................................................................................ KO*RNT
Corinthians ........................................................................................ KR*INTS
corrupt ............................................................................... KRUP, KRUPT
corruptible ........................................................................................ KRUBL
corruption .......................................................................................... KRUPGS
corrupts ............................................................................. KRUPS, KRUPTS
covenant ............................................................................. KOFNT, KOVNT
cradle .................................................................................................. KRAELD
create ..................................................................................................... KRI
created ................................................................................................ KRID
creates ............................................................................................... KRIS
creating ............................................................................................... KRIG
creation ............................................................................................... KRIGS
creator ................................................................................................ KRIR
creature .............................................................................................. KRAOEFP
cross ................................................................................................... KROSZ
crucified ............................................................................................. KRUFD
crucifies ............................................................................................. KRUFS
crucifix ....................................................................... KRUFX, KRAOUFX
crucifixion .............................................................. KRUFGS, KRAOUFGS
crucify ................................................................................................ KRUZ
crucifying ........................................................................................... KRUFG
Cyprian ...................................................................... SPR*IN, SPR–N
Cyrus .................................................................................................. SR*US

**D**

Damascus ........................................................................................... DMAS
Damian ............................................................................................... DA*IM
deacon ................................................................................................ DAO*EK
defile .................................................................................................. DWAOIL
defilement .......................................................................................... DWAOIMT
defiler ................................................................................................. DWAOIRL
deity ................................................................................................... DAO*ET
deliver .................................................................... DLIVR, DLIFR
deliverable ............................................................. DLIVRL, DLIVRBL
deliverance ........................................................... DLIVRNS, DLIFRNS

delivery ............................................................................................................ DLOIVR
demon ....................................................................................... DMON, DM–N
demoralization .......................................................................... DMORLGS
denomination ............................................................................... DNOMGS
descend ........................................................................................... SDEND
descendant ..................................................................................... SDAENT
descent ............................................................................................. SDENT
desert................................................................................................ SDERT
deserter ......................................................................................... SDRERT
desertion ....................................................................................... SDERGS
desolation ..................................................................................... SDOLGS
Deuteronomy .................................................................................. DAORT
devilish ........................................................................................... DLERB
diocesan ..................................................................................... DAOINSZ
diocese ......................................................................................... DAOISZ
disciple ............................................................................................... SDIP
divine .................................................................. DWAO*IN, DWOIN
divinely ............................................................. DWAOINL, DWOINL
divinity ........................................................................................... DWINT
docile ............................................................................................... SDOIL
doctrinal ........................................................................... DROINL, DR–NL
doctrine ............................................................................. DROIN, DR–N
domain ............................................................................................ DMAIN
dominion .......................................................................................... DMOIN
donkey ............................................................................................. DONK
doth .................................................................................................. DOFT
dromedary ..................................................................................... DROMD
dungeon ............................................................................................. D*UJ

**E**

earth ................................................................................................... *ERT
earthly ............................................................................................... *ERLT
Easter .......................................................................................... AO*ERS
ecclesiastic .............................................................................. KLAOEFT
ecclesiastical ......................................................................... KLAOEFLT
ecstasy ........................................................................................... STAOE
Eden ............................................................................................ YAOEND
Egypt .................................................................................................. JIPT
Egyptian ........................................................................................... JIPGS
Elijah ................................................................................................ LAOIJ
Elizabeth ............................................................................................ L*IZ
Emmanuel ................................................................................... MA*ENL
endless ............................................................................................. ENLD
enlighten ................................................................................. SPWLAOINT
enlightened ........................................................................... SPWLAOINTD
enlightener ............................................................................ SPWLAOIRNT
enlightenment ........................................................................ SPWLAOIMT
enrich ...........................................................................................SPWRIFP
enthrone ................................................................................... SPWROEN
Ephesians ........................................................... FAOEGSZ, FAO*EGSZ
Episcopalian .................................................................................. AOEPS
epistle ............................................................................................. POIFLT
eternal ......................................................................................... TAOERNL
eternally ....................................................................................... TAERNL

| | |
|---|---|
| eternity | TAOERNT |
| ether | AO*ET |
| ethereal | AO*ELT |
| Eucharist | AOUKT |
| evangel | JEVL |
| evangelic | JEVK |
| evangelical | JAEVL |
| Evangelical | J–VL |
| evangelically | JLAEVL |
| evangelism | JEVM |
| evangelist | JEVLT |
| Evangelist | J–VLT |
| evangelization | JELGS |
| evangelize | JEV |
| evangelizer | JEVR |
| evangelizing | JEVG |
| eve | AOEV |
| Eve | YAOEV |
| everlasting | EVRLG |
| evil | AOEVL |
| exalt | KPALT |
| exaltation | KPALGS |
| exalted | KPALTD |
| exalting | KPALGT |
| exalts | KPALTS |
| exodus | KPOED |
| Exodus | KPOEDZ |
| expiate | KPA*ET |
| extol | KPOEL |
| extoller | KPOERL |
| exult | KPULT |
| exultation | KPOULGS, KP*ULGS |
| Ezekiel | ZAOEKL, SAOEKL |

# F

| | |
|---|---|
| faith | FA*IT |
| faithful | FAIF |
| faithfully | FAIFL |
| fast | FA*S |
| fasted | FAEFTD, FA*S/–D |
| father | FA, FAU |
| flask | FLAFK |
| flock | FLOK |
| foes | FOES |
| forefather | FOEFR |
| forgave | FRAEV, FOR/GAEV |
| forgive | FRIV, FOR/GIV |
| forgiven | FRIVN, FRIFN, FOR/GIVN |
| forgiveness | FRIVNS, GIVNS |
| forgives | FRIVS, FOR/GIVS |
| forgiving | FRIVG, FO*R/GIVG |
| fornicate | FORNG, FONK |
| fornication | FORNGS, FONKS |
| fornicator | FRORNG, FRONK |

forsake ................................................................................................... FRAIK
forsaken ................................................................... FRA\*IN, FRAIK/–N
foundation ....................................................................................... FOUNGS
Fr. ................................................................................................. FR–FPLT
fragrance ........................................................... FRAIGTS, FRA\*IGS
fragrant ............................................................................................ FRAIGT
frankincense ................................................................................. SFRANK
friar ..................................................................................................... FROIR
Friar .......................................................................................... FRAO\*IR
fruited ............................................................................................ FRAOUTD
fulfill ................................................................................................... F–FL
fulfillment ...................................................................... FL–FMT, FUFMT

## G

Gabriel ............................................................................................ GRAIBL
Galilean .......................................................................................... GLAEL
Galilee ...................................................................... GLEL, GLAOEL
Garden of Eden ........................................................................ GAOEND
garland ............................................................................................ GARLD
generation ................................................................. JAIGS, JENGS
Genesis .................................................................. JENSZ, GENSZ
gentile ............................................................................................ GAOILT
Gentile ............................................................................................. GOILT
genuflect .................................................................... GUFLT, GEFL
genuflecting ................................................................ GUFLGT, GEFLG
genuflection ................................ GUFGS, GEFGS, GUFLGS, GEFLGS
Gethsemane ................................................................................. G\*ETS
Gethsemani ..................................................................................... G\*ET
Gideon .............................................................................................. GIND
Gideon Bible ................................................................................... GIBD
gild ................................................................................. G\*ILD, GLID
gilded .......................................................... GL\*ID, G\*ILD/–D
gilt ................................................................................................... G\*ILT
glorious ................................................................. GLOUS, GLORZ
gloriously ............................................................ GLOULS, GLORLZ
glory .................................................................................................. GLOR
Gnostic ........................................................................................... GOFKT
Gnosticism .................................................................................... GOIFM
Godhead .......................................................................................... G\*ED
Golgotha ................................................................................... GO\*LG
Gomorrah ...................................................................................... GOERM
gospel ..................................................................... GOS, GOPS
grace .............................................................................................. GRAIS
grandeur ..................................................................................... GRAOUR
Greek ......................................................................................... GRAOEK
Gregorian ................................................................................... GROERN
Gregorian chant ...................................................................... GROERNT
hallelujah ................................................................. HA\*L, HO\*UL
hallowed ...................................................................................... WHAOLD

## H

Hanukah ........................................................................................ HAUNK
hark .................................................................................................. HARK
harken ........................................................................................ HA\*ERN

| | |
|---|---|
| hath | HA*T |
| haughty | HAUT |
| heaven | HEVN |
| heavenly | HEVNL |
| Hebrew | HAOEB |
| herald | HAIRLD |
| Herod | H*ERD |
| Him | H*IM |
| Hindu | HOIND |
| Hinduism | HOIFM |
| holocaust | HAUFT |
| Holocaust | HA*UFT |
| holy | HO*IL |
| Holy Ghost | HOILG, HO*ILG |
| Holy Spirit | HOILT |
| homage | HAUM |
| Horeb | HO*ERB |
| hosanna | HAO*NS |
| hymn | YH–M, YHIM |
| idol | DOLD |
| idolater | DORLT, DOLTD |

**I**

| | |
|---|---|
| immaculate | MAKLT |
| Immaculate Conception | MAPGS |
| immortal | KBORLT, KBOERL |
| immortality | KBOERLT |
| impoverish | KBOVR, KBOFR |
| impoverishment | KBOVMT, KBOFMT |
| imprison | KBRIN, KBRIZ, KBRIS |
| imprisonment | KBRIMT, PRIFMT |
| inherit | HERT |
| iniquity | NOIKT |
| intercede | SPWRAOED |
| intercession | SPWR*EGS, SNEGS |
| internal | SPWERNL |
| Isaac | AOIKS |
| Isaiah | YHA |
| Iscariot | SKROT |
| Islam | SLAUM |
| Islamic | SLAUMG |
| isle | YAOIL |
| Israel | IZ |
| Israeli | ILZ |

**J**

| | |
|---|---|
| Jehovah | HOEV |
| Jehovah's Witness | HOEVS |
| Jehovah's Witnesses | HOEVSZ |
| Jeremiah | JAIRM |
| Jerusalem | JAOUM |
| Jesuit | JUZ |
| Jesus | JAOEZ |
| Jesus of Nazareth | JAOEFNZ |

Jew .................................................................................... JAOU
Jewish ........................................................................ JAOURB
Jews ........................................................................... JAOUZ
Jordan ........................................................................... JORD
Jordanian ..................................................................... JORND
Joseph .......................................................................... JOEF
journey ......................................................................... JOIRN
joy ................................................................................... JOI
joyful ............................................................................. JOIF
joyfully ......................................................................... JOIFL
joyfulness .................................................................. JOIFNS
joyless .......................................................................... JOIL
jubilation ................................................................ JAOUBLGS
Judah ........................................................................... JAOD
Judaism ............................................ JUFM, JAOFM, JAOUFM
Judas ..................................................... JAOUDZ, JAODZ
Judas Iscariot ................................... JAOURDZ, JAORDZ
Judea ......................................................................... JAOED

## K

kingdom ...................................................................... KINGD
Koran ......................................................................... KRAUN
kosher ....................................................................... KOERB

## L

Latter-day Saints .................................... LAIRNTS, LA*INTS
Lebanon ........................................................................ L*EB
lector ......................................................................... LORKT
lent .............................................................................. LENT
liar ............................................................................. LAOIR
liturgical ...................................................................... LURJ
liturgy ......................................................................... LOIRJ
lord ............................................................................. LORD
Lord ........................................................................... LO*RD
love ............................................................................... LOV
Luther ..................................................................... LAO*URT
Lutheran .................................................................. LAO*UT
lyre .......................................................................... LAO*IR

## M

Magdalene ................................................................. MAGD
Magi ......................................................................... JAOIM
maiden .................................................... MA*IND, MA*END
maid servant ................................... MAIFRNT, MAIVRNT
majesty ....................................................................... MAJT
manger ...................................................................... MAING
Martin Luther ........................................ MAO*UT, MAO*URT
martyr ....................................................... MIRT, MA*URT
martyrdom ........................................... MIRMD, MAURMD
Mary Magdalene ..................................................... MAIRGD
Mathias .................................................................. MAO*ITS
Mecca .......................................................................... M*EK
meek ........................................................................ MAOEK
meekly ..................................................................... MAOEKL

| | |
|---|---|
| meekness | MAOEKZ |
| Mennonite | M*NT |
| merciful | MEFRL, MEFRS |
| mercifully | MLEFRL, MEFRLS |
| mercifulness | MEFRSZ, MEFRLZ |
| Mesopotamia | MEPT |
| messiah | SMAOI |
| methodism | MOIFMT |
| Methodism | MO*IFMT |
| Methodist | MOIFT |
| Methodist Church | MOIFRT |
| midst | M*ID |
| minister | SMIRNT |
| ministerial | SMERNL |
| ministry | SMERNT |
| miracle | MIRKL |
| miraculous | MIRKLS |
| miraculously | MOIRKL |
| Mohammed | MAUMD |
| monasterial | SMONLT |
| monastery | SMONT |
| monastic | SMONK, SMUNK |
| monastical | SMOKL |
| monastically | SMAOEKL |
| monasticism | SMOFM |
| monk | MUNK |
| Mormon | MORM |
| Mormon Tabernacle | MOIMT |
| Moslem | MOFM |
| mosque | MOFK |
| mourn | MOURN |
| mourner | MROURN |
| mournful | MOUFRL |
| mournfully | MLOUFRL |
| mournfulness | MOUFRLS |
| Muslim | MUFM |
| myrrh | YMIR |
| mysterious | STRAOES |
| mystery | STRAOE |
| mystic | MIFKT |
| mystical | MIFKL |
| mysticism | MIFMT |

**N**

| | |
|---|---|
| naked | NAIKD |
| nakedly | NAIKLD |
| nakedness | NAIKDZ |
| nativity | NAUVT |
| naught | NAUGT |
| Nazarene | NARZ, N*RS |
| Nazareth | N*RT |
| Nehemiah | NAO*EM |
| nourish | NOURB |
| nourishment | NOURMT |

nun ........................................................................................................ NAUN

## O

oracle ................................................................................................. ORKL
ordain ................................................................................... ORND, DA*IN
ordination ..................................................... ORNGZ, ORNGS, DA*INGS
ornament .......................................................................................... ORNT
orthodox ..................................................................... DROX, O*RTD

## P

pagan ................................................................................................ PENG
parable .......................................................................................... PR–BL
pardon ............................................................................................. PARD
pardoning ..................................................................................... PARGD
parish .......................................................................................... PRAERB
parishioner ................................................................................... PR–FRN
parishioners ................................................................................ PR–FRNZ
parish priest ............................................................................... PRAERP
Passover ........................................................................................ POEVR
pasture .......................................................................................... PAUFR
patience ........................................................................................ PAIRBS
Pentecost ......................................................................................... PENK
Pentecostal ..................................................................................... PENKL
Persia ............................................................................................. PERZ
Persian ......................................................................................... PERGS
pharaoh ........................................................................................ FAORP
Pharisee ......................................................................................... FAURZ
Pharisees ..................................................................................... FAURSZ
philosophy ....................................................................................... FLOF
piety ............................................................................................. PYAOET
Pilate ........................................................................................... PLA*ET
pious ............................................................................................. PYOUS
piously ......................................................................................... PYOULS
piousness ...................................................... PYOUSZ, PYOUNS
pontiff ......................................................................................... PAUFNT
Pontius Pilate ................................................................................. PONTS
prayer .......................................................................................... PRAIR
prayerful ..................................................................................... PRAIFRL
prayerfully ................................................. PRAOEFRL, PLAIFRL
prayerfulness ............................................................................ PRAIFRLS
preach ...................................................................................... PRAOEFP
preacher .................................................................................. PRAOEFRP
precious .................................................................. PR–RB, PR*ERB
priest ......................................................................................... PRAO*ES
priestly .......................................................... PRAO*EL, PRAO*ELS
prophecy ...................................................................................... PRAUFS
prophet ...................................................................................... PROEFT
prophetic .................................................................................... PREFKT
proverb ...................................................................................... PROFRB
Proverbs .................................................................................... PROFRBZ
Providence ............................................... PROIFNS, PROIVS
psalm ........................................................................................... ZAUM

## Q

| | |
|---|---|
| Quaker | KWAIRK |
| Quaker Church | KWUFP |
| Quakerism | KWAIFM |
| Quakerly | KWAIRKL |
| quickening | KWENG |

## R

| | |
|---|---|
| rabbi | RA*B |
| radiance | RAINZ |
| Ramadan | RAUMD |
| recompense | WRAEK |
| reconcile | SKAOIL |
| reconciliation | SILGS, RAOILGS, RILGS |
| redeem | RAO*EM, R*M |
| redeemer | RAO*ERM, R*RM |
| Redeemer | RAOERM |
| reign | RA*IN |
| rejoice | JOIFS |
| rejoicing | JOIFG |
| religion | R–J |
| religious | LIJ |
| reparation | RAEPGS |
| repent | PRAOENT |
| repentance | PRAOENZ |
| repentant | PR*ENT |
| repentantly | PRENLT |
| repenter | PRAOERNT |
| resplendence | SPLENTS |
| resplendency | SPLAOENTS |
| resplendent | SPLENT |
| resplendently | SPLENLT |
| resurrect | RURKT |
| resurrection | R*URX |
| resurrection day | RURKD |
| resurrector | RORKT, ROURKT |
| reverence | REVRNS |
| reverend | REVRND |
| reverent | REVRNT |
| reverently | REVRNL |
| Roman Catholic | RAOKT |
| Roman Catholic Church | RAOFP |
| rosaries | RAORSZ |
| rosary | RAORZ |
| Rosh Hashanah | RAURB |

## S

| | |
|---|---|
| Sabbath | SBA*T |
| sacrament | SKRAMT |
| sacred | SKRAID |
| sacredly | SKRAILD |
| sacrifice | SKRAOIF |
| sacrificial | SKRIFL, SKRAOIFL |
| saint | SAINT |

| | |
|---|---|
| salvation | SWALGS |
| Samaritan | SMAIRN |
| sanctification | SFAOIGS |
| sanctifier | SFAOIRK |
| sanctify | SFAOIK |
| sanctuary | SKHAIR |
| sandal | SDAL |
| Satan | ST–N |
| savior | SYOER |
| sayeth | SA*ET, SYA*ET, SYA*IT |
| scepter | SKERPT |
| Scientologist | STO*LT |
| Scientology | STO*LG |
| scoff | SKOF |
| scourge | SKURJ |
| scribe | SKRAOIB |
| scripture | SKRIRT |
| scroll | SKROEL |
| sea | SAE |
| secular | SERKL |
| secularism | SLEFM, SKLURM |
| serpent | SERP |
| Sheba | SHAOEB |
| shepherd | SH*ERD, SHERPD |
| shroud | SHROUD |
| Sikh | SKH– |
| Sikhism | SKH–FM |
| silent | SLENT, SAOILT |
| silently | SLENL |
| Simon | SMIN |
| sin | SIN |
| Sinai | SNAO*I |
| sinful | S*INL |
| sinfully | SL*INL |
| sinfulness | S*INS |
| sinless | S*INLS |
| sinner | SIRN |
| sins | SINZ |
| slave | SLAIV |
| Sodom | SDAM |
| solace | SLAOS |
| solemn | SLEM |
| solemnly | SLOIM |
| solidarity | SDAIRT |
| sorrow | SWO |
| sorrowful | SWOF |
| sorrowfully | SWOFL |
| sorrowfulness | SWOFNS, SWONS |
| sovereignty | SOVRNT, SOFRNT |
| sow | SO*U |
| splendor | SPLEN, SPLOR |
| suffer | SUFR |
| sura | SWUR |
| swaddling | SWAGD |

symbolize ............................................................................................... SBLAOIS
symbolizing .......................................................................................... SBLAOIFG

**T**

tabernacle ................................................................................................ TAEBL
talent ...................................................................................... TAELT, TLENT
Talmud ........................................................................................................ TUD
Taoism .................................................................................................. TAOFM
Taoist .................................................................................................. TAO*FT
Taoists ............................................................................................... TAOFTS
temple ................................................................................................. TEMPL
temptation ......................................................................................... TEMGS
testament ........................................................................................... TEFMT
Thanksgiving ..................................................................................... THAFG
Thanksgiving Day ......................................................................... THAFGD
thee .................................................................................................... THAOE
thence ................................................................................................ THENS
thenceforth ..................................................................................... THEFRNS
Thessalonians ................................................................................. TLOENZ
thine ................................................................................................. THAOIN
thirst ............................................................................... TH*IRS, THIFRT
thou .................................................................................................. THO*U
throne .............................................................................................. THROEN
thy ........................................................................................................ THOI
tiding ............................................................................................... TAOIGD
tidings ............................................................................................ TAOIGDZ
tinsel .................................................................................................... TINZ
tis .......................................................................................................... T–Z
Torah ...................................................................... TRAO, TO*ER
transfiguration .............................................................................. TRIFGS
transfigure ....................................................................................... TRIFG
transfigured ................................................................................... TRIFGD
transfigures .................................................................................... TRIFGZ
transfiguring .................................................................. TR*IFG, TRIFG/–G
trespass ............................................................................................. TREP
tribunal ........................................................................................... BAOUNL
trinity ............................................................................................... TRINT
Trinity ............................................................................................ TRINTD
triumph .......................................................................................... TRUFM
triumphant .................................................................................... TRUFMT
truly ............................................................................................... TRAOUL

**U**

Unitarian ............................................................................................. YAIRN

**V**

Vatican .............................................................................................. VAFK
Vatican City .................................................................................... VAFKT
verse .................................................................................................. VERS
vestibule ........................................................................................... VEFBL
victor .................................................................................................. VIRK
victorious .......................................................................................... VIRKS
victors ............................................................................................... VIRKZ
village ................................................................................................... VIL

vindication ............................................................................................... V–NGS
vineyard ...................................................................................... VOIND, YAVD
virgin .................................................................................................... VIRJ
virtue .................................................................................................... VIR
virtuous ............................................................................................... VIFPS
vulnerability ......................................................................................... VUBLT
vulnerable ........................................................................................... VUBL

## W

wicked .................................................................................................. WIKD
wickedness ........................................................................................... WIKDZ
womb ...................................................................................... WAOM, WAOUM
wonder ................................................................................................. WOND
wondrous .............................................................................................. WORND
worship ................................................................................................ WORP
worshiper ............................................................................................. WRORP
worthily ................................................................................... WOIRLT, WO*IRLT
worthy ..................................................................................... WOIRT, WO*IRT
wrought ............................................................................................... WRAUT

## Y

Yom Kippur ........................................................................................... YIRP
Yule ................................................................................................... YAOUL
Yuletide ............................................................................................... YAOULD

## Z

zeal .................................................................................................... ZAOEL
Zebedee ............................................................................................... ZEBD
Zion ..................................................................................................... Z–N
Zoroaster .............................................................................................. Z–RT
Zoroastrian ........................................................................................... Z–RN
Zoroastrianism ....................................................................................... Z–FM

# COMPASS POINTS (& derivatives)

## CARDINAL POINTS

**North** (N–)

| | |
|---|---|
| north | NO*RT |
| northbound | NORB |
| northeast | NAO*ES |
| northeasterly | NAOERL |
| northeastern | NAOERN |
| northeasterner | NRAOERN |
| northerly | NORL |
| northern | NORN |
| northerner | NRORN |
| north side | N–DZ |
| northwest | N*ES |
| northwesterly | NERL |
| northwestern | NERN |
| northwesterner | NRERN |

**South** (S–)

| | |
|---|---|
| south | SO*UT |
| southbound | SOUB |
| southeast | SAO*ES |
| southeasterly | SERL |
| southeastern | SAOERN |
| southerly | SORL |
| southern | SORN |
| southerner | SRORN |
| south side | S–DZ |
| southwest | SW*ES |
| southwesterly | SWERL |
| southwestern | SWERN |

**East** (AOE–, E–)

| | |
|---|---|
| east | AO*ES |
| eastbound | AOEB |
| easterly | AOERL |
| eastern | AOERN |
| easterner | RAOERN |
| east side | EDZ |
| eastward | AOERD |

**West** (W–)

| | |
|---|---|
| west | W*ES |
| westbound | WAOEB, W–B |
| westerly | WAOERL |
| western | WERN |
| westerner | WRERN |
| west side | W–DZ |

## MID-REGIONAL

**Mideast** (M–, D–)

| | |
|---|---|
| Mideast | MAO*ES, DAO*ES |
| Mideastern | MAO*ERN, DAO*ERN |
| Mideasterner | MRAOERN, DRAOERN |

**Midwest** (DW–)

| | |
|---|---|
| Midwest | DW*ES |
| Midwestern | DWERN |
| Midwesterner | DWRERN |

## DIRECTIONAL

**-bound** (–B)

| | |
|---|---|
| eastbound | AOEB |
| northbound | NORB |
| southbound | SOUB |
| westbound | WAOEB, W–B |

**-east** (–AO*ES)

| | |
|---|---|
| Mideast | MAO*ES |
| northeast | NAO*ES |
| southeast | SAO*ES |

**-easterly** (–ERL)

| | |
|---|---|
| northeasterly | NAOERL |
| southeasterly | SERL |

**-eastern** (–AOERN)

| | |
|---|---|
| Mideastern | MAO*ERN |
| northeastern | NAOERN |
| southeastern | SAOERN |

**-erly** (–RL)

| | |
|---|---|
| easterly | AOERL |
| northerly | NORL |
| southerly | SORL |
| westerly | WAOERL |

**-ern** (–RN)

| | |
|---|---|
| eastern | AOERN |
| Midwestern | DWERN |
| northern | NORN |
| southern | SORN |
| western | WERN |

**-erner** (–ERN, –ORN)

| | |
|---|---|
| easterner | RAOERN |
| Mideasterner | MRAOERN |
| Midwesterner | DWRERN |
| northeasterner | NRAOERN |
| northerner | NRORN |
| northwesterner | NRERN |
| westerner | WRERN |

**-side** (–DZ)

| | |
|---|---|
| east side | EDZ |
| north side | N–DZ |

south side ................................................................................................ S–DZ
west side ................................................................................................ W–DZ

**-west** (*ES)
Midwest ............................................................................................ DW*ES
northwest ........................................................................................... N*ES
southwest .......................................................................................... SW*ES

**-western** (–ERN)
southwestern ..................................................................................... SWERN
northwestern ...................................................................................... NERN

**-westerly** (–ERL)
northwesterly ...................................................................................... NERL
southwesterly ..................................................................................... SWERL

# COMPUTER / INTERNET

## NOTE

Computer/Internet terms are continuously evolving. The origin of many of these terms is typically a manufacturer's trade name or process standard. As these words are assimilated into the English language, they frequently undergo structural modification (initial capitals become lower case, words join together, etc.).

The Computer/Internet terms provided here are styled according to popular usage at the time of printing. To avoid conflicts, create a separate "computer" case dictionary for the specialized terms and use this case dictionary only when you need the computer technical terminology to be active.

**A**

adapter ................................................................................................ DRAPT
adaptor ................................................................................................ DARPT
analog ............................................................................... NAULG, GOUG
application ........................................................................................... PLIGS
archive ................................................................................................ KAOIV

**B**

bi-directional ...................................................................................... BREGS
bi-directional port ............................................................................ BREPGS
binaural ............................................................................................. BAURL
bitmap .................................................................................................. BIPT
bitmapped .......................................................................................... BIPTD
blog ................................................................................. BLO*G, BLA*UG
blogger ............................................................................ BLORG, BLAURG
blogosphere ................................................................. BLOGS, BLAUGZ
Bluetooth .......................................................................................... BLAO*T
browse .............................................................................................. BROUS
browser ........................................................................ BROURS, BROUFR
bulletin ................................................................................................. BLIN
bulletin board ....................................................................................... BLIB
byte ................................................................................................... BAO*IT

**C**

CAD ...................................................................................................... KAD
CAD-CAM ........................................................................................... KAMD
cartridge ............................................................................................. KRAJ
CD-R ................................................................................................. KR–RD
CD-ROM ............................................................................................. DROM
CD-RW ............................................................................................ WR–RD
central processor unit .................................................. SPUNT, SPU/SPU
chatroom ........................................................................................ KHAOMT
client .................................................................................................. KLAOI
client-server ..................................................................................... KLEFRB
CMYK ................................................................................................ SM–K

CMYK image ............................................................................ SMIJ
COM ..................................................................................... KROM
computer .................................................................. KPR–, KPAOURT
computer-aided design ........................................ KPAOIN, KAD/KAD
computer-aided manufacture ......................................................... KPAF
computerize ................................................................................. KPR–R
conventional memory .................................................................. KWEVM
CPU ................................................................................................ SPU
cursor .......................................................................................... KRORZ
cyber .......................................................................... SAOIB, SAOIRB
cyberspace .......................................................... SAOIBS, SAOIRBS

**D**

data ................................................................................................. DAT
database ......................................................................................... D–B
desktop ........................................................................................... D–T
desktop computer ............................................... DR–T, DRAOURT
desktop publishing ................................................................... D–RBT
device driver .......................................................................... DWAOIFR
digital ............................................................................................. DIJT
diskette ......................................................................................... SKET
domain name ........................................................................... DMAIM
DOS .............................................................................................. DOS
DOS protected mode .............................................................. DROED
dot com ........................................................................................ D–M
.com (*"dot com"*) ...................................................................... D*M
dot edu ..................................................................................... DWAOE
.edu (*"dot edu"*) ....................................................................... DWU
dot gov ...................................................................................... DOIVG
.gov (*"dot gov"*) ........................................................................ DAUV
dot matrix printer ................................................................... DMAIX
dot net ......................................................................................... DNET
.net (*"dot net"*) ....................................................................... DN*ET
dot org ................................................................... DAORG, DO*RG
.org (*"dot org"*) ........................................................................ D*RG
dots per inch ............................................................................. DOFP
dots-per-inch ............................................................................ DOFPS
download .................................................................................. DOUNL
DPMI ........................................................................................... DP–M
drum scanner ............................................................................. DRAN
dual processor ..................................................................... DWAORP
duplexer ...................................... DPLERX, DAORPGS, DAOURPGS
DVD ............................................................................................ D–VD
DVD–R ....................................................................................... D–VRD
DVD+R ........................................................... D–VPD, D–VRPD
DVD–RW .......................................................... DW–VD, DW–VRD
DVD+RW .................................................. DWR–VD, DWR–VRD
dye sublimation ...................................................................... DBLIM
dye sublimation printer ......................................................... DBLIRM

**E**

ergonomic keyboard ........................................................ KERG, ERG
Ethernet ................................................................................. AO*ENT
executable ............................................................................... SKUBL

executable file ............................................................ SKUFBL
expanded memory ...................................................... SPAEM
extended memory ......................................................... SKEM

## F

FAQ ........................................................................... FA*K
file transfer protocol ................................................. FAOIP
FireWire .................................................................... FWAOIR
firewall ...................................................................... FWAUL
flatbed scanner ......................................................... FLARN
floating point ............................................................ FLOEPG
floppy disk ................................................................ FLOIPD
format ....................................................................... FORMT
Frequently Asked Questions ..................................... FA*KZ
FTP ........................................................................... F–PT
Future Domain ......................................................... FWAIN

## G

gateway ..................................................................... GAE
gigabit ....................................................................... GIBT
gigabyte ..................................................................... GIGT
Google ....................................................................... GAOG
graphic ....................................................................... GRAFK
graphics file .............................................................. GLAOIL
graphics tablet .......................................................... GLET

## H

hard disk .................................................................... H–RD
hardware ........................................... DWAER, WHAER
Hewlett Packard ....................................................... HAOUP
homepage .................................................................. HAIJ
home page .................................................................. HOEJ
HPGL ........................................................................ H–PLG
HTML ........................................................................ H*MT
http ........................................................................... H–TD
hypertext ................................................................... HAOIPT
Hypertext Markup Language ................... HAOIMT, H*MT/H*MT
Hypertext Transfer Protocol .............. HAOIRPT, H–TD/H–TD

## I

IBM ........................................................................... AOIB
INI file ....................................................................... N*IL
ink jet ........................................................ JINK, JING
ink jet printer ............................................................ JIRNT
Internet ..................................................................... SPW–NT
iTunes ....................................................................... TAOUNZ

## J

JPEG ........................................................... J–PG, JAIG

## K

keyboard ................................................................... KAOEB

## L

laptop .......................................... LAPT, LOPT, LAUP

laptop computer ........................................................................ LORPT, LAURP
laser ............................................................................................................. LAIRZ
laser printer ............................................................................................... LAIRP
local bus ...................................................................................................... LOBL

**M**

Mac ................................................................................................................ MAK
Macintosh ................................................................................................... MAKT
magneto-optical ........................................................................................ MOPT
Manager Information Systems ................................................................ MIFGS
massively parallel computing .................................................................MUGT
megabit ....................................................................................................... MIBT
megabyte ................................................................................................... MEGT
megahertz .................................................................................................. MEGZ
memory manager ...................................................................................... MEMG
Microsoft ................................................................................................. MAUFT
MIS ..............................................................................................................M*IZ
modem ..................................................................................................... MOEMD
monaural ................................................................................................ MAURNL
monitor ....................................................................................................... MONT
monochrome ........................................................................................... KMOEM
Motorola .................................................................................................. MROEL
mouse ........................................................................................................ MOUS
MPEG ........................................................................................................ MA*IG
MP3 ........................................................................................................ MAOEPT
MP3 player .......................................................................................... MAOERPT
multi-frequency ........................................................................................ MEKZ
multimedia ........................................................................................... MAOEMD
multiscan ................................................................................................. MULTS
multisync.................................................................................................. M–NK

**N**

navigator ................................................................................................. NAFRGT
network ..................................................................................... TWORK, NWORK
networking .................................................................. TWO*RG, TWO*RK, NWORG

**O**

OCR ............................................................................................................ O*RK
OCR scanner .......................................................................... SKAORN, O*RKZ
operating system ...................................................................... PRIMG, PR*IM
optical character recognition ........................................... O*RGS, ORPGS, TAULGS
optical disk ................................................................................................. PIFK

**P**

parallel port ........................................................................................... PLOERT
PC ................................................................................................................. P*K
PCI ............................................................................................................... P*IK
PCI bus ......................................................................................................... PIB
PCI slot ....................................................................................... PLAUT, PLO*T
PCMCIA card ....................................................................... P–MD, PAMD
Pentium ...................................................................................................... PENT
personal information manager ............................................................... PIFGS
PIM ............................................................................................................. P*IM
pixel ............................................................................................................ SPIX

plug-n-play ............................................................ PLUN
pointing device ...................................................... PAOIZ
port ...................................................................... PORT
printer .................................................................. PRIRNT
printout ................................................................ PROUT
processor ............................................................. PRORS
protected file ....................................................... PRAO*IL
protocol ............................................................... KPROET

## R

RAM ..................................................................... RA*M
random access memory ........................... RA*MD, RA*M/RA*M
read-only memory ........................... RO*M, ROM/ROM
removable storage ................................................ ROERJ
RGB .................................................................... JAOEB
RGB image ........................................................... JAOEJ
ROM ..................................................................... ROM

## S

screensaver ............................... SKRAIVR, SKRAIFR
SCSI .................................................................... SKWUZ
search engine ...................................................... SN–J
serial port ............................... SAOERP, SAOERPT
server ............................... SR–VR, SR–FR
service provider ................................................ S–VRP
SGML ................................................................. SG–M
shell .................................................................... SHEL
slot ...................................................................... SLOT
software ............................................................. SWAER
Sound Blaster .................................................... SBLA*S
source code ........................................................ SORKD
spreadsheet ....................................................... SPRAOET
Standard Generalized Markup Language ................ SG–L
Standardized Text Markup Language ................... ST–M
STML .................................................................. ST*M
Super VGA .......................................................... SPR–V
surf the Web ....................................................... SWEB
surge protector ................................................... SPURJ
SVGA .................................................................. VAO*EJ
systems analyst ................................................. SNANLT

## T

Tagged Image File Format .................................... TAJD
tape backup ........................................................ TBUP
terminal ............................................................... TAERL
terminal emulation .............................................. TAERLGS
terminator ........................................................... TRERMT
trackball ............................................................. TRABL

## U

Uninterruptible Power Supply ............................... URPS
Universal Resource Locator ............... YAOURL, *URL/*URL
UNIX ................................................................... YAOUX
upload ................................................................. PLOED

uploaded .......................................................................... PL–D, PLOETD, PLO*ED
UPS ............................................................................................................ *UPS
URL ............................................................................................................ *URL
USB ............................................................................................................ UBS
USB port ................................................................................................... UBTS
utility ...................................................................................................... YAOULT

**V**

vector ..................................................................................................... VERKT
VGA ....................................................................................................... VAOEJ
video accelerator ................................................................................. VAORT
Video Graphics Array ........................................................................ VAOEJS
video local bus .................................................................................... V–BLS
VLB ........................................................................................................ V–BL

**W**

Web ........................................................................................................ W*EB
webpage .................................................................................................. WAEJ
Web server ........................................................................................ WREFRB
website .................................................................................. WAOIB, WAOIBT
Web site ............................................................................................ WAO*IB
Wi-Fi ................................................................................... WOIF, FWAOIF
wildcard ............................................................................................ WAOIKD
Winchester disk .................................................................................. WHIFK
wireless ............................................................................................ WAOIRLS
World Wide Web ............................................................. WOIB, WAOIBD
write-protect ...................................................................................... WRAOIK
write-protected .............................................................................. WRAOIKD
www. ........................................................................................................ W–D
www dot ...................................................................... WOTD, W–TD, W*D

# COURT EXAMINATIONS

## IN ALPHABETICAL ORDER

cross-examination ......................................................................................... KR–X
CROSS-EXAMINATION ........................................................... KRO*X, KR–X/KR–X

direct examination .......................................................................................... DR–X
DIRECT EXAMINATION ......................................................... DRIRX, DR–X/DR–X

rebuttal ............................................................................................... R–B, R–BT
REBUTTAL ...................................................... R*B, R*BT, R–B/R–B, R–BT/R–BT

recross-examination .......................................................................................... R–X
RECROSS-EXAMINATION ................................................................. R*X, R–X/R–X

redirect examination ...................................................................................... R–RD
REDIRECT EXAMINATION ...................................................... R*RD, R–RD/R–RD

surrebuttal ............................................................................... SURB, SURBL
SURREBUTTAL .............. SURBLT, S*URB, S*URBL, SURB/SURB, SURBL/SURBL

voir dire ............................................................................... V–RD, VOIRD
voir dire examination ................................................................................. VOIRX
VOIR DIRE EXAMINATION ........................................................ V–RGS, V–RD/V–RD

## IN ORDER OF PROCEDURE

direct examination .......................................................................................... DR–X
DIRECT EXAMINATION ......................................................... DRIRX, DR–X/DR–X

cross-examination ......................................................................................... KR–X
CROSS-EXAMINATION ........................................................... KRO*X, KR–X/KR–X

redirect examination ...................................................................................... R–RD
REDIRECT EXAMINATION ...................................................... R*RD, R–RD/R–RD

recross-examination .......................................................................................... R–X
RECROSS-EXAMINATION ................................................................. R*X, R–X/R–X

rebuttal ............................................................................................... R–B, R–BT
REBUTTAL ...................................................... R*B, R*BT, R–B/R–B, R–BT/R–BT

surrebuttal ............................................................................... SURB, SURBL
SURREBUTTAL .............. SURBLT, S*URB, S*URBL, SURB/SURB, SURBL/SURBL

# DAYS & MONTHS

## DAYS OF THE WEEK

Monday ................................................................................. MOND
Tuesday ................................................................ TAOUS, TAOUZ
Wednesday ........................................................................ WENS
Thursday ............................................................ THURS, THURZ
Friday .................................................................................... FRID
Saturday .............................................................................. SATD
Sunday ................................................................................ SUND

## MONTHS OF THE YEAR

January ................................................................................. JAN
February .............................................................................. FEB
March .................................................................................. MAR
April ..................................................................................... PRIL
May ..................................................................................... MA*I
June ..................................................................................... JUN
July ....................................................................................... JUL
August ................................................................................ AUG
September ......................................................................... SEPT
October ............................................................................. TOEB
November ........................................................................... NOV
December ........................................................................... DEZ

# DEAF & HEARING IMPAIRED

## A

| | |
|---|---|
| access | KRES, KREF |
| accessibility | KREFBLT |
| accessible | KREFBL |
| acoustic | KAO*US |
| acoustical | KAOUFL |
| acoustically | KAOEFL |
| ALDA | ALD |
| American Sign Language | MERNL |
| Americans with Disabilities Act | MERND |
| analog | NAULG, GOUG |
| answering service | SNEFRB |
| answer phone | SNOEN |
| articulation | TARX, TLAEGS |
| ASL | ALS |
| Association of Late-Deafened Adults | ALD/ALD |
| audibility | AUBLT |
| audible | AUBL |
| audibly | AOEBL |
| audio | AOD |
| audiologist | AULD |
| audiology | AULG |
| auditory | AORD |
| auditory canal | AORNL |
| auditory nerve | AORN |
| auditory tube | AORTD |
| aural | AURL |
| auricle | AURK |

## B

| | |
|---|---|
| binaural | BAURL |

## C

| | |
|---|---|
| closed-captioned | KLOEPD |
| closed-captioning | KLOEPG |
| cochlea | KLA |
| cochlear | KLAER |
| cochlear implant | KLAERN |

## D

| | |
|---|---|
| dB | D*B |
| deaf | DAEF |
| deaf and hard of hearing | DHAR, DHARD, DHARGD |
| deaf and hard-of-hearing people | DHARP |
| deaf-blind | DAEFB |
| deaf-blindness | DAEFBS, DEFBS |
| deafen | DAEFN |
| deafly | DAEFL |
| deaf-mute | DMAOUT, DAEFM |
| deafness | DAEFNS, DEFNS |
| deaf or hard of hearing | DHOR, DHORD, DHORGD, DHAORD |

deaf or hard-of-hearing people ................................................................ DHAOERP
deaf or hard-of-hearing person ................................................................. DHORP
decibel ................................................................................................. SDIBL
dizziness ............................................................................................ SDINZ
dizzy ..................................................................................................... SDIZ
dysphonia ........................................................................................... SFOEN

**E**

eardrum ............................................................................................... AOERM
eustachian ........................................................................................ STAIRB
eustachian tube ............................................................................. STAIRBT

**F**

FCC ....................................................................................................... FAOEK
Federal Communications Commission ..................................... FAOEKS, FAOUNGS

**H**

hard of hearing .......................................................................... HARGD, HARG
hearing aid ................................................................................. HAERGD, HIRD
hearing impaired ....................................................... HIRM, HIRMD, HIRP
hearing impairment .......................................................................... HIRMT
hearing loss .................................................................................... HAERLG
hearing people .............................................................................. HAOERPG
hearing person ............................................................................... HAERPG
hearing-sighted .............................................................................. HAERTD
Helen Keller ...................................................................................... HELG
Helen Keller National Center .......................................................... HELGS
Helen Keller National Center for Deaf-Blind Youth and Adults ..................... HELGD
HKNC ................................................................................................... H–KZ

**L**

lipread ................................................................................................. LIRP
listen .................................................................................................... L–N

**M**

maternal rubella ................................................................................ MOUB
Ménière's disease ............................................................................. MAIND
Ménière's syndrome ....................................................................... MAIRND
meningitis .......................................................................................... JAOIT
monaural ......................................................................................... MAURNL

**N**

National Captioning Institute ......................................................... NAPGS

**O**

oral ....................................................................................................... ORL
oral deaf ........................................................................................... AURLD
orally .................................................................................................. OERL

**P**

programmable ................................................................................... PRABL
programmable hearing aid ............................................................. PRABLD
Public Utilities Commission ........................................ PUGS, POIKZ, POIK/POIK
PUC ......................................................................... PYUK, P*UK, PO*IK

## R

relay .................................................................................................... LAE
relay agent ....................................................................................... LAEJ
rubella ............................................................................................. ROUB

## S

Self Help for Hard of Hearing People .............................. SH–D, SH–/SH–
SHHH ............................................................................................... SH–
signed English ............................................................................. SGLIRB
sign language ..................................................................................... S–L
sign language interpreter ............................................................... S–LT
silence ......................................................................................... SLENS
silent ............................................................................................ SLENT
speech impaired ............................................................................. SPIRD
speech impairment ..................................................... SPAIRMT, SPIRMT
speech impediment ..................................................................... SPEFMT
stapes ........................................................................................... STAIPS

## T

TDD ............................................................................................. TAOED
Telecommunications Device for the Deaf ........................ TAOEDZ, TAOED/TAOED
teletypewriter ........................................................... TWOI, TWAOI/TWAOI
tonal ............................................................................................. TOENL
tone deafness .............................................................................. TOEND
TTY .............................................................................................. TWAOI
TTY user .................................................................................. TWAOURS
tympanic ........................................................................................ TIMP
tympanic membrane ...................................................................... TIFRM
tympanic nerve .............................................................................. TIFRN

## U

Usher's syndrome ....................................................................... SHOEM

## V

vertigo ............................................................................... VERG, VERGT

---

# FAMILY MEMBERS

aunt ................................................................................................................ AUNT

brother .......................................................................................................... BRO
brother-in-law ........................................................................... BROL, BROINL

cousin ........................................................................................................ KUFN

daughter.................................................................................... DAUT, DAURT
daughter-in-law ..................................................................................... DAURL

father........................................................................................................ FA, FAU
father-in-law .......................................................................................... FANL

grandfather.................................................................................. GR–FR, GRAFR
grandma....................................................................................................... GR–M
grandmother ................................................................... GROER, GRAMD
grandpa ....................................................................................................... GR–P
grandparent ................................................................................................ GR–PT

mother....................................................................................................... MOER
mother-in-law ....................................................................................... MOERL

sister .................................................................................................. SIS, SIFRT
sister-in-law.................................................................................. SOINL, SIFRL

son ............................................................................................................ SON
son-in-law ............................................................................................... SONL

stepbrother................................................................... SBROE, STP–B, STBRO
stepfather ........................................................... SFA, SFAU, STP–F, STEFR
stepmother ................................................. SMOER, SMOEFR, SMEFR, STP–RM
stepsister ........................................................... STEPZ, STP–Z, STP–R

uncle ......................................................................................................... UNK

# GEOGRAPHIC DATA

## A

| | |
|---|---|
| Afghan | AFG |
| Afghani | AUFG |
| Afghanistan | AFGS |
| Africa | AFRK |
| African | AFN |
| Algeria | JAER |
| Algerian | JAERN |
| America | MERK |
| American | MERN |
| Antarctica | TARKT |
| Antilles | TLAOEZ |
| Arab | A*ERB, RAEB, YAERB |
| Arabian | A*ERN, YAEB |
| Arabic | A*ERK, YAEK, YAERK |
| Argentina | AURGT |
| Argentinean | AURNG |
| Asia | AIZ |
| Asian | AIGS |
| Australia | STRAIL |
| Australian | STRAN, STRAINL |

## B

| | |
|---|---|
| Bahamas | BAUMZ, BA*UMS, BHAMS |
| Bahrain | BHAIN |
| Bahraini | BHI |
| Balkan | BLAUK |
| Balkans | BLAUKS |
| Bangladesh | DERB |
| Bangladeshi | D*IRB, DO*IRB, DHERB |
| Barents | BAIRNT |
| Barents Sea | BAIRNTS |
| Belgian | BELGS |
| Belgium | BELG |
| Bermuda | BAOUMD, BERMD |
| Bhutan | BHAOUT |
| Bolivia | BLIV |
| Bolivian | BLIVN |
| Bosnia | BOZ |
| Bosnia-Herzegovina | BHOZ |
| Bosnian | BONZ |
| Botswana | BAUTS |
| Brazil | BRAZ |
| Brazilian | BRANZ, BRALZ |
| Britain | BRIN, BRINT |
| British | BRIRB |
| British Isles | BRAOIL, BRAOILS |
| Bulgaria | BLAERG |
| Bulgarian | BLAERN |
| Burma | B*URM |

Burmese ........................................................................................... BURMS
Burundi ........................................................................................... BRUND

## C

Cambodia ......................................................................................... KBOED
Cambodian ....................................................................................... KBOEND
Cameroon ........................................................................................ KMAON
Canada ........................................................................................... KRAND
Canadian ......................................................................................... KRAEND
Cashmere ....................................................................................... KMAO*ER
Chad .............................................................................................. KHAD
Chechen .......................................................................................... KHEFP
Chechnya ......................................................................................... KHETS
Chile .............................................................................................. KHAE
Chilean ........................................................................................... KHAEN
China ............................................................................................. KHAOIN
Chinese ................................................................................. KHAOEZ, KH–Z
Colombia ......................................................................................... KLOM
Colombian ............................................................................. KLO*M, KLOB
Congo ............................................................................................ KOENG
Costa Rica ....................................................................................... KOEFRK
Costa Rican ...................................................................................... KOEFRN
Croatia .................................................................................. KROERB, KROET
Croatian .......................................................................................... KROENT
Cuba .............................................................................................. KBA
Cuban ............................................................................................ KBAN
Cyprian .................................................................................. SPR*IN, SPR–N
Cypriot ........................................................................................... SPRIT
Cyprus ........................................................................................... SPRIS
Cyrus ............................................................................................. SR*US
Czech ............................................................................................. ZHEK
Czechoslovakia .................................................................................. ZEK
Czechoslovakian ................................................................................ ZHEN
Czech Republic .................................................................................. ZHERK

## D

Dane .............................................................................................. DAEN
Danish ............................................................................................ DAERB
Denmark .......................................................................................... DAERK
Dominican Republic ............................................................................. DREB
Dutch ............................................................................................. DUFP

## E

Ecuador .......................................................................................... KWAOR
Ecuadorian ....................................................................................... KWAORN
Egypt ............................................................................................. JIPT
Egyptian .......................................................................................... JIPGS
El Salvador ....................................................................................... SAFL
England .................................................................................. ENG, GLAUND
English ........................................................................................... GLIRB
Ethiopia .......................................................................................... TYOEP
Ethiopian ......................................................................................... TYOEN
Europe ........................................................................................... YURP
European .......................................................................................... YURN

## F

Far East ............................................................................................. FRA*ES
Fiji ...................................................................................................... FAOEJ
Fijian .......................................................................... FAOEFNG, FAOENG
Filipino .............................................................................................. FWIP
Finland ............................................................................. FWAN, FWAND
Finn .................................................................................................. FWIN
Finnish ............................................................................................ FWIRB
France ............................................................................................ FRANS
French ............................................................................................ FREFP

## G

German ............................................................................................. JOIM
Germany ......................................................................................... JOIRM
Ghana .............................................................................................. GHAN
Grecian ....................................................................................... GRAOEGS
Great Britain ..................................................................... GRIB, GRINT
Greece ........................................................................................ GRAOES
Greek ........................................................................................... GRAOEK
Grenada ....................................................................................... GRAEND
Guatemala ...................................................................................... GAUT
Guatemalan .................................................................................... GAUN
Guyana ........................................................................................... GAOIG

## H

Haiti ................................................................................................... HOIT
Haitian .............................................................................. HAIGS, HOIRB
Hebrew ......................................................................................... HAOEB
Hindi ............................................................................................ HAOEND
Holland ............................................................................................ HAUN
Honduran ....................................................................................... HOURN
Honduras ...................................................................................... HOURND
Hungarian ....................................................................................... HAIRN
Hungary ......................................................................................... HAUNG

## I

India .............................................................................................. DWIND
Indonesia ...................................................................................... DAOEZ
Indonesian ...................................................... DAOEGS, DAOENZ
Indonesians .............................................................................. DAOENSZ
Iran ................................................................................................. RA*N
Iranian ........................................................................................... RA*EN
Iraq ................................................................................................ AOIRK
Iraqi ............................................................................................... AOERK
Ireland .................................................................... AOIRL, AOIRLD
Irish ................................................................................................ AOIRB
Israel ...................................................................................................... IZ
Israeli .................................................................................................. ILZ
Italian ........................................................................ TLA*N, TLAUN
Italy ................................................................................................ TLAL

## J

Jamaica .......................................................................................... JAEK
Jamaican ........................................................................................ JAEN

Japan ............................................................................................................ JAP
Japanese ......................................................................... JAPS, JAOEPZ
Jordan .......................................................................................... JORD
Jordanian .................................................................................... JORND

## K

Kashmir .......................................................................................... KMIR
Kashmiri ....................................................................................... KMOIR
Korea ........................................................................................... KRAE
Korean ...................................................................................... KRA*EN
Kurd ......................................................................................... KWHURD
Kurdish ..................................................................... KWHURB, KWHIRB
Kurdistan ................................................................................. KWHURN
Kurdistani ................................................................. KWHI, KWHIRD
Kyrgyz .......................................................... KAOERS, KIRGZ, KERGZ
Kyrgyz Republic ....................................... KIRPG, KIRPZ, KERPG
Kyrgyzstan .............................................................. KIRG, KERG
Kuwait ....................................................................................... KWUT

## L

Latin ............................................................................................. LAN
Latino ............................................................................................ LAT
Latvia ......................................................................................... LAUVT
Latvian ....................................................................................... LAUVN
Lebanese ...................................................................................... LEBZ
Lebanon ........................................................................................ L*EB
Liberia ........................................................................................ LAOER
Liberian .................................................................................... LAOERN
Liechtenstein .............................................................................. LIFPT
Luxembourg .............................................................................. LOURG

## M

Malaysia ...................................................................................... MALS
Malaysian .................................................................................... MANZ
Malaysians ................................................................................. MANSZ
Mexican ........................................................................................ MEX
Mexico .................................................................... MAOKS, M*EX
Middle East .............................................................................. MAO*ELS
Middle Eastern ...................................................................... MAOERNL
Mongolia ................................................................................... MOUNG
Morocco ..................................................................................... MAORK
Moroccan ................................................................................. MAORNG
Mozambique ................................................................................. ZAM

## N

Netherlands .............................................................. NELTS, N*ELTS
New Guinea ............................................................................... NAOUG
New Zealand ................................................................................. N–Z
New Zealander ........................................................................... N–RLZ
New Zealanders ....................................................................... N–RLSZ
Niger ........................................................................................ NAOIRG
Nigeria .......................................................................................... NIRJ
Nigerian .................................................................................... NAOERJ
North America .................................................................. NAERK, NA*

North American ................................................................ NAERN, NARN
Norway .............................................................................................. NAUR
Norwegian ............................................................... NAURN, WAOEJ

## P

Pakistan ........................................................................................ PAUKT
Pakistani ........................................................................................ PAIKT
Persia ............................................................................................... PERZ
Persian ........................................................................................... PERGS
Peru ......................................................................................... PRAO*U
Peruvian ................................................................................. PRAOUVN
Philippines ...................................................................................... FIPS
Poland ...................................................................................... PLOEND
Polish ........................................................................... POERB, PLOERB
Portugal ...................................................................................... PORGT
Portuguese .................................................................................. PORGZ

## Q

Quebecker ............................................................................. KW*ERB
Quebecois .................................................................... KAIB, KWAIB

## R

Romania .............................................................................. KPRO, KPRU
Romanian ..................................................................... KPRON, KPRUN
Russia ................................................................... R*URB, RAOURB
Russian ....................................................................... RUGS, RAOURN

## S

Salvadoran ................................................................................ SAFRN
Samoa .......................................................................................... SMOE
Samoan ............................................................... SMAON, SMO*EN
Saudi Arabia ............................................. SAUBD, SA*, SAUD/SAUD
Saudi Arabian .......................................................... SAUND, SA*N
Scandinavia ................................................................................ SKAIV
Scandinavian ........................................................................... SKAIVN
Scotland ............................................................... SKLAND, SKOND
Scottish ...................................................................................... SKORB
Senegal ............................................................................ SGAL, SENG
Senegalese .......................................................................... SGLAOES
Serb ................................................................... SWERB, S*ERB
Serbo-Croatia .................................................................... SKROERB
Serbo-Croatian .................................................................... SKROEN
Sinai .............................................................................................. SNAO*I
Sinai Desert .......................................................................... SNAO*ID
Sinai Peninsula ..................................................................... SNAO*IP
Singapore ................................................................................ SPOERG
Slovakia ....................................................................... SLOEV, SLOEVK
Slovakian ................................................................................. SLOEVN
Slovenia ......................................................................... SLOV, SLAOV
Slovenian ................................................................................ SLAOVN
Somalia ........................................................................................ SMOL
Somalian .................................................................................... SMONL
South Africa .............................................................................. SFAK
South African ............................................................................ SFAN

South America ............................................................. SERK, SA
South American .................................................................. SARN
Soviet ................................................................................. SOVT
Soviet Union ......................................................................... S*U
Spain ................................................................................. SPAIN
Spaniard ........................................................................ SPAURD
Spanish ........................................................................... SPARB
Sri Lanka ....................................................................... SLAUNG
Sri Lankan ..................................................................... SLAUNK
Swede ............................................................................ SWAOED
Sweden ............................................................................ SWAOE
Swedish ...................................................................... SWAOERB
Swiss ............................................................................... SWISZ
Switzerland ..................................................................... SWITS

**T**

Taiwan ............................................................................ TWAUN
Taiwanese ..................................................................... TWAUNZ
Tanzania ............................................................................ TANZ
Tanzanian ...................................................................... TAOENZ
Tanzanians .................................................................. TAOENSZ
Thai ................................................................................ THAO*I
Thailand .............................................. THAOIL, THAOILD
the Netherlands .............................................................. N*ELT
Tibet .................................................................................. TIBT
Tibetan .................................................. TBAEN, TB–NT
Tobago ............................................................................. TBAG
Trinidad .......................................................................... TRIND
Turk ................................................................................. TURK
Turkey ........................................................................... TO*IRK
Turkish .......................................................................... TRURB

**U**

Uganda ....................................................................... YAOUNGD
Ukraine ............................................................................ YAOK
Ukrainian ...................................................... YAOMP, YAO*N
United Kingdom ............................................................... YINGD
United States ................................................ USZ, *US/*US
Uruguay ................................................. YAOURG, YOURG
Uruguayan .................................................................... YOURNG

**V**

Vatican ............................................................................. VAFK
Venezuela ......................................................... VENZ, V–NZ
Venezuelan ....................................................... VAENZ, V–NS
Vietnam ............................................................. VAM, V*N
Vietnamese .................................................................... VAOEZ

**W**

Wales ............................................................................. WAELS
Welsh .................................................................. W*ERBL, WELZ

**Y**

Yemen ............................................................................. Y*EM
Yemeni .......................................................................... YAOEM

Yemenite ............................................................................................... YAOIMT
Yugoslavia ............................................................................................ YAOUG
Yugoslavian ............................................................. YAO*UNG, YAOUVG

# Z

Zaire ....................................................................................................... ZAOIR
Zambia .................................................................................................. ZAMP
Zambian ............................................................................................... ZAFRN
Zimbabwe ............................................................................................ ZIMP

# MEDICAL

## A

| | |
|---|---|
| AARP | ARP |
| abdomen | ABD |
| abdominal | ABL |
| abort | BORT |
| abortion | BORGS |
| abrasion | BRAEGS |
| absorbent | SORNT |
| abstinence | STIBS |
| abstinent | STIBT |
| Achilles | KHAOEL, KHAOELS |
| Achilles tendon | KHAOELT |
| addiction | DIX |
| addictive | DIVT |
| adduction | DUGS |
| adductor | DRUK |
| adenoid | DWOI |
| adhesion | HAOEGS, DHAOEGS |
| adhesive | DHAOEV |
| adhesively | DHAOEVL |
| adhesiveness | DHAOEVNS, DHAOEVZ |
| adrenal | DRAOEN, DRAOENL |
| adrenal gland | DRAOENLG |
| Adrenalin | DREN |
| adrenaline | DRENL |
| aerobic | ROERK |
| afferent | AEFRNT |
| agglutinant | GLAOUNT |
| agglutination | GLAOUNGS |
| agglutinative | GLAOUV |
| agglutinin | GLAOUT |
| agglutinogen | GLAOUJ |
| AIDS | YAIDZ, A*IDZ |
| ailment | AIMT |
| albumin | BAOUM |
| alcohol | KHOL |
| alcoholic | KHOK |
| alcoholic beverage | KHOB |
| Alcoholics Anonymous | KHON |
| alcoholism | KHOFM, KHOM |
| alcohol treatment | KHOMT |
| allergic to | LERJT |
| allergy | L–RJ, LAOERJ |
| Alzheimer's | ALZ |
| Alzheimer's disease | ALDZ |
| American Association of Retired Persons | ARPD |
| amnesia | ZHA, NAOEMZ |
| amnesiac | ZHAK |
| amnesic | ZHIK |
| amphetamine | FET, FA*ET, AEFMT |
| anal | AINL |

anatomical .................................................................. NAEMG
anatomy .................................................... NAEMT, NAT/M*I
androgenous ............................................................... DROJS
androgyny .................................................................... DROJ
anemia ......................................................................... NOIM
anemic ......................................................................... NO*IK
anesthesia ................................................ AEN, THAOERB
anesthesiologist ............................................. THOELT, OELT
anesthesiology ............................................ THOELG, OELG
anesthetic ..................................................................... THET
aneurysm ................................................... NURM, AN/RIFM
angiogram ........................................................... ANG/GRAM
anoretic ...................................................................... NAORK
anorexia ..................................................................... NAORX
anorexia nervosa ..................................................... NAOFRB
anterior .......................................................................... AOR
anterior chamber ....................................................... AORM
anteriorly .................................................................... AORL
antihistamine ........................................... AENTS, ANT/H*IS
anxiety .......................................................................... ZAOI
aorta .......................................................................... AORT
aortic ...................................................... AORKT, AO*RK
aortic valve ................................................................ AOV
appendage ................................................................ PAEJ
appendices ............................................................. PAEXZ
appendicitis ...................................... APDZ, PAETS
appendix .................................................................. PAEX
are you a physician ................................................. RUFGS
are you a physician duly licensed in ........... RAOFGS, RUFGS/DLIND
are you a physician duly licensed to practice medicine .......... RUFMD
are you a physician licensed in ............... RUFGD, RUFGS/LIND
are you a physician licensed to practice medicine ................ RUFM
arterial ....................................................................... AERL
arteriole ...................................................................... ARLT
arteriosclerosis ........................... SKLAERT, AERT/SKLOES
artery ......................................................................... AERT
arthritic .................................................................... THRIKT
arthritis ..................................................................... THRITS
arthroplasty ............................................................ THROPT
articulate ...................................................... TARK, TLAET
articulation .............................................. TARX, TLAEGS
asbestos .................................................... AOBS, STEB
ascend ....................................................................... SAEND
ascension ................................................ SAENGS, SKAENGS
aspirin ......................................................................... SPRIN
asthma ....................................................................... SMAZ
asthmatic ................................................................... SMAKT
astigmatic ..................................................... SNIKT, SGIK
astigmatism ............................................... SGIFM, SNIFM
athlete's foot ............................................................. TLAOF
atria ............................................................... TRA, TRAE
atrium ........................................................................ TRAIM
atrophic ................................................................... TROFK
atrophous ................................................................ TROUFS

atrophy .............................................................. TROF
audibility ......................................................... AUBLT
audible ............................................................. AUBL
audibly ............................................................ AOEBL
audience .......................................................... YENS
audio ................................................................ AOD
audiologist ....................................................... AULD
audiology ......................................................... AULG
auditory ........................................................... AORD
auditory canal ................................................ AORNL
auditory nerve ................................................. AORN
auditory tube ................................................. AORTD
aura .................................................................. AUR
aural ................................................................ AURL
autopsy ............................................................ AUP

**B**

backache ......................................................... BAIK
bacteria ......................................................... BAEKT
bacterial .......................................................... BARL
bacterium ...................................................... BAOERM
barbiturate ...................................................... BRIFP
barium ............................................................ BAIRM
behavior ............................................. BAIFR, BAIVR
behavioral ................................... BAIFRL, BAIVRL
Benzedrine ...................................................... BENS
biceps ............................................................. BEPS
bifocal ........................................................... BAOIFL
bifurcate .......................................................... BIFT
bifurcation ..................................................... BIFGS
bilateral ......................................................... BLARL
bilaterally .................................................... BLAOERL
biologist ........................................................ BOLGT
biology ........................................................... BOLG
biopsy ............................................................. BOIP
birth control .................................................. BROEL
bladder ................................................. BLAD, BLARD
blindness ..................................................... BLAOINS
blister .................................................... BLIFR, BLIS
blockage .......................................................... BLOJ
blood alcohol ................................................... BLOL
blood alcohol level ......................................... BLEVL
blood clot ...................................................... BLUKT
blood clots ................................... BLUX, BLUKTS
blood count .................................................. BLAOK
blood evidence ....................... BLEVD, BLUVD
blood group .................................................. BLAOP
blood poisoning ............................................ BLOIG
blood pressure ............................................... BLUP
blood sugar .................................................... BLUG
blood sugar level .......................................... BLULG
blood test ........................................ BLUT, BL*ES
blood transfusion ................ BLAOUGS, BLAOUFGS
blood type .................................................... BLAOIP

blood vessel .................................................................... BLUFL
bodily ............................................................................... BOL
body ............................................................................... BOD
bonier ......................................................................... BOIRN
bony ............................................................................. BOIN
brachial ..................................................................... BRAIFP
brachial artery ........................................................... BRART
brachial plexus ...................................................... BRAIFPS
bradycardia .............................................................. BRAUR
brain tumor ........................................................... BRAOURM
breast .......................................................................... BR*ES
breast cancer ......................................................... BRAERN
bronchi ..................................................................... BRONG
bronchial ................................................................ BRONLG
bronchial tube ...................................................... BRONLGT
bulimia ................................................................... BLAOEM
bypass ............................................................................ BIP

## C

cadaver .......................................................... DAFR, DAVR
cancer ...................................................................... KAERN
cancerous ............................................................. KAERNZ
cannabis ...................................................................... KBIZ
capillary ................................................................... KPLAIR
capsule ...................................................................... KP–FL
carbon dioxide .............................................. KBOX, KBO*D
carbon monoxide ..................................................... KBOM
carcinogen ................................................................ SKROG
carcinoma ............................................................. SKROEM
cardia ......................................................................... KAUR
cardiac ...................................................................... KAURK
cardiac arrest ........................................................ KAURKT
cardiovascular ....................................................... KAUFRB
cardiovascular system ......................................... KAUFRBS
care and treatment ................................................ KAIRMT
carotid ...................................................................... KROTD
carotid artery ........................................................ KRORTD
carpal .......................................................... KPARL, KARPL
carpal tunnel .......................................................... KPARLT
carpal tunnel syndrome ....................................... KPARLTS
carpus ..................................................................... KARPS
cartilage ..................................................................... KLART
castrate ....................................................................... KRAIF
castration .............................................................. KRAIFGS
CAT ........................................................................... KA*T
catabolic ................................................................ KBLO*K
catabolism ........................................................... KBLOFM
cataract ...................................................................... KAKT
cataract implant ....................................................... KLANT
cataract implant lens surgery ............................... KLENZ
catheter ................................................................... THERT
CAT scan ..................................................... KA*TS, SKRAN
cauterization ................................... KA*UGS, KA*URGS
cauterize ................................................................. KA*UT

| | |
|---|---|
| centigrade | SGRAID |
| centimeter | SMAOERT, KR–M |
| central nervous system | KR–NS |
| centrifugal | STRIF |
| cephalic | SFEK |
| cephalitis | SFAOIT |
| cerebellum | SBLUM |
| cerebral | SBRAL |
| cerebral cortex | SBRORX |
| cerebral palsy | SBRALZ |
| cerebral spinal fluid | SBRAFL |
| cerebrum | SBRUM |
| cervical | SR–FL |
| cervical cancer | SA*ERN |
| cervical spine | SR–FLS |
| cervix | SR–FX |
| cesarean | SAIRN |
| cesarean section | SAIRNGS, SAIRN/S–X |
| chamber | KHAIM |
| check up | KHUP |
| chemical | KHEM |
| chemotherapy | KAOEM, KAOEM/THAERP |
| chickenpox | KHOKZ, KHAUX |
| childbearing | KHAERG |
| child birth | KH*IRT |
| chiropractic | KAOIRT |
| chiropractor | KAOIR |
| chloroform | KLORM |
| cholesterol | KLES, KL*ES |
| chromosome | SMOEM, ZOEM |
| chronic | KRONK |
| chronically | KRONL |
| circulate | SL– |
| circulation | SL–GS |
| circulatory | SIRKT, SLORT |
| circulatory system | SIRKTS, SLORTS |
| circumcise | SKMAOIS |
| circumcision | SKMIGS |
| cirrhosis | KROEZ |
| claustrophobia | KLA*US, KLAUF |
| claustrophobic | KLAUFK |
| clavicle | KLAFL, KLAVL |
| CMV | KM–V |
| CMV retinitis | KM–VR |
| coagulate | KWAG |
| coagulation | KWAGS |
| coccyx | SKOX |
| cochlea | KLA |
| cochlear | KLAER |
| cochlear implant | KLAERN |
| collagen | KAUJ |
| collagenous | KAUJS |
| collarbone | KLARN |
| colloid | KLOID |

| | |
|---|---|
| colon | KLON |
| colorblind | KLORB, KLORND |
| colostomy | KLO*S |
| coma | KO*EM, KMO |
| concussion | KUNGS |
| condom | KMOM |
| condyle | KAUNL |
| congenital | K–JT |
| congenitally | KEJT |
| congest | GEFT |
| congestion | GEGS |
| congestive | GEV |
| conjunctiva | JIV |
| conjunctivitis | JIVT, JAOIVT |
| connective tissue | KIRB |
| conscious | KONS |
| constipate | SKPAIT |
| constipation | SKPAIGS |
| contagious | TAIJ |
| contaminant | TAMT |
| contaminate | TAM |
| contamination | TAMGS, TAJ |
| contract | KR–T |
| contraction | KRAX |
| contusion | TAOGS |
| convalesce | KWLES |
| convalescence | KWLENS |
| convalescent | KWLET |
| convalescent hospital | KWHOP, KWLOP |
| convulse | KWULS |
| convulsion | KWULGS |
| cornea | KR–N |
| corneal | KOERNL, KR–NL |
| corneal transplant | KR–NT |
| corneal transplantation | KR–NGS |
| coronary | KOIRN |
| coronary artery | KOIRT |
| coronary artery disease | KOIRTD |
| coronary bypass | KOIRPS |
| coronary bypass surgery | KOIRPG |
| coronary heart disease | KOIRD |
| coroner | KR–RN |
| coroner's report | KR–RNT, KRORT |
| corpse | KORPS |
| corpuscle | KPUFL |
| cortex | KOERX |
| cortical | KOERLT |
| cranial | KRAINL |
| cuneiform | KAOUN |
| curability | KAOURBLT |
| curable | KAOURBL |
| cuspid | SPID |
| cyanide | KRAOIND |
| cystitis | STAOITS |

cytoplasm ..................................................................... SPLAFM

# D

deaf ................................................................................ DAEF
deaf-blind .......................................................... DAEFB, DEFB
deaf-blindness ............................................... DAEFBS, DEFBS
debride ........................................................................ DBR–D
debridement................................................................ DBR–MT
decedent .................................................................... DAOENT
deformity.................................................................... DWORMT
degeneration ............................................................... JAIRGS
degenerative ................................................................... JAIV
degree............................................................................... DRE
degree of medical certainty ............................... DREFM, DREM
dehydrate ........................................................ DHAOIT, DWAOIT
dehydration ................................................. DHAOIGS, DWAOIGS
delirious ................................................................DLIR, DLAOERS
delirium ........................................................................ DLUM
deltoid................................................................DELTD, DLOITD
dementia .................................................................... DMERB
dendrite ...................................................................... DRAOIT
dendron........................................................................ DRON
dental ............................................................................DENL
dental school ................................................................ DAOL
dentist ....................................................................... D–NTS
dentistry ..................................................................... D–RNT
depress .......................................................................... D–P
depressant ................................................................... DRANT
depression ................................................................... D–PGS
depressor........................................................................DR–P
derange ........................................................... DRAEN, DARNG
derangement ............................................................ DRAEMT
dermatitis .................................................................... DERMT
dermatologist ................................................................ DOLT
dermatology ................................................................... DOLG
descending ................................................................. SDENGD
detached retina .......................................................... DRAENT
deviated septum ........................................................... DWAIP
Dexedrine ...................................................................... DEX
diabetes ...................................................................... DAOIB
diabetes mellitus.......................................................... DMEL
diabetic ..................................................................... DAOIBT
diabetic retinopathy ....................................................DO*PT
diagnose ......................................................................... D–G
diagnosis ...................................................................... D–GS
diagnostic.....................................................................D–GT
diagnostician ...................................................... DIGTS, D–G/TIGS
dialysis ........................................................................... DAL
diaphragm ...................................................... DAOIRM, DAOIFRM
diarrhea ...................................................................... DRAOE
diet ............................................................................... DAET
dietary ....................................................................... DA*ERT
dieter .......................................................................... DAERT
digestive ...................................................................... D–VJ

digestive system ................................................................. D–VJS
diphtheria ............................................................................. D*IPT
disease ................................................................................. D–Z
dislocate ........................................................................... SLOEK
dislocation ........................................................................ SLOEX
dismember ......................................................................... SMEB
dismemberment ............................................................... SMEMT
disorient ............................................................................. DORN
disorientation ................................................................ DORNGS
dispense ......................................................................... SDPENS
dissect ............................................................................... SDEK
dissection ........................................................................... SDEX
dissociate ...................................................................... SDOERB
dissociation .................................................................SDOERBGS
dissociative ..................................................................... SDOEV
dissolve ............................................................................ DOFL
diuretic .............................................................................. DRET
DNA .................................................................................... DAE
doctor ................................................................................. D–R
donor ................................................................................ DOERN
dormant ........................................................................... DORMT
dorsal .............................................................................. DORLS
dosage ............................................................................. DOEJ
drainage ........................................................................... DRAIJ
dressing room ................................................... DR–M, DRAOM
drugs, alcohol and medication ...................................... DRAMZ
drugs, alcohol or medication ......................................... DROMZ
drugstore ......................................................................... DROR
D.U.I. .................................................................... DW–, DY–
duly licensed in ............................................................. DLIND
duly licensed to practice ........................... DLIP, DLIPT
duly licensed to practice medicine ................................ DLIM
duodenum ......................................................................... DWOD
dysfunction ................................................................... SFUNGS
dysfunctional .................................................................. SFUNL
dyslexia ......................................................................... SDLEX
dyslexic ......................................................................... SDLEK

**E**

eardrum ......................................................................... AOERM
eczema ........................................................................... ZAOEM
efferent ........................................................................... EFRNT
ego ................................................................................... GOE
egoist .............................................................................. GOEFT
egomaniac ......................................................................... GOM
egotism ........................................................................... GOEFM
egotistic ........................................................................... GOEK
egotistical ......................................................................... GOL
ejaculate .......................................................................... JAL
ejaculation ..................................................................... JALGS
EKG ................................................................................ AOEJ
elderly .......................................................................... AOERLD
electrocardiogram ........................................................ AOEJD
elongate ......................................................................... LAUNT

| | |
|---|---|
| elongation | LAUNGS |
| embalm | KBAUM |
| embolism | KBLIFM |
| embryo | KBROE |
| emergency | M–RJ |
| emergency room | M–RM, MAOM, ERM |
| emphysema | KBAOEM |
| endocrine | KREN |
| endocrine gland | KRENG |
| enlargement | NARMT |
| environment | VAOIRMT, VIRMT |
| environmental | VIRNL |
| enzymatic | ZAMT, ZAOIMT |
| enzyme | ZAOIM |
| epiglottis | GLOT, EP/GLOT |
| epilepsy | LEPS, EP/LEPS |
| epileptic | LEPG, EP/LEPT |
| esophagus | SOFG |
| estrogen | STREG |
| eustachian | STAIRB |
| eustachian tube | STAIRBT |
| evacuation | VAEX |
| exam | KPAM |
| examination | KP–GS |
| examination room | KPAOM |
| examine | KP– |
| excision | KPIGS |
| excrete | KPRAOET |
| excretion | KPRAOEGS |
| excruciating | SKRAOURB |
| exercise | KP–R |
| exhaustion | KPAUGS |
| expiration | KPRAIGS |
| expire | KPAOIR |
| extensor | STERNS |
| exterior | KPAOR |
| extract | STRAK |
| extraneous | STRAEN |
| extremity | STREMT |
| extrude | KPRAOUD |
| eyeball | AOIBL |

**F**

| | |
|---|---|
| facial | FAIRB |
| Fahrenheit | FAIRNT |
| fallopian | FLOEP |
| fallopian tube | FLOEPT |
| fatal | FAILT |
| fatality | FALT |
| fatigue | FAOEG |
| femur | FERM |
| fertile | FERL |
| fertility | FERLT |
| fertilization | FERLGS |

| | |
|---|---|
| fetal | FAOELT |
| fetal position | FAOEP |
| fetus | FAOETS |
| fiber | FAOIB |
| fibrillar | FRIBL |
| fibrillate | FIBLT |
| fibrillation | FIBLGS |
| fibula | FLIB |
| fibular | FLIBL |
| filter | FIRLT |
| fingernail | FIRN |
| fingertip | FINT |
| first-degree burn | F–BD |
| flaccid | FLAFD |
| flatulence | FLAFP |
| flexion | FL*EX, FL–X, FLEFN |
| flexor | FLERX |
| flu | FL*U |
| fluid | FLAOUD |
| folic acid | FOK |
| follicle | FLOL |
| forceps | FREPS |
| forearm | FROERM |
| forehead | FOERD |
| forensic | FRENS |
| forensic evidence | FREVD |
| fracture | FRAK, FRAKT |
| fragile | FRAJ |
| fragility | FRAJT |
| fragment | FRAMT |
| frontal | FRONL |
| function | FUNGS |

**G**

| | |
|---|---|
| gallbladder | GAUB |
| gallstone | GAULT |
| gamma globulin | GLAUB |
| ganglia | GLA* |
| ganglion | GLAUN |
| gangrene | GRAEN |
| gastritis | GRAOIT, GRAOITS |
| gastroenteric | GAONT |
| gastroenteritis | GAOINT, GAOINTS |
| gastroenterologist | GAONLT |
| gastroenterology | GAONL |
| gastrointestinal | GAOT |
| gender | JERND |
| gene | GAOEN |
| genealogist | GAOENT |
| genealogy | GAOENL |
| genetic | GENT |
| genetically | GENLT |
| genital | GAENL |
| genitalia | GAENT |

genus ............................................................ GAOENZ
geriatric ............................................................ GERT
gerontology ............................................................ GERNT
gestate ............................................................ JEGT
gestation ............................................................ JEGS
glans ............................................................ GLANZ
glaucoma ............................................................ GLAUK
globin ............................................................ GLUB
globulin ............................................................ GLAOUB
glucose ............................................................ GLAOUK
glutin ............................................................ GLUNT
glycemia ............................................................ GLAEM
glycogen ............................................................ GLAOIK
gonad ............................................................ GOEND
gonadal ............................................................ GOENL
gonadic ............................................................ GOENG
grand mal seizure ............................................ G–MS, G–MZ
granulation ............................................................ GRULGS
granule ............................................ GRUL, GRANL
gray matter ............................................................ GRAIMT
group therapy ............................................................ GRAOUPT
gurney ............................................................ GERN
gynecologist ............................................................ GOLT
gynecology ............................................................ GOLG

**H**

hallucinate ............................................................ HAOUL
hallucination ............................................................ HAOULGS
hard of hearing ............................................ HARGD, HARG
headache ............................................................ HAIK
hearing aid ............................................ HAERGD, HIRD
hearing impaired ............................ HIRP, HIRM, HIRMD
hearing impairment ............................................................ HIRMT
hearing loss ............................................................ HAERLG
hearing-sighted ............................................................ HAERTD
heart attack ............................................ HARKT, HAURK
heartbeat ............................................................ HARBT
heartburn ............................................................ HURN
heart disease ............................................................ HARDZ
heart murmur ............................................ HAURM, HURM
heart surgery ............................................................ HARJ
hematoma ............................................................ HAOEMT
hemoglobin ............................................................ HAOEM
hemophilia ............................................................ HAOEF
hemorrhage ............................................................ HERJ
hemorrhoid ............................................................ HEMD
hemostasis ............................................................ HAOEFMT
hepatitis ............................................................ HAEPT
hereditary ............................................................ HA*IRD
hernia ............................................................ HAERN
herniate ............................................................ HAERNT
herniation ............................................ HAERNGS, HERNGS
herpes ............................................................ HERPS
herpes simplex ............................................................ HERPGS

herpes zoster .............................................. HERPZ
heterogeneous .......................................... HAOENS
heterosexual ...................................... H–T, HET
heterosexuality ........................................... HELT
histology ................................................. HOELG
homogeneous ........................................... HAOEMS
homogenous ................................ MOJZ, HOJZ
homosexual ................................................... H–L
homosexuality ............................................ H–LT
horizontal ................................................... ZONL
hormone .................................................. HOERM
hospital ..................................................... HOPT
hospitalization ........................................ HOPGS
hospitalize .................................................. HOF
humerus ................................................. HURMZ
hybrid ..................................................... HAOIBD
hypertension ......................................... HAOIPGS
hypnosis .................................................. SNOP
hypnotic ......................................... SNOPG, SNOPK
hypnotist .................................................. SNOPT
hypochondria ........................................... KHOND
hypochondriac ........................ KHONG, KHONGD
hypodermic ............................................. HAOIM
hypodermic injection ........................... HAOIMGS
hypodermic needle .............................. HAOIMD
hypodermic syringe .............................. HAOIMS
hysterectomy ............................................ HIFRT
hysteria .................................................. ST*ER
hysteric ................................................. STERK
hysterodynia ........................................... HIFRD
hystero-oophorectomy ................... HIFR, HAOFR
hysterosalpingo-oophorectomy .......... HIFRP, HAOFRP

# I

immunoglobulin ..................................... KBLAUB
impairment ........................................... KBAIRMT
impalpable ............................................ KBABL
implant ................................................. KBLANT
impotence ............................................ KBOENS
impotency ....................... KBAOENS, KBOENSZ
impotent ............................................... KBOENT
impregnate ............................................ KBREG
impregnation ...................................... KBRAEGS
impression ........................................... KBREGS
in case of emergency ............................... KERJ
incision ................................................. SNIGS
incisor .............................................. SNAOIRZ
index ....................................................... N–X
indigestion .......................................... SPWEGS
inebriate ............................... NAOEB, BRAIT
inebriation ....................... NAOEBGS, BRAIGS
in emergency ........................................... NERJ
infarct .............................. FAURK, N–FRKT
infarction ........................... FAURX, N–FRX

| | |
|---|---|
| infect | NEFK |
| infection | NEFX, NEFGS |
| inferior | FAOR |
| inflammation | FLAMGS |
| inguinal | GINL |
| inhalation | HALGS, NAELGS |
| inhale | NA*EL |
| inhibition | BIX |
| injure | JIR |
| injury | JAOUR |
| inner | N*R |
| inoperable | NOPBL, NOP/–BL, NOP/RABL |
| inorganic | NANK |
| inpatient | NAIRB, NAIRBT |
| insane | SNAIN |
| insanity | SNANT |
| insomnia | SNOM |
| institutionalization | TAOULGS |
| institutionalize | TAOUL |
| instrument | STRUMT |
| insulin | SLIN |
| interior | NAOR |
| internist | SPWERNT |
| internship | SPWERP |
| interstitial | SPWIRBL |
| intestinal | SPWEL, SPWELS |
| intestine | SPWES |
| intoxicate | SPWOK |
| intoxication | SPWOX |
| intraocular | SPWROK |
| intrauterine | SPWAOUT |
| intravenous | SPWAOEN, SPWRAOEN |
| intravenous feeding | SPWAOEF, SPWRAOEF |
| intravenous injection | SPWREGS |
| introvert | TROEFRT, SPWROFRT |
| intubate | SPWAET |
| intubation | SPWAEGS |
| intubator | SPWAERT |
| inversion | NERGS |
| in vitro | VAOERT |
| ion | AOIN |
| ionization | AOINGS |
| iris | AOIRZ |
| ischemia | SHAOEM |
| ischium | SHUM |

**J**

| | |
|---|---|
| jaundice | JAUN |
| jejunum | GEJ |
| jugular | JAUR, JARL |
| jugular vein | JAUV |
| juxtaposition | JUPGS |

## K

| | |
|---|---|
| keratic | KERKT |
| keratin | KERT |
| keratotomy | K*ERT |
| kidney | KAOEND |
| kidney stone | KAOENT |
| kilo | KLOE |
| kilogram | K–LG |

## L

| | |
|---|---|
| labor | LAIB |
| laboratory | LABT |
| lacerate | LAFRT |
| laceration | LARGS |
| larynx | LAIRNGS |
| laser | LAIRZ |
| lateral | LARL |
| learning disability | LABLT |
| learning disabled | LABL, LABLD |
| left-handed | LEFTD |
| left-hand side | L–NDZ |
| left leg | LEFLG |
| left side | L–DZ |
| lethal | LAO*ET |
| lethargic | THAURJ |
| lethargy | THERJ |
| leukemia | LOUM |
| leukocyte | LOUK |
| licensed in | LIND |
| lifeless | LAOIFL |
| ligament | LIGT |
| linguistic | LING |
| lipid | PID |
| lipoid | PO*ID |
| lithium | L*IT |
| longevity | JEVT |
| longitude | LONT |
| longitudinal | LONL |
| lower back | LOERK, LOERB |
| low-fat | LOEFT |
| lubricate | LAOUBT |
| lumbar | L*UM, L*UB |
| lung cancer | LURNG, LA*ERN |
| lymph | YIMP |
| lymph node | YIMPD |

## M

| | |
|---|---|
| macula | MOUL |
| macula degeneration | MOULGS |
| macular degeneration | MOURLGS |
| major | MAIJ |
| malignancy | MALG |
| malignant | MALGT |
| malpractice | M–P |

mammary .................................................................. MAERM
mammary gland ................................................. MAERMD
mandible ................................................................... MABL
maniac .................................................................... MAINK
manic ...................................................................... MANK
manipulation ........................................................ MIPGS
manual ..................................................................... MANL
mastectomy ............................................................ MEKT
masturbation ........................... MAURBGS, MURBGS
maternal rubella .................................................... MOUB
mature .................................................................... MAUR
maturity ............................................................... MAURT
M.D. ........................................................................... M–D
measurement ..................................................... MURMT
mechanism ........................................................... MEFM
medical ...................................................................... MEL
medical evidence ................................................. MEVD
medical malpractice .............................................. M*M
medical school ..................................................... MAOL
medication ............................................................ MEGS
medicinal ................................................................. M–NL
medicine .................................................................. M–N
memory ................................................................... MEM
Ménière's disease .............................................. MAIND
meningitis ............................................................. JAOIT
menopausal ........................................................ MAUFL
menopause ........................................................... MAUZ
mental ................................................................... MENL
meridian ................................................................ MERD
metabolic ............................................. BL*IK, MET/BLIK
metabolism ....................................... BLIFM, MET/BLIFM
metabolize ............................................ BLAOIZ, BLAOIS
metatarsus ........................................................ MAURZ
methamphetamine ........................................... MAEFM
microscope ...................................................... MAOIRK
microscopic ...................................................... MAOIRP
midwife ............................................................. DWAOIF
midwifery ............................................................... DWIF
millimeter ............................................................... M–M
mineral ................................................................ MIRNL
minor .................................................................. MOIRN
miscarriage ................................... SKAIRJ, SKAERJ
miscarry ............................................................. SKAER
mitral .................................................................... MIRLT
mitral valve ....................................................... MIVRLT
Mongoloid .......................................................... MAUNG
morphine ........................................................... MOFRB
mortal ............................................................... MAORLT
mortality ........................ MAORT, MO*RLT, MOERLT
mucous ............................................................. MAOUK
mucus .................................................. MOUK, MAOUKS
multiple sclerosis ........................................... SKLOEM
muscle ................................................................ MUFL
musculoskeletal ............................................... MUFLZ

| | |
|---|---|
| myopia | MAOP |
| myopic | MAOPG, MAOPK |

## N

| | |
|---|---|
| narcotic | NARKT |
| nasal | NAILZ |
| nausea | NAUZ |
| nauseate | NAURBT |
| nauseous | NAURB |
| navel | NAEVL |
| nearsighted | NAOERTD |
| nearsightedness | NAOERTDZ |
| nephritis | FRAOITS |
| nervous system | N–S |
| neurologically | NAOURL |
| neuron | NAOURN |
| neuroses | NAOURSZ |
| neurosis | NAOURS |
| neurotic | NAOURKT |
| nitrous | NAOIR |
| nitrous oxide | NAOIRD, NAUX |
| nystagmus | N*IS |

## O

| | |
|---|---|
| obstetric | STREK |
| obstetrician | STREGS |
| occipital | SIPT |
| ocular | AUK |
| ocular disorder | AUKD |
| ointment | OIMT |
| olfactory | FLAOK |
| operability | PRAIBLT |
| operable | PRAIBL |
| operate | PRAIT |
| operating room | OERM |
| operation | PRAIGS |
| ophthalmologist | MOLT |
| ophthalmology | MOLG |
| optic | AUPT |
| optical | TA*UL, LAUPT |
| optician | A*UPGS, OPGTS |
| optic nerve | AUN |
| optometrist | TOMT |
| optometry | TROMT |
| oral | ORL |
| oral deaf | AURLD |
| orally | OERL |
| organ | GORN |
| organism | GOFM, GIFM |
| orthodontic | THONK |
| orthodontist | THONT |
| orthopedic | ORPD, ORP |
| orthopedist | ORPT |
| osmosis | SMOES, SMOEZ |

osteoarthritis ............................................................. TWOET
osteopath ................................................................. TWOEPT
osteoporosis ............................................................. TWOEP
osteotomy ................................................................... TWOT
otolaryngologist ......................................................... LARNT
otolaryngology ............................................................ LARN
outpatient ....................................................... TAIRB, TAIRBT
ovarian ................................................................ OIV, OIVN
ovarian cancer ........................................................ VAERN
ovary .......................................................................... OEV
overdose .................................................................... VOEZ
ovulate ...................................................................... OVLT
ovulation ................................................. OVLGS, OEVLGS
ovum ....................................................................... OEVM
oxygen ..................................................................... SHEN
oxygenate ................................................................ SHAIT
oxygenation ............................................................ SHAIGS

## P

palate ......................................................................... PLA
palpitation ............................................................... PALGS
pancreas ................................................ PAENK, PAN/KRAS
paralysis .................................................................. PRALS
paralyze .................................................................... P–RL
paramedic ................................................................ PAIRM
parietal ................................................................... PRAOILT
parietal bone .......................................................... PRAOIBLT
Parkinson's .............................................................. PARNZ
Parkinson's disease ................................................ PARNDZ
parotid ...................................................................... PROTD
parotid gland ......................................................... PROGTD
patella ..................................................................... PAT/LA
patellar ................................................................... PAT/LAR
pathological ................................................... THOJ, THAJ
pathological liar .......................................... THOL, THAOIR
pathologist ..................................................... THOLT, THAOLT
pathology ..................................................... THOLG, THAOLG
patient ............................................................ PAIRB, PAIRBT
pelvic .............................................................. PEFK, PEVK
pelvis .............................................................. PEFL, PEVL
penis ...................................................................... PAOEN
petit mal seizure ....................................................... P–MZ
phalanges ............................................................. FLANGZ
phalanx ................................................................. FLANKZ
pharmaceutical ................................................ FAURL, FARL
pharmacist .................................................. FARMT, FAURMT
pharmacology ........................................................ FAURM
pharmacy ..................................................... FAURMS, FARMZ
pharynx ................................................................. FAIRNGS
Ph.D. ........................................................................ H–PD
phlebitis ............................................................ FLEBT, FLEBTS
phobia ...................................................................... FOEB
photorefractive keratectomy ...................... FRAV, P–RK/P–RK, FRAVT/KAERK,
                                                                   FRAVT/KAERKT

| | |
|---|---|
| physical | F–L |
| physician | F–GS |
| physiological | FLOJ |
| physiology | FOJ |
| pigment | PIMT |
| pigmentation | PIMGS |
| pineal | PAENL |
| pineal gland | PAENLD |
| pituitary | PIRT |
| pituitary gland | PIRTD |
| plantar | PLAURT, PLA*RNT |
| plasma | PLAFM |
| plastic surgeon | PLURN |
| plastic surgery | PLURG |
| platelet | PLAILT |
| pleura | PLER |
| pleural | PLERL |
| pleurisy | PLERS |
| plexus | PLEKZ |
| PMS | P–MS |
| pneumonia | NAOUM |
| poison | POI |
| polyp | PLIP |
| posterior | PAO*R |
| posteriorly | PAO*RL |
| postmortem | PORMT, PO*ERM |
| post mortem | POERM |
| post partum | PAURM |
| potable | POEBT |
| pregnancy | PRAEG |
| pregnant | PREG |
| premature | PRAUR |
| prescribe | PRAOIB |
| prescription | PRIPGS |
| PRK | P*RK |
| procedure | PRAOER |
| proctologist | PROKT |
| proctology | PROK |
| prognosis | PROEG |
| prophylactic | FLAKT |
| prophylaxis | FLAKZ |
| prostate | PRAET |
| prostate cancer | PRAERN |
| prostheses | PRAOETS, PRAO*ETS |
| prosthesis | PRAOET, PRAO*ET |
| prosthetic | PRO*T |
| protein | PROIN |
| prothrombin | THRAUM |
| psoas | SWAS |
| psyche | SKPAOE |
| psychiatric | SKAOIK |
| psychiatrist | SKAOIT |
| psychiatry | SKRAOE |
| psychic | SK*IK |

psycho ............................................................................................ SKOE
psychological ................................................................................ SKOJ
psychologist ................................................................................ SKOLT
psychology .................................................................................. SKOLG
psychoses ................................................................................ SKAOEZ
psychosis .................................................................................. SKOEZ
psychotic ...................................................................................... SKOK
pulmonary ..................................................................................... PLOM
pulmonary artery ......................................................................... PLAOM
pulmonary valve ................................ PLOFM, PLOVM, PLOFL, PLOVL
pulmonary vein ............................................................................... PLOV
pupil ........................................................................................... PAOUP
purulent .................................................................................. PAOURLT
pustule ...................................................................................... PAOUL
pyloric ...................................................................................... PLOERK
pylorus ............................................................... PLOERZ, PLURS

**Q**

quadriceps ................................................................................ KWEPS
quadriplegia .......................................................................... KWAOEJ
quadriplegic .......................................................................... KWAOEK
quadruplet ............................................ DRAOUPLT, KRAOUPT
quarantine ................................................ KWAURNT, KWARN

**R**

radial keratotomy ................................... R–KT, R*K/R*K
radiate .......................................................................................... YAET
radiation .................................................................................. YAEGS
radioactive .................................................................................. RAOV
radiologist .................................................................. ROLT, RAOLT
radiology .................................................................................. RAOLG
radius ............................................................................................ RUS
recovery .............................................................. ROIFR, ROIVR
recovery room .......................................................................... R–RM
recuperate .......................................................................... RAOUPT
recuperation .................................................................. RAOUPGS
red blood cell ........................................................................ REBLZ
red blood count ...................................................................... REBLT
refractive ............................................................................ FRAEVK
regurgitate ............................................................................. GURJ
regurgitation ......................................................................... GURJS
rehabilitate ............................................................................ RABLT
rehabilitation ....................................................................... RABLGS
renal ....................................................................................... RAENL
reproductive ......................................................................... RAOUF
reproductive system .......................................................... RAOUFZ
rescuable ............................................................................ SKWUBL
rescue .................................................................................. SKWUR
rescue team ......................................................................... SKWUT
resistance .................................................... R*INS, RA*NS
respiration ......................................................................... SPAOIRX
respirator ........................................................................ SPRAOIRT
respiratory ....................................................................... SPAOIRT
retina .................................................................................... RAENT

| | |
|---|---|
| retinal detachment | RAENTD |
| retinitis | RAOINTS |
| retinitis pigmentosa | RAOIPTS |
| retinopathy | RO*PT |
| revive | VAOIF |
| rheumatic | ROIMT, RAOUMT |
| rheumatism | ROIFM, RAOUFM |
| rheumatoid arthritis | R*ITS, RAOUMTS, RAOUMTD |
| riboflavin | FLAIVN |
| right arm | RARM |
| right hand | −RND |
| right-hand side | R−NDZ, −RNDZ |
| right leg | R−LG |
| right side | R−DZ |
| rigor mortis | GORMT |
| RK | R*K |
| rubella | ROUB |
| rupture | RUPT |

## S

| | |
|---|---|
| sac | SKRA |
| sacral | SKRAL |
| sacroiliac | SKRAK |
| sacrum | SKRUM |
| sagittal | SAJT |
| saliva | SLAOIV |
| salivary gland | SLAVGD |
| salmonella | SAUL |
| sanatarium | SNAIRM |
| sarcoma | SKOEM |
| sartorius | SAURT |
| scapula | SKLAP |
| schizoid | SKOID |
| schizophrenia | SKIZ, FR*EN |
| schizophrenic | SKIKZ, FRENK |
| sciatica | SKAKT |
| sclera | SKLER |
| scleral | SKLERL |
| scleroderma | SKLERD |
| scleroid | SKLOID |
| scleroma | SKLOERM |
| sclerosis | SKLOEZ |
| scoliosis | SKLOL |
| scrotum | SKROET |
| second-degree burn | S−BD |
| secondhand smoke | SKOEK |
| secrete | SKRAO*ET |
| secretion | SKRAOEGS |
| sedate | SDAET |
| sedation | SDAEGS |
| sedative | SDAEV |
| sedentary | SDAIR, SDAER |
| sedimentation | SD−MGS |
| seizure | SHAOEZ, SHAOES |

| | |
|---|---|
| senile | SNAOIL |
| senility | SNILT |
| sensation | SENGS |
| septum | STEPT |
| shinbone | SHIB |
| shingles | SHINGS |
| shortness of breath | SHORB |
| shoulder | SHOELD, SHOULD |
| sigmoid | SMOID |
| sinusitis | SNUT |
| skeletal | SKALT, SKAELT |
| skeleton | SKELT |
| sober | SOEB |
| sobriety | SOEBT, SBRAOIT, SOBT |
| sociopath | SOEPT |
| soluble | SOBL |
| solution | SLAOUGS |
| sore throat | SOERT |
| spasm | SPAFM |
| spasmodic | SMOD |
| spastic | SPAS |
| specimen | SPEM |
| speech impaired | SPIRD |
| speech impairment | SPAIRMT, SPIRMT |
| speech impediment | SPEFMT |
| sphenoid | SFOID |
| sphincter | SFING, SFINGT |
| spina bifida | SPAOIB |
| spinal | SPAOINL |
| spinal column | SPLUM |
| spinal cord | SKORD |
| splinter | SPLIRNT |
| squamous | SKWAM |
| staph | STAOF |
| staphylococci | STAOFLG, STAOFLS |
| staphylococcus | STAOFL |
| starvation | STARGS, STAFRBGS |
| sterile | STERL |
| sterility | STERLT |
| sterilization | STERLGS |
| sternal | STURNL, ST*ERNL |
| sternum | STURM |
| steroid | STERD |
| stethoscope | STHOEP, THOEP |
| stimulant | STLANT |
| stimulate | STLAIT |
| stimulation | STLAIGS |
| stimuli | STLAOI |
| stimulus | STLUS |
| stirrup | STIRP |
| stoic | STWIK, STWOEK |
| straitjacket | STRAIK |
| strep | STREP |
| strep throat | STREPT |

streptococci ............................................................................. STRAOI
streptococcus .............................................. STREPG, STRAUK
stress and trauma ................................................................ STRAUM
stressful ...................................................................................... STREFL
stretcher .................................................................................... STREFRP
subclavian ................................................................................ SKLAIVN
subdural ........................................................................................ SDURL
subgroup .................................................................................. SGRAOUP
subliminal ...................................................................................... SBLIM
sublingual .................................................................................... SBLING
subluxate ...................................................................................... SBLUK
subluxation ................................................................................... SBLUX
suicidal ........................................................................................ SWAOIL
suicide .......................................................................................... SWAOID
superior ............................................................................. SYOR, SAOR
supine ........................................................................................ SWAOUP
supra ................................................................... SAORP, SPRA
surgeon ............................................................................................ SURN
Surgeon General ...................................................................... SURNG
surgery ........................................................................................... SURG
surgical ............................................................................................ SURL
surgically ..................................................................................... SURLG
suture ......................................................................................... SAOUFP
symbiosis ...................................................................................... SBOES
sympathetic ................................................................................... STHIK
sympathetic nervous system ................................................. STHIKS
symptom ......................................................................................... STOM
symptomatic ................................................................................. STOMT
synapse ....................................................................................... SNAEPZ
synapses ...................................................................................... SNAPSZ
synapsis ......................................................................................... SNAPZ
synchronization ....................................................................... SKROIFGS
synchronize ............................................................................... SKROIF
syndrome ................................................................................... SDROEM
synergism .................................................................................... SNERM
synergy .......................................................................................... SNERJ
synovia ................................................................... SNOV, SNOEV
synovial ................................................................. SNOVL, SNOEVL
synovial cavity ......................................................................... SNOEVK
synovial fluid .............................................. SNOFLD, SNOEFLD
synovial joint .............................................................................. SNOEJ
synovial membrane ...................................... SNOEFM, SNOEVM
syphilis ............................................................................................. SIFLS
syringe ........................................................................................... SRING
system ............................................................................................. S–M
systematic ...................................................................................... S–MT
systolic ......................................................................................... STLOK

## T

tactile ............................................................. TWOIL, TWAO*IL
tactual ............................................................................................ TWUL
tailbone ....................................................................................... TWOEN
tarsal ............................................................................................... TARL
tendon ............................................................................................. TOIN

| | |
|---|---|
| testes | TAO*ES |
| therapeutic | THAOUP, THAOUPT |
| therapeutical | THAOUL |
| therapeutically | THAOEL |
| therapist | THAERPT, THAIRPT |
| therapy | THAERP, THAIRP |
| third-degree burn | TH–BD, THR–BD |
| thoracic | THORK |
| thorax | THORX, THOERX |
| thrombin | THROM |
| thrombocyte | THRAOIT, THROIT |
| thrombus | THRUB |
| thymus | THAOIM |
| thymus gland | THAOIMD |
| thyroid | THAOIRD, THROID |
| thyroid gland | THAOIRG, THAOIRGD |
| tibia | TIB |
| tibial | TIBL |
| tissue | TIRB |
| tonsil | TAUNL |
| tonsillectomy | TAUNG, TAUNLG |
| tonsillitis | TAUNLT |
| topical | TAUPL |
| tourniquet | TOURNT, TOURK |
| toxic | TOX |
| toxin | TOK, TO*X |
| trachea | TRAIK |
| tracheotomy | TRAIKT |
| traction | TRAX |
| trance | TRAENS |
| tranquilize | TRAENK |
| tranquilizer | TRANK |
| transfuse | TR–FS, TRAOUZ |
| transfusion | TR–FGS, TRAOUFGS |
| transplant | TRAPT |
| transverse | TRAFRB |
| transvestism | TREVM, TREFM |
| transvestite | TREVT, TREFT |
| trapezius | TRAPZ |
| trauma | TRAUM |
| traumatic | TRAUMT |
| treatment | TREMT, TRAOEMT |
| triceps | TREPZ |
| trochanter | TROK |
| tubal | TUBL |
| tubal ligation | TUBLGS, TAOUBLGS |
| tubal pregnancy | TUBLG, TRAEG |
| tubercular | BERL |
| tuberculosis | BERK |
| tubular | TAOURBL |
| tubule | TAOUBL |
| tumor | TAOURM |
| turbid | TURBD |
| Tylenol | TLAOIL |

## U

| | |
|---|---|
| ureter | AOURT |
| urethra | AO*URT |
| uric | YAOURK |
| uric acid | YAOURKD |
| urinary | YAIR |
| urinary bladder | YAIRB |
| urinary system | YAIRS |
| urinary tract | YAIRT |
| urinate | YAOURNT |
| urination | YAOURNGS |
| urine | YAOURN |
| urologist | YAOURLT |
| urology | YAOURLG |
| Usher's syndrome | SHOEM |
| uterine | YAOURT |
| uterine cancer | YA*ERN |
| uterus | YAOUT |

## V

| | |
|---|---|
| vaccinate | VAKT |
| vaccination | VAGS |
| vaccine | VAO*EN |
| vagina | VAJ |
| vaporization | VAIRPGS |
| varicose | VAIRKS |
| varicose veins | V–VS |
| vas deferens | VAFD |
| vascular | VAFR |
| vascular tissue | VAFRT |
| vasectomy | VEKT |
| vena cava | VAV |
| venal | VAENL |
| venereal | VAIRL |
| venereal disease | VAIRLD |
| ventricle | VENK |
| ventricular | VANK |
| vertebra | VA |
| vertebrae | VAE |
| vertebral | BRAL |
| vertical | VERL |
| vertigo | VERG, VERGT |
| vessel | VEFL |
| vestibule | VEFBL |
| viral | VAOIRL |
| virile | VIRL |
| virility | VIRLT |
| virus | VAOIR |
| viscous | SKOUS |
| vision | VIGS |
| visual | VIRBL |
| vitamin | VAOIMT, VAOIM |
| vitreous | VIT |
| vocal | VOEKL, VOEFK |

vocal cord .......................................................... VOEKLD, VOEFKD, V–KD
voice box ................................................................................................ VOIB
vomit .................................................................................................... VOMT
vulva ......................................................................................... VUVL, VUFL

## W

wheelchair ........................................................................................ WHAIR
white blood cell ............................................................................ WHAOIBL
white blood count .................................................................... WHAOIBLT

## X

X chromosome ................................................................................. KPOEM
xenophobe ................................................................................ KPOB, SFOB
xenophobia ........................................................................... KPOEB, SFOEB
xenophobic ............................................................................ KPOEK, SFOEK
x-ray ..................................................................................................... KPRAI

## Z

zoophobia ............................................................................................. ZAOF
zygoma ................................................................................................... ZMA
zygomatic ........................................................................................ ZAOIGT
zygomatic arch ................................................................................. ZAUFP
zygomatic bone ................................................................................ ZAOIB
zygomatic process ............................................................................ ZAOIP
zygon .................................................................................................. ZAUN
zygote ................................................................................................ ZAOIG

# -OLOGIST & -OLOGY

anesthesiologist / anesthesiology (1) .......................................................... OELT / OELG
anesthesiologist / anesthesiology (2) ................................................. THOELT / THOELG

anthropologist / anthropology ..................................................................... POLT / POLG

archaeologist / archaeology (1) ............................................................ AERLT / A*ERLG
archaeologist / archaeology (2) ............................................................. KHOLT / KHOLG

astrologist / astrology ....................................................................... STROLT / STROLG

audiologist / audiology .............................................................................. AULD / AULG

biologist / biology ..................................................................................... BOLGT / BOLG

cosmetologist / cosmetology ............................................................... KMOLT / KMOLG

dermatologist / dermatology ......................................................................... DOLT / DOLG

ecologist / ecology ................................................................................. KOELT / KOELG

geologist / geology ................................................................................. JOELT / JOELG

gynecologist / gynecology ........................................................................ GOLT / GOLG

ideologist / ideology ..................................................................................... YOLT / YOLG

ophthalmologist / ophthalmology ............................................................... MOLT / MOLG

otolaryngologist / otolaryngology ............................................................. LARNT / LARN

pathologist / pathology (1) ....................................................................... THOLT / THOLG
pathologist / pathology (2) ................................................................. THAOLT / THAOLG

psychologist / psychology ........................................................................ SKOLT / SKOLG

radiologist / radiology ............................................................................. RAOLT / RAOLG

seismologist / seismology ...................................................................... SMOLT / SMOLG

sociologist / sociology ............................................................................... SOLT / SOLG

zoologist / zoology .................................................................................. ZAOLT / ZAOLG

# Q&A SHORTCUTS

## QUESTIONS (STKPWHR– & STKPWHR*)

**A**

| Q | A | STKPWHR–A |
|---|---|---|
| Q | About | STKPWHR–B |
| Q | About the | STKPWHR–BT |
| Q | About these | STKPWHR–BZ |
| Q | About those | STKPWHR–BS |
| Q | And | STKPWHR–AND |
| Q | All right | STKPWHR–RLT, STKPWHR–IRLT, STKPWHR–ARLT |
| Q | And the | STKPWHR–ANTD |
| Q | And then | STKPWHR–ND |
| Q | And then the | STKPWHR–NTD |
| Q | And these | STKPWHR–ANDZ |
| Q | Are | STKPWHR–R |
| Q | Are the | STKPWHR–RT |
| Q | Are these | STKPWHR–RZ |
| Q | Are those | STKPWHR–RS |
| Q | At | STKPWHR–AT |
| Q | At the | STKPWHR–ATD |
| Q | At those | STKPWHR–ATS |
| Q | All right, sir. | STKPWHR–RLTS, STKPWHR–IRLTS, STKPWHR–ARLTS |

**B**

| Q | But, | STKPWHR–UT |
|---|---|---|

**C**

| Q | Can | STKPWHR–K |
|---|---|---|
| Q | Can these | STKPWHR–KZ |
| Q | Captain, | STKPWHR–PK |
| Q | Correct | STKPWHR–KT |
| Q | Correction | STKPWHR–X |
| Q | Corrections | STKPWHR–XZ |
| Q | Correct, sir. | STKPWHR–KTS |
| Q | Could | STKPWHR–KD |
| Q | Couldn't | STKPWHR–KTD |
| Q | Couldn't these | STKPWHR–KTDZ |
| Q | Could these | STKPWHR–KDZ |

**D**

| Q | Doctor, | STKPWHR–D |
|---|---|---|

**F**

| Q | Fine | STKPWHR–OIN |
|---|---|---|

**H**

| Q | Have | STKPWHR–F |
|---|---|---|
| Q | Have the | STKPWHR–FT |
| Q | Have these | STKPWHR–FZ |
| Q | Have those | STKPWHR–FS |
| Q | He | STKPWHR–E |

| Q | He also | STKPWHR–ELS |
|---|---|---|
| Q | He be | STKPWHR–EB |
| Q | He believe | STKPWHR–EBL |
| Q | He believed | STKPWHR–EBLD |
| Q | He believed so | STKPWHR–EBLDZ |
| Q | He believed the | STKPWHR–EBLTD |
| Q | He believes | STKPWHR–EBLS |
| Q | He believes so | STKPWHR–EBLSZ |
| Q | He believes the | STKPWHR–EBLTS |
| Q | He believe the | STKPWHR–EBLT |
| Q | He believing | STKPWHR–EBLG |
| Q | He believing the | STKPWHR–EBLGT |
| Q | He can | STKPWHR–EK |
| Q | He can't | STKPWHR–EKT |
| Q | He could | STKPWHR–EKD |
| Q | He couldn't | STKPWHR–EKTD |
| Q | He'd | STKPWHR*ED |
| Q | He ever | STKPWHR–EFR, STKPWHR–EVR |
| Q | He feel | STKPWHR–EFL |
| Q | He feeling | STKPWHR–EFLG |
| Q | He feeling the | STKPWHR–EFLGT |
| Q | He feels | STKPWHR–EFLS |
| Q | He feels the | STKPWHR–EFLTS |
| Q | He felt | STKPWHR–EFLT |
| Q | He felt the | STKPWHR–EFLTD |
| Q | He forget | STKPWHR–EFGT |
| Q | He forgets | STKPWHR–EFGTS |
| Q | He forgot | STKPWHR–EFGD |
| Q | He forgotten | STKPWHR–EFN |
| Q | He forgotten the | STKPWHR–EFRNGT |
| Q | He forgot the | STKPWHR–EFGTD |
| Q | He get | STKPWHR–EGT |
| Q | He gets | STKPWHR–EGTS |
| Q | He go | STKPWHR–EG |
| Q | He goes | STKPWHR–EGS |
| Q | He got | STKPWHR–EGD |
| Q | He got the | STKPWHR–EGTD |
| Q | He had | STKPWHR–ED |
| Q | He hadn't | STKPWHR–AENT |
| Q | He hadn't the | STKPWHR–AENTD |
| Q | He had the | STKPWHR–ETD |
| Q | He have | STKPWHR–EF |
| Q | He imagine | STKPWHR–EJ |
| Q | He imagined | STKPWHR–EJD |
| Q | He imagined so | STKPWHR–EJDZ |
| Q | He imagined the | STKPWHR–EJTD |
| Q | He imagines | STKPWHR–EJS |
| Q | He imagines so | STKPWHR–EJSZ |
| Q | He imagines the | STKPWHR–EJTS |
| Q | He imagine the | STKPWHR–EJT |
| Q | He is | STKPWHR–EZ |
| Q | He isn't | STKPWHR–EFNT |
| Q | He isn't the | STKPWHR–EFNTD |
| Q | He'll | STKPWHR*EL |

| Q | He observe | STKPWHR–EFRB |
|---|---|---|
| Q | He observed | STKPWHR–EFRBD |
| Q | He observed the | STKPWHR–EFRBTD |
| Q | He observes | STKPWHR–EFRBS |
| Q | He observes the | STKPWHR–EFRBTS |
| Q | He observe the | STKPWHR–EFRBT |
| Q | He observing | STKPWHR–EFRBG |
| Q | He observing the | STKPWHR–EFRBGT |
| Q | He recall | STKPWHR–ERL |
| Q | He recalled | STKPWHR–ERLD |
| Q | He recalled the | STKPWHR–ERLTD |
| Q | He recalling | STKPWHR–ERLG |
| Q | He recalling the | STKPWHR–ERLGT |
| Q | He recalls | STKPWHR–ERLS |
| Q | He recalls the | STKPWHR–ERLTS |
| Q | He recall the | STKPWHR–ERLT |
| Q | He recognize | STKPWHR–ERN |
| Q | He recognized | STKPWHR–ERND |
| Q | He recognized the | STKPWHR–ERNTD |
| Q | He recognizes | STKPWHR–ERNS |
| Q | He recognizes the | STKPWHR–ERNTS |
| Q | He recognize the | STKPWHR–ERNT |
| Q | He recognizing | STKPWHR–ERNG |
| Q | He recognizing the | STKPWHR–ERNGT |
| Q | He recollect | STKPWHR–ERK |
| Q | He recollected | STKPWHR–ERKD |
| Q | He recollected the | STKPWHR–ERKTD |
| Q | He recollects | STKPWHR–ERKS |
| Q | He recollects the | STKPWHR–ERKTS |
| Q | He recollect the | STKPWHR–ERKT |
| Q | He remember | STKPWHR–ERM |
| Q | He remembered | STKPWHR–ERMD |
| Q | He remembered the | STKPWHR–ERMTD |
| Q | He remembering | STKPWHR–ERMG |
| Q | He remembering the | STKPWHR–ERMGT |
| Q | He remembers | STKPWHR–ERMS |
| Q | He remembers the | STKPWHR–ERMTS |
| Q | He remembers these | STKPWHR–ERMSZ |
| Q | He remember the | STKPWHR–ERMT |
| Q | He remember these | STKPWHR–ERMZ |
| Q | He's | STKPWHR*ES |
| Q | He said | STKPWHR–EDZ |
| Q | He said the | STKPWHR–ETDZ |
| Q | He shall | STKPWHR–ERB |
| Q | He should | STKPWHR–ERBD |
| Q | He shouldn't | STKPWHR–ERBTD |
| Q | He think | STKPWHR–ENG |
| Q | He thinks | STKPWHR–ENGS |
| Q | He thinks the | STKPWHR–ENGTS |
| Q | He thinks so | STKPWHR–ENGSZ |
| Q | He think the | STKPWHR–ENGT |
| Q | He understands | STKPWHR–ENDZ |
| Q | He understands the | STKPWHR–ENTDZ |
| Q | He understood | STKPWHR–END |

| Q | He understood the | STKPWHR–ENTD |
|---|---|---|
| Q | He want | STKPWHR–EPT |
| Q | He wanted | STKPWHR–EPTD |
| Q | He wanting | STKPWHR–EPGT |
| Q | He wants | STKPWHR–EPTS |
| Q | He was | STKPWHR–EFS |
| Q | He wasn't | STKPWHR–EFT |
| Q | He wasn't the | STKPWHR–EFTD |
| Q | He were | STKPWHR–ERP |
| Q | He weren't | STKPWHR–ERPT |
| Q | He weren't the | STKPWHR–ERPTD |
| Q | He will | STKPWHR–EL |
| Q | He will get | STKPWHR–ELGT |
| Q | He will get the | STKPWHR–ELGTD |
| Q | He will go | STKPWHR–ELG |
| Q | He will say | STKPWHR*ELS |
| Q | He will say so | STKPWHR–ELSZ |
| Q | He will see | STKPWHR–ELZ |
| Q | He would | STKPWHR–ELD |
| Q | He wouldn't | STKPWHR–ELTD |
| Q | He would say | STKPWHR–ELDZ |

**I**

| Q | I | STKPWHR–I |
|---|---|---|
| Q | I am | STKPWHR–IM |
| Q | I believe | STKPWHR–IBL |
| Q | I believed | STKPWHR–IBLD |
| Q | I believed so | STKPWHR–IBLDZ |
| Q | I believed the | STKPWHR–IBLTD |
| Q | I believe it is | STKPWHR–IBLTS |
| Q | I believe so | STKPWHR–IBLS |
| Q | I believe the | STKPWHR–IBLT |
| Q | I believing | STKPWHR–IBLG |
| Q | I believing the | STKPWHR–IBLGT |
| Q | I can | STKPWHR–IK |
| Q | I can't | STKPWHR–IKT |
| Q | I could | STKPWHR–IKD |
| Q | I couldn't | STKPWHR–IKTD |
| Q | I'd | STKPWHR–AOID, STKPWHR–AO*ID |
| Q | I feel | STKPWHR–IFL |
| Q | I feeling | STKPWHR–IFLG |
| Q | I felt | STKPWHR–IFLT |
| Q | I felt the | STKPWHR–IFLTD |
| Q | I get | STKPWHR–IGT |
| Q | I go | STKPWHR–IG |
| Q | I got | STKPWHR–IGD |
| Q | I got the | STKPWHR–IGTD |
| Q | I had | STKPWHR–ID |
| Q | I hadn't | STKPWHR–INTD |
| Q | I had the | STKPWHR–ITD, STKPWHR–AOITD |
| Q | I have | STKPWHR–IF |
| Q | I have been | STKPWHR–IFB |
| Q | I have been the | STKPWHR–IFBT |
| Q | I have believed | STKPWHR–IFBLD |

| | | |
|---|---|---|
| Q | I have believed so | STKPWHR–IFBLDZ |
| Q | I have believed the | STKPWHR–IFBLTD |
| Q | I have gone | STKPWHR–IFG |
| Q | I have got | STKPWHR–IFGD |
| Q | I have got the | STKPWHR–IFGTD |
| Q | I have had | STKPWHR–IFD |
| Q | I have had the | STKPWHR–IFTD |
| Q | I have heard | STKPWHR–IFRD |
| Q | I have heard the | STKPWHR–IFRTD |
| Q | I have heard these | STKPWHR–IFRDZ |
| Q | I have known | STKPWHR–IFN |
| Q | I have known the | STKPWHR–IFNT |
| Q | I have known them | STKPWHR–IFNM |
| Q | I have known them the | STKPWHR–IFNMT |
| Q | I have known these | STKPWHR–IFNZ |
| Q | I have known those | STKPWHR–IFNS |
| Q | I haven't | STKPWHR–IVT |
| Q | I have recalled | STKPWHR–IFRLD |
| Q | I have recalled the | STKPWHR–IFRLTD |
| Q | I have recalled these | STKPWHR–IFRLDZ |
| Q | I have recognized | STKPWHR–IFRND |
| Q | I have recognized the | STKPWHR–IFRNTD |
| Q | I have recollected | STKPWHR–IFRKD |
| Q | I have recollected the | STKPWHR–IFRKTD |
| Q | I have recollected these | STKPWHR–IFRKDZ |
| Q | I have remembered | STKPWHR–IFRMD |
| Q | I have remembered the | STKPWHR–IFRMTD |
| Q | I have remembered these | STKPWHR–IFRMDZ |
| Q | I have said | STKPWHR–IFDZ |
| Q | I have said the | STKPWHR–IFTDZ |
| Q | I have the | STKPWHR–IFT |
| Q | I have them | STKPWHR–IFM |
| Q | I have these | STKPWHR–IFZ |
| Q | I have those | STKPWHR*IFS |
| Q | I heard | STKPWHR–IRD |
| Q | I heard the | STKPWHR–IRTD |
| Q | I heard these | STKPWHR–IRDZ |
| Q | I'll | STKPWHR–AOIL, STKPWHR–AO*IL |
| Q | I'm | STKPWHR–AOIM, STKPWHR–AO*IM |
| Q | I mean | STKPWHR*IM |
| Q | I mean to | STKPWHR–IMT, STKPWHR*IMT |
| Q | I mean to say | STKPWHR–IMTS |
| Q | I'm not | STKPWHR–AOIMT |
| Q | I'm not sure | STKPWHR–AOIMTS |
| Q | I'm sorry | STKPWHR–AOIMS |
| Q | I'm sure | STKPWHR–AOIMZ |
| Q | I object | STKPWHR–IB |
| Q | I objected | STKPWHR–IBD |
| Q | I objected to | STKPWHR–IBTD |
| Q | I object to | STKPWHR–IBT |
| Q | I offer | STKPWHR–OIFR |
| Q | I offered | STKPWHR–OIFRD |
| Q | I offered the | STKPWHR–OIFRTD |
| Q | I offer in evidence | STKPWHR–OIFRND |

| Q | I offering | STKPWHR–OIFRG |
|---|---|---|
| Q | I offer the | STKPWHR–OIFRT |
| Q | I observe | STKPWHR–IFRB |
| Q | I observed | STKPWHR–IFRBD |
| Q | I observed the | STKPWHR–IFRBTD |
| Q | I observe the | STKPWHR–IFRBT |
| Q | I observing | STKPWHR–IFRBG |
| Q | I observing the | STKPWHR–IFRBGT |
| Q | I recall | STKPWHR–IRL |
| Q | I recalled | STKPWHR–IRLD |
| Q | I recalled the | STKPWHR–IRLTD |
| Q | I recalling | STKPWHR–IRLG |
| Q | I recalling the | STKPWHR–IRLGT |
| Q | I recognize | STKPWHR–IRN |
| Q | I recognized | STKPWHR–IRND |
| Q | I recognizing | STKPWHR–IRNG |
| Q | I remember | STKPWHR–IRM |
| Q | I remembered | STKPWHR–IRMD |
| Q | I remembering | STKPWHR–IRMG |
| Q | I remembering the | STKPWHR–IRMGT |
| Q | I remembered the | STKPWHR–IRMTD |
| Q | I respect | STKPWHR*IRP |
| Q | I respected | STKPWHR–IRPD |
| Q | I respected the | STKPWHR–IRPTD |
| Q | I respecting | STKPWHR–IRPG |
| Q | I respecting the | STKPWHR–IRPGT |
| Q | I respect the | STKPWHR*IRPT |
| Q | Is | STKPWHR–IS |
| Q | I said | STKPWHR–IDZ |
| Q | I said the | STKPWHR–ITDZ |
| Q | I see | STKPWHR–IZ |
| Q | I should | STKPWHR–IRBD |
| Q | I shouldn't | STKPWHR–IRBTD |
| Q | I think | STKPWHR–ING |
| Q | I think it is | STKPWHR–INGTS |
| Q | I think the | STKPWHR–INGT |
| Q | I think so | STKPWHR–INGS |
| Q | I understand | STKPWHR–INDZ |
| Q | I understood | STKPWHR–IND |
| Q | I understand the | STKPWHR–INTDZ |
| Q | I've | STKPWHR–IV, STKPWHR–AOIV |
| Q | I've also | STKPWHR–IVLS, STKPWHR–AOIVLS |
| Q | I've been | STKPWHR–IVB, STKPWHR–AOIVB |
| Q | I've been the | STKPWHR–IVBT, STKPWHR–AOIVBT |
| Q | I've believed | STKPWHR–IVBLD, STKPWHR–AOIVBLD |
| Q | I've believed so | STKPWHR–IVBLDZ, STKPWHR–AOIVBLDZ |
| Q | I've believed the | STKPWHR–IVBLTD, STKPWHR–AOIVBLTD |
| Q | I've got | STKPWHR–IVGD, STKPWHR–AOIVGD |
| Q | I've got the | STKPWHR–IVGTD, STKPWHR–AOIVGTD |
| Q | I've got these | STKPWHR–IVGDZ, STKPWHR–AOIVGDZ |
| Q | I've had | STKPWHR–IVD, STKPWHR–AOIVD |
| Q | I've had the | STKPWHR–IVTD, STKPWHR–AOIVTD |
| Q | I've heard | STKPWHR–IVRD, STKPWHR–AOIVRD |
| Q | I've heard the | STKPWHR–IVRTD, STKPWHR–AOIVRTD |

| Q | I've heard these | STKPWHR–IVRDZ, STKPWHR–AOIVRDZ |
|---|---|---|
| Q | I've known | STKPWHR–IVN, STKPWHR–AOIVN |
| Q | I've known the | STKPWHR–IVNT, STKPWHR–AOIVNT |
| Q | I've known these | STKPWHR–IVNZ, STKPWHR–AOIVNZ |
| Q | I've known those | STKPWHR–IVNS, STKPWHR–AOIVNS |
| Q | I've recalled | STKPWHR–IVRLD, STKPWHR–AOIVRLD |
| Q | I've recalled the | STKPWHR–IVRLTD, STKPWHR–AOIVRLTD |
| Q | I've recalled these | STKPWHR–IVRLDZ, STKPWHR–AOIVRLDZ |
| Q | I've recognized | STKPWHR–IVRND, STKPWHR–AOIVRND |
| Q | I've recognized the | STKPWHR–IVRNTD, STKPWHR–AOIVRNTD |
| Q | I've recognized these | STKPWHR–IVRNDZ, STKPWHR–AOIVRNDZ |
| Q | I've recollected | STKPWHR–IVRKD, STKPWHR–AOIVRKD |
| Q | I've recollected the | STKPWHR–IVRKTD, STKPWHR–AOIVRKTD |
| Q | I've recollected these | STKPWHR–IVRKDZ, STKPWHR–AOIVRKDZ |
| Q | I've remembered | STKPWHR–IVRMD, STKPWHR–AOIVRMD |
| Q | I've remembered the | STKPWHR–IVRMTD, STKPWHR–AOIVRMTD |
| Q | I've remembered these | STKPWHR–IVRMDZ, STKPWHR–AOIVRMDZ |
| Q | I've said | STKPWHR–IVDZ, STKPWHR–AOIVDZ |
| Q | I've said the | STKPWHR–IVTDZ |
| Q | I want | STKPWHR–IPT |
| Q | I wanted | STKPWHR–IPTD |
| Q | I wanting | STKPWHR–IPGT |
| Q | I was | STKPWHR–IFS |
| Q | I were | STKPWHR–IRP |
| Q | I will | STKPWHR–IL |
| Q | I would | STKPWHR–ILD |
| Q | I wouldn't | STKPWHR–ILTD |
| Q | I would say | STKPWHR–ILDZ |

**L**

| Q | Lieutenant, | STKPWHR–LT |
|---|---|---|

**M**

| Q | Mr. | STKPWHR–M |
|---|---|---|
| Q | Mrs. | STKPWHR–S |
| Q | Miss | STKPWHR–SZ |
| Q | Ms. | STKPWHR–Z |

**N**

| Q | No | STKPWHR–O |
|---|---|---|
| Q | No, | STKPWHR–N |
| Q | No, sir. | STKPWHR–OS |
| Q | No, sir | STKPWHR–OIR |
| Q | Now, | STKPWHR–OU |
| Q | Now, Doctor | STKPWHR–OUD |
| Q | Now, sir, | STKPWHR–OUS |

**O**

| Q | Officer | STKPWHR–OUFR |
|---|---|---|
| Q | Oh, | STKPWHR–OE |
| Q | Okay | STKPWHR–OK |

**P**

| Q | President | STKPWHR–PT |
|---|---|---|

**R**

| | | |
|---|---|---|
| Q | Right | STKPWHR–IRT |
| Q | Right, sir | STKPWHR–IRTS, STKPWHR–RTS |

**S**

| | | |
|---|---|---|
| Q | Sergeant, | STKPWHR–GT |
| Q | Shall | STKPWHR*RB |
| Q | Should | STKPWHR–RBD |
| Q | Shouldn't | STKPWHR–RBNT |
| Q | Shouldn't the | STKPWHR–RBNTD |
| Q | Shouldn't these | STKPWHR–RBNTDZ |
| Q | Shouldn't those | STKPWHR–RBNTS |
| Q | Should the | STKPWHR–RBTD |
| Q | Should these | STKPWHR–RBDZ |
| Q | Sir, | STKPWHR–IRS |
| Q | Sure | STKPWHR–RB |
| Q | Surely | STKPWHR–RBL |

**T**

| | | |
|---|---|---|
| Q | Then | STKPWHR–EN |
| Q | Then the | STKPWHR–ENT |
| Q | Then these | STKPWHR–ENZ |
| Q | Then those | STKPWHR–ENS |

**W**

| | | |
|---|---|---|
| Q | Was | STKPWHR–US |
| Q | Was the | STKPWHR–UTS |
| Q | Well, | STKPWHR–L |
| Q | Would | STKPWHR–LD |
| Q | Wouldn't | STKPWHR–LTD |
| Q | Would these | STKPWHR–LDZ |

**Y**

| | | |
|---|---|---|
| Q | Yeah | STKPWHR–AE |
| Q | Yes | STKPWHR–ES |
| Q | Yes, sir. | STKPWHR–ESZ |
| Q | Yes, sir, | STKPWHR–IR |
| Q | You | STKPWHR–U |
| Q | You allege | STKPWHR–ULG |
| Q | You alleged | STKPWHR–ULGD |
| Q | You alleged the | STKPWHR–ULGTD |
| Q | You alleged these | STKPWHR–ULGDZ |
| Q | You allege the | STKPWHR–ULGT |
| Q | You allege these | STKPWHR–ULGZ |
| Q | You allege those | STKPWHR–ULGS |
| Q | You also | STKPWHR–ULZ |
| Q | You are | STKPWHR–UR |
| Q | You are able | STKPWHR–URBL |
| Q | You are able to | STKPWHR–URBLT |
| Q | You are able to say | STKPWHR–URBLTS |
| Q | You are able to say so | STKPWHR–URBLTSZ |
| Q | You aren't | STKPWHR–URNT |
| Q | You are the | STKPWHR–URT |
| Q | You are these | STKPWHR–URZ |

| Q | You are those | STKPWHR–URS |
|---|---|---|
| Q | You be | STKPWHR–UB |
| Q | You believe | STKPWHR–UBL |
| Q | You believed | STKPWHR–UBLD |
| Q | You believed so | STKPWHR–UBLDZ |
| Q | You believed the | STKPWHR–UBLTD |
| Q | You believe it is | STKPWHR–UBLTS |
| Q | You believe so | STKPWHR–UBLS |
| Q | You believe the | STKPWHR–UBLT |
| Q | You believing | STKPWHR–UBLG |
| Q | You believing the | STKPWHR–UBLGT |
| Q | You be the | STKPWHR–UBT |
| Q | You can | STKPWHR–UK |
| Q | You can't | STKPWHR–UKT |
| Q | You could | STKPWHR–UKD |
| Q | You couldn't | STKPWHR–UKTD |
| Q | You'd | STKPWHR*UD |
| Q | You ever | STKPWHR–UFR, STKPWHR–UVR |
| Q | You feel | STKPWHR–UFL |
| Q | You feeling | STKPWHR–UFLG |
| Q | You feeling the | STKPWHR–UFLGT |
| Q | You felt | STKPWHR–UFLT |
| Q | You felt the | STKPWHR–UFLTD |
| Q | You forget | STKPWHR–UFGT |
| Q | You get | STKPWHR–UGT |
| Q | You go | STKPWHR–UG |
| Q | You got | STKPWHR–UGD |
| Q | You got the | STKPWHR–UGTD |
| Q | You got these | STKPWHR–UGDZ |
| Q | You had | STKPWHR–UD |
| Q | You had the | STKPWHR–UTD |
| Q | You have | STKPWHR–UF |
| Q | You have been | STKPWHR–UFB |
| Q | You have been the | STKPWHR–UFBT |
| Q | You have believed | STKPWHR–UFBLD |
| Q | You have believed so | STKPWHR–UFBLDZ |
| Q | You have believed the | STKPWHR–UFBLTD |
| Q | You have forgotten | STKPWHR–UFNG |
| Q | You have forgotten the | STKPWHR–UFNGT |
| Q | You have gone | STKPWHR–UFG |
| Q | You have got | STKPWHR–UFGD |
| Q | You have got the | STKPWHR–UFGTD |
| Q | You have had | STKPWHR–UFD |
| Q | You have had the | STKPWHR–UFTD |
| Q | You have heard | STKPWHR–UFRD |
| Q | You have heard the | STKPWHR–UFRTD |
| Q | You have heard these | STKPWHR–UFRDZ |
| Q | You have known | STKPWHR–UFN |
| Q | You have known the | STKPWHR–UFNT |
| Q | You have known them | STKPWHR–UFNM |
| Q | You have known them the | STKPWHR–UFNMT |
| Q | You have known these | STKPWHR–UFNZ |
| Q | You have known those | STKPWHR–UFNS |
| Q | You haven't | STKPWHR–UVT, STKPWHR–UFNT |

| Q | You have recalled | STKPWHR–UFRLD |
|---|---|---|
| Q | You have recalled the | STKPWHR–UFRLTD |
| Q | You have recalled these | STKPWHR–UFRLDZ |
| Q | You have recognized | STKPWHR–UFND |
| Q | You have recognized the | STKPWHR–UFNTD |
| Q | You have recognized these | STKPWHR–UFNDZ |
| Q | You have recollected | STKPWHR–UFRKD |
| Q | You have recollected the | STKPWHR–UFRKTD |
| Q | You have recollected these | STKPWHR–UFRKDZ |
| Q | You have remembered | STKPWHR–UFRMD |
| Q | You have remembered the | STKPWHR–UFRMTD |
| Q | You have remembered these | STKPWHR–UFRMDZ |
| Q | You have said | STKPWHR–UFDZ |
| Q | You have said the | STKPWHR–UFTDZ |
| Q | You have the | STKPWHR–UFT |
| Q | You have them | STKPWHR–UFM |
| Q | You have these | STKPWHR–UFZ |
| Q | You have those | STKPWHR–UFS |
| Q | You heard | STKPWHR–URD |
| Q | You heard the | STKPWHR–URTD |
| Q | You heard these | STKPWHR–URDZ |
| Q | You imagine | STKPWHR–UJ |
| Q | You imagined | STKPWHR–UJD |
| Q | You imagined so | STKPWHR–UJDZ |
| Q | You imagined the | STKPWHR–UJTD |
| Q | You imagine so | STKPWHR–UJS |
| Q | You imagine the | STKPWHR–UJT |
| Q | You'll | STKPWHR*UL |
| Q | You mean | STKPWHR–UM |
| Q | You mean to | STKPWHR–UMT |
| Q | You mean to say | STKPWHR–UMTS |
| Q | You observe | STKPWHR–UFRB |
| Q | You observed | STKPWHR–UFRBD |
| Q | You observed the | STKPWHR–UFRBTD |
| Q | You observe the | STKPWHR–UFRBT |
| Q | You observing | STKPWHR–UFRBG |
| Q | You observing the | STKPWHR–UFRBGT |
| Q | You're | STKPWHR*UR |
| Q | You recall | STKPWHR–URL |
| Q | You recalled | STKPWHR–URLD |
| Q | You recalled the | STKPWHR–URLTD |
| Q | You recalling | STKPWHR–URLG |
| Q | You recalling the | STKPWHR–URLGT |
| Q | You recall the | STKPWHR–URLT |
| Q | You recognize | STKPWHR–URN |
| Q | You recognized | STKPWHR–URND |
| Q | You recognized the | STKPWHR–URNTD |
| Q | You recollect | STKPWHR–URK |
| Q | You recollected | STKPWHR–URKD |
| Q | You recollected the | STKPWHR–URKTD |
| Q | You recollecting | STKPWHR–URG |
| Q | You recollect the | STKPWHR–URKT |
| Q | You remember | STKPWHR–URM |
| Q | You remembered | STKPWHR–URMD |

| Q | You remembered the | STKPWHR–URMTD |
|---|---|---|
| Q | You remembered these | STKPWHR–URMDZ |
| Q | You remembering | STKPWHR–URMG |
| Q | You remembering the | STKPWHR–URMGT |
| Q | You remember the | STKPWHR–URMT |
| Q | You remember these | STKPWHR–URMZ |
| Q | You remember those | STKPWHR–URMS |
| Q | You're the | STKPWHR*URT |
| Q | You said | STKPWHR–UDZ |
| Q | You said the | STKPWHR–UTDZ |
| Q | You shall | STKPWHR*URB |
| Q | You should | STKPWHR–URBD |
| Q | You shouldn't | STKPWHR–URBTD |
| Q | You sure | STKPWHR–URB |
| Q | You surely | STKPWHR*URBL |
| Q | You think | STKPWHR–UNG |
| Q | You think it is | STKPWHR–UNGTS |
| Q | You think so | STKPWHR–UNGS |
| Q | You think the | STKPWHR–UNGT |
| Q | You think these | STKPWHR–UNGZ |
| Q | You've | STKPWHR–UV |
| Q | You've been | STKPWHR–UVB |
| Q | You've been the | STKPWHR–UVBT |
| Q | You've believed | STKPWHR–UVBLD |
| Q | You've believed so | STKPWHR–UVBLDZ |
| Q | You've believed the | STKPWHR–UVBLTD |
| Q | You've got | STKPWHR–UVGD |
| Q | You've got the | STKPWHR–UVGTD |
| Q | You've had | STKPWHR–UVD |
| Q | You've had the | STKPWHR–UVTD |
| Q | You've heard | STKPWHR–UVRD |
| Q | You've heard the | STKPWHR–UVRTD |
| Q | You've heard these | STKPWHR–UVRDZ |
| Q | You've known | STKPWHR–UVN |
| Q | You've known the | STKPWHR–UVNT |
| Q | You've known these | STKPWHR–UVNZ |
| Q | You've known those | STKPWHR–UVNS |
| Q | You've recalled | STKPWHR–UVRLD |
| Q | You've recalled the | STKPWHR–UVRLTD |
| Q | You've recalled these | STKPWHR–UVRLDZ |
| Q | You've recognized | STKPWHR–UVRND |
| Q | You've recognized the | STKPWHR–UVRNTD |
| Q | You've recognized these | STKPWHR–UVRNDZ |
| Q | You've recollected | STKPWHR–UVRKD |
| Q | You've recollected the | STKPWHR–UVRKTD |
| Q | You've recollected these | STKPWHR–UVRKDZ |
| Q | You've remembered | STKPWHR–UVRMD |
| Q | You've remembered the | STKPWHR–UVRMTD |
| Q | You've remembered these | STKPWHR–UVRMDZ |
| Q | You've said | STKPWHR–UVDZ |
| Q | You've said the | STKPWHR–UVTDZ |
| Q | You want | STKPWHR–UPT |
| Q | You wanted | STKPWHR–UPTD |
| Q | You wanting | STKPWHR–UPGT |

| Q | You wanting the | STKPWHR–UPGTD |
|---|---|---|
| Q | You want those | STKPWHR–UPTS |
| Q | You were | STKPWHR–URP |
| Q | You weren't | STKPWHR*URPT |
| Q | You were the | STKPWHR–URPT |
| Q | You will | STKPWHR–UL |
| Q | You would | STKPWHR–ULD |
| Q | You wouldn't | STKPWHR–ULTD |
| Q | You would say | STKPWHR–ULDZ |

## ANSWERS (–FRPBLGTS & *FRPBLGTS)

### A

| A | A | A–FRPBLGTS |
|---|---|---|
| A | About | BOU–FRPBLGTS |
| A | Actually | TWAE–FRPBLGTS |
| A | All right | TR–FRPBLGTS |
| A | Always | SL–FRPBLGTS |
| A | And | A*FRPBLGTS, SKP–FRPBLGTS |
| A | And a | SKPA–FRPBLGTS |
| A | And he | SKPE–FRPBLGTS |
| A | And I | SKPI–FRPBLGTS |
| A | And she | SKPHE–FRPBLGTS |
| A | And they | SKPAI–FRPBLGTS, SKPHAI–FRPBLGTS |
| A | And we | SKPWE–FRPBLGTS |
| A | And you | SKPU–FRPBLGTS |
| A | Another | AO–FRPBLGTS |
| A | Are | R–FRPBLGTS |
| A | Are you | RU–FRPBLGTS |
| A | As | ZA–FRPBLGTS |
| A | As far as | SFA–FRPBLGTS |
| A | As I | SI–FRPBLGTS |
| A | As I recall | SLI–FRPBLGTS |
| A | Ask | SK–FRPBLGTS |
| A | Assistant District Attorney | SDA–FRPBLGTS, SDAE–FRPBLGTS |
| A | At | TA–FRPBLGTS |

### B

| A | Be | B–FRPBLGTS |
|---|---|---|
| A | Below | BLO–FRPBLGTS |
| A | Both | BO–FRPBLGTS |
| A | Boy, | BOI–FRPBLGTS |
| A | But | BU–FRPBLGTS |
| A | But the | TBU–FRPBLGTS |
| A | Buy | BAOI–FRPBLGTS |
| A | By | BI–FRPBLGTS |

### C

| A | Can | K–FRPBLGTS |
|---|---|---|
| A | Can he | KE–FRPBLGTS |
| A | Can I | KI–FRPBLGTS |
| A | Can you | KU–FRPBLGTS |
| A | Captain | KP–FRPBLGTS |

| A | Correct | KR–FRPBLGTS |
| A | Could | KO–FRPBLGTS |
| A | Could you | KOU–FRPBLGTS |

**D**

| A | D.A. | DA–FRPBLGTS |
| A | Day | DAI–FRPBLGTS |
| A | Did | D–FRPBLGTS |
| A | Did he | DE–FRPBLGTS |
| A | Did I | DI–FRPBLGTS |
| A | Did we | DWE–FRPBLGTS |
| A | Did you | DU–FRPBLGTS |
| A | District Attorney | DAE–FRPBLGTS |
| A | Do | DO–FRPBLGTS |
| A | Doctor | DR*FRPBLGTS |
| A | Do I | DOI–FRPBLGTS |
| A | Down | DWOU–FRPBLGTS |
| A | Do you | DOU–FRPBLGTS |
| A | Dr. | DR–FRPBLGTS |

**E**

| A | Exactly | SAE–FRPBLGTS |

**F**

| A | False | FL–FRPBLGTS |
| A | Few | FAOU–FRPBLGTS |
| A | Fine | FOI–FRPBLGTS, FAOI–FRPBLGTS |
| A | For | FO–FRPBLGTS |
| A | Friday | FRI–FRPBLGTS |
| A | From | FR–FRPBLGTS |
| A | From a | FRA–FRPBLGTS |
| A | From me | FRE–FRPBLGTS |
| A | From you | FRU–FRPBLGTS |

**G**

| A | Go | GO–FRPBLGTS |
| A | Good | G–FRPBLGTS |

**H**

| A | Have | V–FRPBLGTS |
| A | Have I | VI–FRPBLGTS |
| A | Have you | VU–FRPBLGTS |
| A | He | HE–FRPBLGTS, E–FRPBLGTS |
| A | He can | K*E–FRPBLGTS |
| A | He will | L*E–FRPBLGTS |
| A | He would | WO*E–FRPBLGTS |
| A | High | HAOI–FRPBLGTS |
| A | How | HOU–FRPBLGTS |

**I**

| A | I | AOI–FRPBLGTS |
| A | I can | K*I–FRPBLGTS |
| A | I cannot recall | KRA*E–FRPBLGTS |
| A | I cannot remember | KR*E–FRPBLGTS |
| A | I can't | YA–FRPBLGTS |

| A | I can't recall | KRAE–FRPBLGTS |
|---|---|---|
| A | I can't remember | KRE–FRPBLGTS |
| A | I couldn't | YU–FRPBLGTS |
| A | I did not | YAOI–FRPBLGTS |
| A | I didn't | YI–FRPBLGTS |
| A | I do not really recall | RA*U–FRPBLGTS |
| A | I do not recall | YA*U–FRPBLGTS |
| A | I do not remember | YAO*E–FRPBLGTS |
| A | I don't | YO–FRPBLGTS |
| A | I don't know | YOE–FRPBLGTS |
| A | I don't really recall | RAU–FRPBLGTS |
| A | I don't really remember | RAO*E–FRPBLGTS |
| A | I don't recall | YAU–FRPBLGTS |
| A | I don't remember | YAOE–FRPBLGTS |
| A | If | F–FRPBLGTS |
| A | If a | FA–FRPBLGTS |
| A | If he | FE–FRPBLGTS |
| A | If I | FI–FRPBLGTS |
| A | If you | FU–FRPBLGTS |
| A | I have | V*I–FRPBLGTS |
| A | I have no idea | YOI–FRPBLGTS |
| A | In | N–FRPBLGTS |
| A | Into | NAO–FRPBLGTS |
| A | I really don't remember | RAOE–FRPBLGTS |
| A | Is | S–FRPBLGTS |
| A | Is it | ST–FRPBLGTS |
| A | Is it right | STR–FRPBLGTS |
| A | Isn't | SN–FRPBLGTS |
| A | Is that | STHA–FRPBLGTS |
| A | Is that he | STHAE–FRPBLGTS |
| A | Is that I | STHAI–FRPBLGTS |
| A | Is that you | STHAU–FRPBLGTS |
| A | Is there | STHR–FRPBLGTS |
| A | Is this | STH–FRPBLGTS |
| A | Is to | STO–FRPBLGTS |
| A | Is what | SWHA–FRPBLGTS |
| A | Is what he | SWHAE–FRPBLGTS |
| A | Is what I | SWHAI–FRPBLGTS |
| A | Is what you | SWHAU–FRPBLGTS |
| A | Is when | SWH–FRPBLGTS |
| A | Is when he | SWHE–FRPBLGTS |
| A | Is when I | SWHI–FRPBLGTS |
| A | Is when you | SWHU–FRPBLGTS |
| A | Is where | SWR–FRPBLGTS |
| A | Is where he | SWRE–FRPBLGTS |
| A | Is where I | SWRI–FRPBLGTS |
| A | Is where you | SWRU–FRPBLGTS |
| A | Is whether | SWHR–FRPBLGTS |
| A | Is whether he | SWHRE–FRPBLGTS |
| A | Is whether I | SWHRI–FRPBLGTS |
| A | Is whether or not | SWHRO–FRPBLGTS |
| A | Is whether or not he | SWHROE–FRPBLGTS |
| A | Is whether or not I | SWHROI–FRPBLGTS |
| A | Is whether or not you | SWHROU–FRPBLGTS |

| | | |
|---|---|---|
| A | Is whether you | SWHRU–FRPBLGTS |
| A | It | TI–FRPBLGTS |
| A | It is | ST*FRPBLGTS |
| A | It is right | STR*FRPBLGTS |
| A | It seems to me | SME–FRPBLGTS |
| A | It was | TWA–FRPBLGTS |
| A | It wasn't | TWAU–FRPBLGTS |
| A | I will | L*I–FRPBLGTS |
| A | I would | WO*I–FRPBLGTS |
| A | I wouldn't | YAO–FRPBLGTS |

**L**

| | | |
|---|---|---|
| A | Lieutenant | LAOU–FRPBLGTS |
| A | Low | LOE–FRPBLGTS |

**M**

| | | |
|---|---|---|
| A | Many | M–FRPBLGTS |
| A | May | MAI–FRPBLGTS |
| A | Maybe | MOI–FRPBLGTS |
| A | Me | ME–FRPBLGTS |
| A | Miss | SMI–FRPBLGTS |
| A | Monday | MO–FRPBLGTS |
| A | Mr. | MR–FRPBLGTS |
| A | Mrs. | SMR–FRPBLGTS |
| A | Ms. | Z–FRPBLGTS, ZM–FRPBLGTS |
| A | My | MI–FRPBLGTS |

**N**

| | | |
|---|---|---|
| A | Neither | NAOE–FRPBLGTS |
| A | Never | NE–FRPBLGTS, N*E–FRPBLGTS |
| A | Night | NAOI–FRPBLGTS |
| A | No | NO–FRPBLGTS |
| A | No, | O–FRPBLGTS |
| A | No, I can't | NAI–FRPBLGTS |
| A | No idea | OI–FRPBLGTS |
| A | No, I didn't | NI–FRPBLGTS |
| A | No, I do not recall | RAO–FRPBLGTS |
| A | No, I don't | DOE–FRPBLGTS |
| A | No, I don't recall | RO–FRPBLGTS |
| A | No, ma'am | NA–FRPBLGTS |
| A | None | NU–FRPBLGTS |
| A | No, sir | NOI–FRPBLGTS |
| A | Not | N*FRPBLGTS |
| A | Nothing | NO*FRPBLGTS |
| A | Not that I can recall | NA*U–FRPBLGTS |
| A | Not that I can remember | NA*E–FRPBLGTS |
| A | Not that I knew | NAOU–FRPBLGTS |
| A | Not that I know | NOE–FRPBLGTS |
| A | Not that I recall | NAU–FRPBLGTS |
| A | Not that I remember | NAE–FRPBLGTS |
| A | Not to my knowledge | JO–FRPBLGTS |
| A | Not to my recollection | ROI–FRPBLGTS |
| A | Now. | NOU–FRPBLGTS |
| A | Now, sir. | SNOU–FRPBLGTS |

## O

| | | |
|---|---|---|
| A | Officer | SAU–FRPBLGTS |
| A | Oh, | OE–FRPBLGTS |
| A | Okay, | KAI–FRPBLGTS |
| A | Out | TOU–FRPBLGTS |

## P

| | | |
|---|---|---|
| A | Please | PLE–FRPBLGTS |
| A | President | PR–FRPBLGTS |

## R

| | | |
|---|---|---|
| A | Right | RI–FRPBLGTS |

## S

| | | |
|---|---|---|
| A | Saturday | STA–FRPBLGTS |
| A | Say | SAI–FRPBLGTS |
| A | See | SAOE–FRPBLGTS |
| A | Sergeant | SA–FRPBLGTS |
| A | She | SHE–FRPBLGTS |
| A | Show | SHOE–FRPBLGTS |
| A | So | SO–FRPBLGTS |
| A | So he | SOE–FRPBLGTS |
| A | So I | SOI–FRPBLGTS |
| A | Some | SM–FRPBLGTS |
| A | Somebody | SB–FRPBLGTS |
| A | Somebody else | SBL–FRPBLGTS |
| A | Somehow | SMOU–FRPBLGTS |
| A | Some kind | SKAOI–FRPBLGTS |
| A | Some more | SMO–FRPBLGTS |
| A | Someone | SWU–FRPBLGTS |
| A | Someplace | SP–FRPBLGTS |
| A | Something | SG–FRPBLGTS |
| A | Sometime | STI–FRPBLGTS, STAOI–FRPBLGTS |
| A | Somewhat | SMA–FRPBLGTS |
| A | Soon | SAO–FRPBLGTS |
| A | So you | SO*U–FRPBLGTS |
| A | Sunday | SNU–FRPBLGTS |
| A | Sure | SH–FRPBLGTS |

## T

| | | |
|---|---|---|
| A | That | THA–FRPBLGTS |
| A | That he | THAE–FRPBLGTS |
| A | That I | THAI–FRPBLGTS |
| A | That is | STHA*FRPBLGTS |
| A | That is correct | SKR–FRPBLGTS |
| A | That is right | TRA–FRPBLGTS |
| A | That's all | TAU–FRPBLGTS |
| A | That's correct | SKRE–FRPBLGTS |
| A | That's right | TRAE–FRPBLGTS |
| A | That you | THAU–FRPBLGTS |
| A | The | T–FRPBLGTS |
| A | There | THR–FRPBLGTS |
| A | They | THE–FRPBLGTS |
| A | This | TH–FRPBLGTS |

| | | |
|---|---|---|
| A | This is | STH*FRPBLGTS |
| A | Though | THO–FRPBLGTS |
| A | Through | THRU–FRPBLGTS |
| A | Thursday | THU–FRPBLGTS |
| A | To | TO–FRPBLGTS |
| A | Too | TAO–FRPBLGTS |
| A | To you | TO*U–FRPBLGTS |
| A | True | TRU–FRPBLGTS, TRAOU–FRPBLGTS |
| A | Tuesday | TU–FRPBLGTS |
| A | Two | TWO–FRPBLGTS |

## U

| | | |
|---|---|---|
| A | Uh-huh | HU–FRPBLGTS |
| A | Up | PU–FRPBLGTS |

## V

| | | |
|---|---|---|
| A | Very | VE–FRPBLGTS, VAI–FRPBLGTS |

## W

| | | |
|---|---|---|
| A | Was | WA–FRPBLGTS, WU–FRPBLGTS |
| A | Was it | TWA*FRPBLGTS, TWU–FRPBLGTS |
| A | We | WE–FRPBLGTS |
| A | Wednesday | DW–FRPBLGTS |
| A | Well | WL–FRPBLGTS |
| A | What | WHA–FRPBLGTS |
| A | What he | WHAE–FRPBLGTS |
| A | What I | WHAI–FRPBLGTS |
| A | What is | SWHA*FRPBLGTS |
| A | What you | WHAU–FRPBLGTS |
| A | When | WH–FRPBLGTS |
| A | When he | WHE–FRPBLGTS |
| A | When I | WHI–FRPBLGTS |
| A | When is | SWH*FRPBLGTS |
| A | When you | WHU–FRPBLGTS |
| A | Where | WR–FRPBLGTS |
| A | Where he | WRE–FRPBLGTS |
| A | Where I | WRI–FRPBLGTS |
| A | Where is | SWR*FRPBLGTS |
| A | Where you | WRU–FRPBLGTS |
| A | Whether | WHR*FRPBLGTS |
| A | Whether a | WHRA–FRPBLGTS |
| A | Whether he | WHRE–FRPBLGTS |
| A | Whether I | WHRI–FRPBLGTS |
| A | Whether or not | WHRO–FRPBLGTS |
| A | Whether or not he | WHROE–FRPBLGTS |
| A | Whether or not I | WHROI–FRPBLGTS |
| A | Whether or not you | WHROU–FRPBLGTS |
| A | Whether you | WHRU–FRPBLGTS |
| A | Which | KH–FRPBLGTS |
| A | Which he | KHE–FRPBLGTS |
| A | Which I | KHI–FRPBLGTS |
| A | Which you | KHU–FRPBLGTS |
| A | While | WHAOI–FRPBLGTS |
| A | Who | WHO–FRPBLGTS |

| A | Who he | WHOE–FRPBLGTS |
|---|--------|---------------|
| A | Who I | WHOI–FRPBLGTS |
| A | Who you | WHOU–FRPBLGTS |
| A | Will | L–FRPBLGTS |
| A | Will he | LE–FRPBLGTS |
| A | Will I | LI–FRPBLGTS |
| A | Will you | LU–FRPBLGTS |
| A | With | W*FRPBLGTS |
| A | Without | TWOU–FRPBLGTS |
| A | Would | WO–FRPBLGTS |
| A | Would he | WOE–FRPBLGTS |
| A | Would I | WOI–FRPBLGTS |
| A | Would you | WOU–FRPBLGTS |
| A | Wrong | WRO–FRPBLGTS |

**Y**

| A | Yeah | YAE–FRPBLGTS |
|---|------|--------------|
| A | Yes | YE–FRPBLGTS |
| A | Yes, I can | YAI–FRPBLGTS |
| A | Yes, I did | D*I–FRPBLGTS |
| A | Yes, I do | YAOU–FRPBLGTS |
| A | Yes, ma'am | YA*FRPBLGTS, YA*E–FRPBLGTS |
| A | Yes, sir | SYE–FRPBLGTS |
| A | You | U–FRPBLGTS, YOU–FRPBLGTS |
| A | You are | R*U–FRPBLGTS |
| A | You can | K*U–FRPBLGTS |
| A | You could | KO*U–FRPBLGTS |
| A | You do | DO*U–FRPBLGTS |
| A | You have | V*U–FRPBLGTS |
| A | You will | L*U–FRPBLGTS |
| A | You would | WO*U–FRPBLGTS |

# SPEAKER IDENTIFICATION

If RIGHT1 or RIGHT2 is going to ask a question after colloquy, K– (*for "question"*) can be used with the right-bank speaker identification. Same system applies for left bank.

| | |
|---|---|
| BY RIGHT1: | |
| Q | K–EURBGS |
| BY RIGHT2: | |
| Q | K–EUFPLT |
| BY LEFT1: | |
| Q | SKWRAO–K |
| BY LEFT2: | |
| Q | STPHAO–K |

The first letter of speaker's name or title can be used with the answer bank. Names should be entered into a "case" dictionary as they vary from job to job.

| | |
|---|---|
| THE CLERK: | KL–FRPBLGTS |
| THE COURT: | STKPWHR–FRPBLGTS |
| THE DEFENDANT: | D–*FRPBLGTS |
| THE WITNESS: | W–FRPBLGTS |
| THE JUROR: | J–FRPBLGTS |
| PROSPECTIVE JUROR NO. 1: | J–FRPBLGTS/1 |

For conferences, lectures and meetings, names and/or titles of speakers can be written in a variety of ways. Again, these should be entered into a "case" dictionary only. Some examples:

| | |
|---|---|
| PROFESSOR BAKER: | SKWRAO–B |
| PROFESSOR BAKER: | SKWRAO/BAIRK |
| PROFESSOR BAKER: | BAIRK/BAIRK |
| *or* | |
| JOHN BAKER: | SKWRAO–B |
| JOHN BAKER: | SKWRAO/BAIRK |
| JOHN BAKER: | BAIRK/BAIRK |

The following examples consist of speaker identification plus a commonly used word or phrase.

| | |
|---|---|
| LEFT1: Objection | SKWRAO–BGS<br>(SKWRAO *plus* BGS) |
| LEFT2: Objection | STPHAO–BGS<br>(STPHAO *plus* BGS) |
| LEFT1: Objection, your Honor | SKWRAO–RBGS<br>(SKWRAO *plus* RBGS) |
| LEFT2: Objection, your Honor | STPHAO–RBGS<br>(STPHAO *plus* RBGS) |
| RIGHT1: Objection | KWR*EURBGS<br>(KWR *plus* *EURBGS) |

RIGHT2: Objection ........................................................... KWR–EUFPLT
(KWR *plus* EUFPLT)

RIGHT1: Objection, your Honor ......................................... SKWR–EURBGS
(SKWR *plus* EURBGS)

RIGHT2: Objection, your Honor ......................................... SKWR–EUFPLT
(SKWR *plus* EUFPLT)

Examples of some variations:

RIGHT1: Objection ........................................................... O–EURBGS
(O *for* "Objection")

RIGHT2: Objection ........................................................... OEUFPLT
(O *for* "Objection")

RIGHT1: Objection ........................................................... KP–EURBGS
(KP *for* "Objection")

RIGHT2: Objection ........................................................... KP–EUFPLT
(KP *for* "Objection")

# UNITED STATES & TERRITORIES

## THE 50 UNITED STATES

### A

| | |
|---|---|
| Alabama | A*L |
| Alaska | A*K |
| Arizona | A*Z |
| Arkansas | A*R |

### C

| | |
|---|---|
| California | KRA* |
| Colorado | KRO* |
| Connecticut | KR*T |

### D - H

| | |
|---|---|
| Delaware | DWE, D*EL |
| Florida | FL* |
| Georgia | GA* |
| Hawaii | H*I |

### I

| | |
|---|---|
| Idaho | DHOE, *ID/*ID |
| Illinois | *IL |
| Indiana | DWIN, *IN/*IN |
| Iowa | A*I |

### K - L

| | |
|---|---|
| Kansas | K*S |
| Kentucky | KAO*I |
| Louisiana | LA* |

### M

| | |
|---|---|
| Maine | M*E |
| Maryland | M*D |
| Massachusetts | MA* |
| Michigan | M*I |
| Minnesota | M*N |
| Mississippi | M*S |
| Missouri | MO* |
| Montana | M*T |

### N

| | |
|---|---|
| Nebraska | N*E |
| Nevada | NAEVD, NEVS, NEVDZ |
| New Hampshire | H*N |
| New Jersey | N*J |
| New Mexico | N*M |
| New York | NORK |
| North Carolina | N*K |
| North Dakota | N*D |

## O

Ohio ........................................................................................................ HO*
Oklahoma ......................................................................................... KLOEM
Oregon .................................................................................................. O*R

## P - R

Pennsylvania ........................................................................................ PA*
Rhode Island ........................................................................................ R*I

## S

South Carolina ..................................................................................... S*K
South Dakota ........................................................................................ S*D

## T

Tennessee ............................................................................................ T*N
Texas .................................................................................................... T*X

## U - V

Utah .................................................................................................... *UT
Vermont .............................................................................................. V*T
Virginia ............................................................................................... VA*

## W

Washington ......................................................................................... WA*
West Virginia ...................................................................................... W*V
Wisconsin ............................................................................................. W*I
Wyoming ............................................................................... WAO*I, WOEM

## THE 50 UNITED STATES (ABBREVIATED)

AK ..................................................................................................... A*KZ
AL ...................................................................................................... A*LZ
AR ..................................................................................................... A*RZ
AZ ...................................................................................................... A*SZ
CA .................................................................................................... KRA*Z
CO ................................................................................................... KRO*Z
CT ................................................................................................... KR*TS
DE .................................................................................................... D*EZ
FL ...................................................................................................... FL*Z
GA .................................................................................................... GA*Z
HI ....................................................................................................... H*IZ
IA ....................................................................................................... A*IZ
ID ...................................................................................................... *IDZ
IL ....................................................................................................... *ILZ
IN ...................................................................................................... *INZ
KS ..................................................................................................... K*SZ
KY ................................................................................................. KAO*IZ
LA ..................................................................................................... LA*Z
MA ................................................................................................... MA*Z
MD ................................................................................................... M*DZ
ME ................................................................................................... M*EZ
MI ...................................................................................................... M*IZ
MN ................................................................................................... M*NZ

| | |
|---|---|
| MO | MO*Z |
| MS | M*SZ |
| MT | M*TS |
| NC | N*KZ |
| ND | N*DZ |
| NE | N*EZ |
| NH | H*NZ |
| NJ | N*JZ |
| NM | N*MZ |
| NV | N–FZ, NEVZ |
| NY | NY*Z, Y*NZ |
| OH | HO*Z |
| OK | O*K, KLOEMZ, O*KZ |
| OR | O*RZ |
| PA | PA*Z |
| RI | R*IZ |
| SC | S*KZ |
| SD | S*DZ |
| TN | T*NZ |
| TX | T*XZ |
| UT | *UTS |
| VA | VA*Z |
| VT | V*TS |
| WA | WA*Z |
| WI | W*IZ |
| WV | W*VZ |
| WY | WAO*IZ, WOEMS, WOEMZ |

## U.S. TERRITORIES & POSSESSIONS

| | |
|---|---|
| D.C. | D*K |
| District of Columbia | D–KD, D*K/D*K, DRIK/KLUM |
| Guam | GAUM |
| Puerto Rico | P*R |
| Virgin Islands | VAOIJ |
| Washington, D.C. | WARBDZ, WA*DZ |

# UNITS OF MEASURE

**A**

acre ............................................................................................. AEK
alternating current .................................................................. TURNT
amp .............................................................................................. AMP
ampere ..................................................................................... AEMP
Ångstrom .................................................................................. GROM

**B**

barrel ...................................................................................... BAERL

**C**

Celsius ...................................................................................... SELZ
centigrade ............................................................................... SGRAID
centimeter ............................................................. SMAOERT, KR–M
cord ............................................................................................ KORD
cubic .......................................................................................... KBIK
cubic centimeter ................................................................. SKMAOERT
cubic feet ................................................................................ KBAOET
cubic foot ................................................................................. KBAOT
cubic inch ................................................................................ KBIFP
cubic meter ........................................................................... KMAOERT
cup ............................................................................................. K*UP

**D**

dB ................................................................................................ D*B
decibel ..................................................................................... SDIBL
degree .......................................................................................DRE
direct current .......................................................................... DRURNT

**F**

fathom ...................................................................................... FAOM
feet ........................................................................................... FAOET
foot ............................................................................................. FAOT
foot-pound ............................................................................... FAOPD
Fahrenheit ............................................................................... FAIRNT

**G**

gallon ......................................................................................... GAL
gram ......................................................................................... GRAM

**H**

hertz ........................................................................... HERZ, H–RTS
hour ......................................................................................... HOUR

**I**

inch ........................................................................................... N–FP

**J**

joule ....................................................................................... JAO*UL

**K**

kelvin ....................................................................................... KEVNL

kg ....................................................................................................... K–G
kilo ..................................................................................................... KLOE
kilogram ........................................................................................... K–LG
kilometer ........................................................................................... K–M
kilos .................................................................................................. KLOEZ

## L

liter ................................................................................................... LAOERT

## M

mega~ ( *prefix* ) ............................................................................... MEG
megabit .............................................................................................. MIBT
megabyte ............................................................................................ MEGT
megacycle .......................................................................................... SMEG
megahertz .......................................................................................... MEGZ
mg ...................................................................................................... M*G
milligram ........................................................................................... M*LG
minute ................................................................................................ MIN
meter .................................................................................................. MAOERT
mileage .............................................................................................. MAOIJ
mile-an-hour ...................................................................................... MIR
mile-per-hour ..................................................................................... MIRP
miles an hour ..................................................................................... MIRS
miles per hour .................................................................................... MIRPS
millimeter ........................................................................................... M–M

## N

nano ................................................................................................... NA*N
nanosecond ....................................................................................... NA*NS
nautical mile ...................................................................................... NAUMT

## O

ounce ................................................................................................. OUNS

## P

pound ................................................................................................. POUND
pint ..................................................................................................... PAOINT

## Q

quart .................................................................................................. KWART

## S

second ............................................................................................... SEK
seconds ............................................................................................. SEKZ
square feet ........................................................................................ SKWAOEFT
square foot ........................................................................................ SKWAOFT
square inch ........................................................................................ SKWIFP
square meter ................................................... SKWAOERM, SKWAOERMT
square mile ........................................................................................ SKWAIM
square yard ....................................................................................... SKWARD

## T

tablespoon ........................................................................................ TAIBLZ
tablespoons ...................................................................................... TAIBLSZ

teaspoon ........................................................................... TAEPZ
teaspoons ....................................................................... TAEPSZ
tesla ..................................................................................... TELZ
ton ........................................................................................ TON
tonne ................................................................................. TO*N

# V

volt ...................................................................................... VOLT
volt-ampere ................................................................... VAEMP
volt-amperes ............................................................... VAEMPS

# W

watt ...................................................................................... WAT

# Y

yard .................................................................................... YARD

# PART 3

# ALPHABETS & NUMBERS

**3**

# ALPHABETS & NUMBERS

## GENERAL

Part 3 lists 16 alphabet-writing styles followed by a large variety of number-writing styles, from the bare essentials to advanced and complex numbering techniques. Much of the material is intended to be used for reference, i.e., to be called upon when needed rather than dutifully absorbed into mind and dictionary, especially now that high-tech CAT systems are able to automatically or easily convert numbers into some of these formats. It is therefore advisable to locate and focus on the desired material and techniques.

## HINTS AND TIPS

Part 3 contains "hints and tips" boxes to aid the transition to realtime. Intended mainly for students, "hints and tips" boxes generally provide ideas for easy learning and/or specifics for CAT dictionary building. The boxes are identified by a "mortarboard" symbol, as shown in the following example for military time:

*Associate M with "Military" or*
*UM with "Units Military."*

# ALPHABET STYLES

The following 16 alphabet styles are found in this section:

| *STYLE* | *EXAMPLE* |
|---|---|
| A B C | A–RBGS |
| ABC | A\*RBGS |
| a b c | A\*RBGSZ |
| abc | B\*Z (A\*S) |
| -A-B-C | A–RBGSZ |
| -a-b-c | A\* |
| A. B. C. | A–FPLT |
| A.B.C. | A\*FPLT |
| a. b. c. | A–FPLS |
| a.b.c. | A–FPLD |
| A, B, C, | A–RBGTS |
| a, b, c, | A\*RBGTS |
| (A) (B) (C) | A\*FPLTD |
| (a) (b) (c) | A–FPLTD |
| (A), (B), (C), | A\*FPLTS |
| (a), (b), (c), | A–FPLTS |

In all of the alphabets, the left-bank steno for the letter "Z" is STK–.

At times, it is necessary to use a combination of alphabet styles, as in the following examples:

- *"I found it at ABC Electronics."*
  To write **ABC** in this sentence, use a stand-alone **A** followed by left-attached **B** and **C** =
  A–RBGS/B*RBGS/C*RBGS

- *"His name is P.J. Johnson."*
  To write **P.J.** in this sentence, use a stand-alone **P.** followed by a left-attached **J.** =
  P–FPLT/J*FPLT

- *"Send it c.o.d. today."*
  To write **c.o.d.** in this sentence, use a stand-alone **c.** followed by left-attached **o.** and **d.** =
  C–FPLS/O–FPLD/D–FPLD

- *"Check boxes (A), (B), (C) and (D) on page two."*
  To write **(A), (B), (C)** and **(D)**, use a comma-attached **(A),** and **(B),** followed by stand-alone **(C)** and **(D)** =
  A*FPLTS/B*FPLTS/C*FPLTD/AND/D*FPLTD

- *"Smith, spelled S-m-i-t-h."*
  To write/spell-out **S-m-i-t-h** in this style, use a stand-alone **S** followed by stitched **-m-i-t-h** =
  S–RBGS/M*/I*/T*/H*

- *"Smith, spelled S-M-I-T-H."*
  To write/spell-out **S-M-I-T-H** in this style, use a stand-alone **S** followed by stitched **-M-I-T-H** =
      S–RBGS/M–RBGSZ/I–RBGSZ/T–RBGSZ/H–RBGSZ

*The first eight alphabets are required for writing and spelling words and names. It is advisable to learn these alphabets before taking the CSR or RPR. The remaining eight alphabets are optional; that is, you will not need them until you start working as a reporter and/or realtime writer.*

*Some CAT programs will stitch spelled words (S-M-I-T-H) upon command or even automatically. If your software does not stitch automatically, it is advisable to be prepared to stitch words without the help of software, as you may not have time to give the stitch command when writing in realtime.*

*If you have trouble programming any of the alphabets into your CAT software, consult the documentation supplied with the program or check with your CAT vendor.*

## ALPHABETS:
## A B C and ABC

| | |
|---|---|
| **STYLE:** | Uppercase letters: standing alone and attached on left. |
| **EXAMPLES:** | *"Exhibit A"* (standing alone), *"room 2C"* (attached on left). |
| **CAT DICTIONARY:** | A (standing alone), ~A (attached left). |

| | STANDING ALONE | ATTACHED ON LEFT |
|---|---|---|
| A | A–RBGS | A*RBGS |
| B | B–RBGS | B*RBGS |
| C | C–RBGS | C*RBGS |
| D | D–RBGS | D*RBGS |
| E | E–RBGS | E*RBGS |
| F | F–RBGS | F*RBGS |
| G | G–RBGS | G*RBGS |
| H | H–RBGS | H*RBGS |
| I | *(exception)* I | I*RBGS |
| J | J–RBGS | J*RBGS |
| K | K–RBGS | K*RBGS |
| L | L–RBGS | L*RBGS |
| M | M–RBGS | M*RBGS |
| N | N–RBGS | N*RBGS |
| O | O–RBGS | O*RBGS |
| P | P–RBGS | P*RBGS |
| Q | Q–RBGS | Q*RBGS |
| R | R–RBGS | R*RBGS |
| S | S–RBGS | S*RBGS |
| T | T–RBGS | T*RBGS |
| U | U–RBGS | U*RBGS |
| V | V–RBGS | V*RBGS |
| W | W–RBGS | W*RBGS |
| X | X–RBGS | X*RBGS |
| Y | Y–RBGS | Y*RBGS |
| Z | STK–RBGS | STK*RBGS |

# ALPHABETS:
## a b c  and  abc

> **STYLE:**              Lowercase letters: standing alone and attached on left.
>
> **EXAMPLES:**          *"sections b to f"* (standing alone),
>                        *"room 2c"* (attached on left).
>
> **CAT DICTIONARY:**    a (standing alone), ~a (attached left).

|   | STANDING ALONE | ATTACHED ON LEFT |
|---|---|---|
| a | A*RBGSZ | *(exception)* A*S |
| b | B*RBGSZ | B*Z |
| c | C*RBGSZ | C*Z |
| d | D*RBGSZ | D*Z |
| e | E*RBGSZ | E*Z |
| f | F*RBGSZ | F*Z |
| g | G*RBGSZ | G*Z |
| h | H*RBGSZ | H*Z |
| i | I*RBGSZ | I*Z |
| j | J*RBGSZ | J*Z |
| k | K*RBGSZ | K*Z |
| l | L*RBGSZ | L*Z |
| m | M*RBGSZ | M*Z |
| n | N*RBGSZ | N*Z |
| o | O*RBGSZ | O*Z |
| p | P*RBGSZ | P*Z |
| q | Q*RBGSZ | Q*Z |
| r | R*RBGSZ | R*Z |
| s | S*RBGSZ | S*Z |
| t | T*RBGSZ | T*Z |
| u | U*RBGSZ | U*Z |
| v | V*RBGSZ | V*Z |
| w | W*RBGSZ | W*Z |
| x | X*RBGSZ | X*Z |
| y | Y*RBGSZ | Y*Z |
| z | STK*RBGSZ | STK*Z |

## ALPHABET:
### -A-B-C

**STYLE:** Uppercase letters, preceded by hyphen and attached on left.
Used to spell words in capital letters, but the first letter of the word is written using the "standing alone" alphabet on page 3-4.

**EXAMPLE:** *"Smith, spelled S-M-I-T-H"*

**CAT DICTIONARY:** ~-A

| | |
|---|---|
| -A | A–RBGSZ |
| -B | B–RBGSZ |
| -C | C–RBGSZ |
| -D | D–RBGSZ |
| -E | E–RBGSZ |
| -F | F–RBGSZ |
| -G | G–RBGSZ |
| -H | H–RBGSZ |
| -I | I–RBGSZ |
| -J | J–RBGSZ |
| -K | K–RBGSZ |
| -L | L–RBGSZ |
| -M | M–RBGSZ |
| -N | N–RBGSZ |
| -O | O–RBGSZ |
| -P | P–RBGSZ |
| -Q | Q–RBGSZ |
| -R | R–RBGSZ |
| -S | S–RBGSZ |
| -T | T–RBGSZ |
| -U | U–RBGSZ |
| -V | V–RBGSZ |
| -W | W–RBGSZ |
| -X | X–RBGSZ |
| -Y | Y–RBGSZ |
| -Z | STK–RBGSZ |

# ALPHABET:
## -a-b-c

**STYLE:** Lowercase letters, preceded by hyphen and attached on left.
Used to spell words in lowercase letters, but the first letter of the word is written using the "standing alone" alphabet on page 3-4 (if capitalized) or page 3-5.

**EXAMPLE:** "byte, spelled b-y-t-e"

**CAT DICTIONARY:** ~-a

| | |
|---|---|
| -a | A* |
| -b | B* |
| -c | C* |
| -d | D* |
| -e | E* |
| -f | F* |
| -g | G* |
| -h | H* |
| -i | I* |
| -j | J* |
| -k | K* |
| -l | L* |
| -m | M* |
| -n | N* |
| -o | O* |
| -p | P* |
| -q | Q* |
| -r | R* |
| -s | S* |
| -t | T* |
| -u | U* |
| -v | V* |
| -w | W* |
| -x | X* |
| -y | Y* |
| -z | STK* |

## ALPHABETS:
## A. B. C. and A.B.C.

| | |
|---|---|
| **STYLE:** | **Uppercase letters with period: standing alone and attached on left.** |
| **EXAMPLES:** | *"J. Smith"* (standing alone), *"C.O.D."* (attached on left). |
| **CAT DICTIONARY:** | A. (standing alone), ~A. (attached on left). |

| | STANDING ALONE | ATTACHED ON LEFT |
|---|---|---|
| A. | A–FPLT | A*FPLT |
| B. | B–FPLT | B*FPLT |
| C. | C–FPLT | C*FPLT |
| D. | D–FPLT | D*FPLT |
| E. | E–FPLT | E*FPLT |
| F. | F–FPLT | F*FPLT |
| G. | G–FPLT | G*FPLT |
| H. | H–FPLT | H*FPLT |
| I. | *(exception)* I/FPLT | I*FPLT |
| J. | J–FPLT | J*FPLT |
| K. | K–FPLT | K*FPLT |
| L. | L–FPLT | L*FPLT |
| M. | M–FPLT | M*FPLT |
| N. | N–FPLT | N*FPLT |
| O. | O–FPLT | O*FPLT |
| P. | P–FPLT | P*FPLT |
| Q. | Q–FPLT | Q*FPLT |
| R. | R–FPLT | R*FPLT |
| S. | S–FPLT | S*FPLT |
| T. | T–FPLT | T*FPLT |
| U. | U–FPLT | U*FPLT |
| V. | V–FPLT | V*FPLT |
| W. | W–FPLT | W*FPLT |
| X. | X–FPLT | X*FPLT |
| Y. | Y–FPLT | Y*FPLT |
| Z. | STK–FPLT | STK*FPLT |

## ALPHABETS:
### a. b. c.  and  a.b.c.

**STYLE:**      Lowercase letters with period: standing alone and attached on left.

**EXAMPLES:**      *"options b. to g."* (standing alone),
*"c.o.d."* (attached on left).

**CAT DICTIONARY:**  a. (standing alone), ~a. (attached on left).

| | STANDING ALONE | ATTACHED ON LEFT |
|---|---|---|
| a. | A–FPLS | A–FPLD |
| b. | B–FPLS | B–FPLD |
| c. | C–FPLS | C–FPLD |
| d. | D–FPLS | D–FPLD |
| e. | E–FPLS | E–FPLD |
| f. | F–FPLS | F–FPLD |
| g. | G–FPLS | G–FPLD |
| h. | H–FPLS | H–FPLD |
| i. | I–FPLS | I–FPLD |
| j. | J–FPLS | J–FPLD |
| k. | K–FPLS | K–FPLD |
| l. | L–FPLS | L–FPLD |
| m. | M–FPLS | M–FPLD |
| n. | N–FPLS | N–FPLD |
| o. | O–FPLS | O–FPLD |
| p. | P–FPLS | P–FPLD |
| q. | Q–FPLS | Q–FPLD |
| r. | R–FPLS | R–FPLD |
| s. | S–FPLS | S–FPLD |
| t. | T–FPLS | T–FPLD |
| u. | U–FPLS | U–FPLD |
| v. | V–FPLS | V–FPLD |
| w. | W–FPLS | W–FPLD |
| x. | X–FPLS | X–FPLD |
| y. | Y–FPLS | Y–FPLD |
| z. | STK–FPLS | STK–FPLD |

## ALPHABET:
### A, B, C,

| | |
|---|---|
| **STYLE:** | Uppercase letters, followed by a comma. Used for reference letter sequences. |
| **EXAMPLE:** | *"Exhibits A, B, C, including the diagrams, etc."* |
| **CAT DICTIONARY:** | A, |

| | |
|---|---|
| A, | A–RBGTS |
| B, | B–RBGTS |
| C, | C–RBGTS |
| D, | D–RBGTS |
| E, | E–RBGTS |
| F, | F–RBGTS |
| G, | G–RBGTS |
| H, | H–RBGTS |
| I, | I–RBGTS |
| J, | J–RBGTS |
| K, | K–RBGTS |
| L, | L–RBGTS |
| M, | M–RBGTS |
| N, | N–RBGTS |
| O, | O–RBGTS |
| P, | P–RBGTS |
| Q, | Q–RBGTS |
| R, | R–RBGTS |
| S, | S–RBGTS |
| T, | T–RBGTS |
| U, | U–RBGTS |
| V, | V–RBGTS |
| W, | W–RBGTS |
| X, | X–RBGTS |
| Y, | Y–RBGTS |
| Z, | STK–RBGTS |

# ALPHABET:
## a, b, c,

| | |
|---|---|
| **STYLE:** | Lowercase letters, followed by a comma. Used for reference letter sequences. |
| **EXAMPLE:** | *"Schedules a, b, c, including the diagrams, etc."* |
| **CAT DICTIONARY:** | **a,** |

| | |
|---|---|
| a, | A*RBGTS |
| b, | B*RBGTS |
| c, | C*RBGTS |
| d, | D*RBGTS |
| e, | E*RBGTS |
| f, | F*RBGTS |
| g, | G*RBGTS |
| h, | H*RBGTS |
| i, | I*RBGTS |
| j, | J*RBGTS |
| k, | K*RBGTS |
| l, | L*RBGTS |
| m, | M*RBGTS |
| n, | N*RBGTS |
| o, | O*RBGTS |
| p, | P*RBGTS |
| q, | Q*RBGTS |
| r, | R*RBGTS |
| s, | S*RBGTS |
| t, | T*RBGTS |
| u, | U*RBGTS |
| v, | V*RBGTS |
| w, | W*RBGTS |
| x, | X*RBGTS |
| y, | Y*RBGTS |
| z, | STK*RBGTS |

# ALPHABET:
## (A)  (B)  (C)

| | |
|---|---|
| **STYLE:** | Uppercase letters, in parentheses, standing alone. |
| **EXAMPLE:** | *"Exhibit (A)"* and *"paragraph (G)"* |
| **CAT DICTIONARY:** | (A) |

(A) .......................................................................................................... A*FPLTD
(B) .......................................................................................................... B*FPLTD
(C) .......................................................................................................... C*FPLTD
(D) .......................................................................................................... D*FPLTD
(E) .......................................................................................................... E*FPLTD
(F) .......................................................................................................... F*FPLTD
(G) .......................................................................................................... G*FPLTD
(H) .......................................................................................................... H*FPLTD
(I) ........................................................................................................... I*FPLTD
(J) ........................................................................................................... J*FPLTD
(K) .......................................................................................................... K*FPLTD
(L) ........................................................................................................... L*FPLTD
(M) .......................................................................................................... M*FPLTD
(N) .......................................................................................................... N*FPLTD
(O) .......................................................................................................... O*FPLTD
(P) ........................................................................................................... P*FPLTD
(Q) .......................................................................................................... Q*FPLTD
(R) .......................................................................................................... R*FPLTD
(S) ........................................................................................................... S*FPLTD
(T) ........................................................................................................... T*FPLTD
(U) .......................................................................................................... U*FPLTD
(V) .......................................................................................................... V*FPLTD
(W) .......................................................................................................... W*FPLTD
(X) .......................................................................................................... X*FPLTD
(Y) .......................................................................................................... Y*FPLTD
(Z) ....................................................................................................... STK*FPLTD

# ALPHABET:
## (a) (b) (c)

| | |
|---|---|
| **STYLE:** | Lowercase letters, in parentheses, standing alone. |
| **EXAMPLE:** | *"box (k)"* and *"paragraph (q)"* |
| **CAT DICTIONARY:** | (a) |

| | |
|---|---|
| (a) | A–FPLTD |
| (b) | B–FPLTD |
| (c) | C–FPLTD |
| (d) | D–FPLTD |
| (e) | E–FPLTD |
| (f) | F–FPLTD |
| (g) | G–FPLTD |
| (h) | H–FPLTD |
| (i) | I–FPLTD |
| (j) | J–FPLTD |
| (k) | K–FPLTD |
| (l) | L–FPLTD |
| (m) | M–FPLTD |
| (n) | N–FPLTD |
| (o) | O–FPLTD |
| (p) | P–FPLTD |
| (q) | Q–FPLTD |
| (r) | R–FPLTD |
| (s) | S–FPLTD |
| (t) | T–FPLTD |
| (u) | U–FPLTD |
| (v) | V–FPLTD |
| (w) | W–FPLTD |
| (x) | X–FPLTD |
| (y) | Y–FPLTD |
| (z) | STK–FPLTD |

## ALPHABET:
### (A), (B), (C),

| | |
|---|---|
| **STYLE:** | Uppercase letters, in parentheses, followed by a comma. Used for quoting references. |
| **EXAMPLE:** | *"sections (A), (B), (C), etc."* |
| **CAT DICTIONARY:** | **(A),** |

(A), .................................................................................................. A*FPLTS
(B), .................................................................................................. B*FPLTS
(C), .................................................................................................. C*FPLTS
(D), .................................................................................................. D*FPLTS
(E), .................................................................................................. E*FPLTS
(F), .................................................................................................. F*FPLTS
(G), .................................................................................................. G*FPLTS
(H), .................................................................................................. H*FPLTS
(I), .................................................................................................. I*FPLTS
(J), .................................................................................................. J*FPLTS
(K), .................................................................................................. K*FPLTS
(L), .................................................................................................. L*FPLTS
(M), .................................................................................................. M*FPLTS
(N), .................................................................................................. N*FPLTS
(O), .................................................................................................. O*FPLTS
(P), .................................................................................................. P*FPLTS
(Q), .................................................................................................. Q*FPLTS
(R), .................................................................................................. R*FPLTS
(S), .................................................................................................. S*FPLTS
(T), .................................................................................................. T*FPLTS
(U), .................................................................................................. U*FPLTS
(V), .................................................................................................. V*FPLTS
(W), .................................................................................................. W*FPLTS
(X), .................................................................................................. X*FPLTS
(Y), .................................................................................................. Y*FPLTS
(Z), .................................................................................................. STK*FPLTS

# ALPHABET:
## (a), (b), (c),

**STYLE:**            **Lowercase letters, in parentheses, followed by a comma. Used for quoting references.**

**EXAMPLE:**          *"items (a), (b), (c), etc."*

**CAT DICTIONARY:**   **(a),**

(a),  .................................................................................................................. A–FPLTS

(b),  .................................................................................................................. B–FPLTS

(c),  .................................................................................................................. C–FPLTS

(d),  .................................................................................................................. D–FPLTS

(e),  .................................................................................................................. E–FPLTS

(f),  .................................................................................................................. F–FPLTS

(g),  .................................................................................................................. G–FPLTS

(h),  .................................................................................................................. H–FPLTS

(i),  .................................................................................................................. I–FPLTS

(j),  .................................................................................................................. J–FPLTS

(k),  .................................................................................................................. K–FPLTS

(l),  .................................................................................................................. L–FPLTS

(m),  ................................................................................................................. M–FPLTS

(n),  .................................................................................................................. N–FPLTS

(o),  .................................................................................................................. O–FPLTS

(p),  .................................................................................................................. P–FPLTS

(q),  .................................................................................................................. Q–FPLTS

(r),  .................................................................................................................. R–FPLTS

(s),  .................................................................................................................. S–FPLTS

(t),  .................................................................................................................. T–FPLTS

(u),  .................................................................................................................. U–FPLTS

(v),  .................................................................................................................. V–FPLTS

(w),  ................................................................................................................. W–FPLTS

(x),  .................................................................................................................. X–FPLTS

(y),  .................................................................................................................. Y–FPLTS

(z),  ............................................................................................................... STK–FPLTS

# NUMBERS

Numbering systems are given for the following, both with and without use of the number bar:

> 0-99 (plain, with a comma, in parentheses & plurals)
> decimals & fractions
> ordinals & Roman numerals
> US currency
> time formats, dates & years
> counts & "Nos."
> adjective compounds & phrases

Three different writing styles are given for most of the above:

| | Translation | Steno | Number Bar |
|---|---|---|---|
| 1 | figures (1, 2, 3) | words (W*UN, TWO*, THR*E) | no |
| 2 | figures (1, 2, 3) | figures (1, 2, 3) | yes |
| 3 | words (one, two, three) | words (WUN, TWO, THRE) | no |

> *Writing numbers on a steno machine can be cumbersome and complicated. Some reporters have an affinity to the number bar while others ignore it. The information provided here goes far beyond the essentials necessary to pass the CSR and/or RPR examinations.*
> *Start with numbers from 0-99, then work on higher numbers. Students who do not have a CAT dictionary may prefer to postpone the incorporation of complex, higher numbers.*

The number-writing systems in this section follow the basic rule of spelling out numbers from one through ten and using figures for numbers above ten in the following sense:

- Numbers one through ten in words are all written without an asterisk (one = WUN, two = TWO) since they are more likely to be used than numbers 1-10 in figures (1 = W*UN, 2 = TWO*), which are written with an asterisk or otherwise modified form.

- Numbers in words above ten are mostly written with an asterisk (thirteen = THRAO*EN, fourteen = FRAO*EN) since they are less likely to be used than figures (13 = THRAOEN, 14 = FRAOEN).

## DELETE-SPACE COMMAND IN CAT DICTIONARY

Suggestions for CAT dictionary entries are given for some of the writing styles. A "delete-space" dictionary command (CAT software typically uses a tilde: ~) is used to remove unwanted spaces between digits in fractions, time formats, compound numbers, etc. Most CAT systems automatically join number strings entered with the number bar (7/5/0 translates as 750) but do not join number strings written in words (SEV/VI translates as 7 50).

The following outlines are used in conjunction with the delete-space command:

delete space (CAT entry = ~) ............................................................ DL–RBGS, HU–RBGS

delete space, with comma (CAT entry = ~,~) ................................. *RBGS, THOU–RBGS, MI–RBGS, BL–RBGS, TR–RBGS

## NUMBER BAR STRATAGEMS

There are two time- and stroke-saving enhancements that are used throughout this section.

- **E** is used to reverse the order of two digits. Examples:

21 ............................................................................................... 12–E
43 ............................................................................................... 34–E
75 ............................................................................................... 5–E7
98 ............................................................................................... E89

- **U** doubles a digit.

11 ............................................................................................... 1–U
22 ............................................................................................... 2–U
33 ............................................................................................... 3–U
44 ............................................................................................... 4–U
55 ............................................................................................... 5–U
66 ............................................................................................... U6
77 ............................................................................................... U7
88 ............................................................................................... U8
99 ............................................................................................... U9

Variations are developed in the section "Advanced Numbering Tactics" (Page 3-117).

## PLAIN NUMBERS:
### 0  1  2  3 ... 99

| | |
|---|---|
| **STYLE:** | **Figure format, plain.** |
| **NUMBER BAR USED?** | **No** |
| **ENGLISH TRANSLATION:** | **Figures** |

## IN NUMERICAL ORDER (0 - 99)

**0 - 19**

| | |
|---|---|
| 0 | ZAOER |
| 1 | W*UN |
| 2 | TWO* |
| 3 | THR*E |
| 4 | FO*UR |
| 5 | FAOIF |
| 6 | SWIX |
| 7 | SEV |
| 8 | YAIT |
| 9 | NAO*IN |
| 10 | T*EN |
| 11 | LEV |
| 12 | TWEL |
| 13 | THRAOEN |
| 14 | FRAOEN |
| 15 | FAOEN |
| 16 | SKAOEN |
| 17 | SFAOEN |
| 18 | YAOEN, AO*EN |
| 19 | NAOEN |

**20 - 29** ("twenty-" = TW–)

| | |
|---|---|
| 20 | TWI |
| 21 | TWUN |
| 22 | TWAO |
| 23 | TWAOE |
| 24 | TWOER |
| 25 | TWAOIV |
| 26 | TWIK |
| 27 | TWEV |
| 28 | TWAI |
| 29 | TWAEN |

**30 - 39** ("thirty-" = THR–)

| | |
|---|---|
| 30 | THRI |
| 31 | THRUN |
| 32 | THRAO |
| 33 | THRAOE |
| 34 | THROER |

```
35 .......................................................................................... THRAOIF
36 ............................................................................................ THRIK
37 ........................................................................................... THREV
38 ............................................................................................ THRAI
39 ......................................................................................... THRAEN
```

**40 - 49** ("forty-" = FR–)
```
40 .............................................................................................. FRI
41 ............................................................................................ FRUN
42 ............................................................................................ FRAO
43 ........................................................................................... FRAOE
44 ...........................................................................................FROER
45 ......................................................................................... FRAOIV
46 ............................................................................................ FRIK
47 ........................................................................................... FREV
48 ............................................................................................ FRAI
49 ......................................................................................... FRAEN
```

**50 - 59** ("fifty-" = V–)
```
50 ............................................................................................... VI
51 .............................................................................................. VUN
52 .............................................................................................. VAO
53 ............................................................................................. VAOE
54 ............................................................................................ VOER
55 ........................................................................................... VAOIV
56 .............................................................................................. VIK
57 .............................................................................................. VEV
58 .............................................................................................. VAI
59 ............................................................................................. VAEN
```

**60 - 69** ("sixty-" = SK–)
```
60 ............................................................................................... SKI
61 ............................................................................................. SKUN
62 ............................................................................................. SKAO
63 ............................................................................................ SKAOE
64 ........................................................................................... SKO*ER
65 ........................................................................................... SKAOIV
66 ............................................................................................. SKIK
67 ............................................................................................ SKEV
68 ............................................................................................. SKAI
69 ............................................................................................ SKAEN
```

**70 - 79** ("seventy-" = SF–)
```
70 ............................................................................................... SFI
71 ............................................................................................. SFUN
72 ............................................................................................. SFAO
73 ............................................................................................ SFAOE
74 ............................................................................................ SFOER
75 ........................................................................................... SFAOIV
76 .............................................................................................. SFIK
77 ............................................................................................. SFEV
78 .............................................................................................. SFAI
79 ............................................................................................ SFAEN
```

**80 - 89** ("eighty-" = Y–)
```
80 ............................................................................................... Y*I
81 ............................................................................................. Y*UN
```

| | |
|---|---|
| 82 | YAO* |
| 83 | YAOE |
| 84 | YOER |
| 85 | YAOIV |
| 86 | YIK |
| 87 | YEV |
| 88 | YAI |
| 89 | YAEN |

**90 - 99** ("ninety-" = N–)

| | |
|---|---|
| 90 | NAOI |
| 91 | N*UN |
| 92 | NAO* |
| 93 | NAO*E |
| 94 | NOER |
| 95 | NAOIV |
| 96 | N*IK |
| 97 | NEF |
| 98 | NA*I |
| 99 | NAEN |

## ARRANGED BY COMMON ENGLISH/STENO SUFFIX (13 - 99)

*This arrangement organizes numbers by suffix for easy learning and practice.*

**-teen = –AOEN**

| | |
|---|---|
| 13 | THRAOEN |
| 14 | FRAOEN |
| 15 | FAOEN |
| 16 | SKAOEN |
| 17 | SFAOEN |
| 18 | AO*EN |
| 19 | NAOEN |

**-ty = –I**

| | |
|---|---|
| 20 | TWI |
| 30 | THRI |
| 40 | FRI |
| 50 | VI |
| 60 | SKI |
| 70 | SFI |
| 80 | Y*I |
| 90 | NAOI |

**-ty-one = –UN**

| | |
|---|---|
| 21 | TWUN |
| 31 | THRUN |
| 41 | FRUN |
| 51 | VUN |

61 ................................................................................................................... SKUN
71 ................................................................................................................... SFUN
81 ................................................................................................................... Y*UN
91 ................................................................................................................... N*UN

## -ty-two = –AO

22 ................................................................................................................... TWAO
32 ................................................................................................................ THRAO
42 ................................................................................................................... FRAO
52 ...................................................................................................................... VAO
62 ................................................................................................................... SKAO
72 ................................................................................................................ SFAO
82 ................................................................................................................... YAO*
92 ................................................................................................................... NAO*

## -ty-three = –AOE

23 ................................................................................................................ TWAOE
33 ............................................................................................................. THRAOE
43 ................................................................................................................ FRAOE
53 ................................................................................................................... VAOE
63 ............................................................................................................... SKAOE
73 ............................................................................................................... SFAOE
83 ................................................................................................................ YAOE
93 ............................................................................................................... NAO*E

## -ty-four = –OER

24 ............................................................................................................... TWOER
34 ............................................................................................................. THROER
44 ............................................................................................................... FROER
54 ................................................................................................................. VOER
64 .............................................................................................................. SKO*ER
74 ............................................................................................................... SFOER
84 ................................................................................................................ YOER
94 ................................................................................................................ NOER

## -ty-five = –AOIV

25 ............................................................................................................. TWAOIV
35 ............................................................................................................. THRAOIF
45 ............................................................................................................. FRAOIV
55 ............................................................................................................... VAOIV
65 ............................................................................................................ SKAOIV
75 ............................................................................................................ SFAOIV
85 ............................................................................................................. YAOIV
95 ............................................................................................................ NAOIV

## -ty-six = –IK

26 ................................................................................................................. TWIK
36 ............................................................................................................... THRIK
46 ................................................................................................................. FRIK
56 ...................................................................................................................... VIK
66 ................................................................................................................. SKIK
76 ................................................................................................................. SFIK
86 ..................................................................................................................... YIK
96 ................................................................................................................ N*IK

## -ty-seven = –EV

27 ................................................................................................................. TWEV
37 ............................................................................................................... THREV

47 ................................................................................................................... FREV
57 ..................................................................................................................... VEV
67 ................................................................................................................. SKEV
77 ................................................................................................................. SFEV
87 ................................................................................................................... YEV
97 .................................................................................................................... NEF

**-ty-eight = –AI**

28 .................................................................................................................. TWAI
38 ................................................................................................................ THRAI
48 .................................................................................................................. FRAI
58 ..................................................................................................................... VAI
68 ................................................................................................................... SKAI
78 ................................................................................................................... SFAI
88 .................................................................................................................... YAI
98 .................................................................................................................. NA*I

**-ty-nine = –AEN**

29 ................................................................................................................ TWAEN
39 .............................................................................................................. THRAEN
49 ................................................................................................................ FRAEN
59 ................................................................................................................. VAEN
69 ............................................................................................................... SKAEN
79 ............................................................................................................... SFAEN
89 ................................................................................................................ YAEN
99 ................................................................................................................ NAEN

## PLAIN NUMBERS:
## 0   1   2   3  ...  99

| STYLE: | Figure format, plain. |
|---|---|
| **NUMBER BAR USED?** | **Yes** |
| **ENGLISH TRANSLATION:** | **Figures** |

**0 - 9**

| | |
|---|---|
| 0 | 0 |
| 1 | 1 |
| 2 | 2 |
| 3 | 3 |
| 4 | 4 |
| 5 | 5 |
| 6 | 6 |
| 7 | 7 |
| 8 | 8 |
| 9 | 9 |

**10 - 19**

| | |
|---|---|
| 10 | 10 |
| 11 | 1–U |
| 12 | 12 |
| 13 | 13 |
| 14 | 14 |
| 15 | 15 |
| 16 | 16 |
| 17 | 17 |
| 18 | 18 |
| 19 | 19 |

**20 - 29**

| | |
|---|---|
| 20 | 20 |
| 21 | 12–E |
| 22 | 2–U |
| 23 | 23 |
| 24 | 24 |
| 25 | 25 |
| 26 | 26 |
| 27 | 27 |
| 28 | 28 |
| 29 | 29 |

**30 - 39**

| | |
|---|---|
| 30 | 30 |
| 31 | 13–E |
| 32 | 23–E |
| 33 | 3–U |
| 34 | 34 |

## PLAIN NUMBERS:
### zero one two three ... ninety-nine

| | |
|---|---|
| **STYLE:** | **Numbers in words, plain.** |
| **NUMBER BAR USED?** | **No** |
| **ENGLISH TRANSLATION:** | **Words** |

**0 - 9**

zero ......................................................................................................... ZER
one ......................................................................................................... WUN
two ......................................................................................................... TWO
three ...................................................................................................... THRE
four ........................................................................................................ FOUR
five ......................................................................................................... FAOIV
six .......................................................................................................... SIX
seven ..................................................................................................... SEVN
eight ....................................................................................................... AIT
nine ........................................................................................................ NAOIN

**10 - 19**

ten .......................................................................................................... TEN
eleven .................................................................................................... LEVN
twelve ..................................................................................................... TWEFL
thirteen ................................................................................................... THRAO*EN
fourteen .................................................................................................. FRAO*EN
fifteen ..................................................................................................... FAO*EN
sixteen .................................................................................................... SKAO*EN
seventeen ............................................................................................... SFAO*EN
eighteen .................................................................................................. YAO*EN
nineteen .................................................................................................. NAO*EN

**20 - 29** (TW–)

twenty ..................................................................................................... TW*I, TWENT
twenty-one .............................................................................................. TW*UN
twenty-two .............................................................................................. TWAO*
twenty-three ........................................................................................... TWAO*E
twenty-four ............................................................................................. TWO*ER
twenty-five .............................................................................................. TWAOIF
twenty-six ............................................................................................... TW*IK
twenty-seven .......................................................................................... TWEF
twenty-eight ............................................................................................ TWA*I
twenty-nine ............................................................................................. TWA*EN

**30 - 39** (THR–)

thirty ....................................................................................................... THR*I, THIRT
thirty-one ................................................................................................ THR*UN
thirty-two ................................................................................................ THRAO*
thirty-three .............................................................................................. THRAO*E
thirty-four ................................................................................................ THRO*ER

thirty-five ........................................................................................... THRAOIFT
thirty-six ............................................................................................... THR*IK
thirty-seven ......................................................................................... THREF
thirty-eight .......................................................................................... THRA*I
thirty-nine ........................................................................................... THRA*EN

## 40 - 49 (FR–)
forty ........................................................................... FR*I, FOURT
forty-one .............................................................................................. FR*UN
forty-two ............................................................................................. FRAO*
forty-three ......................................................................................... FRAO*E
forty-four ........................................................................................... FRO*ER
forty-five ............................................................................................ FRAOIF
forty-six ............................................................................................... FR*IK
forty-seven .......................................................................................... FREF
forty-eight ........................................................................................... FRA*IT
forty-nine ........................................................................................... FRA*EN

## 50 - 59 (V–)
fifty ........................................................................................................ FIFT
fifty-one .............................................................................................. V*UN
fifty-two .............................................................................................. VAO*
fifty-three ........................................................................................... VAO*E
fifty-four ............................................................................................. VO*ER
fifty-five ................................................................... VAOIVT, VAOIFT
fifty-six ................................................................................................ V*IK
fifty-seven .......................................................................................... VEVN
fifty-eight ............................................................................................ VA*I
fifty-nine ............................................................................................ VAO*IN

## 60 - 69 (SK–)
sixty ......................................................................................... SK*I, SIKT
sixty-one ............................................................................................. SK*UN
sixty-two .............................................................................................. SKAO*
sixty-three ......................................................................................... SKWAO*E
sixty-four ............................................................................................ SKO*R
sixty-five ............................................................................................ SKWAOIV
sixty-six .............................................................................................. SKWIK
sixty-seven .......................................................................................... SKEF
sixty-eight ........................................................................................... SKA*I
sixty-nine ............................................................................................ SKA*IN

## 70 - 79 (SF–)
seventy ...................................................................................... SF*I, SEVT
seventy-one ......................................................................................... SF*UN
seventy-two .......................................................................................... SFAO*
seventy-three ...................................................................................... SFAO*E
seventy-four ........................................................................................ SFO*ER
seventy-five ........................................................................................ SFAOIF
seventy-six .......................................................................................... SF*IK
seventy-seven ...................................................................................... SFEF
seventy-eight ....................................................................................... SFA*I
seventy-nine ........................................................................................ SFA*EN

## 80 - 89 (Y–)
eighty ......................................................................................... Y–, AOIGT
eighty-one ........................................................................................... YAIN

eighty-two ................................................................................................... YAO*T
eighty-three ................................................................................................. YAO*E
eighty-four ................................................................................................... YOERT
eighty-five .................................................................................................... YAOIF
eighty-six ...................................................................................................... Y*IK
eighty-seven ................................................................................................ YEF
eighty-eight .................................................................................................. YA*I
eighty-nine ................................................................................................... YA*EN

**90 - 99** (N–)
ninety ........................................................................................ NWAOI, NAOINT
ninety-one ................................................................................................ NWUN
ninety-two ................................................................................................ NWAO
ninety-three .............................................................................................. NWAOE
ninety-four ................................................................................. NWOER, NO*ER
ninety-five .................................................................................................. NWAOIV
ninety-six .................................................................................................... NWIK
ninety-seven .............................................................................................. NWEF
ninety-elght ................................................................................................ NWAI
ninety-nine ................................................................................. NWAEN, NA*EN

## NUMBERS (with comma):
## 0,  1,  2,  ... 19,

| STYLE: | Figures, with comma attached on right. |
|---|---|
| **NUMBER BAR USED?** | **No** |
| **ENGLISH TRANSLATION:** | **Figures** |

**NOTE: This format is used for number sequences. To extend this format beyond 19, use the numbers given on pages 3-18 to 3-20, followed by a comma.**

**0 - 9**
| | |
|---|---|
| 0, | ZAOER/–RBGS |
| 1, | W*UN/–RBGS |
| 2, | TWO*/–RBGS |
| 3, | THR*E/–RBGS |
| 4, | FO*UR/–RBGS |
| 5, | FAOIF/–RBGS |
| 6, | SWIX/–RBGS |
| 7, | SEV/–RBGS |
| 8, | YAIT/–RBGS |
| 9, | NAO*IN/–RBGS |

**10 - 19**
| | |
|---|---|
| 10, | T*EN/–RBGS |
| 11, | LEV/–RBGS |
| 12, | TWEL/–RBGS |
| 13, | THRAOEN/–RBGS |
| 14, | FRAOEN/–RBGS |
| 15, | FAOEN/–RBGS |
| 16, | SKAOEN/–RBGS |
| 17, | SFAOEN/–RBGS |
| 18, | YAOEN, AO*EN/–RBGS |
| 19, | NAOEN/–RBGS |

## NUMBERS (with comma):
## 0, 1, 2, ... 99,

| | |
|---|---|
| **STYLE:** | **Figures, with comma attached on right.** |
| **NUMBER BAR USED?** | **Yes** |
| **ENGLISH TRANSLATION:** | **Figures** |

**NOTE: This format is used for number sequences. Where physically possible, the full comma symbol RBGS is used and vice versa on left bank (SKWR).**

**0, - 9,**

| | |
|---|---|
| 0, | 0–RBGS |
| 1, | 1–RBGS |
| 2, | 2–RBGS |
| 3, | 3–RBGS |
| 4, | 4–RBGS |
| 5, | 5–RBGS |
| 6, | SKWR–6 |
| 7, | SKWR–7 |
| 8, | SKWR–8 |
| 9, | SKWR–9 |

**10, - 19,**

| | |
|---|---|
| 10, | 10–RBGS |
| 11, | 1–URBGS |
| 12, | 12–RBGS |
| 13, | 13–RBGS |
| 14, | 14–RBGS |
| 15, | 15–RBGS |
| 16, | 1–6BGS |
| 17, | 1–7GS |
| 18, | 1–RB8 |
| 19, | 1–RB9 |

**20, - 29,**

| | |
|---|---|
| 20, | 20–RBGS |
| 21, | 12–ERBGS, 2/1–RBGS |
| 22, | 2–URBGS |
| 23, | 23–RBGS |
| 24, | 24–RBGS |
| 25, | 25–RBGS |
| 26, | 2–6BGS |
| 27, | 2–7GS |
| 28, | 2–RB8 |
| 29, | 2–RB9 |

**30, - 39,**

| | |
|---|---|
| 30, | 30–RBGS |
| 31, | 13–ERBGS, 3/1–RBGS |

| | |
|---|---|
| 32, | 23–ERBGS, 3/2–RBGS |
| 33, | 3–URBGS |
| 34, | 34–RBGS |
| 35, | 35–RBGS |
| 36, | 3–6BGS |
| 37, | 3–7GS |
| 38, | 3–RB8 |
| 39, | 3–RB9 |

**40, - 49,**

| | |
|---|---|
| 40, | 40–RBGS |
| 41, | 14–ERBGS, 4/1–RBGS |
| 42, | 24–ERBGS, 4/2–RBGS |
| 43, | 34–ERBGS, 4/3–RBGS |
| 44, | 4–URBGS |
| 45, | 45–RBGS |
| 46, | 4–6BGS |
| 47, | 4–7GS |
| 48, | KW4–8, 4/SKWR–8 |
| 49, | KW4–9, 4/SKWR–9 |

**50, - 59,**

| | |
|---|---|
| 50, | 50–RBGS |
| 51, | 15–ERBGS, 5/1–RBGS |
| 52, | 25–ERBGS, 5/2–RBGS |
| 53, | 35–ERBGS, 5/3–RBGS |
| 54, | 45–ERBGS, 5/4–RBGS |
| 55, | 5–URBGS |
| 56, | 5–6BGS |
| 57, | 5–7GS |
| 58, | 5–RB8 |
| 59, | 5–RB9 |

**60, - 69,**

| | |
|---|---|
| 60, | SKWR0–E6, 6/0–RBGS |
| 61, | 1–E6BGS, 6/1–RBGS |
| 62, | 2–E6BGS, 6/2–RBGS |
| 63, | 3–E6BGS, 6/3–RBGS |
| 64, | 4–E6BGS, 6/4–RBGS |
| 65, | 5–E6BGS, 6/5–RBGS |
| 66, | U6BGS |
| 67, | 67GS |
| 68, | SKWR–68 |
| 69, | SKWR–69 |

**70, - 79,**

| | |
|---|---|
| 70, | SKWR0–E7, 7/0–RBGS |
| 71, | 1–E7GS, 7/1–RBGS |
| 72, | 2–E7GS, 7/2–RBGS |
| 73, | 3–E7GS, 7/3–RBGS |
| 74, | 4–E7GS, 7/4–RBGS |
| 75, | 5–E7GS, 7/5–RBGS |
| 76, | SKWR–E67, 7/6BGS |
| 77, | SKWR–U7, U7GS |
| 78, | SKWR–78 |
| 79, | SKWR–79 |

**80, - 89,**

**90, - 99,**

## NUMBERS (in parentheses):
### (1)  (2)  (3) ... (99)

**STYLE:**                    **Figures, enclosed in parentheses.**

**NUMBER BAR USED?**          **Yes**

**ENGLISH TRANSLATION:**      **Figures**

**NOTE:   Right bank = WR–   Left bank = –RB**

**(1) - (9)**
    (1) ............................................................................................................ 1–RB
    (2) ............................................................................................................ 2–RB
    (3) ............................................................................................................ 3–RB
    (4) ............................................................................................................ 4–RB
    (5) ............................................................................................................ 5–RB
    (6) ........................................................................................................... WR–6
    (7) ........................................................................................................... WR–7
    (8) ........................................................................................................... WR–8
    (9) ........................................................................................................... WR–9

**(10) - (19)**
    (10) ........................................................................................................ 10–RB
    (11) ........................................................................................................ 1–URB
    (12) ........................................................................................................ 12–RB
    (13) ........................................................................................................ 13–RB
    (14) ........................................................................................................ 14–RB
    (15) ........................................................................................................ 15–RB
    (16) ....................................................................................................... 1WR–6
    (17) ....................................................................................................... 1WR–7
    (18) ....................................................................................................... 1WR–8
    (19) ....................................................................................................... 1WR–9

**(20) - (29)**
    (20) ........................................................................................................ 20–RB
    (21) ...................................................................................................... 12–ERB
    (22) ....................................................................................................... 2–URB
    (23) ........................................................................................................ 23–RB
    (24) ........................................................................................................ 24–RB
    (25) ........................................................................................................ 25–RB
    (26) ...................................................................................................... 2WR–6
    (27) ...................................................................................................... 2WR–7
    (28) ...................................................................................................... 2WR–8
    (29) ...................................................................................................... 2WR–9

**(30) - (39)**
    (30) ........................................................................................................ 30–RB
    (31) ...................................................................................................... 13–ERB

(32) ..................................................................................................... 23–ERB
(33) ...................................................................................................... 3–URB
(34) ...................................................................................................... 34–RB
(35) ...................................................................................................... 35–RB
(36) ...................................................................................................... 3WR–6
(37) ...................................................................................................... 3WR–7
(38) ...................................................................................................... 3WR–8
(39) ...................................................................................................... 3WR–9

**(40) - (49)**

(40) ...................................................................................................... 40–RB
(41) ..................................................................................................... 14–ERB
(42) ..................................................................................................... 24–ERB
(43) ..................................................................................................... 34–ERB
(44) ...................................................................................................... 4–URB
(45) ...................................................................................................... 45–RB
(46) ...................................................................................................... 46–RB
(47) ...................................................................................................... 4–RB7
(48) ...................................................................................................... 4–RB8
(49) ...................................................................................................... 4–RB9

**(50) - (59)**

(50) ...................................................................................................... 50–RB
(51) ..................................................................................................... 15–ERB
(52) ..................................................................................................... 25–ERB
(53) ..................................................................................................... 35–ERB
(54) ..................................................................................................... 45–ERB
(55) ...................................................................................................... 5–URB
(56) ..................................................................................................... WR5–6
(57) ..................................................................................................... WR5–7
(58) ..................................................................................................... WR5–8
(59) ..................................................................................................... WR5–9

**(60) - (69)**

(60) ..................................................................................................... WR0–E6
(61) ..................................................................................................... 1WR–E6
(62) ..................................................................................................... 2WR–E6
(63) ..................................................................................................... 3WR–E6
(64) ..................................................................................................... WR4–E6
(65) ..................................................................................................... WR5–E6
(66) ..................................................................................................... WR–U6
(67) ..................................................................................................... WR–67
(68) ..................................................................................................... WR–68
(69) ..................................................................................................... WR–69

**(70) - (79)**

(70) ..................................................................................................... WR0–E7
(71) ..................................................................................................... 1WR–E7
(72) ..................................................................................................... 2WR–E7
(73) ..................................................................................................... 3WR–E7
(74) ..................................................................................................... 4WR–E7
(75) ..................................................................................................... WR5–E7
(76) ..................................................................................................... WR–E67
(77) ..................................................................................................... WR–U7
(78) ..................................................................................................... WR–78
(79) ..................................................................................................... WR–79

**(80) - (89)**

(80) ............................................................................................... WR0–E8
(81) ............................................................................................... 1WR–E8
(82) ............................................................................................... 2WR–E8
(83) ............................................................................................... 3–ERB8
(84) ............................................................................................... 4–ERB8
(85) ............................................................................................... 5–ERB8
(86) ............................................................................................... WR–E68
(87) ............................................................................................... WR–E78
(88) ............................................................................................... WR–U8
(89) ............................................................................................... WR–89

**(90) - (99)**

(90) ............................................................................................... 0–ERB9
(91) ............................................................................................... 1–ERB9
(92) ............................................................................................... 2–ERB9
(93) ............................................................................................... 3–ERB9
(94) ............................................................................................... 4–ERB9
(95) ............................................................................... 5–ERB9, WR5–E9
(96) ............................................................................................... WR–E69
(97) ............................................................................................... WR–E79
(98) ............................................................................................... WR–E89
(99) ............................................................................................... WR–U9

## NUMBERS (plurals):
### 0s  1s  2s  3s etc.

| | |
|---|---|
| **STYLE:** | **Figures, with attached "s" ending.** |
| **NUMBER BAR USED?** | **No** |
| **ENGLISH TRANSLATION:** | **Figures** |

**NOTE:  Add the plural ending to numbers on pages 3-18 to 3-20 to complete the range 0-100.**

| | |
|---|---|
| 0s | ZAOERS |
| 1s | W*UNZ, WUN/–Z |
| 2s | TWOZ |
| 3s | THR*ES |
| 4s | FO*URS |
| 5s | FAOIV/–Z |
| 6s | SIX/–Z |
| 7s | SEVZ |
| 8s | YAITS |
| 9s | NAOINZ |

| | |
|---|---|
| 10s | T*ENS |
| 20s | TWIZ |
| 30s | THRIZ |
| 40s | FR*IZ |
| 50s | V*IS |
| 60s | SK*IZ |
| 70s | SFIZ |
| 80s | Y*IZ |
| 90s | NAO*IZ, NAOI/–S |
| 100s | HUN/–Z |

## NUMBERS (plurals):
## 0s  1s  2s  3s etc.

| | |
|---|---|
| **STYLE:** | **Figures, with attached "s" ending.** |
| **NUMBER BAR USED?** | **Yes** |
| **ENGLISH TRANSLATION:** | **Figures** |

**NOTE:  Add the plural ending to numbers on pages 3-23 to 3-25 to complete the range 0-100.**

| | |
|---|---|
| 0s | 0–Z |
| 1s | 1–Z |
| 2s | 2–Z |
| 3s | 3–Z |
| 4s | 4–Z |
| 5s | 5–Z |
| 6s | 6Z |
| 7s | 7Z |
| 8s | 8Z |
| 9s | 9/–S, 9/–Z |
| 10s | 10–Z |
| 20s | 20–Z |
| 30s | 30–Z |
| 40s | 40–Z |
| 50s | 50–Z |
| 60s | 0–E6Z, 6/0–Z |
| 70s | 0–E7Z, 7/0–Z |
| 80s | 0–E8Z, 8/0–Z |
| 90s | 9/0–Z |
| 100s | 10–UZ |

## NUMBERS (plurals):
### zeros  ones  twos  ...  ninety-nines

| | |
|---|---|
| **STYLE:** | **Numbers in words, with attached "s" ending.** |
| **NUMBER BAR USED?** | **No** |
| **ENGLISH TRANSLATION:** | **Words** |

**0 - 9**

zeros ............................................................................................. ZERS
ones ................................................................................ WUNZ, WUN/–S
twos ............................................................................................. TWOS
threes ......................................................................................... THRES
fours .......................................................................................... FOURS
fives ....................................................................................... FAOIV/–S
sixes ......................................................................................... SIX/–S
sevens ............................................................................. SEVS, SEVNS
eights ............................................................................................ AITS
nines ........................................................................................ NAOINS

**10 - 19**

tens ................................................................................ TENZ, TEN/–S
elevens ........................................................................... LEVS, LEVNS
twelves ...................................................................... TWELS, TWEFLS
thirteens ............................................................................... THRAOENS
fourteens ............................................................................... FRAOENS
fifteens ................................................................................... FAOENS
sixteens ................................................................................. SKAOENS
seventeens ............................................................................ SFAOENS
eighteens ............................................................................... AO*ENS
nineteens ............................................................................... NAOENZ

**20 - 29**

twenties ......................................................................... TWIS, TWENTS
twenty-ones ........................................................... TWUNZ, TWUN/–S
twenty-twos ........................................................................... TWAOS
twenty-threes ....................................................................... TWAOES
twenty-fours ......................................................................... TWOERS
twenty-fives .......................................................................... TWAOIVS
twenty-sixes .......................................................................... TWIKS
twenty-sevens ....................................................................... TWEVS
twenty-eights ........................................................................ TWAIS
twenty-nines ......................................................................... TWAENS

**30 - 39**

thirties ......................................................................... THRIS, THIRTS
thirty-ones ............................................................................ THRUNS
thirty-twos ............................................................................ THRAOS
thirty-threes ......................................................................... THRAOES
thirty-fours ........................................................................... THROERS

thirty-fives ........................................................................ THRAOIFS
thirty-sixes ........................................................................ THRIKS
thirty-sevens ..................................................................... THREVS
thirty-eights ...................................................................... THRAIS
thirty-nines ....................................................................... THRAENS

**40 - 49**
forties ............................................................................... FRIS, FOURTS
forty-ones ......................................................................... FRUNS
forty-twos .......................................................................... FRAOS
forty-threes ..................................................... FRAO*ES, FRAOE/–S
forty-fours ........................................................................ FROERS
forty-fives ......................................................................... FRAOIVS
forty-sixes ......................................................................... FRIKS
forty-sevens ...................................................................... FREVS
forty-eights ....................................................................... FRAIZ
forty-nines ..................................................... FRA*ENS, FRAENZ

**50 - 59**
fifties ............................................................................... FIFTS, VI/–S
fifty-ones .......................................................................... VUNS
fifty-twos .......................................................................... VAOS
fifty-threes ..................................................... VAO*ES, VAOE/–S
fifty-fours ......................................................................... VOERS
fifty-fives .......................................................................... VAOIVS
fifty-sixes ......................................................................... VIKZ, VIK/–S
fifty-sevens ...................................................................... VEVS
fifty-eights ........................................................................ VAIS
fifty-nines ......................................................................... VAENS

**60 - 69**
sixties ............................................................................... SKIS
sixty-ones ......................................................................... SKUNS
sixty-twos .......................................................................... SKAOS
sixty-threes ....................................................................... SKAO*ES
sixty-fours ......................................................................... SKOERS
sixty-fives ......................................................................... SKAOIVS
sixty-sixes ......................................................................... SKIKS
sixty-sevens ...................................................................... SKEVS
sixty-eights ....................................................................... SKAIS
sixty-nines ........................................................................ SKAENS

**70 - 79**
seventies .......................................................... SFIS, SEVTS, SFENTS
seventy-ones ..................................................................... SFUNS
seventy-twos ..................................................................... SFAOS
seventy-threes ................................................................... SFAOES
seventy-fours .................................................................... SFOERS
seventy-fives ..................................................................... SFAOIVS
seventy-sixes .................................................... SF*IKS, SFIK/–S
seventy-sevens .................................................................. SFEVS
seventy-eights ................................................................... SFAIS
seventy-nines .................................................................... SFAENS

**80 - 89**
eighties ............................................................................. AOIGTS, Y–S
eighty-ones ........................................................................ Y*UNS

eighty-twos ....................................................................................... YAO*Z, YAO/–S
eighty-threes ................................................................................................ YAOES
eighty-fours ................................................................................................. YOERS
eighty-fives ................................................................................................ YAOIVS
eighty-sixes ..................................................................................................... YIKS
eighty-sevens ................................................................................................ YEVS
eighty-eights .................................................................................................. YAIS
eighty-nines ................................................................................................. YAENS

## 90 - 99

nineties ..................................................................................... NAOINTS, NAO*IS
ninety-ones ............................................................................... N*UNS, N*UN/–S
ninety-twos ..................................................................................... NAO*S , NAO/–S
ninety-threes .......................................................................... NAO*EZ, NAO*E/–S
ninety-fours .............................................................................................. NOERS
ninety-fives ............................................................................................... NAOIVS
ninety-sixes ....................................................................................... NIKZ, NIK/–S
ninety-sevens ................................................................................... NEFZ, NEF/–S
ninety-eights ................................................................................................. NAIZ
ninety-nines ................................................................................ NA*ENS, NAEN/–S

## DECIMAL NUMBERING:
### .01  .02  .03 ... .99

| | |
|---|---|
| **STYLE:** | **Decimal numbers attached on left, expressed as "decimal point-digits."** |
| **NUMBER BAR USED?** | **Yes** |
| **ENGLISH TRANSLATION:** | **Figures** |

**NOTE:  This format is used to attach a decimal value to a whole number (e.g., ".43" in the number 26.43).**

*Associate –S with "cents"
or "hundredths."
When building your CAT dictionary, include a
"delete space" command before the decimal
point (example: ~.01).*

**.01 - .09**

| | |
|---|---|
| .01 | 1S |
| .02 | 2S |
| .03 | 3S |
| .04 | 4S |
| .05 | 5S |
| .06 | 6S |
| .07 | 7S |
| .08 | 8S |
| .09 | 9S |

**.10 - .19**

| | |
|---|---|
| .10 | 10S |
| .11 | 1–US |
| .12 | 12S |
| .13 | 13S |
| .14 | 14S |
| .15 | 15S |
| .16 | 16S |
| .17 | 17S |
| .18 | 18S |
| .19 | 19S |

**.20 - .29**

| | |
|---|---|
| .20 | 20S |
| .21 | 12–ES, 2/1S |
| .22 | 2–US |
| .23 | 23S |
| .24 | 24S |

.25 .......................................................................................................... 25S
.26 .......................................................................................................... 26S
.27 .......................................................................................................... 27S
.28 .......................................................................................................... 28S
.29 .......................................................................................................... 29S

**.30 - .39**
.30 .......................................................................................................... 30S
.31 ............................................................................................ 13–ES, 3/1S
.32 ............................................................................................ 23–ES, 3/2S
.33 ................................................................................................... 3–US
.34 .......................................................................................................... 34S
.35 .......................................................................................................... 35S
.36 .......................................................................................................... 36S
.37 .......................................................................................................... 37S
.38 .......................................................................................................... 38S
.39 .......................................................................................................... 39S

**.40 - .49**
.40 .......................................................................................................... 40S
.41 ............................................................................................ 14–ES, 4/1S
.42 ............................................................................................ 24–ES, 4/2S
.43 ............................................................................................ 34–ES, 4/3S
.44 ................................................................................................... 4–US
.45 .......................................................................................................... 45S
.46 .......................................................................................................... 46S
.47 .......................................................................................................... 47S
.48 .......................................................................................................... 48S
.49 .......................................................................................................... 49S

**.50 - .59**
.50 .......................................................................................................... 50S
.51 ............................................................................................ 15–ES, 5/1S
.52 ............................................................................................ 25–ES, 5/2S
.53 ............................................................................................ 35–ES, 5/3S
.54 ............................................................................................ 45–ES, 5/4S
.55 ................................................................................................... 5–US
.56 .......................................................................................................... 56S
.57 .......................................................................................................... 57S
.58 .......................................................................................................... 58S
.59 .......................................................................................................... 59S

**.60 - .69**
.60 ........................................................................................... 0–E6S, 6/0S
.61 ........................................................................................... 1–E6S, 6/1S
.62 ........................................................................................... 2–E6S, 6/2S
.63 ........................................................................................... 3–E6S, 6/3S
.64 ........................................................................................... 4–E6S, 6/4S
.65 ........................................................................................... 5–E6S, 6/5S
.66 ......................................................................................................... U6S
.67 .......................................................................................................... 67S
.68 .......................................................................................................... 68S
.69 .......................................................................................................... 69S

**.70 - .79**
.70 ........................................................................................... 0–E7S, 7/0S
.71 ........................................................................................... 1–E7S, 7/1S

.72 ...................................................................................................................... 2–E7S, 7/2S
.73 ...................................................................................................................... 3–E7S, 7/3S
.74 ...................................................................................................................... 4–E7S, 7/4S
.75 ...................................................................................................................... 5–E7S, 7/5S
.76 ...................................................................................................................... E67S, 7/6S
.77 ...................................................................................................................................... U7S
.78 ...................................................................................................................................... 78S
.79 ...................................................................................................................................... 79S

**.80 - .89**
.80 ...................................................................................................................... 0–E8S, 8/0S
.81 ...................................................................................................................... 1–E8S, 8/1S
.82 ...................................................................................................................... 2–E8S, 8/2S
.83 ...................................................................................................................... 3–E8S, 8/3S
.84 ...................................................................................................................... 4–E8S, 8/4S
.85 ...................................................................................................................... 5–E8S, 8/5S
.86 ...................................................................................................................... E68S, 8/6S
.87 ...................................................................................................................... E78S, 8/7S
.88 ...................................................................................................................................... U8S
.89 ...................................................................................................................................... 89S

**.90 - .99**
.90 ...................................................................................................................... 0–E9S, 9/0S
.91 ...................................................................................................................... 1–E9S, 9/1S
.92 ...................................................................................................................... 2–E9S, 9/2S
.93 ...................................................................................................................... 3–E9S, 9/3S
.94 ...................................................................................................................... 4–E9S, 9/4S
.95 ...................................................................................................................... 5–E9S, 9/5S
.96 ...................................................................................................................... E69S, 9/6S
.97 ...................................................................................................................... E79S, 9/7S
.98 ...................................................................................................................... E89S, 9/8S
.99 ...................................................................................................................................... U9S

## DECIMAL NUMBERING:
### 0.  1.  2.  ...  10.

| STYLE: | Whole numbers with decimal point, and attached on right, expressed as *"digit-decimal point."* |
|---|---|
| NUMBER BAR USED? | No |
| ENGLISH TRANSLATION: | Figures |

NOTE: This format is used in combination with the styles on pages 3-18 to 3-25 to form complete decimal numbers (e.g., "1." in the number 1.3). The system is developed on pages 3-45 (without number bar) and 3-46 (with number bar).

*Associate OINT with "point."*
*When building your dictionary, include a*
*"delete space" command after the decimal*
*point (example: 1.~).*

| | |
|---|---|
| 0. | ZOINT |
| 1. | WOINT |
| 2. | TWOINT |
| 3. | THROINT |
| 4. | FOINT |
| 5. | VOINT |
| 6. | SOINT |
| 7. | SFOINT |
| 8. | OINT |
| 9. | NO*INT |
| 10. | TOINT |

## DECIMAL NUMBERING:
### 0.1  0.2  0.3 etc.

| STYLE: | Numbers expressed as *"digit-dec. point-digit."* |
|---|---|
| NUMBER BAR USED? | No |
| ENGLISH TRANSLATION: | Figures |

**0.1 - 0.9**

| | |
|---|---|
| 0.1 | ZOINT/W*UN |
| 0.2 | ZOINT/TWO* |
| 0.3 | ZOINT/THR*E |
| 0.4 | ZOINT/FO*UR |
| 0.5 | ZOINT/FAOIF |
| 0.6 | ZOINT/SWIX |
| 0.7 | ZOINT/SEV |
| 0.8 | ZOINT/YAIT |
| 0.9 | ZOINT/NAO*IN |

**1.0 - 1.9**

| | |
|---|---|
| 1.0 | WOINT/ZAOER |
| 1.1 | WOINT/W*UN |
| 1.2 | WOINT/TWO* |
| 1.3 | WOINT/THR*E |
| 1.4 | WOINT/FO*UR |
| 1.5 | WOINT/FAOIF |
| 1.6 | WOINT/SWIX |
| 1.7 | WOINT/SEV |
| 1.8 | WOINT/YAIT |
| 1.9 | WOINT/NAO*IN |

**2.0 onward** follow the same progression. Examples:

| | |
|---|---|
| 2.3 | TWOINT/THR*E |
| 3.4 | THROINT/FO*UR |
| 4.5 | FOINT/FAOIF |
| 5.6 | VOINT/SWIX |
| 6.7 | SOINT/SEV |
| 7.8 | SFOINT/YAIT |
| 8.9 | OINT/NAO*IN |
| 9.0 | NO*INT/YAIT |
| 10.7 | TOINT/SEV |

## DECIMAL NUMBERING:
### 0.1  0.2  0.3  etc.

| | |
|---|---|
| **STYLE:** | **Numbers expressed as** *"digit-dec. point-digit."* |
| **NUMBER BAR USED?** | **Yes** |
| **ENGLISH TRANSLATION:** | **Figures** |

**0.1 - 0.9**

| | |
|---|---|
| 0.1 | ZOINT/1 |
| 0.2 | ZOINT/2 |
| 0.3 | ZOINT/3 |
| 0.4 | ZOINT/4 |
| 0.5 | ZOINT/5 |
| 0.6 | ZOINT/6 |
| 0.7 | ZOINT/7 |
| 0.8 | ZOINT/8 |
| 0.9 | ZOINT/9 |

**1.0 - 1.9**

| | |
|---|---|
| 1.0 | WOINT/0 |
| 1.1 | WOINT/1 |
| 1.2 | WOINT/2 |
| 1.3 | WOINT/3 |
| 1.4 | WOINT/4 |
| 1.5 | WOINT/5 |
| 1.6 | WOINT/6 |
| 1.7 | WOINT/7 |
| 1.8 | WOINT/8 |
| 1.9 | WOINT/9 |

**2.0 onward** follow the same progression. Examples:

| | |
|---|---|
| 2.3 | TWOINT/3 |
| 3.4 | THROINT/4 |
| 4.5 | FOINT/5 |
| 5.6 | VOINT/6 |
| 6.7 | SOINT/7 |
| 7.8 | SFOINT/8 |
| 8.9 | OINT/9 |
| 9.0 | NO*INT/0 |
| 10.7 | TOINT/7 |

## DECIMAL NUMBERING:
### 0.1   0.2   0.3   ...   9.9

| | |
|---|---|
| **STYLE:** | **Numbers expressed as** *"digit-dec. point-digit."* |
| **NUMBER BAR USED?** | **Yes** |
| **ENGLISH TRANSLATION:** | **Figures** |

**0.1 - 0.9**
```
0.1 .......................................................................... 0/P*/1
0.2 .......................................................................... 0/P*/2
0.3 .......................................................................... 0/P*/3
0.4 .......................................................................... 0/P*/4
0.5 .......................................................................... 0/P*/5
0.6 .......................................................................... 0/P*/6
0.7 .......................................................................... 0/P*/7
0.8 .......................................................................... 0/P*/8
0.9 .......................................................................... 0/P*/9
```

**1.0 - 1.9**
```
1.0 .......................................................................... 1/P*/0
1.1 .......................................................................... 1/P*/1
1.2 .......................................................................... 1/P*/2
1.3 .......................................................................... 1/P*/3
1.4 .......................................................................... 1/P*/4
1.5 .......................................................................... 1/P*/5
1.6 .......................................................................... 1/P*/6
1.7 .......................................................................... 1/P*/7
1.8 .......................................................................... 1/P*/8
1.9 .......................................................................... 1/P*/9
```

**2.0 - 9.9** follow the same progression. Examples:
```
2.0 .......................................................................... 2/P*/0
3.1 .......................................................................... 3/P*/1
4.2 .......................................................................... 4/P*/2
5.3 .......................................................................... 5/P*/3
6.4 .......................................................................... 6/P*/4
7.5 .......................................................................... 7/P*/5
8.6 .......................................................................... 8/P*/6
9.7 .......................................................................... 9/P*/7
9.8 .......................................................................... 9/P*/8
9.9 .......................................................................... 9/P*/9
```

## FRACTIONS:
### 1/5   2/5   3/5   etc.

| | |
|---|---|
| **STYLE:** | **Fractions in figures.** |
| **NUMBER BAR USED?** | **Example 1: yes    Example 2: no** |
| **ENGLISH TRANSLATION:** | **Figures** |

*Associate SL–RB with "slash."*
*CAT dictionary entry for SL–RB = ~/~*
*This slash can be used with or without the*
*number bar.*

### EXAMPLE 1 (with number bar)
1/5 ................................................................................................ 1/SL–RB/5
2/5 ................................................................................................ 2/SL–RB/5
3/5 ................................................................................................ 3/SL–RB/5
4/5 ................................................................................................ 4/SL–RB/5
115/130 ................................................................................. 1/15/SL–RB/1/30

### EXAMPLE 2 (without number bar)
1/5 .............................................................................. W*UN/SL–RB/FAOIF
2/5 ............................................................................. TWO*/SL–RB/FAOIF
3/5 ............................................................................ THR*E/SL–RB/FAOIF
4/5 ............................................................................ FO*UR/SL–RB/FAOIF
115/130 ............................................... WUN/HUN/FAOEN/SL–RB/WUN/HUN/THRI

## NUMBERS (ordinals):
### 1st  2nd  3rd  ...  99th

| | |
|---|---|
| **STYLE:** | **Figures, with attached ending "st," "nd," "rd" or "th."** |
| **NUMBER BAR USED?** | **Yes** |
| **ENGLISH TRANSLATION:** | **Figures** |

**NOTE: Forms ordinals using the number bar plus *R or R*.**

### 1st - 9th

| | |
|---|---|
| 1st | 1*R |
| 2nd | 2*R |
| 3rd | 3*R |
| 4th | 4*R |
| 5th | 5*R |
| 6th | R*6 |
| 7th | R*7 |
| 8th | R*8 |
| 9th | R*9 |

### 10th - 19th

| | |
|---|---|
| 10th | 10*R |
| 11th | 1*RU, 1R*U |
| 12th | 12*R |
| 13th | 13*R |
| 14th | 14*R |
| 15th | 15*R |
| 16th | 1R*6 |
| 17th | 1*R7, 1R*7 |
| 18th | 1*R8, 1R*8 |
| 19th | 1*R9, 1R*9 |

### 20th - 29th

| | |
|---|---|
| 20th | 20*R |
| 21st | 12*ER, 2/1*R |
| 22nd | 2*UR |
| 23rd | 23*R |
| 24th | 24*R |
| 25th | 25*R |
| 26th | 2R*6, 2*R6 |
| 27th | 2*R7 |
| 28th | 2*R8 |
| 29th | 2*R9 |

### 30th - 39th

| | |
|---|---|
| 30th | 30*R |
| 31st | 13*ER, 3/1*R |
| 32nd | 23*ER, 3/2*R |

33rd ................................................................................................... 3*UR
34th ................................................................................................ 34*R
35th ................................................................................................ 35*R
36th ................................................................................ 3*6R, 3R*6
37th ................................................................................ 3*R7, 3R*7
38th ................................................................................ 3*R8, 3R*8
39th ................................................................................ 3*R9, 3R*9

## 40th - 49th

40th ............................................................................................ 40*R
41st ................................................................................ 14*ER, 4/1*R
42nd ............................................................................... 24*ER, 4/2*R
43rd ................................................................................ 34*ER, 4/3*R
44th ............................................................................................ 4*UR
45th ............................................................................................ 45*R
46th ................................................................................ 4*6R, 4R*6
47th ............................................................................................ 4*R7
48th ............................................................................................ 4*R8
49th ............................................................................................ 4*R9

## 50th - 59th

50th ............................................................................................ 50*R
51st ................................................................................ 15*ER, 5/1*R
52nd ............................................................................... 25*ER, 5/2*R
53rd ................................................................................ 35*ER, 5/3*R
54th ................................................................................ 45*ER, 5/4*R
55th ............................................................................................ 5*UR
56th ................................................................................ 5*6R, R5*6
57th ................................................................................ 5*R7, R5*7
58th ............................................................................................ 5*R8
59th ............................................................................................ 5*R9

## 60th - 69th

60th ......................................................................................... R0*E6
61st ................................................................. 1R*E6, 1*E6R, 6/1*R
62nd ................................................................ 2R*E6, 2*E6R, 6/2*R
63rd ................................................................. 3R*E6, 3*E6R, 6/3*R
64th ................................................................. 4R*E6, 4*E6R, 6/4*R
65th ............................................................................ 5*E6R, 6/5*R
66th ......................................................................................... R*U6
67th ......................................................................................... R*67
68th ......................................................................................... R*68
69th ......................................................................................... R*69

## 70th - 79th

70th ......................................................................................... 0*ER7
71st ................................................................................ 1*ER7, 7/1*R
72nd ............................................................................... 2*ER7, 7/2*R
73rd ................................................................................ 3*ER7, 7/3*R
74th ................................................................................ 4*ER7, 7/4*R
75th ................................................................................ 5*ER7, 7/5*R
76th ................................................................................ R*E67, 7/R*6
77th ................................................................................ *UR7, R*U7
78th ................................................................................ *R78, R*78
79th ................................................................................ *R79, R*79

**80th - 89th**

| | |
|---|---|
| 80th | 0*ER8 |
| 81st | 1*ER8, 8/1*R |
| 82nd | 2*ER8, 8/2*R |
| 83rd | 3*ER8, 8/3*R |
| 84th | 4*ER8, 8/4*R |
| 85th | 5*ER8, 8/5*R |
| 86th | R*E68, 8/R*6 |
| 87th | *ER78, R*E78, 8/R*7 |
| 88th | *UR8, R*U8 |
| 89th | *R89, R*89 |

**90th - 99th**

| | |
|---|---|
| 90th | 0*ER9 |
| 91st | 1*ER9, 9/1*R |
| 92nd | 2*ER9, 9/2*R |
| 93rd | 3*ER9, 9/3*R |
| 94th | 4*ER9, 9/4*R |
| 95th | 5*ER9, 9/5*R |
| 96th | R*E69, 9/R*6 |
| 97th | R*E79, 9/R*7 |
| 98th | *ER89, R*E89, 9/R*8 |
| 99th | *UR9, R*U9 |

## NUMBERS (ordinals):
### first   second   third ... ninety-ninth

| | |
|---|---|
| **STYLE:** | **Ordinals in words.** |
| **NUMBER BAR USED?** | **No** |
| **ENGLISH TRANSLATION:** | **Words** |

**1 - 9**

| | |
|---|---|
| first | FIRS |
| second | SEK |
| third | THIRD |
| fourth | FO*URT |
| fifth | F*IFT |
| sixth | S*IX |
| seventh | SWEFT |
| eighth | A*IT |
| ninth | N*INT |

**10 - 19**

| | |
|---|---|
| tenth | T*ENT |
| eleventh | LEVNT |
| twelfth | TWELT, TW*ELT |
| thirteenth | THRAOENT |
| fourteenth | FRAOENT |
| fifteenth | FAOENT |
| sixteenth | SKAOENT |
| seventeenth | SFAOENT |
| eighteenth | YAOENT |
| nineteenth | NAOENT |

**20 - 29**

| | |
|---|---|
| twentieth | TW*ENT |
| twenty-first | TWIRS |
| twenty-second | TWEND |
| twenty-third | TWIRD |
| twenty-fourth | TWOURT |
| twenty-fifth | TWIF |
| twenty-sixth | TWIKT |
| twenty-seventh | TWEFNT |
| twenty-eighth | TWA*IT |
| twenty-ninth | TWAENT |

**30 - 39**

| | |
|---|---|
| thirtieth | TH*IRT |
| thirty-first | THRIRS |
| thirty-second | THREKD |
| thirty-third | THRIRD |
| thirty-fourth | THROURT |
| thirty-fifth | THRIF |

thirty-sixth .............................................................. THR\*IX
thirty-seventh ...................................................... THREFNT
thirty-eighth ........................................................ THRA\*IT
thirty-ninth .......................................................... THRAENT

**40 - 49**

fortieth ................................................................. FWOURT
forty-first ............................................................... FWIRS
forty-second ............................................... FWEN, FWREN
forty-third ............................................................. FWIRD
forty-fourth ........................................................ FWOERT
forty-fifth .............................................................. FWIF
forty-sixth ............................................................. FWIK
forty-seventh ....................................................... FWEFT
forty-eighth ......................................................... FWAIT
forty-ninth ................................................ FWAOINT, FWINT

**50 - 59**

fiftieth .................................................................. DWIFT
fifty-first ............................................................... DWIRZ
fifty-second .................................................... DW\*EKD
fifty-third .............................................................. DWIRD
fifty-fourth ........................................................ DWOURT
fifty-fifth ............................................................ DW–FT
fifty-sixth .......................................................... DW\*IK
fifty-seventh .................................... DWEFN, DWEFNT
fifty-eighth ....................................................... DWA\*IT
fifty-ninth .......................................................... DW\*INT

**60 - 69**

sixtieth ................................................................ SK\*IT
sixty-first ............................................................. SKIRS
sixty-second ............................................ SK\*EK, SKWEK
sixty-third ............................................................ SKIRD
sixty-fourth ...................................................... SKO\*URT
sixty-fifth ............................................................ SKWIF
sixty-sixth ........................................................... SKIKT
sixty-seventh .................................... SKEFN, SKEVN
sixty-eighth ...................................................... SKA\*IT
sixty-ninth .......................................................... SK\*INT

**70 - 79**

seventieth ............................................................ SFIT
seventy-first ........................................................ SFIRS
seventy-second ................................................. SFEKD
seventy-third ...................................................... SFIRD
seventy-fourth ................................................... SFOURT
seventy-fifth ..................................................... SFAOIFT
seventy-sixth ..................................................... SFIKT
seventy-seventh ................................................ SFEFT
seventy-eighth ................................................... SFA\*IT
seventy-ninth .................................................... SF\*INT

**80 - 89**

eightieth .............................................................. YA\*IT
eighty-first ........................................................... YIRS

eighty-second ..................................................................................... YEK
eighty-third ........................................................................................ YIR
eighty-fourth ................................................................................. YOURT
eighty-fifth ................................................................................... YAOIFT
eighty-sixth ..................................................................................... YIKT
eighty-seventh ............................................................................... YEFT
eighty-eighth ................................................................................ YAO*IT
eighty-ninth ................................................................................. YAENT

## 90 - 99

ninetieth ..................................................................................... NWAOIT
ninety-first ...................................................................................... NIRS
ninety-second ............................................................................... NEND
ninety-third .................................................................................... NIRD
ninety-fourth .............................................................................. NO*URT
ninety-fifth .................................................................................... NWIF
ninety-sixth .................................................................................. NWIX
ninety-seventh ........................................................................... NWEFT
ninety-eighth ............................................................................... NWAIT
ninety-ninth ................................................................................ NWINT

## NUMBERS (ordinals):
### First   Second   Third   ...   Ninety-ninth

| STYLE: | Ordinals in words with initial capital letter. |
|---|---|
| **NUMBER BAR USED?** | No |
| **ENGLISH TRANSLATION:** | Words |

### 1 - 9

| | |
|---|---|
| First | F*IRS |
| Second | S*EKD |
| Third | TH*IRD |
| Fourth | FO*ERT |
| Fifth | FWIFT, FW*IFT |
| Sixth | SW*IX |
| Seventh | SW*EFT |
| Eighth | A*ITD |
| Ninth | NAO*INT |

### 10 - 19

| | |
|---|---|
| Tenth | T*ENTD |
| Eleventh | LEFNT |
| Twelfth | TWEFLT, TW*EFLT |
| Thirteenth | THRAO*ENT |
| Fourteenth | FRAO*ENT |
| Fifteenth | FAO*ENT |
| Sixteenth | SKAO*ENT |
| Seventeenth | SFAO*ENT |
| Eighteenth | YAO*ENT |
| Nineteenth | NAO*ENT |

### 20 - 29

| | |
|---|---|
| Twentieth | TW*INT |
| Twenty-first | TW*IRS |
| Twenty-second | TW*END |
| Twenty-third | TW*IRD |
| Twenty-fourth | TWO*URT |
| Twenty-fifth | TW*IFT |
| Twenty-sixth | TW*IKT |
| Twenty-seventh | TWEVNT |
| Twenty-eighth | TWA*ET |
| Twenty-ninth | TWA*ENT |

### 30 - 39

| | |
|---|---|
| Thirtieth | TH*IRTD |
| Thirty-first | THR*IRS |
| Thirty-second | THR*EKD |
| Thirty-third | THR*IRD |
| Thirty-fourth | THRO*URT |
| Thirty-fifth | THR*IFT |

Thirty-sixth ............................................................................. THR*IKT
Thirty-seventh ........................................................................ THREVNT
Thirty-eighth ........................................................................... THRA*ET
Thirty-ninth ............................................................................ THRA*ENT

## 40 - 49

Fortieth ................................................................................... FWO*URT
Forty-first ................................................................................. FW*IRS
Forty-second ........................................................... FWEND, FWREND
Forty-third ................................................................................ FWIRD
Forty-fourth ............................................................................. FWO*ERT
Forty-fifth ................................................................................. FW*IF
Forty-sixth ............................................................................... FW*IK
Forty-seventh .......................................................................... FWEVT
Forty-eighth ............................................................................. FWA*IT
Forty-ninth ............................................................ FWAO*INT, FW*INT

## 50 - 59

Fiftieth ..................................................................................... DW*IFT
Fifty-first ................................................................................. DW*IRS
Fifty-second ............................................................................ DW*END
Fifty-third ................................................................................ DW*IRD
Fifty-fourth .............................................................................. DWO*URT
Fifty-fifth ................................................................................. DW*FT
Fifty-sixth ................................................................................ DW*IX
Fifty-seventh ............................................................. DWEVN, DWEVNT
Fifty-eighth .............................................................................. DWA*ET
Fifty-ninth ............................................................................... DWAO*INT

## 60 - 69

Sixtieth .................................................................................... SKAO*ET
Sixty-first ................................................................................ SK*IRS
Sixty-second ........................................................... SK*EKD, SKWEKD
Sixty-third ............................................................................... SK*IRD
Sixty-fourth ............................................................................. SKO*ERT
Sixty-fifth ................................................................................ SKWIFT
Sixty-sixth ............................................................................... SK*IKT
Sixty-seventh ........................................................... SKEFNT, SKEVNT
Sixty-eighth ............................................................................. SKA*ET
Sixty-ninth ............................................................. SKAOINT, SKAO*INT

## 70 - 79

Seventieth ............................................................................... SF*IT
Seventy-first ............................................................................ SF*IRS
Seventy-second ....................................................................... SF*EKD
Seventy-third ........................................................................... SF*IRD
Seventy-fourth ......................................................................... SFO*URT
Seventy-fifth ............................................................. SF*IFT, SFAO*IFT
Seventy-sixth ........................................................................... SF*IKT
Seventy-seventh ...................................................................... SF*EFT
Seventy-eighth ......................................................................... SFA*ET
Seventy-ninth ........................................................................... SFAO*INT

## 80 - 89

Eightieth .................................................................................. YA*ET
Eighty-first ............................................................................... Y*IRS

Eighty-second ................................................................................................. Y*EK
Eighty-third ................................................................................................... Y*IRD
Eighty-fourth ................................................................................................ YO*URT
Eighty-fifth .................................................................................................. YAO*IFT
Eighty-sixth .................................................................................................. Y*IKT
Eighty-seventh ............................................................................................. YEVT
Eighty-eighth ............................................................................................... YO*IT
Eighty-ninth ................................................................................................. YA*ENT

**90 - 99**

Ninetieth ..................................................................................................... NWAO*IT
Ninety-first .................................................................................................. N*IRS
Ninety-second ............................................................................................. N*END
Ninety-third ................................................................................................. N*IRD
Ninety-fourth ............................................................................................... NO*ERT
Ninety-fifth .................................................................................................. NWIFT
Ninety-sixth ................................................................................................. NWIKT
Ninety-seventh ............................................................................................ NWEVT
Ninety-eighth .............................................................................................. NWA*IT
Ninety-ninth ............................................................................ NW*INT, NWAOINT

## NUMBERS (Roman numerals):
## I   II   III   IV ... X

| | |
|---|---|
| **STYLE:** | **Roman numerals, uppercase.** |
| | **Range: 1 through 10.** |
| **NUMBER BAR USED?** | **No** |
| **ENGLISH TRANSLATION:** | **Roman numerals** |

To construct this **two-stroke** number style, spell out the number in question, followed by the letter "R" (steno R–RBGS).

**Examples:**

| | |
|---|---|
| I | WUN/R–RBGS |
| II | TWO/R–RBGS |
| III | THRE/R–RBGS |
| IV | FOUR/R–RBGS |
| V | FAOIV/R–RBGS |
| VI | SIX/R–RBGS |
| VII | SEVN/R–RBGS |
| VIII | AIT/R–RBGS |
| IX | NAOIN/R–RBGS |
| X | TEN/R–RBGS |

To write **one-stroke** Roman numerals without using the number bar, where possible without creating conflicts, insert the letter "R" into the number in words.

**Examples:**

| | |
|---|---|
| I | WURN |
| II | TWRO |
| III | THR*ER |
| IV | FROUR |
| V | FAOIVR |

## NUMBERS (Roman numerals):
## I  II  III  IV  ...  CM

| | |
|---|---|
| **STYLE:** | **Roman numerals, uppercase.** |
| | **Range: 1 through 900.** |
| **NUMBER BAR USED?** | **Yes** |
| **ENGLISH TRANSLATION:** | **Roman numerals** |

*Associate R with "Roman."*

**1 - 9**

| | | |
|---|---|---|
| I | ( = 1 ) | 1–R |
| II | ( = 2 ) | 2–R |
| III | ( = 3 ) | 3–R |
| IV | ( = 4 ) | 4–R |
| V | ( = 5 ) | 5–R |
| VI | ( = 6 ) | R–6 |
| VII | ( = 7 ) | R–7 |
| VIII | ( = 8 ) | R–8 |
| IX | ( = 9 ) | R–9 |

**10 - 19**

| | | |
|---|---|---|
| X | ( = 10 ) | 10–R |
| XI | ( = 11 ) | 1–RU, 1–UR |
| XII | ( = 12 ) | 12–R |
| XIII | ( = 13 ) | 13–R |
| XIV | ( = 14 ) | 14–R |
| XV | ( = 15 ) | 15–R |
| XVI | ( = 16 ) | 1R–6, 1–6R |
| XVII | ( = 17 ) | 1R–7, 1–R7 |
| XVIII | ( = 18 ) | 1R–8, 1–R8 |
| XIX | ( = 19 ) | 1R–9, 1–R9 |

**20 - 29**

| | | |
|---|---|---|
| XX | ( = 20 ) | 20–R |
| XXI | ( = 21 ) | 12–ER, 2/1–R |
| XXII | ( = 22 ) | 2–UR, 2R–U |
| XXIII | ( = 23 ) | 23–R |
| XXIV | ( = 24 ) | 24–R |
| XXV | ( = 25 ) | 25–R |
| XXVI | ( = 26 ) | 2R–6, 2–R6 |
| XXVII | ( = 27 ) | 2R–7, 2–R7 |
| XXVIII | ( = 28 ) | 2R–8, 2–R8 |
| XXIX | ( = 29 ) | 2R–9, 2–R9 |

**30 - 39**

| | | |
|---|---|---|
| XXX | ( = 30 ) | 30–R |
| XXXI | ( = 31 ) | 13–ER, 3/1–R |
| XXXII | ( = 32 ) | 23–ER, 3/2–R |
| XXXIII | ( = 33 ) | 3–UR, 3R–U |
| XXXIV | ( = 34 ) | 34–R |
| XXXV | ( = 35 ) | 35–R |
| XXXVI | ( = 36 ) | 3R–6, 3–6R |
| XXXVII | ( = 37 ) | 3R–7, 3–R7 |
| XXXVIII | ( = 38 ) | 3R–8, 3–R8 |
| XXXIX | ( = 39 ) | 3R–9, 3–R9 |

**40 - 49**

| | | |
|---|---|---|
| XL | ( = 40 ) | 40–R |
| XLI | ( = 41 ) | 14–ER, 4/1–R |
| XLII | ( = 42 ) | 24–ER, 4/2–R |
| XLIII | ( = 43 ) | 34–ER, 4/3–R |
| XLIV | ( = 44 ) | 4–UR, 4R–U |
| XLV | ( = 45 ) | 45–R |
| XLVI | ( = 46 ) | 4–6R, 4–6R |
| XLVII | ( = 47 ) | 4–R7, 4–7R |
| XLVIII | ( = 48 ) | 4–R8, 4–8R |
| XLIX | ( = 49 ) | 4–R9, 4–9R |

**50 - 59**

| | | |
|---|---|---|
| L | ( = 50 ) | 50–R |
| LI | ( = 51 ) | 15–ER, 5/1–R |
| LII | ( = 52 ) | 25–ER, 5/2–R |
| LIII | ( = 53 ) | 35–ER, 5/3–R |
| LIV | ( = 54 ) | 45–ER, 5/4–R |
| LV | ( = 55 ) | 5–UR, R5–U |
| LVI | ( = 56 ) | 5R–6, 56–R |
| LVII | ( = 57 ) | 5R–7, 5–R7 |
| LVIII | ( = 58 ) | 5R–8, 5–R8 |
| LIX | ( = 59 ) | 5R–9, 5–R9 |

**60 - 69**

| | | |
|---|---|---|
| LX | ( = 60 ) | R0–E6, 6/0–R |
| LXI | ( = 61 ) | 1R–E6, 6/1–R |
| LXII | ( = 62 ) | 2R–E6, 6/2–R |
| LXIII | ( = 63 ) | 3R–36, 6/3–R |
| LXIV | ( = 64 ) | 4R–E6, 6/4–R |
| LXV | ( = 65 ) | 5R–E6, 6/5–R |
| LXVI | ( = 66 ) | R–U6, U6R |
| LXVII | ( = 67 ) | R–67 |
| LXVIII | ( = 68 ) | R–68 |
| LXIX | ( = 69 ) | R–69 |

**70 - 79**

| | | |
|---|---|---|
| LXX | ( = 70 ) | R0–E7, 0–ER7, 7/0–E |
| LXXI | ( = 71 ) | 1R–E7, 1–ER7, 7/1–R |
| LXXII | ( = 72 ) | 2R–E7, 7/2–R |
| LXXIII | ( = 73 ) | 3R–E7, 7/3–R |
| LXXIV | ( = 74 ) | 4R–E7, 4–ER7, 7/4–R |
| LXXV | ( = 75 ) | 5–ER7, 7/5–R |
| LXXVI | ( = 76 ) | R–E67, 7/R–6 |

LXXVII  *( = 77 )*..................................................................................................... R–U7, UR7
LXXVIII  *( = 78 )*.................................................................................................. R–78, –R78
LXXVIX  *( = 79 )*................................................................................................. R–79, –R79

## 80 - 89
LXXX    *( = 80 )*.................................................................................................. 0–ER8, 8/0–R
LXXXI   *( = 81 )*................................................................................................... 1–ER8, 8/1–R
LXXXII  *( = 82 )*................................................................................................... 2–ER8, 8/2–R
LXXXIII  *( = 83 )*.................................................................................................. 3–ER8, 8/3–R
LXXXIV  *( = 84 )*................................................................................................. 4–ER8, 8/4–R
LXXXV  *( = 85 )*.................................................................................................. 5–ER8, 8/5–R
LXXXVI  *( = 86 )*.............................................................................................. R–E68, 8/R–6
LXXXVII *( = 87 )*..................................................................................... R–E78, ER78, 8/–R7
LXXXVIII *( = 88 )*................................................................................................. R–U8, UR8
LXXXIX  *( = 89 )*................................................................................................ R–89, –R89

## 90 - 99
XC       *( = 90 )*.................................................................................................. 0–ER9, 9/0–R
XCI      *( = 91 )*................................................................................................... 1–ER9, 9/1–R
XCII     *( = 92 )*.................................................................................................. 2–ER9, 9/2–R
XCIII    *( = 93 )*................................................................................................. 3–ER9, 9/3–R
XCIV    *( = 94 )*................................................................................................. 4–ER9, 9/4–R
XCV     *( = 95 )*....................................................................................... 5–ER9, R5–E9, 9/5–R
XCVI    *( = 96 )*................................................................................................ R–E69, 9/R–6
XCVII   *( = 97 )*...................................................................................... R–E79, ER79, 9/R–7
XCVIII  *( = 98 )*.................................................................................... R–E89, ER89, 9/R–8
XCVIX  *( = 99 )*................................................................................................ R–U9, UR9, 9/R–9

## 100 - 900 multiples
C         *( = 100 )*.................................................................................................... 10–UR
CC       *( = 200 )*.................................................................................................... 20–UR
CCC     *( = 300 )*.................................................................................................... 30–UR
CD      *( = 400 )*.................................................................................................... 40–UR
D        *( = 500 )*.................................................................................................... 50–UR
DC      *( = 600 )*................................................................................................. R0–EU6
DCC    *( = 700 )*.................................................................................... 0–EUR7, R0–EU7
DCCC  *( = 800 )*.................................................................................... 0–EUR8, R0–EU8
CM     *( = 900 )*.................................................................................... 0–EUR9, R0–EU9

---

## US CURRENCY:
### $1  $2  $3  ...  $99

| | |
|---|---|
| **STYLE:** | **Figures, with attached "$" symbol.** |
| **NUMBER BAR USED?** | **No** |
| **ENGLISH TRANSLATION:** | **Figures** |

*Associate –D with "dollars."*

## IN NUMERICAL SEQUENCE

**$1 - $9 (___D)**

| | |
|---|---|
| $1 | WUND |
| $2 | TWOD |
| $3 | THR*ED |
| $4 | FOURD |
| $5 | FAOIVD |
| $6 | SIKD |
| $7 | SEVD |
| $8 | AITD |
| $9 | NAOIND |

**$10 - $19 (___D)**

| | |
|---|---|
| $10 | T*END |
| $11 | LEVD |
| $12 | TWEFLD |
| $13 | THRAOEND |
| $14 | FRAOEND |
| $15 | FAO*END |
| $16 | SKAOEND |
| $17 | SFAOEND |
| $18 | AO*END |
| $19 | NAOEND |

**$20 - $29 (TW___D)**

| | |
|---|---|
| $20 | TWID |
| $21 | TWUND |
| $22 | TWAOD |
| $23 | TWAO*ED |
| $24 | TWOERD |
| $25 | TWAOIVD |
| $26 | TWIKD |
| $27 | TWEVD |

$28 ................................................................................................................ TWAID
$29 ............................................................................................................. TWAEND

## $30 - $39 (THR___D)

$30 ................................................................................................................. THRID
$31 ............................................................................................................. THRUND
$32 ............................................................................................................. THRAOD
$33 ........................................................................................................... THRAOED
$34 ........................................................................................................... THROERD
$35 ......................................................................................................... THRAOIFD
$36 .............................................................................................................. THRIKD
$37 ............................................................................................................. THREVD
$38 ............................................................................................................... THRAID
$39 .......................................................................................................... THRAEND

## $40 - $49 (FR___D)

$40 ............................................................................................................... FR*ID
$41 .............................................................................................................. FRUND
$42 .............................................................................................................. FRAOD
$43 ........................................................................................................... FRAO*ED
$44 ............................................................................................................. FROERD
$45 .......................................................................................................... FRAOIVD
$46 ............................................................................................................... FRIKD
$47 .............................................................................................................. FREFD
$48 .............................................................................................................. FRA*ID
$49 ........................................................................................................... FRAEND

## $50 - $59 (V___D)

$50 ................................................................................................................... V*ID
$51 ............................................................................................................... V*UND
$52 .............................................................................................................. VAO*D
$53 .............................................................................................................. VAOED
$54 .............................................................................................................. VOERD
$55 ............................................................................................................. VAOIVD
$56 ................................................................................................................. VIKD
$57 ................................................................................................................ VEVD
$58 ............................................................................................................... VA*ID
$59 .............................................................................................................. VAEND

## $60 - $69 (SK___D)

$60 ................................................................................................................ SK*ID
$61 .............................................................................................................. SKUND
$62 .............................................................................................................. SKAOD
$63 ........................................................................................................... SKAO*ED
$64 ............................................................................................................ SKO*ERD
$65 .......................................................................................................... SKAOIVD
$66 ............................................................................................................... SKIKD
$67 .............................................................................................................. SKEFD
$68 .............................................................................................................. SKAID
$69 ........................................................................................................... SKAEND

## $70 - $79 (SF___D)

$70 ................................................................................................................. SFID
$71 ............................................................................................................... SFUND
$72 ............................................................................................................... SFAOD
$73 ............................................................................................................. SFAOED
$74 ............................................................................................................. SFOERD

$75 .................................................................................................. SFAOIVD
$76 .................................................................................................... SFIKD
$77 .................................................................................................... SFEVD
$78 ..................................................................................................... SFAID
$79 .................................................................................................. SFAEND

**$80 - $89** (Y___D)

$80 ...................................................................................................... Y*ID
$81 .................................................................................................... YUND
$82 .................................................................................................. YAO*D
$83 ................................................................................................. YAO*ED
$84 .................................................................................................. YOERD
$85 ................................................................................................ YAOIVD
$86 ..................................................................................................... YIKD
$87 ..................................................................................................... YEVD
$88 ...................................................................................................... YAID
$89 .................................................................................................. YAEND

**$90 - $99** (N___D)

$90 ....................................................................................... NAOID, NID
$91 ................................................................................................... NUND
$92 .................................................................................................... NAOD
$93 ..................................................................... NAO*ERD, NYAO*ED
$94 .................................................................................................. NOERD
$95 ................................................................................................ NAOIVD
$96 ..................................................................................................... NIKD
$97 .................................................................................................... NEFD
$98 ...................................................................................................... NAID
$99 .................................................................................................. NAEND

## ARRANGED BY COMMON ENGLISH/STENO SUFFIX ($13 - $99)

*This arrangement organizes the numbers by
suffix for easy learning and practice.*

**$ -teen** = –AOEND

$13 ............................................................................................ THRAOEND
$14 ............................................................................................. FRAOEND
$15 ............................................................................................. FAO*END
$16 ............................................................................................. SKAOEND
$17 ............................................................................................. SFAOEND
$18 ................................................................................................ AO*END
$19 .............................................................................................. NAOEND

**$ -ty** = –ID

$20 .................................................................................................. TWID
$30 ................................................................................................. THRID
$40 ................................................................................................... FR*ID
$50 ..................................................................................................... V*ID
$60 ................................................................................................... SK*ID

$70 ............................................................................................ SFID
$80 ............................................................................................ Y*ID
$90 .................................................................................. NAOID, NID

**$ -ty-one = –UND**

$21 .......................................................................................... TWUND
$31 ....................................................................................... THRUND
$41 ......................................................................................... FRUND
$51 .......................................................................................... V*UND
$61 ......................................................................................... SKUND
$71 ......................................................................................... SFUND
$81 ............................................................................................ YUND
$91 ........................................................................................... NUND

**$ -ty-two = –AOD**

$22 ......................................................................................... TWAOD
$32 ...................................................................................... THRAOD
$42 ........................................................................................ FRAOD
$52 ......................................................................................... VAO*D
$62 ........................................................................................ SKAOD
$72 ......................................................................................... SFAOD
$82 ......................................................................................... YAO*D
$92 .......................................................................................... NAOD

**$ -ty-three = –AOED**

$23 ..................................................................................... TWAO*ED
$33 ..................................................................................... THRAOED
$43 ...................................................................................... FRAO*ED
$53 ........................................................................................ VAOED
$63 ...................................................................................... SKAO*ED
$73 ....................................................................................... SFAOED
$83 ........................................................................................ YAO*ED
$93 ............................................................ NAO*ERD, NYAO*ED

**$ ty-four = –OERD**

$24 ...................................................................................... TWOERD
$34 ..................................................................................... THROERD
$44 ....................................................................................... FROERD
$54 .......................................................................................... VOERD
$64 ....................................................................................... SKO*ERD
$74 ........................................................................................ SFOERD
$84 .......................................................................................... YOERD
$94 .......................................................................................... NOERD

**$ ty-five = –AOIVD**

$25 ..................................................................................... TWAOIVD
$35 .................................................................................. THRAOIFD
$45 ...................................................................................... FRAOIVD
$55 ........................................................................................ VAOIVD
$65 ...................................................................................... SKAOIVD
$75 ....................................................................................... SFAOIVD
$85 ........................................................................................ YAOIVD
$95 ....................................................................................... NAOIVD

**$ ty-six = –IKD**

$26 ......................................................................................... TWIKD
$36 ...................................................................................... THRIKD
$46 ......................................................................................... FRIKD

$56 ............................................................................................. VIKD
$66 .......................................................................................... SKIKD
$76 ........................................................................................... SFIKD
$86 ............................................................................................. YIKD
$96 .............................................................................................NIKD

**$ ty-seven** = –EVD

$27 ....................................................................................... TWEVD
$37 ...................................................................................... THREVD
$47 ......................................................................................... FREFD
$57 ........................................................................................ . VEVD
$67 ....................................................................................... SKEFD
$77 ......................................................................................... SFEVD
$87 ........................................................................................ YEVD
$97 ....................................................................................... NEFD

**$ ty-eight** = –AID

$28 ......................................................................................... TWAID
$38 ....................................................................................... THRAID
$48 ......................................................................................... FRA*ID
$58 ........................................................................................ VA*ID
$68 ......................................................................................... SKAID
$78 .......................................................................................... SFAID
$88 .......................................................................................... . YAID
$98 ...........................................................................................NAID

**$ ty-nine** = –AEND

$29 ..................................................................................... TWAEND
$39 .................................................................................... THRAEND
$49 ...................................................................................... FRAEND
$59 ........................................................................................ VAEND
$69 ........................................................................................ SKAEND
$79 ........................................................................................ SFAEND
$89 ......................................................................................... YAEND
$99 ........................................................................................ NAEND

## US CURRENCY:
### $1  $2  $3  etc.

| | |
|---|---|
| **STYLE:** | **Figures, with attached "$" symbol.** |
| **NUMBER BAR USED?** | **Yes** |
| **ENGLISH TRANSLATION:** | **Figures** |

*Associate –D with "dollars."*
*Some CAT programs include a predefined*
*command to insert a $ sign before a number.*

### $1 - $9

| | |
|---|---|
| $1 | 1–D |
| $2 | 2–D |
| $3 | 3–D |
| $4 | 4–D |
| $5 | 5–D |
| $6 | 6D |
| $7 | 7D |
| $8 | 8D |
| $9 | 9D |

### $10 - $19

| | |
|---|---|
| $10 | 10–D |
| $11 | 1–UD |
| $12 | 12–D |
| $13 | 13–D |
| $14 | 14–D |
| $15 | 15–D |
| $16 | 1–6D |
| $17 | 1–7D |
| $18 | 1–8D |
| $19 | 1–9D |

### $20 - $29

| | |
|---|---|
| $20 | 20–D |
| $21 | 12–ED, 2/1–D |
| $22 | 2–UD |
| $23 | 23–D |
| $24 | 24–D |
| $25 | 25–D |
| $26 | 2–6D |
| $27 | 2–7D |
| $28 | 2–8D |
| $29 | 2–9D |

## $30 - $39

| | |
|---|---|
| $30 | 30–D |
| $31 | 13–ED, 3/1–D |
| $32 | 23–ED, 3/2–D |
| $33 | 3–UD |
| $34 | 34–D |
| $35 | 35–D |
| $36 | 3–6D |
| $37 | 3–7D |
| $38 | 3–8D |
| $39 | 3–9D |

## $40 - $49

| | |
|---|---|
| $40 | 40–D |
| $41 | 14–ED, 4/1–D |
| $42 | 24–ED, 4/2–D |
| $43 | 34–ED, 4/3–D |
| $44 | 4–UD |
| $45 | 45–D |
| $46 | 4–6D |
| $47 | 4–7D |
| $48 | 4–8D |
| $49 | 4–9D |

## $50 - $59

| | |
|---|---|
| $50 | 50–D |
| $51 | 15–ED, 5/1–D |
| $52 | 25–ED, 5/2–D |
| $53 | 35–ED, 5/3–D |
| $54 | 45–ED, 5/4–D |
| $55 | 5–UD |
| $56 | 5–6D |
| $57 | 5–7D |
| $58 | 5–8D |
| $59 | 5–9D |

## $60 - $69

| | |
|---|---|
| $60 | 0–E6D, 6/0–D |
| $61 | 1–E6D, 6/1–D |
| $62 | 2–E6D, 6/2–D |
| $63 | 3–E6D, 6/3–D |
| $64 | 4–E6D, 6/4–D |
| $65 | 5–E6D, 6/5–D |
| $66 | U6D |
| $67 | 67D |
| $68 | 68D |
| $69 | 69D |

## $70 - $79

| | |
|---|---|
| $70 | 0–E7D, 7/0–D |
| $71 | 1–E7D, 7/1–D |
| $72 | 2–E7D, 7/2–D |
| $73 | 3–E7D, 7/3–D |
| $74 | 4–E7D, 7/4–D |
| $75 | 5–E7D, 7/5–D |
| $76 | E67D, 7/6D |

$77 ........................................................................................................................ U7D
$78 ........................................................................................................................ 78D
$79 ........................................................................................................................ 79D

**$80 - $89**
$80 ..................................................................................................... 0–E8D, 8/0–D
$81 ..................................................................................................... 1–E8D, 8/1–D
$82 ..................................................................................................... 2–E8D, 8/2–D
$83 ..................................................................................................... 3–E8D, 8/3–D
$84 ..................................................................................................... 4–E8D, 8/4–D
$85 ..................................................................................................... 5–E8D, 8/5–D
$86 ........................................................................................... E68D, 8/6D
$87 ........................................................................................... E78D, 8/7D
$88 ........................................................................................................ U8D
$89 ........................................................................................................ 89D

**$90 - $99**
$90 ..................................................................................................... 0–E9D, 9/0–D
$91 ..................................................................................................... 1–E9D, 9/1–D
$92 ..................................................................................................... 2–E9D, 9/2–D
$93 ..................................................................................................... 3–E9D, 9/3–D
$94 ..................................................................................................... 4–E9D, 9/4–D
$95 ..................................................................................................... 5–E9D, 9/5–D
$96 ........................................................................................... E69D, 9/6D
$97 ........................................................................................... E79D, 9/7D
$98 ........................................................................................... E89D, 9/8D
$99 ........................................................................................................ U9D

**$100 - $950** (in $50 increments)
$100 ................................................................................................... 10–UD
$150 ................................................................................................. 150–D

$200 ................................................................................................... 20–UD
$250 ................................................................................................. 250–D

$300 ................................................................................................... 30–UD
$350 ................................................................................................. 350–D

$400 ................................................................................................... 40–UD
$450 ................................................................................................. 450–D

$500 ................................................................................................... 50–UD
$550 ................................................................................................. 5/50–D

$600 ..................................................................................... 0–EU6D, 6/0–UD
$650 ................................................................................................. 6/50–D

$700 ..................................................................................... 0–EU7D, 7/0–UD
$750 ................................................................................................. 7/50–D

$800 ..................................................................................... 0–EU8D, 8/0–UD
$850 ................................................................................................. 8/50–D

$900 ..................................................................................... 0–EU9D, 9/0–UD
$950 ................................................................................................. 9/50–D

## US CURRENCY:
### $1,000　$2,000　$3,000 ... $99,000

| STYLE: | Figures in exact thousands, with attached "$" symbol. |
| --- | --- |
| NUMBER BAR USED? | No |
| ENGLISH TRANSLATION: | Figures |

*Associate THOUD with "thousand dollars."*

**$1,000 - $9,000**

| | |
| --- | --- |
| $1,000 | WUN/THOUD |
| $2,000 | TWO/THOUD |
| $3,000 | THRE/THOUD |
| $4,000 | FOUR/THOUD |
| $5,000 | FAOIV/THOUD |
| $6,000 | SIX/THOUD |
| $7,000 | SEV/THOUD |
| $8,000 | AIT/THOUD |
| $9,000 | NAOIN/THOUD |

**$10,000 - $19,000**

| | |
| --- | --- |
| $10,000 | TEN/THOUD |
| $11,000 | LEV/THOUD |
| $12,000 | TWEL/THOUD |
| $13,000 | THRAOEN/THOUD |
| $14,000 | FRAOEN/THOUD |
| $15,000 | FAOEN/THOUD |
| $16,000 | SKAOEN/THOUD |
| $17,000 | SFAOEN/THOUD |
| $18,000 | AOEN/THOUD |
| $19,000 | NAOEN/THOUD |

**$20,000 - $29,000**

| | |
| --- | --- |
| $20,000 | TWI/THOUD |
| $21,000 | TWUN/THOUD |
| $22,000 | TWAO/THOUD |
| $23,000 | TWAOE/THOUD |
| $24,000 | TWOER/THOUD |
| $25,000 | TWAOIV/THOUD |
| $26,000 | TWIK/THOUD |
| $27,000 | TWEV/THOUD |
| $28,000 | TWAI/THOUD |
| $29,000 | TWAEN/THOUD |

## $30,000 - $39,000

$30,000 ............................................................................ THRI/THOUD
$31,000 ........................................................................ THRUN/THOUD
$32,000 ........................................................................ THRAO/THOUD
$33,000 ..................................................................... THRAOE/THOUD
$34,000 ...................................................................... THROER/THOUD
$35,000 ..................................................................... THRAOIF/THOUD
$36,000 ........................................................................ THRIK/THOUD
$37,000 ....................................................................... THREV/THOUD
$38,000 ........................................................................ THRAI/THOUD
$39,000 ...................................................................... THRAEN/THOUD

## $40,000 - $49,000

$40,000 .............................................................................. FRI/THOUD
$41,000 .......................................................................... FRUN/THOUD
$42,000 ........................................................................... FRAO/THOUD
$43,000 ........................................................................ FRAOE/THOUD
$44,000 .......................................................................... FROER/THOUD
$45,000 ......................................................................... FRAOIV/THOUD
$46,000 ............................................................................ FRIK/THOUD
$47,000 ............................................................................ FREV/THOUD
$48,000 ............................................................................ FRAI/THOUD
$49,000 ......................................................................... FRAEN/THOUD

## $50,000 - $59,000

$50,000 ............................................................................... VI/THOUD
$51,000 ............................................................................ VUN/THOUD
$52,000 ............................................................................ VAO/THOUD
$53,000 .......................................................................... VAOE/THOUD
$54,000 ........................................................................... VOER/THOUD
$55,000 .......................................................................... VAOIV/THOUD
$56,000 ............................................................................. VIK/THOUD
$57,000 ............................................................................ VEV/THOUD
$58,000 ............................................................................. VAI/THOUD
$59,000 .......................................................................... VAEN/THOUD

## $60,000 - $69,000

$60,000 ............................................................................. SKI/THOUD
$61,000 ......................................................................... SKUN/THOUD
$62,000 ......................................................................... SKAO/THOUD
$63,000 ....................................................................... SKAOE/THOUD
$64,000 ........................................................................ SKOER/THOUD
$65,000 ....................................................................... SKAOIV/THOUD
$66,000 .......................................................................... SKIK/THOUD
$67,000 ......................................................................... SKEV/THOUD
$68,000 .......................................................................... SKAI/THOUD
$69,000 ....................................................................... SKAEN/THOUD

## $70,000 - $79,000

$70,000 ............................................................................. SFI/THOUD
$71,000 ......................................................................... SFUN/THOUD
$72,000 ......................................................................... SFAO/THOUD
$73,000 ....................................................................... SFAOE/THOUD
$74,000 ........................................................................ SFOER/THOUD
$75,000 ....................................................................... SFAOIV/THOUD
$76,000 .......................................................................... SFIK/THOUD

$77,000 ............................................................................................ SFEV/THOUD
$78,000 ............................................................................................. SFAI/THOUD
$79,000 .......................................................................................... SFAEN/THOUD

**$80,000 - $89,000**

$80,000 ................................................................................................. YI/THOUD
$81,000 ............................................................................................ YUN/THOUD
$82,000 ............................................................................................ YAO/THOUD
$83,000 .......................................................................................... YAOE/THOUD
$84,000 .......................................................................................... YOER/THOUD
$85,000 ......................................................................................... YAOIV/THOUD
$86,000 ............................................................................................. YIK/THOUD
$87,000 ............................................................................................ YEV/THOUD
$88,000 ............................................................................................. YAI/THOUD
$89,000 .......................................................................................... YAEN/THOUD

**$90,000 - $99,000**

$90,000 ......................................................................................... NAOI/THOUD
$91,000 ............................................................................................ NUN/THOUD
$92,000 ............................................................................................ NAO/THOUD
$93,000 .......................................................................................... NAOE/THOUD
$94,000 .......................................................................................... NOER/THOUD
$95,000 ......................................................................................... NAOIV/THOUD
$96,000 ............................................................................................. NIK/THOUD
$97,000 ............................................................................................. NEF/THOUD
$98,000 ............................................................................................. NAI/THOUD
$99,000 .......................................................................................... NAEN/THOUD

## US CURRENCY:
### $1,000  $2,000  $3,000  etc.

---

**STYLE:**                           **Figures in thousands, with attached "$" symbol.**

**NUMBER BAR USED?**       **Yes**

**ENGLISH TRANSLATION:**     **Figures**

**NOTE: This format uses 0–EUD to (a) place a dollar sign at the front of the number and (b) add the ",000" ending.**

---

### $1,000 - $9,000

| | |
|---|---|
| $1,000 | 10–EUD |
| $2,000 | 20–EUD |
| $3,000 | 30–EUD |
| $4,000 | 40–EUD |
| $5,000 | 50–EUD |
| $6,000 | 0*EU6D, 6/0–EUD |
| $7,000 | 0*EU7D, 7/0–EUD |
| $8,000 | 0*EU8D, 8/0–EUD |
| $9,000 | 0*EU9D, 9/0–EUD |

### $10,000 - $19,000

| | |
|---|---|
| $10,000 | 10/0–EUD |
| $11,000 | 1–U/0–EUD |
| $12,000 | 12/0–EUD |
| $13,000 | 13/0–EUD |
| $14,000 | 14/0–EUD |
| $15,000 | 15/0–EUD |
| $16,000 | 16/0–EUD |
| $17,000 | 17/0–EUD |
| $18,000 | 18/0–EUD |
| $19,000 | 19/0–EUD |

### $20,000 - $100,000 (examples)

| | |
|---|---|
| $20,000 | 20/0–EUD |
| $30,000 | 30/0–EUD |
| $40,000 | 40/0–EUD |
| $50,000 | 50/0–EUD |
| $60,000 | 0–E6/0–EUD |
| $70,000 | 0–E7/0–EUD |
| $80,000 | 0–E8/0–EUD |
| $90,000 | 0–E9/0–EUD |
| $100,000 | 10–U/0–EUD |

---

## US CURRENCY:
### one thousand dollars ... ninety-nine thousand dollars

| | |
|---|---|
| **STYLE:** | **Numbers in words, followed by** *"thousand dollars."* |
| **NUMBER BAR USED?** | **No** |
| **ENGLISH TRANSLATION:** | **Words** |

*Associate THOUD with
"thousand dollars."*

**$1,000 - $9,000**

| | |
|---|---|
| one thousand dollars | W*UN/THOUD |
| two thousand dollars | TWO*/THOUD |
| three thousand dollars | THR*E/THOUD |
| four thousand dollars | FO*UR/THOUD |
| five thousand dollars | FAOIF/THOUD |
| six thousand dollars | SWIX/THOUD |
| seven thousand dollars | SEV/THOUD |
| eight thousand dollars | YAIT/THOUD |
| nine thousand dollars | NAO*IN/THOUD |

**$10,000 - $19,000**

| | |
|---|---|
| ten thousand dollars | T*EN/THOUD |
| eleven thousand dollars | LEVN/THOUD |
| twelve thousand dollars | TWEFL/THOUD |
| thirteen thousand dollars | THRAO*EN/THOUD |
| fourteen thousand dollars | FRAO*EN/THOUD |
| fifteen thousand dollars | FAO*EN/THOUD |
| sixteen thousand dollars | SKAO*EN/THOUD |
| seventeen thousand dollars | SFAO*EN/THOUD |
| eighteen thousand dollars | YAO*EN/THOUD |
| nineteen thousand dollars | NAO*EN/THOUD |

**$20,000 - $29,000**

| | |
|---|---|
| twenty thousand dollars | TW*I/THOUD, TWENT/THOUD |
| twenty-one thousand dollars | TW*UN/THOUD |
| twenty-two thousand dollars | TWAO*/THOUD |
| twenty-three thousand dollars | TWAO*E/THOUD |
| twenty-four thousand dollars | TWO*ER/THOUD |
| twenty-five thousand dollars | TWAOIF/THOUD |
| twenty-six thousand dollars | TW*IK/THOUD |
| twenty-seven thousand dollars | TWEF/THOUD |
| twenty-eight thousand dollars | TWA*I/THOUD |
| twenty-nine thousand dollars | TWA*EN/THOUD |

## $30,000 - $39,000

thirty thousand dollars ............................................... THR*I/THOUD, THIRT/THOUD
thirty-one thousand dollars ................................................................. THR*UN/THOUD
thirty-two thousand dollars ................................................................. THRAO*/THOUD
thirty-three thousand dollars ........................................................... THRAO*E/THOUD
thirty-four thousand dollars .............................................................. THRO*ER/THOUD
thirty-five thousand dollars ............................................................. THRAOIFT/THOUD
thirty-six thousand dollars .................................................................. THR*IK/THOUD
thirty-seven thousand dollars ............................................................. THREF/THOUD
thirty-eight thousand dollars .............................................................. THRA*I/THOUD
thirty-nine thousand dollars ........................................................... THRA*EN/THOUD

## $40,000 - $49,000

forty thousand dollars ................................................. FR*I/THOUD, FOURT/THOUD
forty-one thousand dollars .................................................................. FR*UN/THOUD
forty-two thousand dollars ................................................................. FRAO*/THOUD
forty-three thousand dollars .............................................................. FRAO*E/THOUD
forty-four thousand dollars ................................................................ FRO*ER/THOUD
forty-five thousand dollars ................................................................ FRAOIF/THOUD
forty-six thousand dollars ..................................................................... FR*IK/THOUD
forty-seven thousand dollars ................................................................. FREF/THOUD
forty-eight thousand dollars ............................................................... FRA*IT/THOUD
forty-nine thousand dollars ................................................................ FRA*EN/THOUD

## $50,000 - $59,000

fifty thousand dollars ........................................................................... FIFT/THOUD
fifty-one thousand dollars ..................................................................... V*UN/THOUD
fifty-two thousand dollars ..................................................................... VAO*/THOUD
fifty-three thousand dollars .................................................................. VAO*E/THOUD
fifty-four thousand dollars .................................................................... VO*ER/THOUD
fifty-five thousand dollars ................................................................... VAOIVT/THOUD
fifty-six thousand dollars ........................................................................ V*IK/THOUD
fifty-seven thousand dollars .................................................................. VEVN/THOUD
fifty-eight thousand dollars ..................................................................... VA*I/THOUD
fifty-nine thousand dollars ................................................................... VAO*IN/THOUD

## $60,000 - $69,000

sixty thousand dollars ..................................................... SK*I/THOUD, SIKT/THOUD
sixty-one thousand dollars .................................................................. SK*UN/THOUD
sixty-two thousand dollars ................................................................. SKAO*/THOUD
sixty-three thousand dollars ............................................................ SKWAO*E/THOUD
sixty-four thousand dollars ................................................................. SKO*R/THOUD
sixty-five thousand dollars .............................................................. SKWAOIV/THOUD
sixty-six thousand dollars ................................................................. SKWIK/THOUD
sixty-seven thousand dollars ................................................................ SKEF/THOUD
sixty-eight thousand dollars ................................................................ SKA*I/THOUD
sixty-nine thousand dollars ............................................................... SKA*IN/THOUD

## $70,000 - $79,000

seventy thousand dollars ................................................ SF*I/THOUD, SEVT/THOUD
seventy-one thousand dollars ............................................................. SF*UN/THOUD
seventy-two thousand dollars ............................................................. SFAO*/THOUD
seventy-three thousand dollars .......................................................... SFAO*E/THOUD
seventy-four thousand dollars ............................................................ SFO*ER/THOUD
seventy-five thousand dollars ........................................................... SFAOIF/THOUD
seventy-six thousand dollars ............................................................... SF*IK/THOUD

---

seventy-seven thousand dollars ........................................................... SFEF/THOUD
seventy-eight thousand dollars ............................................................ SFA*I/THOUD
seventy-nine thousand dollars ......................................................... SFA*EN/THOUD

## $80,000 - $89,000

eighty thousand dollars ................................................. Y–/THOUD, AOIGT/THOUD
eighty-one thousand dollars ................................................................. Y*UNT/THOUD
eighty-two thousand dollars ................................................................ YAO*T/THOUD
eighty-three thousand dollars ............................................................. YAO*E/THOUD
eighty-four thousand dollars .............................................................. YOERT/THOUD
eighty-five thousand dollars ................................................................ YAOIF/THOUD
eighty-six thousand dollars ..................................................................... Y*IK/THOUD
eighty-seven thousand dollars ................................................................ YEF/THOUD
eighty-eight thousand dollars ................................................................ YA*I/THOUD
eighty-nine thousand dollars ............................................................. YA*EN/THOUD

## $90,000 - $99,000

ninety thousand dollars ................................................................ NAOINT/THOUD
ninety-one thousand dollars ................................................................ NWUN/THOUD
ninety-two thousand dollars ................................................................. NWAO/THOUD
ninety-three thousand dollars ............................................................ NWAOE/THOUD
ninety-four thousand dollars ................................. NWOER/THOUD, NO*ER/THOUD
ninety-five thousand dollars .............................................................. NWAOIV/THOUD
ninety-six thousand dollars ..................................................................... NWIK/THOUD
ninety-seven thousand dollars ............................................................. NWEF/THOUD
ninety-eight thousand dollars .............................................................. NWAI/THOUD
ninety-nine thousand dollars ................................. NWAEN/THOUD, NA*EN/THOUD

## US CURRENCY:
**one-thousand-dollar ... ninety-nine-thousand-dollar**

| STYLE: | Words, with attached *"-thousand-dollar."* |
|---|---|
| NUMBER BAR USED? | No |
| ENGLISH TRANSLATION: | Words |

*Associate THO\*UD with "-thousand-dollar."*
*This style is used when the $-sum is an*
*adjective preceeding a noun.*
*(Example: "A ten-thousand-dollar car.")*
*Note that this list incorporates steno from*
*both of the Plain Numbers lists given previously*
*and provides the steno that uses fewer asterisks.*

**$1,000 - $9,000**

| | |
|---|---|
| one-thousand-dollar | WUN/THO*UD |
| two-thousand-dollar | TWO/THO*UD |
| three-thousand-dollar | THRE/THO*UD |
| four-thousand-dollar | FOUR/THO*UD |
| five-thousand-dollar | FAOIV/THO*UD |
| six-thousand-dollar | SIX/THO*UD |
| seven-thousand-dollar | SEV/THO*UD |
| eight-thousand-dollar | AIT/THO*UD |
| nine-thousand-dollar | NAOIN/THO*UD |

**$10,000 - $19,000**

| | |
|---|---|
| ten-thousand-dollar | TEN/THO*UD |
| eleven-thousand-dollar | LEV/THO*UD |
| twelve-thousand-dollar | TWEL/THO*UD, TWEFL/THO*UD |
| thirteen-thousand-dollar | THRAOEN/THO*UD |
| fourteen-thousand-dollar | FRAOEN/THO*UD |
| fifteen-thousand-dollar | FAOEN/THO*UD |
| sixteen-thousand-dollar | SKAOEN/THO*UD |
| seventeen-thousand-dollar | SFAOEN/THO*UD |
| eighteen-thousand-dollar | AOEN/THO*UD |
| nineteen-thousand-dollar | NAOEN/THO*UD |

**$20,000 - $29,000**

| | |
|---|---|
| twenty-thousand-dollar | TWI/THO*UD |
| twenty-one-thousand-dollar | TWUN/THO*UD |
| twenty-two-thousand-dollar | TWAO/THO*UD |
| twenty-three-thousand-dollar | TWAOE/THO*UD |
| twenty-four-thousand-dollar | TWOER/THO*UD |
| twenty-five-thousand-dollar | TWAOIV/THO*UD |

twenty-six-thousand-dollar ............................................................ TWIK/THO*UD
twenty-seven-thousand-dollar ...................................................... TWEV/THO*UD
twenty-eight-thousand-dollar ........................................................ TWAI/THO*UD
twenty-nine-thousand-dollar ....................................................... TWAEN/THO*UD

**$30,000 - $39,000**
thirty-thousand-dollar ................................................................... THRI/THO*UD
thirty-one-thousand-dollar .......................................................... THRUN/THO*UD
thirty-two-thousand-dollar ............................................................ THRAO/THO*UD
thirty-three-thousand-dollar ....................................................... THRAOE/THO*UD
thirty-four-thousand-dollar ........................................................... THROER/THO*UD
thirty-five-thousand-dollar ........................................................ THRAOIF/THO*UD
thirty-six-thousand-dollar .............................................................. THRIK/THO*UD
thirty-seven-thousand-dollar ........................................................ THREV/THO*UD
thirty-eight-thousand-dollar .......................................................... THRAI/THO*UD
thirty-nine-thousand-dollar ......................................................... THRAEN/THO*UD

**$40,000 - $49,000**
forty-thousand-dollar ...................................................................... FRI/THO*UD
forty-one-thousand-dollar .............................................................. FRUN/THO*UD
forty-two-thousand-dollar ............................................................... FRAO/THO*UD
forty-three-thousand-dollar ........................................................... FRAOE/THO*UD
forty-four-thousand-dollar .............................................................. FROER/THO*UD
forty-five-thousand-dollar ............................................................. FRAOIV/THO*UD
forty-six-thousand-dollar ................................................................. FRIK/THO*UD
forty-seven-thousand-dollar ............................................................ FREV/THO*UD
forty-eight-thousand-dollar ............................................................. FRAI/THO*UD
forty-nine-thousand-dollar ............................................................. FRAEN/THO*UD

**$50,000 - $59,000**
fifty-thousand-dollar ......................................................................... VI/THO*UD
fifty-one-thousand-dollar ................................................................. VUN/THO*UD
fifty-two-thousand-dollar .................................................................. VAO/THO*UD
fifty-three-thousand-dollar ............................................................... VAOE/THO*UD
fifty-four-thousand-dollar ................................................................. VOER/THO*UD
fifty-five-thousand-dollar ................................................................ VAOIV/THO*UD
fifty-six-thousand-dollar .................................................................... VIK/THO*UD
fifty-seven-thousand-dollar ............................................................... VEV/THO*UD
fifty-eight-thousand-dollar ................................................................. VAI/THO*UD
fifty-nine-thousand-dollar ................................................................ VAEN/THO*UD

**$60,000 - $69,000**
sixty-thousand-dollar ...................................................................... SKI/THO*UD
sixty-one-thousand-dollar .............................................................. SKUN/THO*UD
sixty-two-thousand-dollar ............................................................... SKAO/THO*UD
sixty-three-thousand-dollar ........................................................... SKAOE/THO*UD
sixty-four-thousand-dollar .............................................................. SKOER/THO*UD
sixty-five-thousand-dollar ............................................................. SKAOIV/THO*UD
sixty-six-thousand-dollar ................................................................. SKIK/THO*UD
sixty-seven-thousand-dollar ............................................................ SKEV/THO*UD
sixty-eight-thousand-dollar ............................................................. SKAI/THO*UD
sixty-nine-thousand-dollar ............................................................. SKAEN/THO*UD

**$70,000 - $79,000**
seventy-thousand-dollar .................................................................. SFI/THO*UD
seventy-one-thousand-dollar .......................................................... SFUN/THO*UD
seventy-two-thousand-dollar ........................................................... SFAO/THO*UD

seventy-three-thousand-dollar ....................................................... SFAOE/THO*UD
seventy-four-thousand-dollar ......................................................... SFOER/THO*UD
seventy-five-thousand-dollar .......................................................... SFAOIV/THO*UD
seventy-six-thousand-dollar ................................................................ SFIK/THO*UD
seventy-seven-thousand-dollar ....................................................... SFEV/THO*UD
seventy-eight-thousand-dollar ......................................................... SFAI/THO*UD
seventy-nine-thousand-dollar ........................................................ SFAEN/THO*UD

**$80,000 - $89,000**
eighty-thousand-dollar ........................................................................... YI/THO*UD
eighty-one-thousand-dollar ................................................................ YUN/THO*UD
eighty-two-thousand-dollar ................................................................. YAO/THO*UD
eighty-three-thousand-dollar .......................................................... YAOE/THO*UD
eighty-four-thousand-dollar ............................................................. YOER/THO*UD
eighty-five-thousand-dollar .............................................................. YAOIV/THO*UD
eighty-six-thousand-dollar .................................................................... YIK/THO*UD
eighty-seven-thousand-dollar ............................................................. YEV/THO*UD
eighty-eight-thousand-dollar ................................................................ YAI/THO*UD
eighty-nine-thousand-dollar ............................................................. YAEN/THO*UD

**$90,000 - $99,000**
ninety-thousand-dollar .................................................................... NAOI/THO*UD
ninety-one-thousand-dollar .............................................................. NUN/THO*UD
ninety-two-thousand-dollar ............................................................... NAO/THO*UD
ninety-three-thousand-dollar ........................................................... NAOE/THO*UD
ninety-four-thousand-dollar ............................................................. NOER/THO*UD
ninety-five-thousand-dollar ............................................................. NAOIV/THO*UD
ninety-six-thousand-dollar ................................................................... NIK/THO*UD
ninety-seven-thousand-dollar ............................................................. NEF/THO*UD
ninety-eight-thousand-dollar ............................................................... NAI/THO*UD
ninety-nine-thousand-dollar ............................................................ NAEN/THO*UD

## US CURRENCY:
### 1 cent   2 cents   3 cents  ...  9 cents

| | |
|---|---|
| **STYLE:** | **Figures, followed by** *"cents"* |
| **NUMBER BAR USED?** | **No** |
| **ENGLISH TRANSLATION:** | **Figures** |

**NOTE: To extend this system, use the number format given on pages 3-18 to 3-20.**

1 cent ......................................................................................................... W*UN/KRENT
2 cents ...................................................................................................... TWO*/KRENTS
3 cents ....................................................................................................... THR*E/KRENTS
4 cents ...................................................................................................... FO*UR/KRENTS
5 cents ....................................................................................................... FAOIF/KRENTS
6 cents ......................................................................................................... SWIX/KRENTS
7 cents ........................................................................................................... SEV/KRENTS
8 cents ........................................................................................................... YAIT/KRENTS
9 cents ....................................................................................................... NAO*IN/KRENTS

## US CURRENCY:
### 1 cent   2 cents   3 cents  ...  99 cents

| | |
|---|---|
| **STYLE:** | **Figures, followed by** *"cents."* |
| **NUMBER BAR USED?** | **Yes** |
| **ENGLISH TRANSLATION:** | **Figures** |

*Associate –SZ with "cents."*

**1 cent - 9 cents**

| | |
|---|---|
| 1 cent | 1–SZ |
| 2 cents | 2–SZ |
| 3 cents | 3–SZ |
| 4 cents | 4–SZ |
| 5 cents | 5–SZ |
| 6 cents | 6SZ |
| 7 cents | 7SZ |
| 8 cents | 8SZ |
| 9 cents | 9SZ |

**10 cents - 19 cents**

| | |
|---|---|
| 10 cents | 10–SZ |
| 11 cents | 1–USZ |
| 12 cents | 12–SZ |
| 13 cents | 13–SZ |
| 14 cents | 14–SZ |
| 15 cents | 15–SZ |
| 16 cents | 1–6SZ |
| 17 cents | 1–7SZ |
| 18 cents | 1–8SZ |
| 19 cents | 1–9SZ |

**20 cents - 29 cents**

| | |
|---|---|
| 20 cents | 20–SZ |
| 21 cents | 12–ESZ, 2/1–SZ |
| 22 cents | 2–USZ |
| 23 cents | 23–SZ |
| 24 cents | 24–SZ |
| 25 cents | 25–SZ |
| 26 cents | 2–6SZ |
| 27 cents | 2–7SZ |
| 28 cents | 2–8SZ |
| 29 cents | 2–9SZ |

**30 cents - 39 cents**

30 cents ............................................................................... 30–SZ
31 cents ................................................... 13–ESZ, 3/1–SZ
32 cents ................................................... 23–ESZ, 3/2–SZ
33 cents ............................................................................... 3–USZ
34 cents ............................................................................... 34–SZ
35 cents ............................................................................... 35–SZ
36 cents ............................................................................... 3–6SZ
37 cents ............................................................................... 3–7SZ
38 cents ............................................................................... 3–8SZ
39 cents ............................................................................... 3–9SZ

**40 cents - 49 cents**

40 cents ............................................................................... 40–SZ
41 cents ................................................... 14–ESZ, 4/1–SZ
42 cents ................................................... 24–ESZ, 4/2–SZ
43 cents ................................................... 34–ESZ, 4/3–SZ
44 cents ............................................................................... 4–USZ
45 cents ............................................................................... 45–SZ
46 cents ............................................................................... 4–6SZ
47 cents ............................................................................... 4–7SZ
48 cents ............................................................................... 4–8SZ
49 cents ............................................................................... 4–9SZ

**50 cents - 59 cents**

50 cents ............................................................................... 50–SZ
51 cents ................................................... 15–ESZ, 5/1–SZ
52 cents ................................................... 25–ESZ, 5/2–SZ
53 cents ................................................... 35–ESZ, 5/3–SZ
54 cents ................................................... 45–ESZ, 5/4–SZ
55 cents ............................................................................... 5–USZ
56 cents ............................................................................... 5–6SZ
57 cents ............................................................................... 5–7SZ
58 cents ............................................................................... 5–8SZ
59 cents ............................................................................... 5–9SZ

**60 cents - 69 cents**

60 cents ................................................... 0–E6SZ, 6/0–SZ
61 cents ................................................... 1–E6SZ, 6/1–SZ
62 cents ................................................... 2–E6SZ, 6/2–SZ
63 cents ................................................... 3–E6SZ, 6/3–SZ
64 cents ................................................... 4–E6SZ, 6/4–SZ
65 cents ................................................... 5–E6SZ, 6/5–SZ
66 cents ............................................................................... U6SZ
67 cents ............................................................................... 67SZ
68 cents ............................................................................... 68SZ
69 cents ............................................................................... 69SZ

**70 cents - 79 cents**

70 cents ................................................... 0–E7SZ, 7/0–SZ
71 cents ................................................... 1–E7SZ, 7/1–SZ
72 cents ................................................... 2–E7SZ, 7/2–SZ
73 cents ................................................... 3–E7SZ, 7/3–SZ
74 cents ................................................... 4–E7SZ, 7/4–SZ
75 cents ................................................... 5–E7SZ, 7/5–SZ
76 cents ................................................... E67SZ, 7/6SZ

77 cents ............................................................................. U7SZ, 7/7SZ
78 cents ............................................................................................ 78SZ
79 cents ............................................................................................ 79SZ

**80 cents - 89 cents**

80 cents ................................................................. 0–E8SZ, 8/0–SZ
81 cents ................................................................. 1–E8SZ, 8/1–SZ
82 cents ................................................................. 2–E8SZ, 8/2–SZ
83 cents ................................................................. 3–E8SZ, 8/3–SZ
84 cents ................................................................. 4–E8SZ, 8/4–SZ
85 cents ................................................................. 5–E8SZ, 8/5–SZ
86 cents ...................................................................... E68SZ, 8/6SZ
87 cents ...................................................................... E78SZ, 8/7SZ
88 cents ....................................................................... U8SZ, 8/8SZ
89 cents ............................................................................................ 89SZ

**90 cents - 99 cents**

90 cents ................................................................. 0–E9SZ, 9/0–SZ
91 cents ................................................................. 1–E9SZ, 9/1–SZ
92 cents ................................................................. 2–E9SZ, 9/2–SZ
93 cents ................................................................. 3–E9SZ, 9/3–SZ
94 cents ................................................................. 4–E9SZ, 9/4–SZ
95 cents ................................................................. 5–E9SZ, 9/5–SZ
96 cents ...................................................................... E69SZ, 9/6SZ
97 cents ...................................................................... E79SZ, 9/7SZ
98 cents ...................................................................... E89SZ, 9/8SZ
99 cents ....................................................................... U9SZ, 9/9SZ

# US CURRENCY:
## one cent   two cents   three cents  ...  ninety-nine cents

| | |
|---|---|
| **STYLE:** | Words, followed by *"cents."* |
| **NUMBER BAR USED?** | No |
| **ENGLISH TRANSLATION:** | Words |

*Associate –SZ with "cents."*

### 1 cent - 9 cents
one cent ................................................................................................................. WUNSZ
two cents ................................................................................................................ TWOSZ
three cents ............................................................................................................ THRESZ
four cents .............................................................................................................. FOURSZ
five cents ............................................................................................................. FAOIVSZ
six cents .................................................................................................................... SIXZ
seven cents ................................................................................................ SEFSZ, SEVSZ
eight cents ................................................................................................................ AITSZ
nine cents ............................................................................................................ NAOINSZ

### 10 cents - 19 cents
ten cents .................................................................................................................. TENSZ
eleven cents .............................................................................................. LEFSZ, LEVSZ
twelve cents ........................................................................................................... TWELSZ
thirteen cents .................................................................................................. THRAOENSZ
fourteen cents ................................................................................................... FRAOENSZ
fifteen cents ...................................................................................................... VAO*ENSZ
sixteen cents .................................................................................................... SKAOENSZ
seventeen cents ............................................................................................... SFAOENSZ
eighteen cents ..................................................................................................... AOENSZ
nineteen cents .................................................................................................. NAOENSZ

### 20 cents - 29 cents
twenty cents ............................................................................................................ TWISZ
twenty-one cents ................................................................................................ TWUNSZ
twenty-two cents ................................................................................................. TWAOSZ
twenty-three cents ............................................................................................ TWAOESZ
twenty-four cents .............................................................................................. TWOERSZ
twenty-five cents .......................................................... TWAOIFSZ, TWAOIVSZ
twenty-six cents ..................................................................................................... TWIXZ
twenty-seven cents ...................................................................... TWEFSZ, TWEVSZ
twenty-eight cents ............................................................................................... TWAISZ
twenty-nine cents ............................................................................................ TWAENSZ

## 30 cents - 39 cents
thirty cents ............................................................................... THRISZ
thirty-one cents ..................................................................... THRUNSZ
thirty-two cents ...................................................................... THRAOSZ
thirty-three cents .................................................................. THRAOESZ
thirty-four cents ..................................................................... THROERSZ
thirty-five cents ........................................... THRAOIFSZ, THRAOIVSZ
thirty-six cents ......................................................................... THRIXZ
thirty-seven cents ...................................... THREFSZ, THREVSZ
thirty-eight cents ..................................................................... THRAISZ
thirty-nine cents ................................................................... THRAENSZ

## 40 cents - 49 cents
forty cents ................................................................................. FRISZ
forty-one cents ........................................................................ FRUNSZ
forty-two cents ......................................................................... FRAOSZ
forty-three cents ................................................................... FRAO*ESZ
forty-four cents ...................................................................... FROERSZ
forty-five cents ............................................... FRAOIFSZ, FRAOIVSZ
forty-six cents ........................................................................... FRIXZ
forty-seven cents ........................................... FREFSZ, FREVSZ
forty-eight cents .................................................................... FRA*ISZ
forty-nine cents ..................................................................... FRAENSZ

## 50 cents - 59 cents
fifty cents ................................................................................... VISZ
fifty-one cents .......................................................................... VUNSZ
fifty-two cents ........................................................................... VAOSZ
fifty-three cents ....................................................................... VAOESZ
fifty-four cents .......................................................................... VOERSZ
fifty-five cents ................................................... VAOIFSZ, VAOIVSZ
fifty-six cents ............................................................................. VIXZ
fifty-seven cents ............................................... VEFSZ, VEVSZ
fifty-eight cents ........................................................................ VA*ISZ
fifty-nine cents ....................................................................... VAENSZ

## 60 cents - 69 cents
sixty cents ................................................................................. SKISZ
sixty-one cents ....................................................................... SKUNSZ
sixty-two cents ....................................................................... SKAOSZ
sixty-three cents ................................................................... SKAOESZ
sixty-four cents ..................................................................... SKOERSZ
sixty-five cents ............................................ SKAOIFSZ, SKAOIVSZ
sixty-six cents ......................................................................... SKIXZ
sixty-seven cents ......................................... SKEFSZ, SKEVSZ
sixty-eight cents ..................................................................... SKAISZ
sixty-nine cents .................................................................... SKAENSZ

## 70 cents - 79 cents
seventy cents ......................................................................... SFISZ
seventy-one cents ................................................................. SFUNSZ
seventy-two cents .................................................................. SFAOSZ
seventy-three cents ............................................................. SFAOESZ
seventy-four cents ............................................................... SFOERSZ
seventy-five cents ....................................... SFAOIFSZ, SFAOIVSZ
seventy-six cents .................................................................. SFIXZ

---

seventy-seven cents ........................................................................ SFEFSZ, SFEVSZ
seventy-eight cents ..................................................................................... SFAISZ
seventy-nine cents ................................................................................... SFAENSZ

## 80 cents - 89 cents

eighty cents ................................................................................................ Y*ISZ
eighty-one cents ........................................................................................ YUNSZ
eighty-two cents ...................................................................................... YAO*SZ
eighty-three cents ..................................................................................... YAOESZ
eighty-four cents ....................................................................................... YOERSZ
eighty-five cents ......................................................................... YAOIFSZ, YAOIVSZ
eighty-six cents ............................................................................................ YIXZ
eighty-seven cents ........................................................................... YEFSZ, YEVSZ
eighty-eight cents ........................................................................................ YAISZ
eighty-nine cents ...................................................................................... YAENSZ

## 90 cents - 99 cents

ninety cents ................................................................................... NAOISZ, NISZ
ninety-one cents ........................................................................................ NUNSZ
ninety-two cents ......................................................................................... NAOSZ
ninety-three cents .................................................................................... NAOESZ
ninety-four cents ....................................................................................... NOERSZ
ninety-five cents ...................................................................... NAOIFSZ, NAOIVSZ
ninety-six cents ............................................................................................ NIXZ
ninety-seven cents .......................................................................... NEFSZ, NEVSZ
ninety-eight cents ....................................................................................... NAISZ
ninety-nine cents ..................................................................................... NAENSZ

## TIME FORMAT:
### 1:  2:  3:  ... 12:

| | |
|---|---|
| **STYLE:** | **Figures, with colon and added minutes attached to colon.** |
| **NUMBER BAR USED?** | **Yes** |
| **ENGLISH TRANSLATION:** | **Figures** |

*Associate FPLT and (counterpart) STPH with the colon.*
*When building your dictionary, include a "delete space" command after the colon (example: 1:~).*

| | |
|---|---|
| 1: | 1–FPLT |
| 2: | 2–FPLT |
| 3: | 3–FPLT |
| 4: | 4–FPLT |
| 5: | 5–FPLT |
| 6: | STPH–6 |
| 7: | STPH–7 |
| 8: | STPH–8 |
| 9: | STPH–9 |
| 10: | 10–FPLT |
| 11: | 1–UFPLT |
| 12: | 12–FPLT |

To add minutes, use the number style on pages 3-23 to 3-25. Examples:

| | |
|---|---|
| 1:23 | 1–FPLT/23 |
| 2:10 | 2–FPLT/10 |
| 3:50 | 3–FPLT/50 |
| 4:21 | 4–FPLT/12–E, 4–FPLT/2/1 |
| 5:55 | 5–FPLT/5–U |
| 6:34 | STPH–6/34 |
| 7:49 | STPH–7/49 |
| 8:02 | STPH–8/20–E, STPH–8/0/2 |
| 9:19 | STPH–9/19 |
| 10:22 | 10–FPLT/2–U |
| 11:11 | 1–UFPLT/1–U |
| 12:35 | 12–FPLT/35 |

## TIME FORMAT:
### 1:00  1:15  1:30  1:45 ... 12:45

| | |
|---|---|
| **STYLE:** | **Figures, with colon and added quarter hour (15-minute interval).** |
| **NUMBER BAR USED?** | **Yes** |
| **ENGLISH TRANSLATION:** | **Figures** |

**Number + attached ":00" (makes even o'clock number)**

*Associate –K with "o'clock."*

| | |
|---|---|
| 1:00 | 1–K |
| 2:00 | 2–K |
| 3:00 | 3–K |
| 4:00 | 4–K |
| 5:00 | 5–K |
| 6:00 | K–6 |
| 7:00 | K–7 |
| 8:00 | K–8 |
| 9:00 | K–9 |
| 10:00 | 10–K |
| 11:00 | 1–UK |
| 12:00 | 12–K |

**Number + attached ":15" (makes "quarter past" number)**

*On the left, associate KW– with "quarter."*
*On the right, associate –G or fourth finger with "quarter."*

| | |
|---|---|
| 1:15 | 1–G |
| 2:15 | 2–G |
| 3:15 | 3–G |
| 4:15 | 4–G |
| 5:15 | 5–G |
| 6:15 | KW–6 |
| 7:15 | KW–7 |
| 8:15 | KW–8 |
| 9:15 | KW–9 |
| 10:15 | 10–G |
| 11:15 | 1–UG |
| 12:15 | 12–G |

**Number + attached ":30" (makes half-hour or "half-past" numbers)**

*The –B and W– fingers are the middle fingers,
thus half or midway between hours.*

| | |
|---|---|
| 1:30 | 1–B |
| 2:30 | 2–B |
| 3:30 | 3–B |
| 4:30 | 4–B |
| 5:30 | 5–B |
| 6:30 | W–6 |
| 7:30 | W–7 |
| 8:30 | W–8 |
| 9:30 | W–9 |
| 10:30 | 10–B |
| 11:30 | 1–UB |
| 12:30 | 12–B |

**Number + attached ":45" (makes "quarter-to" numbers)**

*On the left, associate KWR– with "quarter."
On the right, associate –GS (fourth finger plus
plural –S) with "quarters."*

| | |
|---|---|
| 1:45 | 1–GS |
| 2:45 | 2–GS |
| 3:45 | 3–GS |
| 4:45 | 4–GS |
| 5:45 | 5–GS |
| 6:45 | KWR–6 |
| 7:45 | KWR–7 |
| 8:45 | KWR–8 |
| 9:45 | KWR–9 |
| 10:45 | 10–GS |
| 11:45 | 1–UGS |
| 12:45 | 12–GS |

## TIME FORMAT:
### 1:00 o'clock   2:00 o'clock  ...  12:00 o'clock

| | |
|---|---|
| **STYLE:** | **Figures, with ":00 o'clock."** |
| **NUMBER BAR USED?** | **Example 1: no   Example 2: yes** |
| **ENGLISH TRANSLATION:** | **Figures** |

*Associate KLAOK with "o'clock."*
*When building your dictionary, include*
*a "delete space" command before the*
*":00 o'clock."*

### EXAMPLE 1 (without number bar)

| | |
|---|---|
| 1:00 o'clock | W*UN/KLAOK |
| 2:00 o'clock | TWO*/KLAOK |
| 3:00 o'clock | THR*E/KLAOK |
| 4:00 o'clock | FO*UR/KLAOK |
| 5:00 o'clock | FAOIF/KLAOK |
| 6:00 o'clock | SWIX/KLAOK |
| 7:00 o'clock | SEV/KLAOK |
| 8:00 o'clock | YAIT/KLAOK |
| 9:00 o'clock | NAO*IN/KLAOK |
| 10:00 o'clock | T*EN/KLAOK |
| 11:00 o'clock | LEV/KLAOK |
| 12:00 o'clock | TWEL/KLAOK |

### EXAMPLE 2 (with number bar)

| | |
|---|---|
| 1:00 o'clock | 1/KLAOK |
| 2:00 o'clock | 2/KLAOK |
| 3:00 o'clock | 3/KLAOK |
| 4:00 o'clock | 4/KLAOK |
| 5:00 o'clock | 5/KLAOK |
| 6:00 o'clock | 6/KLAOK |
| 7:00 o'clock | 7/KLAOK |
| 8:00 o'clock | 8/KLAOK |
| 9:00 o'clock | 9/KLAOK |
| 10:00 o'clock | 10/KLAOK |
| 11:00 o'clock | 1–U/KLAOK |
| 12:00 o'clock | 12/KLAOK |

## TIME FORMAT:
### 1 o'clock  2 o'clock  ...  12 o'clock

| | |
|---|---|
| **STYLE:** | **Figures, with** *"o'clock."* |
| **NUMBER BAR USED?** | **Example 1: no    Example 2: yes** |
| **ENGLISH TRANSLATION:** | **Figures** |

*Associate KL–K with "o'clock."*

### EXAMPLE 1 (without number bar)

| | |
|---|---|
| 1 o'clock | W*UN/KL–K |
| 2 o'clock | TWO*/KL–K |
| 3 o'clock | THR*E/KL–K |
| 4 o'clock | FO*UR/KL–K |
| 5 o'clock | FAOIF/KL–K |
| 6 o'clock | SWIX/KL–K |
| 7 o'clock | SEV/KL–K |
| 8 o'clock | YAIT/KL–K |
| 9 o'clock | NAO*IN/KL–K |
| 10 o'clock | T*EN/KL–K |
| 11 o'clock | LEV/KL–K |
| 12 o'clock | TWEL/KL–K |

### EXAMPLE 2 (with number bar)

| | |
|---|---|
| 1 o'clock | 1/KL–K |
| 2 o'clock | 2/KL–K |
| 3 o'clock | 3/KL–K |
| 4 o'clock | 4/KL–K |
| 5 o'clock | 5/KL–K |
| 6 o'clock | 6/KL–K |
| 7 o'clock | 7/KL–K |
| 8 o'clock | 8/KL–K |
| 9 o'clock | 9/KL–K |
| 10 o'clock | 10/KL–K |
| 11 o'clock | 1–U/KL–K |
| 12 o'clock | 12/KL–K |

## TIME FORMAT:
### one o'clock  two o'clock  ...  twelve o'clock

| | |
|---|---|
| **STYLE:** | **Words, with *"o'clock."*** |
| **NUMBER BAR USED?** | **No** |
| **ENGLISH TRANSLATION:** | **Words** |

*Associate KL–K with "o'clock."*

one o'clock ............................................................................................... WUN/KL–K

two o'clock ............................................................................................ TWO/KL–K

three o'clock ......................................................................................... THRE/KL–K

four o'clock ........................................................................................... FOUR/KL–K

five o'clock ........................................................................................... FAOIV/KL–K

six o'clock ............................................................................................... SIX/KL–K

seven o'clock ........................................................................................ SEVN/KL–K

eight o'clock ............................................................................................ AIT/KL–K

nine o'clock .......................................................................................... NAOIN/KL–K

ten o'clock ............................................................................................. TEN/KL–K

eleven o'clock ....................................................................................... LEVN/KL–K

twelve o'clock .......................................................... TWEFL/KL–K, TWEVL/KL–K

## TIME FORMAT (military time):
### 0100   0200   0300  ...  2400

| | |
|---|---|
| **STYLE:** | **Four-digit figures.** |
| **NUMBER BAR USED?** | **Yes** |
| **ENGLISH TRANSLATION:** | **Figures** |

*Associate M with "Military," or
UM with "Units Military."*

| | |
|---|---|
| 0100 | 10–EUM |
| 0200 | 20–EUM |
| 0300 | 30–EUM |
| 0400 | 40–EUM |
| 0500 | 50–EUM |
| 0600 | M0–EU6 |
| 0700 | M0–EU7 |
| 0800 | M0–EU8 |
| 0900 | M0–EU9 |
| 1000 | 10–UM |
| 1100 | 1–UM |
| 1200 | 12–UM |
| 1300 | 13–UM |
| 1400 | 14–UM |
| 1500 | 15–UM |
| 1600 | 16–UM, 1M–U6 |
| 1700 | 1M–U7 |
| 1800 | 1M–U8 |
| 1900 | 1M–U9 |
| 2000 | 20–UM |
| 2100 | 12–EUM |
| 2200 | 2–UM |
| 2300 | 23–UM |
| 2400 | 24–UM |

## DATES:
### 11/1/06   2/28/09   9/20/99 etc.

---

**STYLE:**                    **Figures in mm/dd/yy format.**

**NUMBER BAR USED?**          **Example 1: no    Example 2: yes**

**ENGLISH TRANSLATION:**      **Figures**

---

*Associate Z– with "zero" when using words for 00-09 below.*

*Associate SL–RB with "slash."*
*CAT dictionary entry for SL–RB = ~/~*
*This slash can be used with or without the number bar.*

| | | |
|---|---|---|
| 00 | ZO | 0–U |
| 01 | ZWUN | 10–E |
| 02 | ZWAO | 20–E |
| 03 | ZE | 30–E |
| 04 | ZFOUR | 40–E |
| 05 | ZFOIV | 50–E |
| 06 | Z–X | 0–6 |
| 07 | ZWEVN | 0–7 |
| 08 | ZWAIT | 0–8 |
| 09 | ZNAION, ZWAOIN | 0–9 |

### EXAMPLE 1 (without number bar)

| | |
|---|---|
| 1/16/06 | W*UN/SL–RB/SKAOEN/SL–RB/Z–X |
| 3/13/03 | THR*E/SL–RB/THRAOEN/SL–RB/ZE |
| 09/12/99 | ZAOER/NAO*IN/SL–RB/TWEL/SL–RB/NAEN |
| 10/31/87 | T*EN/SL–RB/THRUN/SL–RB/YEV |
| 11/16/81 | LEV/SL–RB/SKAOEN/SL–RB/YUN |
| 12/11/50 | TWEL/SL–RB/LEV/SL–RB/VI |

### EXAMPLE 2 (with number bar)

| | |
|---|---|
| 1/16/06 | 1/SL–RB/16/SL–RB/0–6 |
| 3/13/03 | 3/SL–RB/13/SL–RB/30–E |
| 3/12/92 | 3/SL–RB/12/SL–Rʙ/2–E9, 3/SL–RB/12/SL–RB/9/2 |
| 4/25/89 | 4/SL–RB/25/SL–RB/89 |
| 5/21/78 | 5/SL–RB/12E/SL–RB/78, 5/SL–RB/2/1/SL–RB/78 |
| 06/02/95 | 06/SL–RB/20E/SL–RB/5E9, 06/SL–RB/0/2/SL–RB/9/5 |

---

## YEARS (in full):
## 1995　2000　2006 ... 2020

| STYLE: | Figures in YYYY format. |
|---|---|
| NUMBER BAR USED? | No |
| ENGLISH TRANSLATION: | Figures |

| | |
|---|---|
| 1995 | NOIV |
| 1996 | NOIK |
| 1997 | NEVN, NEFN |
| 1998 | NAENT |
| 1999 | NOIN |
| 2000 | TWOU |
| 2001 | TWAOUN |
| 2002 | TWAOU |
| 2003 | TWE |
| 2004 | TWAOUR |
| 2005 | TWOIF, TWIV |
| 2006 | TWOUX, TWAOUX |
| 2007 | TWEVN, TWEFN |
| 2008 | TWAE |
| 2009 | TWOIN |
| 2010 | TWEN |
| 2011 | TLEFN |
| 2012 | TWOEFL |
| 2013 | THAOEN |
| 2014 | TWOURN |
| 2015 | TWAOIFN, TWIFN |
| 2016 | TWAO*EX |
| 2017 | TWAOEFN |
| 2018 | TYAEN, TYAO*EN |
| 2019 | TAOENT |
| 2020 | TYEN, TYENT |

## YEARS (abbreviated):
### '00  '01  '02 ...  '20

| STYLE: | Two-digit figures, preceded by apostrophe. |
|---|---|
| NUMBER BAR USED? | Example 1: no    Example 2: yes |
| ENGLISH TRANSLATION: | Figures |

NOTE: In this format, the letters KR– (left bank) and –RG (right bank) are used for the initial apostrophe. The zero is omitted on the number bar for years starting with a zero (e.g. '01 = 1–RG and '06 = KR–6).

*Example 1:*
*Associate the "T" with "two thousand" and associate the steno*
*with the corresponding steno for years on the previous page.*

*Example 2:*
*On the left, associate KR– with "Centuries Replaced."*
*On the right, associate (counterpart) –RG with "ReplacinG."*

| | EXAMPLE 1 (wihout number bar) | EXAMPLE 2 (with number bar) |
|---|---|---|
| '00 | TWO*U | 0–URG |
| '01 | TWAO*UN | 10–ERG |
| '02 | TWAO*U | 20–ERG |
| '03 | TW*E | 30–ERG |
| '04 | TWAO*UR | 40–ERG |
| '05 | TWOIV | 50–ERG |
| '06 | TWO*UX, TWAO*UX | KR0–6 |
| '07 | TWOIFN, TWOIVN | KR0–7 |
| '08 | TWA*E | KR0–8 |
| '09 | TWO*IN | KR0–9 |
| '10 | TW*EN | 10–RG |
| '11 | TLEVN | 1–URG |
| '12 | TWOEVL | 12–RG |
| '13 | THAO*EN | 13–RG |
| '14 | TWO*URN | 14–RG |
| '15 | TWAO*IFN, TW*IFN | 15–RG |
| '16 | TW*EX | 1R–6G |
| '17 | TWAO*EFN | 1R–7G |
| '18 | TYA*EN | 1KR–8 |
| '19 | TAO*ENT | 1KR–9 |
| '20 | TY*EN, TY*ENT | 20–RG |

## COUNTS:
## count one   count two   count IV  ...  count X

| | |
|---|---|
| **STYLE:** | **"count" followed by count number in words or Roman numerals.** |
| **NUMBER BAR USED?** | **Yes** |
| **ENGLISH TRANSLATION:** | **Words, Roman numerals** |

### NUMBER SPELLED

*Associate –KT and (counterpart) TKW–*
*with "count."*

| | |
|---|---|
| count one | 1–KT |
| count two | 2–KT |
| count three | 3–KT |
| count four | 4–KT |
| count five | 5–KT |
| count six | TKW–6 |
| count seven | TKW–7 |
| count eight | TKW–8 |
| count nine | TKW–9 |
| count ten | 10–KT |

### NUMBER AS ROMAN NUMERAL

*Associate –RKT and (counterpart) TKWR–*
*with "Roman count."*

| | |
|---|---|
| count I | 1–RKT |
| count II | 2–RKT |
| count III | 3–RKT |
| count IV | 4–RKT |
| count V | 5–RKT |
| count VI | TKWR–6 |
| count VII | TKWR–7 |
| count VIII | TKWR–8 |
| count IX | TKWR–9 |
| count X | 10–RKT |

## No. #:
## No. 1   No. 2   No. 3   etc.

| | |
|---|---|
| **STYLE:** | *"No."* **followed by number in figures.** |
| **NUMBER BAR USED?** | **No** |
| **ENGLISH TRANSLATION:** | **Figures** |

*Associate NOIB with NUB,*
*the brief for "number."*

**1 - 9**

| | |
|---|---|
| No. 1 | NOIB/W*UN |
| No. 2 | NOIB/TWO* |
| No. 3 | NOIB/THR*E |
| No. 4 | NOIB/FO*UR |
| No. 5 | NOIB/FAO*IV |
| No. 6 | NOIB/SWIX |
| No. 7 | NOIB/SEV |
| No. 8 | NOIB/YAIT |
| No. 9 | NOIB/NAO*IN |

**10 - 19**

| | |
|---|---|
| No. 10 | NOIB/T*EN |
| No. 11 | NOIB/LEV |
| No. 12 | NOIB/TWEL |
| No. 13 | NOIB/THRAOEN |
| No. 14 | NOIB/FRAOEN |
| No. 15 | NOIB/FAOEN |
| No. 16 | NOIB/SKAOEN |
| No. 17 | NOIB/SFAOEN |
| No. 18 | NOIB/YAOEN |
| No. 19 | NOIB/NAOEN |

**20 +** (examples)

| | |
|---|---|
| No. 20 | NOIB/TWI |
| No. 21 | NOIB/TWUN |
| No. 22 | NOIB/TWAO |
| No. 23 | NOIB/TWAOE |
| No. 24 | NOIB/TWOER |
| No. 25 | NOIB/TWAOIV |
| No. 100 | NOIB/HUN |

## No. #:
## No. 1  No. 2  No. 3  etc.

| | |
|---|---|
| **STYLE:** | *"No."* **followed by number in figures.** |
| **NUMBER BAR USED?** | **Yes** |
| **ENGLISH TRANSLATION:** | **Figures** |

*Associate B– and (counterpart) –N with NUB, the brief for "number."*

**1 - 9**

| | |
|---|---|
| No. 1 | 1–N |
| No. 2 | 2–N |
| No. 3 | 3–N |
| No. 4 | 4–N |
| No. 5 | 5–N |
| No. 6 | B–6 |
| No. 7 | B–7 |
| No. 8 | B–8 |
| No. 9 | B–9 |

**10 - 19**

| | |
|---|---|
| No. 10 | 10–N |
| No. 11 | 1–UN |
| No. 12 | 12–N |
| No. 13 | 13–N |
| No. 14 | 14–N |
| No. 15 | 15–N |
| No. 16 | 1B–6, 1–6N |
| No. 17 | 1B–7 |
| No. 18 | 1B–8, 1–N8 |
| No. 19 | 1B–9, 1–N9 |

**20 +** (examples)

| | |
|---|---|
| No. 20 | 20–N |
| No. 21 | 12–EN, 2/1–N |
| No. 22 | 2–UN |
| No. 23 | 23–N |
| No. 24 | 24–N |
| No. 25 | 25–N |
| No. 100 | 10–UN |

## NUMBERS (compound adjectives and more):
### *twofold   three-piece   foursome   etc.*

| | |
|---|---|
| **STYLE:** | **Words and phrases containing numbers, spelled out.** |
| **NUMBER BAR USED?** | **No** |
| **ENGLISH TRANSLATION:** | **Words** |

## FRACTIONS

| | |
|---|---|
| one-and-a-quarter | WA*RT |
| one-eighth | WA*IT |
| one-fourth | WO*URT |
| one-half | WAF |
| one-half of the | WAFT |
| one-half of them | WAFM |
| one-half of these | WAFZ |
| one-half of those | WAFS |
| one-ninth | WAO*INT |
| one-quarter | WAERT |
| one-seventh | WEVNT |
| one-sixth | W*IX |
| one-tenth | W*ENT |
| one-third | WIRD |
| three-fourths | THRO*URTS |
| three-quarters | THRAERTS |
| two-thirds | TWIRDZ |

## COMPOUND ADJECTIVES

**-fold** (–FLD)

| | |
|---|---|
| twofold | TWOFLD |
| threefold | THREFLD |
| fourfold | FOUFRLD |
| fivefold | FAOIVLD |
| sixfold | SWIFLD |
| sevenfold | SEVLD |

**-piece** (–P)

| | |
|---|---|
| two-piece | TWOP |
| three-piece | THREP |
| four-piece | FOURP |
| five-piece | FAOIVP |
| six-piece | SW*IP |
| seven-piece | SEVP |

**-some** (–M)

twosome ................................................................................................ TWOM
threesome ........................................................................................... THREM
foursome .............................................................................................. FOURM

## PHRASES & COMPOUND ADJECTIVES

### one

one and two .......................................................................... WAOT, WAONT
one of ..................................................................................................... WUF
one of the ............................................................................................. WUFT
one of them .......................................................................................... WUFM
one of these .......................................................................................... WUFZ
one of those ...........................................................................................WUFS
one or two ........................................................................................... WAORT
one time .............................................................................................. WAOIM

### two

twofold ............................................................................................. TWOFLD
two of the ........................................................................................... TWOFT
two of them ........................................................................................TWOFM
two of these ........................................................................................ TWOFZ
two of those ........................................................................................ TWOFS
two-piece ............................................................................................. TWOP
twosome ............................................................................................. TWOM

### three

threefold ............................................................................................ THREFLD
three of the .......................................................................................... THREFT
three of them ...................................................................................... THREFM
three of these ...................................................................................... THREFZ
three of those ....................................................................................... THREFS
three-piece ........................................................................................... THREP
threesome ........................................................................................... THREM

### four

fourfold ............................................................................................. FOUFRLD
four of the ........................................................................................... FOUFT
four of them ........................................................................................ FOUFM
four of these ........................................................................................ FOUFZ
four of those ........................................................................................ FOUFS
four-piece ........................................................................................... FOURP
foursome ............................................................................................. FOURM

### five

fivefold ............................................................................................ FAOIVLD
five of the ...........................................................................................FAOIFT
five of them ........................................................................................ FAOIFM
five of these ........................................................................ FAOIFZ, FAOIVZ
five of those ........................................................................................ FAOIVS
five-piece ........................................................................................... FAOIVP

### six

sixfold................................................................................................ SWIFLD
six of ..................................................................................................... SWIF
six of them .......................................................................................... SWIFM
six of these .......................................................................................... SWIFZ
six-piece .............................................................................................. SW*IP

**seven**
  sevenfold ................................................................................................ SEVLD
  seven-piece ............................................................................................. SEVP

**eight**
  eight of the ............................................................................................ AIFT
  eight of them .......................................................................................... AIFM
  eight of these ......................................................................................... AIFZ
  eight of those ......................................................................................... AIFS

**nine**
  nine of the ............................................................................................. NAOIFT
  nine of them ........................................................................................... NAOIFM
  nine of these .......................................................................................... NAOIFZ
  nine of those .......................................................................................... NAOIFS

# "LARGE NUMBER"TACTICS

The numbering styles introduced in the previous section typically end at 99 (the main exception being US currency). In order to rapidly record numbers in excess of 99, it is necessary to master the styles so far defined and establish follow-on systems. This section absorbs and builds on the previously defined strategies.

This section begins with a few methods of entering numbers in the range 100-999, then continues with truly large numbers, i.e., numbers that traditionally employ a "group separation comma" to allow rapid visualization of the magnitude of the value.

The extent to which a stenographer will require immediate access to the different styles and methods (and the total range available) naturally differs according to personal preference, CAT software capabilities and the predominant work environment. This section offers and illustrates a variety of number writing tactics, both with and without use of the number bar. Elements of the different techniques can be combined and fine-tuned to suit individual writing styles.

## RAW AND REFINED NUMBER SYSTEMS

At times it may not be possible to write numbers as refined or perfectly as desired. In such situations, numbers can be written in raw form, for later "cleanup." Raw numbers are typically written:

- with a space or gap between adjoining digits
  (e.g., 1,5 25,3 50 instead of 1,525,350)

- without group separation comma(s)
  (e.g., 1525350 instead of 1,525,350)

- without a zero or place-holder
  (e.g., 10,50,200 instead of 10,050,200).

Where applicable, examples are given of both raw and refined methods of writing numbers. The delete-space dictionary commands introduced here convert many raw numbers to their refined state:

```
000 (CAT entry = ~000) ................................................. HO–RBGSZ, 0–EU
,000 (CAT entry = ~,000) ................................................ HO*RBGSZ, 0*EU
,000, (CAT entry = ~,000,~) .................................................... 0*EURBGS
00 (CAT entry = ~00) ........................................................................ 0–U
00 (CAT entry = 00~) ........................................................................ 0*U
,00 (CAT entry = ~,00~) ............................................................. 0*URBGS
```

---

## NUMBER MULTIPLES:
### hundreds   thousands   millions   etc.

| | |
|---|---|
| **STYLE:** | **Various number multiples in words.** |
| **NUMBER BAR USED?** | **No** |
| **ENGLISH TRANSLATION:** | **Words** |

**hundred**

| | |
|---|---|
| hundred | HUN |
| hundred-dollar | HUND |
| hundred dollars | HUNDZ |
| hundreds | HUNS |
| hundredth | H*NT, H*UNT |

**thousand**

| | |
|---|---|
| thousand | THOU |
| thousand-dollar | THOUD |
| thousand dollars | THOUDZ |
| thousands | THOUS |
| thousandth | THO*UT |

**million**

| | |
|---|---|
| million | M–L |
| million-dollar | M–LD |
| million dollars | M–LDZ |
| millions | M–LS |
| millionth | M–LT, M*ILT |

**billion**

| | |
|---|---|
| billion | B–L |
| billion-dollar | B–LD |
| billion dollars | B–LDZ |
| billions | B–LS |
| billionth | B–LT, B*ILT |

**trillion**

| | |
|---|---|
| trillion | TR–L |
| trillion-dollar | TR–LD |
| trillion dollars | TR–LDZ |
| trillions | TR–LS |
| trillionth | TR*LT, TR*ILT |

## HUNDREDS:
### 100 200 300 ... 900

| STYLE: | Figures in hundreds. |
|---|---|
| NUMBER BAR USED? | No |
| ENGLISH TRANSLATION: | Figures |

### EXACT HUNDREDS

| | |
|---|---|
| 100 | W*UN/HUN |
| 200 | TWO*/HUN |
| 300 | THR*E/HUN |
| 400 | FO*UR/HUN |
| 500 | FAOIF/HUN |
| 600 | SWIX/HUN |
| 700 | SEV/HUN |
| 800 | YAIT/HUN |
| 900 | NAO*IN/HUN |

### INTERMEDIATE VALUES

For all other numbers in the hundreds, use either HO–RBGS or HU–RBGS for a delete space when the speaker says "hundred," per the following:

- Use HO–RBGS when the middle number is a zero, in numbers such as 101. CAT dictionary entry = ~0~

- Use HU–RBGS when the middle number is not a zero, in numbers such as 235. CAT dictionary entry = ~

*Associate the HO in HO–RBGS with "hundred zero" or "zero in hundreds."*
*Associate the HU in HU–RBGS with "hundred."*

**Examples:**

| | |
|---|---|
| 121 | W*UN/HU–RBGS/TWUN |
| 289 | TWO*/HU–RBGS/YAEN |
| 362 | THR*E/HU–RBGS/SKAO |
| 403 | FO*UR/HO–RBGS/THR*E |
| 506 | FAOIF/HO–RBGS/SWIX |
| 660 | SWIX/HU–RBGS/SKI |
| 780 | SEV/HU–RBGS/Y*I |
| 888 | YAIT/HU–RBGS/YAI |
| 909 | NAO*IN/HO–RBGS/NAO*IN |

## "NUMBERS ONLY" METHOD

This is the most simple method of writing numbers without the number bar but often requires more strokes than other methods. For the "numbers only" method, use the outlines given on pages 3-18 to 3-20. Numbers will translate in the raw form (2 36 or 2 3 6 instead of 236).

**Examples:**

128 .......................................................................... W*UN/TWAI, W*UN/TWO*/YAIT
(translates as 1 28 or 1 2 8)
566 ............................................................... FAOIF/SKIK, FAOIF/SWIX/SWIX
(translates as 5 66 or 5 6 6)

To refine the "numbers only" method (i.e., eliminate the spaces between numbers), define the following sequences of numbers as outlines:

00, 01, 02, 03, 04, 05, 06, 07, 08, 09
000, 001, 002, 003, 004, 005, 006, 007, 008, 009
010, 011, 012, 013, 014, 015, 016, 017, 018, 019
020 through 099
100 through 999

**Examples:**

00 ............................................................................... ZAO*ER/ZAO*ER
01 ...................................................................................... ZAO*ER/W*UN
02 ..................................................................................... ZAO*ER/TWO*

000 ............................................................... ZAO*ER/ZAO*ER/ZAO*ER
001 ....................................................................... ZAO*ER/ZAO*ER/W*UN
002 ...................................................................... ZAO*ER/ZAO*ER/TWO*

010 .............................................. ZAO*ER/T*EN, ZAO*ER/W*UN/ZAO*ER
011 ............................................... ZAO*ER/LEV, ZAO*ER/W*UN/W*UN
012 .............................................. ZAO*ER/TWEL, ZAO*ER/W*UN/TWO*

020 .............................................. ZAO*ER/TWI, ZAO*ER/TWO*/ZAO*ER
021 .............................................. ZAO*ER/TWUN, ZAO*ER/TWO*/W*UN
022 .............................................. ZAO*ER/TWAO, ZAO*ER/TWO*/TWO*

101 ........................................................................ W*UN/ZAO*ER/W*UN
102 ........................................................................ W*UN/ZAO*ER/TWO*
199 ................................................ W*UN/NAEN, W*UN/NAO*IN/NAO*IN
550 .................................................. FAOIF/VI, FAOIF/FAOIF/ZAO*ER

To write numbers above 999, use commas where necessary (example: 1,101 = W*UN/*RBGS/W*UN/ZAO*ER/W*UN).

---

## HUNDREDS:
### 100  200  300 ... 900

| | |
|---|---|
| **STYLE:** | **Figures in hundreds.** |
| **NUMBER BAR USED?** | **Yes** |
| **ENGLISH TRANSLATION:** | **Figures** |

### EXACT HUNDREDS

| | |
|---|---|
| 100 | 10–U |
| 200 | 20–U |
| 300 | 30–U |
| 400 | 40–U |
| 500 | 50–U |
| 600 | 0–EU6 |
| 700 | 0–EU7 |
| 800 | 0–EU8 |
| 900 | 0–EU9 |

### INTERMEDIATE VALUES

**Examples:**

| | |
|---|---|
| 121 | 12/1 |
| 289 | 289 |
| 362 | 36/2, 3/2–E6 |
| 403 | 40/3 |
| 506 | 506 |
| 660 | 6/0–E6 |
| 780 | 78/0 |
| 888 | 8/U8 |
| 909 | 9/09 |

## HUNDREDS:
### one hundred   two hundred  ...  nine hundred

| STYLE: | Numbers in words and hundreds. |
| --- | --- |
| NUMBER BAR USED? | No |
| ENGLISH TRANSLATION: | Words |

## EXACT HUNDREDS

| | |
| --- | --- |
| one hundred | WUN/HUN |
| two hundred | TWO/HUN |
| three hundred | THRE/HUN |
| four hundred | FOUR/HUN |
| five hundred | FAOIV/HUN |
| six hundred | SIX/HUN |
| seven hundred | SEVN/HUN |
| eight hundred | AIT/HUN |
| nine hundred | NAOIN/HUN |

## INTERMEDIATE VALUES

**Examples:**

| | |
| --- | --- |
| one hundred twenty-one | WUN/HUN/TW*UN |
| two hundred eighty-nine | TWO/HUN/YA*EN |
| three hundred sixty-two | THRE/HUN/SKAO* |
| four hundred three | FOUR/HUN/THRE |
| five hundred six | FAOIV/HUN/SIX |
| six hundred sixty | SIX/HUN/SK*I |
| seven hundred eighty | SEVN/HUN/Y– |
| eight hundred eighty-eight | AIT/HUN/YA*I |
| nine hundred nine | NAOIN/HUN/NAOIN |

## LARGE NUMBERS:
### 1,000  5,000  250,000  etc.

| | |
|---|---|
| **STYLE:** | **Figures in exact thousands.** |
| **NUMBER BAR USED?** | **No** |
| **ENGLISH TRANSLATION:** | **Figures** |

### 1,000 - 9,000

| | |
|---|---|
| 1,000 | WUN/THOU |
| 2,000 | TWO/THOU |
| 3,000 | THRE/THOU |
| 4,000 | FOUR/THOU |
| 5,000 | FAOIV/THOU |
| 6,000 | SIX/THOU |
| 7,000 | SEVN/THOU |
| 8,000 | AIT/THOU |
| 9,000 | NAOIN/THOU |

### 10,000 - 900,000 (examples)

| | |
|---|---|
| 10,000 | TEN/THOU |
| 25,000 | TWAOIV/THOU |
| 50,000 | VI/THOU |
| 100,000 | WUN/HUN/THOU |
| 250,000 | TWO/HUN/VI/THOU |
| 500,000 | FAOIV/HUN/THOU |
| 900,000 | NAOIN/HUN/THOU |

## LARGE NUMBERS:
### 1,000  5,000  250,000 etc.

| STYLE: | Figures in exact thousands. |
|---|---|
| NUMBER BAR USED? | Yes |
| ENGLISH TRANSLATION: | Figures |

**1,000 - 9,000**

| | |
|---|---|
| 1,000 | 10*EU |
| 2,000 | 20*EU |
| 3,000 | 30*EU |
| 4,000 | 40*EU |
| 5,000 | 50*EU |
| 6,000 | 0*EU6 |
| 7,000 | 0*EU7 |
| 8,000 | 0*EU8 |
| 9,000 | 0*EU9 |

**10,000 - 900,000** (examples)

| | |
|---|---|
| 10,000 | 10/0*EU |
| 25,000 | 25/0*EU |
| 50,000 | 50/0*EU |
| 100,000 | 10–U/0*EU |
| 250,000 | 250/0*EU |
| 500,000 | 50–U/0*EU |
| 900,000 | 9/0–U/0*EU |

## LARGE NUMBERS:
### one thousand   five hundred thousand  etc.

| | |
|---|---|
| **STYLE:** | **Numbers in words, exact thousands.** |
| **NUMBER BAR USED?** | **No** |
| **ENGLISH TRANSLATION:** | **Words** |

### 1,000 - 9,000

| | |
|---|---|
| one thousand | WUN/THO*U |
| two thousand | TWO/THO*U |
| three thousand | THRE/THO*U |
| four thousand | FOUR/THO*U |
| five thousand | FAOIV/THO*U |
| six thousand | SIX/THO*U |
| seven thousand | SEVN/THO*U |
| eight thousand | AIT/THO*U |
| nine thousand | NAOIN/THO*U |

### 10,000 - 900,000 (examples)

| | |
|---|---|
| ten thousand | TEN/THO*U |
| twenty-five thousand | TWAOIF/THO*U |
| fifty thousand | FIFT/THO*U |
| one hundred thousand | WUN/HUN/THO*U |
| two hundred fifty thousand | TWO/HUN/FIFT/THO*U |
| five hundred thousand | FAOIV/HUN/THO*U |
| nine hundred thousand | NAOIN/HUN/THO*U |

## LARGE NUMBERS:
### 1,206  92,400,230  etc.

| | |
|---|---|
| **STYLE:** | **Figures using outlines for commas in numbers greater than 1,000.** |
| **NUMBER BAR USED?** | **No** |
| **ENGLISH TRANSLATION:** | **Figures** |

**NOTE: Numbers in this section use the group-related commas listed below. CAT dictionary entry = ~,~**

For a comma with "delete space" on either side:

- Use THOU–RBGS when speaker says *"thousand."*

- Use MI–RBGS when speaker says *"million."*

- Use BL–RBGS when speaker says *"billion."*

- Use TR–RBGS when speaker says *"trillion."*

*Two reasons some reporters prefer to use these ways of writing ~,~ are: (1) They prefer to write a stroke for what they hear, as opposed to thinking about inserting a comma; (2) When editing the document, they can easily spot errors.*
*For example, if your translation reads 10,50,200, one digit has been omitted.*
*Your notes reading*
T*EN/MI-RBGS/VI/THOU-RBGS/TWO*/HUN
*will indicate that the correct number should be 10,050,200.*

**Examples:**

| | |
|---|---|
| 1,206 | W*UN/THOU–RBGS/TWO*/HO–RBGS/SWIX |
| 12,312 | TWEL/THOU–RBGS/THR*E/HU–RBGS/TWEL |
| 1,500,250 | W*UN/MI–RBGS/FAOIF/HUN/THOU–RBGS/TWO*/ HU–RBGS/VI |
| 92,400,230 | NAO*/MI–RBGS/FO*UR/HUN/THOU–RBGS/ TWO*/HU–RBGS/THRI |
| 135,440,500 | W*UN/HU–RBGS/THRAOIF/MI–RBGS/FO*UR/ HU–RBGS/FRI/THOU–RBGS/FAOIF/HUN |
| 50,500,100,532 | VI/BL–RBGS/FAIOIF/HUN/MI–RBGS/W*UN/HUN/ THOU–RBGS/FAOIF/HU–RBGS/THRAO |

## LARGE NUMBERS:
### 1,001   92,400,230   etc.

| | |
|---|---|
| **STYLE:** | **Figures using outlines for commas in numbers greater than 1,000.** |
| **NUMBER BAR USED?** | **Yes** |
| **ENGLISH TRANSLATION:** | **Figures** |

**NOTE: Numbers in this section use the group-related commas listed below. CAT dictionary entry = ~,~**

For a comma with "delete space" on either side:

- Use THOU–RBGS when speaker says *"thousand."*
- Use MI–RBGS when speaker says *"million."*
- Use BL–RBGS when speaker says *"billion."*
- Use TR–RBGS when speaker says *"trillion."*

> *Two reasons some reporters prefer to use these ways of writing ~,~ are: (1) They prefer to write a stroke for what they hear, as opposed to thinking about inserting a comma; (2) When editing the document, they can easily spot errors. For example, if your translation reads 10,50,200, one digit has been omitted.*
> *Your notes reading* 10/MI–RBGS/50/THOU–RBGS/20–U *will indicate that the correct number should be 10,050,200.*

### Examples

| | |
|---|---|
| 1,001 | 1/THOU–RBGS/0–U/1 |
| 12,020 | 12/THOU–RBGS/0/20 |
| 123,300 | 123/THOU–RBGS/30–U |
| 1,500,250 | 1/MI–RBGS/50–U/THOU–RBGS/250 |
| 92,400,230 | 2–E9/MI–RBGS/40–U/THOU–RBGS/230 |
| 135,400,044 | 135/MI–RBGS/40–U/THOU–RBGS/0/4–U |
| 5,555,200,000 | 5/BL–RBGS/5/5–U/MI–RBGS/20–U/THOU–RBGS/0–EU |
| 50,500,100,500 | 50/BL–RBGS/50–U/MI–RBGS/10–U/THOU–RBGS/50–U |
| 100,236,450,000 | 10–U/BL–RBGS/236/MI–RBGS/450/THOU–RBGS/0–EU |

# LARGE NUMBERS:
## 1, 2, 3, etc.

| | |
|---|---|
| **STYLE:** | **Figures, with comma following, attached to previous and next numbers.** |
| **NUMBER BAR USED?** | **No** |
| **ENGLISH TRANSLATION:** | **Figures** |

**NOTE: This format is used to build numbers that require the 3-digit grouping comma (i.e., numbers greater than 999).**
**To build the desired range, use the numbers given on pages 3-18 to 3-20 (Plain Numbers) in combination with the attached comma \*RBGS.**
**CAT dictionary entry = ~1,~**

| | |
|---|---|
| 1, | W*UN/*RBGS |
| 2, | TWO*/*RBGS |
| 3, | THR*E/*RBGS |
| 4, | FO*UR/*RBGS |
| 5, | FAOIF/*RBGS |
| 6, | SWIX/*RBGS |
| 7, | SEV/*RBGS |
| 8, | YAIT/*RBGS |
| 9, | NAO*IN/*RBGS |

*For refined writing of digits in the hundreds, use HO–RBGS and HU–RBGS where applicable, as explained on page 3-105.*

**Examples:**

| | |
|---|---|
| 1,200 | W*UN/*RBGS/TWO*/HUN |
| 10,525 ( *raw* ) | T*EN/*RBGS/FAOIF/TWAOIV |
| *(translates as 10,5 25)* | |
| 10,525 ( *refined* ) | T*EN/*RBGS/FAOIF/HU–RBGS/TWAOIV |
| *(translates as 10,525)* | |
| 21,250 ( *raw* ) | TWUN/*RBGS/TWO*/VI |
| *(translates as 21,2 50)* | |
| 21,250 ( *refined* ) | TWUN/*RBGS/TWO*/HU–RBGS/VI |
| *(translates as 21,250)* | |
| 100,101 ( *raw* ) | W*UN/HUN/*RBGS/W*UN/ZAO*ER/W*UN |
| *(translates as 100,1 0 1)* | |
| 100,101 ( *refined* ) | W*UN/HUN/*RBGS/W*UN/HO–RBGS/W*UN |
| *(translates as 100,101)* | |

## LARGE NUMBERS:
### 1, 2, 3, ... 19,

| | |
|---|---|
| **STYLE:** | **Figures, with comma following, attached to previous and next numbers.** |
| **NUMBER BAR USED?** | **Yes** |
| **ENGLISH TRANSLATION:** | **Figures** |

**NOTE: This format is used to build numbers that require the 3-digit grouping comma (i.e., numbers greater than 999). Where physically possible, the full comma symbol with asterisk (\*RBGS) is used and vice versa on left bank (SKWR\*). To extend this format beyond 25, use the numbers given on pages 3-29 to 3-32: "Numbers (with comma)." CAT dictionary entry = ~1,~**

**1, - 9,**

| | |
|---|---|
| 1, | 1\*RBGS |
| 2, | 2\*RBGS |
| 3, | 3\*RBGS |
| 4, | 4\*RBGS |
| 5, | 5\*RBGS |
| 6, | SKWR\*6 |
| 7, | SKWR\*7 |
| 8, | SKWR\*8 |
| 9, | SKWR\*9 |

**10, - 19,**

| | |
|---|---|
| 10, | 10\*RBGS |
| 11, | 1\*URBGS |
| 12, | 12\*RBGS |
| 13, | 13\*RBGS |
| 14, | 14\*RBGS |
| 15, | 15\*RBGS |
| 16, | 1\*6BGS |
| 17, | 1\*7GS |
| 18, | 1\*RB8 |
| 19, | 1\*RB9 |

**Examples:**

| | |
|---|---|
| 10,525 | 10\*RBGS/5/25 |
| 21,250 | 12\*ERBGS/250, 2/1\*RBGS,250 |
| 222,100 | 2–U/2\*RBGS/10–U |
| 913,689 | 9/13\*RBGS/689 |

## LARGE NUMBERS:
### 1,001  13,300  100,000 etc.

| | |
|---|---|
| **STYLE:** | **Figures in thousands.** |
| **NUMBER BAR USED?** | **Yes** |
| **ENGLISH TRANSLATION:** | **Figures** |

**NOTE: With this system, all numbers from 1,000 - 999,999 can be defined in 2-3 strokes.**

### Examples:

| | |
|---|---|
| 1,001 | 1*RBGS/0–U/1 |
| 2,020 | 2*RBGS/0/20 |
| 3,300 | 3*RBGS/30–U |
| 4,044 | 4*RBGS/0/4–U |
| 5,555 | 5*RBGS/5/5–U |
| 6,987 | SKWR*6/9/E78 |
| 7,789 | SKWR*7/789 |
| 8,100 | SKWR*8/10–U |
| 9,150 | SKWR*9/150 |
| | |
| 10,000 | 10*RBGS/0–EU, 10/0*EU |
| 11,001 | 1*URBGS/0–U/1 |
| 12,020 | 12*RBGS/0/20 |
| 13,300 | 13*RBGS/30–U |
| 14,044 | 14*RBGS/0/4–U |
| 15,280 | 15*RBGS/28/0 |
| 16,987 | 16*BGS/9/E78 |
| 17,798 | 1*7GS/79/8 |
| 18,100 | 1*RB8/10–U |
| 19,150 | 1*RB9/150 |
| | |
| 20,689 | 20*RBGS/689 |
| 31,550 | 13*ERBGS/5/50 |
| 42,888 | 24*ERBGS/8/U8 |
| 53,379 | 35*ERBGS/379 |
| 67,225 | SKWR*67/2/25 |
| 75,600 | 5*E7GS/0–EU6 |
| 86,900 | SKWR*E68/0–EU9 |
| 99,467 | SKWR*U9/467 |
| | |
| 100,000 | 10*URBGS/0–EU, 10–U/0*EU |
| 200,100 | 20*URBGS/10–U |
| 300,287 | 30*URBGS/28/7 |
| 401,359 | 40/1*RBGS/359 |
| 520,200 | 5/20*RBGS/20–U |

# ADVANCED NUMBERING TACTICS

It is not often necessary to write numbers in figures in the millions and beyond. However, it is useful to know how such numbers can be constructed. The possibilities are almost infinite. This section is intended to be used for reference in situations where the reporter is required to write complicated large numbers in their refined form.

## MIX AND MATCH

A popular advanced tactic is to mix and match the various styles previously defined.

**Example: 100,250,450,500**

**using number bar:**
10*URBGS/250*RBGS/450/50*U

**spelled out:**
W*UN/HUN/BL–RBGS/TWO*/HU–RBGS/VI/MI–RBGS/FO*UR/HU–RBGS/
VI/THOU–RBGS/FAOIF/HUN

**mix and match:**
10–U/BL–RBGS/250/MI–RBGS/450/THOU–RBGS/FAOIF/HUN

As discussed on page 3-103, the techniques used so far for large numbers may at times leave a space between digits in the translated version, for later "cleanup" (e.g., 1,5 25,3 50 instead of 1,525,350). If the working environment will not tolerate using numbers in the "raw" translation, a variety of **refinement tactics** can be employed where needed to avoid unwanted spaces. Some add an extra stroke while others do not.

1. In order to join numbers using "mix and match" methods, you will at times need a "delete space" command. Use DL–RBGS for "delete space." CAT dictionary entry = ~

*Associate the DL in DL–RBGS with "delete space."*

**Example: 1,525,350**

**using number bar:**
1*RBGS/5/25*RBGS/350
*(translates as 1,525,350)*

**spelled out - raw:**
W*UN/MI–RBGS/FAOIF/TWAOIV/THOU–RBGS/THR*E/VI
*(translates as 1,5 25,3 50)*

**spelled out - refined:**
W*UN/*RBGS/FAOIF/DL–RBGS/TWAOIV/*RBGS/THR*E/**DL–RBGS**/VI
*(translates as 1,525,350)*

W*UN/MI–RBGS/FAOIF/HU–RBGS/TWAOIV/THOU–RBGS/THR*E/
HU–RBGS/VI
*(translates as 1,525,350)*

**mix and match - raw:**
W*UN/MI–RBGS/FAOIF/25/THOU–RBGS/THR*E/50
*(translates as 1,5 25,3 50)*

**mix and match - refined:**
W*UN/MI–RBGS/FAOIF/DL–RBGS/25/THOU–RBGS/THR*E/**DL–RBGS**/50
*(translates as 1,525,350)*

2. For numbers with *"000"* use HO–RBGSZ.
   CAT dictionary entry = ~000

*Associate the HO in HO–RBGSZ with
"hundred zero" or "zero in hundreds."*

**Example: 100,236,450,000**

**using number bar:**
10*URBGS/23*6–BGS/450/0*EU
*(translates as 100,236,450,000)*

**spelled out - raw:**
W*UN/HUN/BL–RBGS/TWO*/THRIK/MI–RBGS/FO*UR/HU–RBGS/VI/
THOU
*(translates as 100,2 36,450,000)*

**spelled out - refined:**
W*UN/HUN/BL–RBGS/TWO*/DL–RBGS/THRIK/MI–RBGS/FO*UR/
HU–RBGS/VI/THOU
*(translates as 100,236,450,000)*

**mix and match:**
10–U/BL–RBGS/236/MI–RBGS/450/THOU–RBGS/0–EU
*(translates as 100,236,450,000)*

**mix and match:**
W*UN/HUN/BL–RBGS/236/MI–RBGS/450/THOU–RBGS/**HO–RBGSZ**
*(translates as 100,236,450,000)*

3. To include a comma, use HO*RBGSZ for *",000"*
   CAT dictionary entry = ~,000~

*Associate the HO in HO*RBGSZ with
"hundred zero" or "zero in hundreds."*

**Example: 100,000,000,500**

**using number bar:**
10*URBGS/0–EU/0*EU/50*U

**spelled out:**
W*UN/HUN/BL–RBGS/**HO*RBGSZ/HO*RBGSZ**/FAOIF/HUN

**mix and match:**
10–U/BL–RBGS/**HO*RBGSZ/HO*RBGSZ**/50–U

**mix and match:**
10*URBGS/**HO*RBGSZ/HO*RBGSZ**/50–U

**mix and match:**
W*UN/HUN/BL–RBGS/**HO*RBGSZ/HO*RBGSZ**/50–U

4. For a zero following a comma, attached on both sides, SKWR0* for ",0"
   CAT dictionary entry = ~,0~

*Associate the SKWR in SKWR0\* with a comma
and the asterisk with "delete space."*

**Example: 3,000,025**

**using number bar:**
3–RBGS/0*EU/**SKWR*0**/25
*(translates as 3,000,025)*

**spelled out - raw:**
THR*E/MI–RBGS/HO*RBGSZ/ZAOER/TWAOIV
*(translates as 3,000,0 25)*

**spelled out - refined:**
THR*E/MI–RBGS/HO–RBGSZ/**SKWR*0**/TWAOIV
*(translates as 3,000,025)*

**mix and match:**
3–RBGS/HO–RBGSZ/**SKWR*0**/25
*(translates as 3,000,025)*

5. For 500 following a comma, attached on the left side, use 50*U
   CAT dictionary entry = ~,500

*Associate the 50U in 50\*U with 500
and the asterisk with "delete space comma."*

**Example: 20,000,500**

**using number bar:**
20*RBGS/0–EU/**50*U**
*(translates as 20,000,500)*

**spelled out:**
TWI/MI–RBGS/HO*RBGSZ/FAOIF/HUN
*(translates as 20,000,500)*

**mix and match:**
TWI/MI–RBGS/0–EU/**50*U**
*(translates as 20,000,500)*

## WITH NUMBER BAR ONLY

### Millions (examples)

| | |
|---|---|
| 1,000,000 | 1*RBGS/0–EU/0*EU, 10*EU/0*EU, 1/0*EURBGS/0–EU |
| 2,000,005 | 2*RBGS/0–EU/0*URBGS/5, 20*EU/0*URBGS/5, 2/0*EURBGS/0*U/5 |
| 3,000,238 | 3*RBGS/0–EU/*RBGS/238, 30*EU/*RBGS/238, 3/0*EURBGS/238 |
| 4,000,100 | 4*RBGS/0–EU/*RBGS/10–U, 40*EU/*RBGS/10–U, 4/0*EURBGS/10–U |
| 5,088,333 | 5*RBGS/0/SKWR*U8/3/3–U |
| 6,519,030 | SKWR*6/15*E/SKWR*9/0/30 |
| 7,896,002 | SKWR*7/89/SKWR*6/0*U/2 |
| 8,500,000 | SKWR*8/50–U/0*EU, 8/50*U/0*EU |
| 9,250,000 | SKWR*9/250/0*EU |
| 10,000,000 | 10*RBGS/0–EU/0*EU, 10/0*EU/0*EU |
| 50,500,000 | 50*RBGS/50–U/0*EU, 50/50*U/0*EU |

### Billions (examples)

| | |
|---|---|
| 1,000,000,000 | 1*RBGS/0–EU/0*EU/0*EU, 10*EU/0*EU/0*EU |
| 2,500,000,000 | 2*RBGS/50–U/0*EU/0*EU, 2/50*U/0*EU/0*EU |
| 3,000,600,000 | 3*RBGS/0–EU/*RBGS/0–EU6/O*EU, 3/0*EU/*RBGS/0–EU6/0*EU |
| 4,001,500,000 | 4*RBGS/0*U/1/50*U/0*EU |
| 5,015,600,000 | 5*RBGS/0/15*RBGS/0–E6U/0*EU |
| 6,500,000,000 | SKWR*6/5–0U/0*EU/0*EU, 6/50*U/0*EU/0*EU |
| 7,850,500,000 | SKWR*7/8/50/50*U/0*EU |
| 8,350,440,500 | SKWR*8/350*RBGS/4/40/50*U |
| 9,555,800,000 | SKWR*9/5/5*URBGS/0–EU8/0*EU |
| 10,000,000,000 | 10*RBGS/0–EU/0*EU/0*EU, 10/0*EU/0*EU/0*EU |
| 100,000,000,000 | 10*URBGS/0–EU/0*EU/0*EU, 10–U/0*EU/0*EU/0*EU |

## DOUBLE NUMBERS

The basic rule "U doubles a digit" will suffice for writing all double numbers. However, in numbers over 100, this basic rule may leave a space between some numbers. The following enhancements will eliminate spaces in this situation.

- Use *U to double the first digit and attach it on its right.
  Examples:
  112 ........................................................................................... 1*U/2
  998 ........................................................................................... 9*U/8

- Use U to double the last digit and attach it on its left.
  Examples:
  122 ........................................................................................... 12–U
  988 ........................................................................................... 9/U8

- To include a comma, use number to be doubled with URBGS or SKWR–U.
  Examples:
  211, ................................................................................... 2/1–URBGS
  988, ................................................................................... 9/SKWR–U8

- To include a comma attached on both sides, use number to be doubled with *URBGS or SKWR*U.
  Examples:
  122,026 ....................................................................... 12*URBGS/0/26
  988,102 ....................................................................... 9/SKWR*U8/10/2

# PART 4

# LEXICON OF WORD ASSOCIATIONS

**4**

general
lexicon a-z
numbers

# A LEXICON OF
# WORD ASSOCIATIONS

## GENERAL

This section contains a lexicon of various forms of word association that can be used to resolve conflicts and to facilitate the learning of briefs and phrases. It is intended to be used mainly for reference. Included are:

- homonyms (*there, they're, their* )
- stenonyms (KANT, KA*NT, K–NT)
- other soundalikes, lookalikes and easily confused words (*accelerate, exhilarate*)
- antonyms (*honesty, dishonesty* )
- word pairs and families by suffix/final word (*arrest warrant, bench warrant, death warrant, search warrant, traffic warrant* )
- rhyming words (carotid, parotid / KROTD, PROTD)
- combinations of these elements (*backyard, backward, bard, barred* / BARD, BAURD, BA*URD, BA*RD).

Refer to this lexicon when you have questions about specific words, phrases and steno outlines. Words and phrases are arranged alphabetically by "keyword" entry in bold. The initial keyword is separated from related secondary entries by a bullet.

Entries appear more than once. Thus [**resource** • source] listed under "R" can also be found under "S" as [**source** • resource]. In this context, the words in one entry may appear again in the very next entry, in reverse order. For example, [**pride** • pried] is followed by [**pried** • pride]. This is to enable you to search quickly through the lists, looking down the left column at the word or phrase in bold.

Some homonym entries are grouped with related stenonyms. For example, if you are wondering how to write *"peace"* and *"piece"* conflict-free, look up either of these words. In addition to finding *"peace"* and *"piece,"* you will find other words closely related to them, either by steno or English: *"appease"* and *"peas."* These (potential) conflicts are resolved in one lexicon entry so you do not have to search further to check them all.

Sometimes the keyword in one entry will appear again as the keyword in the next entry, followed by a different secondary entry from the line above. In the example of *"peace,"* a separate entry for [**peace** • pace] is given, as these two words have a different relationship than [**peace** • appease, peas, piece]. The entry [**peace** • pace] covers stenonyms [PAES • PAIS], whereas *"peace," "peas"* and *"piece"* are homonyms. The word *"appease"* is included in the first entry because in its one-stroke brief form, it becomes a stenonym related to *"peace," "peas"* and *"piece,"* but has no connection with the [PAES • PAIS] relationship.

Some words/phrases have more than one possible outline, but generally only one outline is given. See ***Brief Encounters*** for a more complete listing of outline options.

---

An "-ed," "-ing" or "-s" ending can always be written as a separate stroke, and these are sometimes included as an alternative solution. Where it is possible to write an outline with an asterisk to save a stroke, the short (asterisk) form is given since **CATegorically Speaking** is largely about saving strokes. For example, *"salaried"* can be written SAL/–D and also SA\*LD, but is given as SA\*LD to (a) eliminate the second stroke and (b) prevent a conflict with *"saddle"* (SALD).

A tilde ~ indicates a "delete-space" command in your CAT dictionary. For example, **~fold** heads a list that includes *"twofold"* and *"sixfold."*

# A

abdominal • able ..................................................... ABL • AIBL

abhor • hoar, whore ............................................... HOER • HAOR, WHOER

abhorred • hoard, horde ........................................ HOERD • HAORD, HORD

abhors • hoarse, horse ......................................... HOERS • HAORS, HORS

ability • disability .................................................. AIBLT • DAIBLT

able • abdominal .................................................. AIBL • ABL

able

    able ............................................................... AIBL

    are able ......................................................... RAIBL

    be able .......................................................... BAIBL

    disable .......................................................... DAIBL

    enable ........................................................... NA*IBL

    payable ......................................................... PAIBL

    unable ........................................................... NAIBL

about how late • how late ...................................... BOULT • HOULT

about the same time • basement ......................... BAEMT • BAIMT

abrasion • inebriation ............................................ BRAEGS • BRAIGS

abridge • bridge .................................................... BRAIJ • BRIJ

abroad • brood ...................................................... BRAOD I BRAO*D

absolute • salute ................................................... SLU • SLAOUT

absoluteness • sullenness ................................... SLUNS • SLUNZ

absorb • associate ................................................ SORB • SOERB

abuse

    abuse ............................................................ BAOUS

    child abuse .................................................... KHAOUS

    sexual abuse ................................................. SWAOUS

    spousal abuse ............................................... SPAOUS

accelerate • exhilarate .......................................... SLERT • ZIL

acceleration • exhilaration .................................... SLERGS • ZILGS

accent • ascent, assent ........................................ SKWANT • SKAENT, SAENT

accept • except ..................................................... SEP • KPEP

acceptability • unacceptability ............................. SEBLT • SNEBLT

acceptable • unacceptable .................................... SEBL • SNEBL

access • assess, excess ....................................... KRES • SAES, KPESZ

accident • descent ................................................ SDEN • SDENT

accident • Occident ............................................... SDEN • SDON

accidental • Occidental ......................................... SDENL • SDONL

acclaim • claim ...................................................... KLAEM • KLAIM

accompany • company .......................................... KPOIN • KPAEN

accountant • cant, can't ........................................ KANT • KA*NT, K–NT

| | |
|---|---|
| **accrual** • cruel | KRUL • KRAOUL |
| **accruement** • cruel and unusual punishment, recruitment | KR*UMT *or* KRAO*UMT • KRUMT, KRAOUMT |
| **accurate** • carat | KRAT • KRA*T |
| **accurate** • inaccurate | KRAT • NAEK |
| **accuse** • cues | KAOUS • KAOUZ |
| **accustom** • cause of them | KA*UFM • KAUFM |
| **ache** • acre | AIK • AEK |
| **ache** • backache | AIK • BAIK |
| **acid** • decided | SD*ID • SDID |
| **acknowledge** • knowledge | NAOJ • NOJ |
| **acquire** • choir | KWAOIR • KWOIR |
| **acre** • ache | AEK • AIK |
| **across** • cross | KROS • KROSZ |
| **act** • Alaska | AK • A*K |
| **action** • acts, ax | AX • AKZ, A*X |
| **actions** • axes ( *tools* ) | AXZ • A*XZ |
| **activate** • actuate | TWAET • TWAIT |
| **actor** • aortic | AORK • AORKT *or* AO*RK |
| **acts** • action, ax | AKZ • AX, A*X |
| **actuate** • activate | TWAIT • TWAET |
| **ad** • add | A*D • AD |
| **add** • ad | AD • A*D |
| **add here** • adhere | AD/HAOER • DHAOER *or* HAO*ER |
| **addict** • edict | DIKT • DAOEKT *or* DAOEK |
| **addiction** • addition | DIX • DIGS |
| **addition** • addiction, edition, in addition | DIGS • DIX, YIGS, NIGS |
| **addition** • digs | DIGS • DIGZ |
| **address** • dress | DRAES • DRESZ |
| **adept** • deadly weapon, did he want | DWEPT • DWEP, DEPT |
| **adhere** • add here | DHAOER *or* HAO*ER • AD/HAOER |
| **adherence** • adherents | HAOERNS • HAOERNTS |
| **adherents** • adherence | HAOERNTS • HAOERNS |
| **adjusted** • maladjusted, readjusted | JAUFD • MAUFD, RAUFD |
| **administrative** • might have | MIV • MIF |
| **admissibility** • inadmissibility | MIFLT • NIFLT |
| **admissible** • inadmissible | MIFL • NIFL |
| **admit** • mitt | MIT • MOIT |

**adolescence** • adolescents ................................... DLENS • DLENTS

**adolescents** • adolescence ................................... DLENTS • DLENS

**advance** • vans ...................................................... VANS • VANZ

**adverse** • averse, diverse ...................................... DWERZ • WERS, DWERS

**advice** • advise ....................................................... VIS • VIZ

**advocates** • advocation ......................................... VOEKZ • VOEX

**advocation** • vocation, Volkswagen ...................... VOEX • VOEGS, VO*EX

**aerial** • airline, arterial ............................................ A*ERL • AIRL, AERL

**affable** • alphabet, alphabetical ............................. AFBL • AFL, AEFL

**affair** • fair ............................................................... AIFR • FAIR

**affect** • effect, fake ................................................. FAEK • FEK, FAIK

**affection** • effectuation ........................................... AFX • EFX

**affiliation** • fillings .................................................. FILGS • F*ILGS *or* FILGZ

**afraid** • forelady, frayed ......................................... FRAID • FRAED, FRA*ED

**aft** • after the .......................................................... A*FT • AFT

**afternoon**
    afternoon ......................................................... AFRN
    good afternoon ............................................... GAFRN
    in the afternoon .............................................. NAFRN
    that afternoon ................................................. THAFN
    this afternoon .................................................. TH–FRN
    tomorrow afternoon ......................................... TWAFRN
    yesterday afternoon ........................................ YAFRN

**after the** • aft .......................................................... AFT • A*FT

**afterward** • afterword ............................................. AFRD • AOFRD

**afterword** • afterward ............................................. AOFRD • AFRD

**agenda** • gender .................................................... JEND • JERND

**ago** • agriculture ..................................................... AG • A*G

**agree** • disagree ..................................................... GRE • SGRE

**agreeable** • disagreeable ....................................... GREBL • SGREBL

**agreement** • disagreement ..................................... GREMT • SGREMT

**agriculture** • ago ..................................................... A*G • AG

**ah** • awe ................................................................. AU • A*U

**ahead of** • hateful ................................................... HAIF • HAIFL

**aid** • aide ................................................................ AID • AED

**aide** • aid ................................................................ AED • AID

**aids** • AIDS, aides .................................................. AIDZ • A*IDZ, AEDZ

**AIDS** • aids ............................................................. A*IDZ • AIDZ

**ail** • ale, alley .......................................................... AIL • A*EL, AEL

**ailment** • element .................................................... AIMT • L–MT

| | |
|---|---|
| **air** • area | AIR • AER |
| **air** • err, heir | AIR • *ER, HIR *or* HA*IR |
| **air-condition** • Aryan | AIRN • AERN |
| **airline** • aerial, arterial | AIRL • A*ERL, AERL |
| **aisle** • I'll, isle | YAOIL • AOIL, YAOIL |
| **Alaska** • act | A*K • AK |
| **alcoholics** • chickenpox | KHOKS • KHOKZ |
| **ale** • ail, alley | A*EL • AIL, AEL |
| **allegiance** • legion, lesion | LAOEJ • LAO*EJ, LAOEGS |
| **allegiance** • pledge of allegiance | LAOEJ • PLAOEJS |
| **alleviate** • elicit | LAOEVT • LAOEFT |
| **alley** • ale | AEL • A*EL |
| **alliance** • lInes | LAOINZ • LAOINS |
| **allot** • a lot | AI/LOT • A/LOT |
| **allow** • disallow | LOU • DLOU |
| **allow** • lieu, Lou | LOU • LAOU, LO*U |
| **allowed** • loud | LO*UD • LOUD |
| **all ready** • already | AUL/R–D • L–R |
| **all together** • altogether | AUL/TOEG • L–GT |
| **alluvial** • Louisville | LAOUVL • LAOUV |
| **all ways** • always | AUL/WAIS • AUZ |
| **alone** • loan, lone, loon | LAON • LOEN, LO*EN, LAO*N |
| **a lot** • allot | A/LOT • AI/LOT |
| **alphabet** • affable, alphabetical | AFL • AFBL, AEFL |
| **already** • all ready | L–R • AUL/R–D |
| **altar** • alter | A*LT • ALT |
| **alter** • altar | ALT • A*LT |
| **alternating current** • current, direct current | TURNT • KURNT, DRURNT |
| **alternative** • tern, turn | TERN • T*ERN, TURN |
| **alternatively** • eternal | TERNL • TAOERNL |
| **altitude** • attitude | TAO*UD • TAOUD |
| **altogether** • all together | L–GT • AUL/TOEG |
| **aluminum** • lumbar | LUM • L*UM |
| **always** • all ways | AUZ • AUL/WAIS |
| **a.m.** • p.m. | A*M • P*M *or* P–M |
| **amaze** • maze | MAES • MAEZ |
| **ambience** • cabins | KBINS • KBINZ |
| **ambition** • biggest | BIGS • B*IGS |

**amendment**

| | |
|---|---|
| amendment | AEMT |
| Fifth Amendment | FAEMT |
| First Amendment | FIRMT |

**America**

| | |
|---|---|
| America | MERK |
| Central America | STRERK |
| Latin America | LERK |
| North America | NAERK |
| South America | SERK |

**American**

| | |
|---|---|
| American | MERN |
| American Sign Language | MERNL |
| Americans with Disabilities Act | MERND |

**American**

| | |
|---|---|
| Central American | STRARN |
| Latin American | LAERN |
| Native American | NAIRN |
| North American | NAERN, NARN |
| South American | SARN |

| | |
|---|---|
| **ammunition** • musician | NAOUGS • MAOUGS |
| **amp** • ampere, volt-ampere | AMP • AEMP, VAEMP |
| **ampere** • amp, volt-ampere | AEMP • AMP, VAEMP |
| **amuse** • mews, muse | MAOUS • MAO*US, MAOUZ |
| **and a quarter** • one-and-a-quarter | NART • NAERT |
| **annals** • annuals, animals | ANLZ • YULS, ANLS |
| **annihilate** • Nile | NAOIL • NAO*IL |
| **announce** • nouns | NOUNS • NOUNZ |
| **annoyed** • no idea | NO*ID • NOID |
| **annoys** • noise | NOIZ • NOIS |
| **annual** • annul, null | YUL • N*UL, NUL |
| **annuals** • annals, animals | YULS • ANLZ, ANLS |
| **annul** • annual, null | N*UL • YUL, NUL |
| **another** • at another time | AOT • TAONT |
| **answering service** • customer service | SNEFRB • KMEFRB |
| **ant** • aunt | ANT • AUNT |
| **ante** • anti | AENT • AOINT |

**anterior**

| | |
|---|---|
| anterior | AOR |
| exterior | KPAOR |
| inferior | FAOR |
| interior | NAOR |
| posterior | PAO*R |
| superior | SAOR |

**anterior** • oar .......................................................... AOR • AO*R

**anti** • ante .............................................................. AOINT • AENT

**anybody** • nib .......................................................... NIB • N*IB

**any body** • anybody .............................................. NI/BOD • NIB

**anybody else** • nibble ........................................... NIBL • N*IBL

**anybody else's** • nibbles ...................................... NIBLS • N*IBLS

**anyhow** • now ......................................................... NO*U • NOU

**anymore** • no more ................................................ NIM • NOM

**any more** • anymore ............................................... NI/MOR • NIM

**any one** • anyone ................................................... NI/WUN • NIN

**anyone else** • anyone else's ................................. NINL • NINLS

**anyplace** • nape ..................................................... NAIP • NAEP

**any place** • anyplace ............................................. NI/PLAIS • NAIP

**any thing** • anything ............................................... NI/THING • NIG

**anything further** • nothing further ........................ NIRT • NORT

**anything unusual** • unusual .................................. THURB • NURB

**anytime** • knit ......................................................... NIT • N*IT

**any time** • anytime ................................................. NI/TAOIM • NIT

**anyway** • nay, neigh, 98 ....................................... NAI • NAE, NAEG, NA*I

**any way** • anyway ................................................... NI/WAI • NAI

**any where** • anywhere ........................................... NI/WR– • NIR

**aortic** • actor ........................................................... AORKT *or* AO*RK • AORK

**apartment** • compartment ...................................... PARMT • KPARMT

**apologies** • Jesus .................................................. JAOES • JAOEZ

**apology** • gee ......................................................... JAOE • GAOE

**apparently** • paternal ............................................. PAERNL • PARNL

**appeal** • peal, peel ................................................. PAEL • PA*EL, PAOEL

**appear** • disappear ................................................ PAER • SPAER

**appear** • pear ......................................................... PAER • PA*ER

**appearance** • disappearance ................................ PAERNS • SPAERNS

**appearance** • patterns ........................................... PAERNS • PAERNZ

**appears** • peers, pierce ......................................... PAERS • PAOERZ, PAOERS

**appease** • peace, peas, piece .............................. PAOEZ • PAES, PAEZ, PAOES

**appellant** • appellate .............................................. PAELT • PEL

**appellate** • appellant .............................................. PEL • PAELT

**appellate** • appellate court .................................... PEL • PELT

**appellate court** • appellate, pelt ........................... PELT • PEL, P*ELT

**appellee** • plea ....................................................... PLAOE • PLAE

| | |
|---|---|
| **application** • politician | PLIGS • POLGS |
| **applied** • plied | PLAOID • PLAO*ID |
| **apply** • ply, reply | PLAOI • PLAO*I, PLI |
| **appoint** • disappoint | POIN • SPOIN |
| **appoint** • point | POIN • POINT |
| **appointment** • disappointment | POIMT • SPOIMT |
| **apportion** • portion, proportion | PAORGS • PORGS, PRORGS |
| **appraise** • preys | PRAES • PRAEZ |
| **appropriate** • misappropriate | PROEPT • MOEPT |
| **appropriate** • propose | PROEPT • PROEP |
| **appropriation** • misappropriation | PROEPGS • MOEPGS |
| **appropriation** • proposition | PROEPGS • PROPGS |
| **approval** • disapproval | PROVL • SPROVL |
| **approve** • disapprove | PRAOV • SPRAOV |
| **approximate** • proximate | P– • PR–KT |
| **approximation** • proxy | PROX • PRO*X |
| **arbitrate** • ash | ARB • A*RB |
| **arc** • ark | ARK • A*RK |
| **area** • air | AER • AIR |
| **areas** • arrears | AERS • RAOERZ |
| **argue** • arresting | AERG • ARG |
| **argument** • arrangement | AERMT • ARMT |
| **Arizona** • as | A*Z • AZ |
| **ark** • arc | A*RK • ARK |
| **Arkansas** • arrest | A*R • AR |
| **arm** • disarm | ARM • DARM |
| **around** • surround | ARND • SROUN |
| **arraign** • arrange | RARN • ARNG |
| **arraignment** • arrangement | RAIMT • ARMT |
| **arrange** • arraign | ARNG • RARN |
| **arrange** • derange, disarrange | ARNG • DARNG, SARNG |
| **arrangement** • argument, arraignment | ARMT • AERMT, RAIMT |
| **arrears** • areas | RAOERZ • AERS |
| **arrest** • Arkansas | AR • A*R |
| **arresting** • argue | ARG • AERG |
| **arrival** • rival | RAOIVL • R–VL |
| **art** • artery | ART • AERT |
| **arterial** • aerial | AERL • A*ERL |

| | |
|---|---|
| **artery** • art | AERT • ART |
| **Aryan** • air-condition | AERN • AIRN |
| **as** • Arizona | AZ • A*Z |
| **ascends** • accents, assents | SAENDZ • SKWANTS, SAENTS |
| **ascension** • sanitation | SAENGS • SAINGS |
| **ascent** • accent, assent | SKAENT • SKWANT, SAENT |
| **ascertain** • certain | SAERN • SERN |
| **asked and answered** • scanned | SKARND • SKAND |
| **assail** • sale, sail | SW–L • SAEL, SAIL |
| **assassin** • cinnamon | SNIN • SNON |
| **assault with a deadly weapon** • deadly weapon | SWEP *or* SDWEP • DWEP |
| **assent** • accent, ascent | SAENT • SKWANT, SKAENT |
| **assents** • accents, ascends | SAENTS • SKWANTS, SAENDZ |
| **assess** • access, excess | SAES • KRES, KPESZ |
| **assess** • seas | SAES • SA*ES |
| **assessment** • segment | SAEFMT • SAEMT |
| **assign** • sign, sine | SOIN • SAOIN, SAO*IN |
| **assist** • cyst | S*IS • KR*IS |
| **assistance** • assistants | SNINS • SNINTS |
| **assistants** • assistance | SNINTS • SNINS |
| **as smart as** • smarts | SMARTS • SMAURTS *or* SMARTSZ |
| **associate** • absorb | SOERB • SORB |
| **associate** • disassociate, dissociate | SOERB • SDOERBT, SDOERB |
| **association** • disassociation, dissociation | SOERBGS • SDORBGS, SDOERBGS |
| **assurance** • insurance, sureness | SHAOURNZ • SHURNS, SHAOURNS |
| **assure** • insure, shower | SHOUR • SHUR, SHAUR |
| **as well as** • swells | SWELS • SWELZ |
| **at another time** • another | TAONT • AOT |
| **at another time** • at no time | TAONT • TOENT |
| **at any rate** • retreat, trait | TRAET • TRA*ET, TRAIT |
| **ate** • eight | AET • AIT |
| **at home** • home, hometown | THOEM • HOEM, HOEMT |
| **Atlanta** • Atlantic, tolerant | TLAN • TLAK, TLANT |
| **Atlantic** • Atlanta, tolerant | TLAK • TLAN, TLANT |
| **atmosphere** • sphere | SFAER • SFAOER |
| **at no time** • at another time | TOENT • TAONT |
| **at no time** • tonight | TOENT • TONT |

| | | |
|---|---|---|
| **atrocity** • controvert | ............................................... | TROFT • TROVT |
| **attach** • detach | ..................................................... | TAFP • DAFP |
| **attachment** • detachment | ..................................... | TAFMT • DAFMT |
| **attain** • twain | ....................................................... | TWAIN • TWA*IN |
| **attainder** • bill of attainder | ..................................... | TWAIRND • BAIRND |
| **attempt** • tempt | .................................................... | TAEMT • TEMT |
| **attendance** • attendants | ........................................ | TAENZ • TAENTS |
| **attendance** • instantaneous | .................................. | TAENZ • TAENS |
| **attendant** • tenant | .................................................. | TAENT • TANT |
| **attendants** • attendance | ........................................ | TAENTS • TAENZ |
| **attention** • tension | ................................................. | TAENGS • TENGS |
| **at that particular time** • at this particular time | ..... | TAPT • TIPT |
| **at the same time** • same time | ............................... | TAIMT • SAIMT |
| **at the very most** • most, very most | ...................... | TO*S • MO*S, VO*S |
| **attitudinal** • institutionalized | ................................. | TAOULD • TAOU*LD *or* TAOUFLD |
| **attitude** • altitude | .................................................... | TAOUD • TAO*UD |
| **attractively** • travel | ................................................ | TRAVL • TRAFL |
| **at which time** • at what time | ................................. | TWIT • TWAT |
| **at which time** • therewith, twit | .............................. | TWIT • TW*IT, TWOIT |
| **audible** • automobile | ............................................. | AUBL • AUB |
| **audible** • inaudible, no audible response | .............. | AUBL • NAUBL, NAUBLS |
| **audit** • auditor, auditory | ......................................... | AUD • AURD, AORD |
| **aunt** • ant | ............................................................. | AUNT • ANT |
| **aural** • binaural, monaural | ..................................... | AURL • BAURL *or* BAURNL, MAURNL |
| **aural** • oral | ............................................................ | AURL • ORL |
| **auto** • ought | ......................................................... | AOUT • AUT |
| **automobile** • audible | ............................................. | AUB • AUBL |
| **averse** • adverse, diverse | ..................................... | WERS • DWERZ, DWERS |
| **averse** • averts | ..................................................... | WERS • WERTS |
| **averse** • worse | ...................................................... | WERS • WORS |
| **aversion** • subversion | ........................................... | WERGS • SWERGS |
| **avert** • subvert | ...................................................... | WERT • SWERT |
| **averts** • averse | ...................................................... | WERTS • WERS |
| **awaken** • wane, Wayne | ......................................... | WAEN • WAIN, WA*IN |
| **award** • reward | ...................................................... | WAURD • RAUR |
| **aware** • ware, wear, where | ................................... | WAIR • WA*ER, WAER, WR– |
| **away** • Washington | ............................................... | WA • WA* |
| **away** • way | ........................................................... | WA • WAI |

**awe** • ah .................................................................... A*U • AU

**awed** • audit, odd ...................................................... A*UD • AUD, O*D

**a while** • awhile ........................................................ A/WHAOIL • AI/WHAOIL

**ax** • action, acts ....................................................... A*X • AX, AKZ

**axes**
    actions ............................................................. AXZ
    axes ( *tools* ) .................................................... A*XZ
    axes ( *lines* ) ................................................... SKWISZ, A*XZ
    axis .................................................................. SKWIS

**aye** • eye, I ............................................................... AO*I • AOI, I

# B

| | |
|---|---|
| **babe** • baby | BAEB • BAIB |
| **baby** • babe | BAIB • BAEB |
| **backache** • ache | BAIK • AIK |
| **backache** • bake | BAIK • BAEK |
| **backward** • backyard, bard, barred | BAURD • BARD, BA*URD, BA*RD |
| **backyard** • backward, bard, barred | BARD • BAURD, BA*URD, BA*RD |
| **bad faith** • good faith | B–F • G–F |
| **badly** • balanced, bald | BALD • BA*LD, BAULD |
| **bail** • bale | BAIL • BAEL |
| **bait** • bate | BAIT • BA*ET |
| **bait** • beat | BAIT • BAET |
| **bake** • backache | BAEK • BAIK |
| **balance** • ball, bawl | BAL • BAUL, BA*UL |
| **balanced** • badly, bald | BA*LD • BALD, BAULD |
| **bald** • badly, balanced | BAULD • BALD, BA*LD |
| **bald** • balled, bawled | BAULD • BAUL/–D, BA*ULD |
| **bale** • bail | BAEL • BAIL |
| **ball** • balance, bawl | BAUL • BAL, BA*UL |

**ball**

| | |
|---|---|
| baseball | BAEBL |
| basketball | BAUBL |
| billiard ball | BLIBL |
| blackball | BLABL |
| bowling ball | BOUBL |
| croquet ball | KROEBL |
| eyeball | AOIBL |
| fireball | FAOIRBL |
| football | FAOBL |
| fur ball | FURBL |
| golf ball | GOFBL |
| goofball | GAOFBL, GAOBL |
| hairball | HAIRBL |
| handball | H–BL |
| highball | HAOIBL |
| meatball | MAEBL |
| oddball | OBL |
| pinball | P–BL |
| racquetball | KWABL |
| screwball | SKRAOUBL |
| snowball | SNOEBL |
| soccer ball | SKR–BL |
| softball | SOFBL |
| tennis ball | TEBL |
| trackball | TRABL |

| | |
|---|---|
| volley ball | VOBL |
| **ballad** • ballet, ballot | BLALD • BLAI, BLAOT |
| **balled** • bald, bawled | BAUL/–D • BAULD, BA*ULD |
| **ballet** • ballad, ballot | BLAI • BLALD, BLAOT |
| **ballot** • ballad, ballet | BLAOT • BLALD, BLAI |
| **balm** • bomb, bottom | BAUM • BOEM, BOM |
| **band** • banned | BAND • BA*ND *or* BAN/–D |
| **bands** • bans | BANDZ • BANS |
| **bane** • obtain | BAEN • BAIN |
| **banned** • band | BAN/–D *or* BA*ND • BAND |
| **bans** • bands | BANS • BANDZ |
| **barb** • bash | BAURB • BARB |
| **bard** • backward, backyard, barred | BA*URD • BAURD, BARD, BA*RD |
| **bare** • bear | BAIR • BAER |
| **barely** • barrel | BAIRL • BAERL |
| **baron** • barren | BRON • BAIRN |
| **barred** • backward, backyard, bard | BA*RD • BAURD, BARD, BA*URD |
| **barrel** • barely | BAERL • BAIRL |
| **barren** • baron | BAIRN • BRON |
| **base** • basis, bass | BAIS • BAZ, BASZ |
| **baseball** • be able | BAEBL • BAIBL |
| **based** • baste | BAIFD • BA*IS |
| **basement** • about the same time | BAIMT • BAEMT |
| **bases** • basis | BAISZ • BAZ |
| **bash** • barb | BARB • BAURB |
| **basis** • base, bass | BAZ • BAIS, BASZ |
| **basis** • bases | BAZ • BAISZ |
| **basketball** • bauble, bobble | BAUBL • BA*UBL, BOBL |
| **bass** • base, basis | BASZ • BAIS, BAZ |
| **baste** • based | BA*IS • BAIFD |
| **bate** • bait, beat | BA*ET • BAIT, BAET |
| **bate** • bath, bathe | BA*ET • BA*T, BA*IT |
| **bathe** • bate, bath | BA*IT • BA*ET, BA*T |
| **bathroom** • bedroom | BARM • BERM |
| **baud** • bawdy, bod, body | BAUD • BA*UD, BO*D, BOD |
| **bawdy** • baud, bod, body | BA*UD • BAUD, BO*D, BOD |
| **bawl** • balance, ball | BA*UL • BAL, BAUL |
| **bawled** • bald, balled | BA*ULD • BAULD, BAUL/–D |

| | |
|---|---|
| **be** • bee | B– • BAOE |
| **beach** • beech | BAEFP • BAOEFP |
| **bean** • been | BAOEN • B–N |
| **bear** • bare | BAER • BAIR |
| **beat** • beet | BAET • BAOET |
| **beater** • batter | BAOERT • BAERT |
| **beau** • bow ( *& arrow* ) | BO*E • BOU |
| **because** • cause | BAUZ • KAUZ |
| **bedroom** • berm, master bedroom | BERM • B*ERM, MARM |
| **bee** • be | BAOE • B– |
| **beech** • beach | BAOEFP • BAEFP |
| **been** • bean, bin | B–N • BAOEN, BIN |
| **beer** • bier | BAOER • BAO*ER *or* BIR |
| **beet** • beat | BAOET • BAET |
| **begun** • bun | BUN • B*UN |
| **belief** • disbelief | BLAOEF • SBLAOEF |
| **believable** • unbelievable | BLEFBL • NEFBL |
| **believe** • disbelieve | BLAOEV • SBLAOEV |
| **belittle** • little | BLIL • LIL |
| **bell** • belle | BEL • B*EL |
| **Benzedrine** • Benz | BENS • BENZ |
| **berm** • bedroom | B*ERM • BERM |
| **berry** • bury | BRER • BRU |
| **berth** • birth | B*ERT • B*IRT |
| **beseech** • besiege | SAOEFP • BAOEJ |
| **besiege** • beseech | BAOEJ • SAOEFP |
| **best of my knowledge** • best of your knowledge | BEJ • BURJ |
| **best of my memory** • best of your memory | BIRM • BURM |
| **best of my recollection** • best of your recollection | BEX • BURX |
| **betrayed** • bread | BRA*ED • BRAED |
| **better** • bettor | BERT • BOERT |
| **bettor** • better | BOERT • BERT |
| **beyond a reasonable doubt** • reasonable doubt | Y–RD • –RD |
| **beyond the scope** • scope | YOEP • SKOEP |
| **bias or prejudice** • bop | BOP • BO*P |
| **bier** • beer | BIR *or* BAO*ER • BAOER |

| | |
|---|---|
| **biggest** • ambition | B*IGS • BIGS |
| **bill** • Bill | BIL • B*IL |
| **billed** • build | B*ILD • BILD |
| **billings** • Billings | BILGS • B*ILGS |
| **billion** • million, trillion | B–L • M–L, TR–L |
| **bill of attainder** • attainder | BAIRND • TWAIRND |
| **bin** • bean, been | BIN • BAOEN, B–N |
| **biaural** • aural, monaural | BAURL *or* BAURNL • AURL, MAURNL |
| **birth** • berth | B*IRT • B*ERT |
| **bite** • byte | BAOIT • BAO*IT |
| **black man** • bedlam | BLAN • BLAM |
| **black market** • market | BLAERK • MAERK |
| **blasting** • burglarizing | BLAFGT • BLAFG |
| **bleak** • oblique | BLAEK • BLAOEK |
| **bleu** • blew, blue | BL*U • BLU, BLAOU |
| **blew** • bleu, blue | BLU • BL*U, BLAOU |
| **bloc** • block | BLO*K • BLOK |
| **block** • bloc | BLOK • BLO*K |
| **blood poisoning** • poisoning | BLOIG • POIG |
| **blood transfusion** • transfusion | BLAOUFGS • TRAOUFGS |
| **blue** • bleu, blew | BLAOU • BL*U, BLU |
| **blurb** • blush | BL*URB • BLURB |
| **blush** • blurb | BLURB • BL*URB |
| **boar** • boor, bore | BO*ER • BAOR, BOER |
| **board** • bored | BORD • BOERD |
| **board** • circuit board | BORD • SKBORD |
| **boarder** • border | BRAORD • BROERD |
| **bobble** • basketball, bauble | BOBL • BAUBL, BA*UBL |
| **bod** • baud, bawdy, body | BO*D • BAUD, BA*UD, BOD |
| **bodily** • bole, boll, bowl | BOL • BOEL, BO*L, BOUL |
| **body** • baud, bawdy, bod | BOD • BAUD, BA*UD, BO*D |
| **bold** • bowled | BOLD • BOULD |
| **bolder** • boulder | BOERLD • BOURLD |
| **bole** • bodily, boll, bowl | BOEL • BOL, BO*L, BOUL |
| **bomb** • balm, bottom | BOEM • BAUM, BOM |
| **boor** • boar, bore | BAOR • BO*ER, BOER |
| **boos** • booze | BAOS • BAOZ |
| **booze** • boos | BAOZ • BAOS |

**bop** • bias or prejudice ................................ BO*P • BOP

**border** • boarder ................................ BROERD • BRAORD

**border** • brotherhood ................................ BROERD • BRORD

**bore** • boar, boor ................................ BOER • BO*ER, BAOR

**bore** • borrow ................................ BOER • BOR

**bored** • board, borrowed ................................ BOERD • BORD, BO*RD

**born** • borne, bourn ................................ BORN • BOERN, BOURN

**borough** • bureau, burro, burrow ................................ BROUG • BUR, BROE, BRO*E

**borrow** • bore ................................ BOR • BOER

**borrowed** • bored ................................ BO*RD • BOERD

**bottom** • balm, bomb ................................ BOM • BAUM, BOEM

**bough** • bow ................................ BOUG • BOU

**bouillon** • bullion ................................ BAO*UL • BAOUL

**boulder** • bolder ................................ BOURLD • BOERLD

**bounce** • bounds ................................ BOUNS • BOUNDZ

**bounds** • bounce ................................ BOUNDZ • BOUNS

**bourn** • born, borne ................................ BOURN • BORN, BOERN

**bow** *( & arrow )* • beau, bow *( bend )* ................................ BOE • BO*E, BOU

**bow** *( bend )* • bough ................................ BOU • BOUG

**bowel** • bowl ................................ BO*UL • BOUL

**bowing** • bough ................................ BO*UG • BOUG

**bowl** • bodily, bole, boll ................................ BOUL • BOL, BOEL, BO*L

**bowl** • bowel ................................ BOUL • BO*UL

**bowled** • bold ................................ BOULD • BOLD

**boy** • buoy ................................ BOI • BO*I

**boyfriend** • girlfriend ................................ BOIF • GOIF

**brace** • braise, brays ................................ BRAIS • BRAIZ, BRA*IS

**bradycardia** • cardia ................................ BRAUR • KAUR

**braid** • brayed ................................ BRAID • BRA*ID

**brainstorm** • storm ................................ BRORM • STORM

**brain tumor** • tumor ................................ BRAOURM • TAOURM

**braise** • brace, brays ................................ BRAIZ • BRAIS, BRA*IS

**brake** • break ................................ BRAIK • BRAEK

**brayed** • braid ................................ BRA*ID • BRAID

**brays** • brace, braise ................................ BRA*IS • BRAIS, BRAIZ

**breach** • breech ................................ BRAEFP • BRAOEFP

**bread** • betrayed ................................ BRAED • BRA*ED

**bread** • bred ................................ BRAED • BRED

---

| | | |
|---|---|---|
| **breadth** • breath | BR*ETD *or* BRA*ET • BR*ET |
| **break** • brake | BRAEK • BRAIK |
| **breaker** • circuit breaker | BRAERK • SKBRAERK |
| **breath** • breadth | BR*ET • BR*ETD *or* BRA*ET |
| **bred** • bread | BRED • BRAED |
| **breech** • breach | BRAOEFP • BRAEFP |
| **brewed** • abroad, brood | BRAOUD • BRAOD, BRAO*D |
| **brewer** • brochure | BRAOUR • BRUR |
| **brews** • Bruce, bruise | BRAOUS • BRAO*US, BRAOUZ |
| **bridal** • bridle | BRAOILD • BRELD |
| **bridge** • abridge | BRIJ • BRAIJ |
| **brilliant** • brittle | BRIL • BRILT |
| **brittle** • brilliant | BRILT • BRIL |
| **bro** • brother | BRO* • BRO |
| **broach** • brooch | BROEFP • BRAOFP |
| **brochure** • brewer | BRUR • BRAOUR |
| **brooch** • broach | BRAOFP • BROEFP |
| **brood** • abroad, brewed | BRAO*D • BRAOD, BRAOUD |
| **brother** • bro | BRO • BRO* |
| **brotherhood** • border | BRORD • BROERD |
| **brother-in-law** • brotherly | BROL • BRORL |
| **brother-in-law** • sister-in-law | BROINL • SOINL |
| **brows** • browse | BROUZ • BROUS |
| **Bruce** • brews, bruise | BRAO*US • BRAOUS, BRAOUZ |
| **bruise** • brews, Bruce | BRAOUZ • BRAOUS, BRAO*US |
| **budge** • budget | BUJ • BOIJ |
| **budget** • budge | BOIJ • BUJ |
| **buffed** • bunch of stuff, bused | BUFD • BUFT, B*UFD |
| **build** • billed | BILD • B*ILD |
| **bulletproof** • soundproof, waterproof | BLAOF • SPRAOF, WRAOF |
| **bullion** • bouillon | BAOUL • BAO*UL |
| **bun** • begun | B*UN • BUN |
| **bunch of stuff** • buffed | BUFT • BUFD |
| **buoy** • boy | BO*I • BOI |

**bureau**

| | |
|---|---|
| borough | BROUG |
| bro | BRO* |
| brochure | BRUR |
| brother | BRO |
| bureau | BUR |

| | |
|---|---|
| burro | BROE |
| burrow | BRO*E |
| **bureau** • burr | BUR • B*UR |
| **burglarizing** • blasting | BLAFG • BLAFGT |
| **burn** | |
| first-degree burn | F–BD |
| second-degree burn | S–BD |
| third-degree burn | TH–BD, THR–BD |
| **burr** • bureau | B*UR • BUR |
| **burro** • borough, bureau, burrow | BROE • BROUG, BUR, BRO*E |
| **burrow** • borough, bureau, burro | BRO*E • BROUG, BUR, BROE |
| **bury** • berry | BRU • BRER |
| **bus** • buzz | BUS • BUZ |
| **bus driver** • driver | BRIR • DRIR |
| **bused** • buffed, bust | BUS/–D *or* B*UFD • BUFD, B*US |
| **business** | |
| home business | HOEBS |
| none of your business | NURBS |
| place of business | PLAIBS |
| show business | SHOEBS |
| state your business | STURBS |
| what is your business | WHAURBS |
| **businessman** • businessmen | BAM • BEM |
| **businessmen** • businessman | BEM • BAM |
| **businesswoman** • businesswomen | BA*M • B*EM |
| **businesswomen** • businesswoman | B*EM • BA*M |
| **bust** | |
| buffed | BUFD |
| bunch of stuff | BUFT |
| bused | B*UFD, BUS/–D |
| bust | B*US |
| **but** • butt, but the | BU • B*UT, BUT |
| **butt** • but, but the | B*UT • BU, BUT |
| **but the** • but, butt | BUT • BU, B*UT |
| **buy** • by, bye | BAOI • BI, BAO*I |
| **buzz** • bus | BUZ • BUS |
| **by** • buy, bye | BI • BAOI, BAO*I |
| **bye** • buy, by | BAO*I • BAOI, BI |
| **byte** • bite | BAO*IT • BAOIT |
| **by the way** • way, weigh | BAE • WAI, WAE |

# C

| | |
|---|---|
| **cabal** • cable | KAUBL • KAIBL |
| **cabins** • ambience | KBINZ • KBINS |
| **cable** • counsel table | KAIBL • KAEBL *or* KAEB |
| **cache** • cash | KAERB • KARB |
| **Cairo** • chiropractor | KRO • KAOIR |
| **Cairo** • Colorado | KRO • KRO* |
| **calf** • castle | KAF • KAFL |
| **California** • criminal law | KRA* • KRA |
| **caller** • collar | KAURL • KLAR |
| **calling your attention** • cauterization | KAURGS • KA*URGS |
| **call your attention** • calling your attention | KAURT • KAURGS |
| **campaigner** • comparison | KPRAIN • KPAIRN |

**cancer**

| | |
|---|---|
| breast cancer | BRAERN |
| cancer | KAERN |
| cervical cancer | SA*ERN |
| lung cancer | LA*ERN |
| ovarian cancer | VAERN |
| prostate cancer | PRAERN |
| uterine cancer | YA*ERN |

| | |
|---|---|
| **can he understand** • contends | KENDZ • K*ENDZ *or* KAENDZ |
| **can I recall** • killer | K*IRL • KIRL |
| **cannabis** • emphasis | KBIZ • KBIS |
| **can not** • can knot, cannot | KWO*T • K–/NO*T, K–/NOT *or* KWOT |
| **can't** • accountant, cant | K–NT • KANT, KA*NT |
| **can you recall** • curl | KURL • K*URL |
| **can you tell** • cut | KUT • K*UT |
| **capital** • capitol | KPAL • KPOL |
| **capitalism** • chasm | KAFM • KHAFM |
| **capitol** • capital | KPOL • KPAL |
| **capitol** • Capitol Hill | KPOL • KPOIL |
| **caption** • realtime captioning | KAPGS • RAPGS |
| **carat** • accurate | KRA*T • KRAT |

**carat**

| | |
|---|---|
| carat | KRA*T |
| caret | KR*ET, KRA*ET |
| carrot | KAERT |
| karat | KA*ERT |

| | |
|---|---|
| **carbon dioxide** • embody | KBOX *or* KBO*D • KBOD |
| **carcinoma** • sarcoma, scrotum | SKROEM • SKOEM, SKROET |

**cardia** • bradycardia ............................................... KAUR • BRAUR

**care** • carry ............................................................. KAIR • KAER

**car go** • cargo ....................................................... KAR/GO • KARG

**carotid** • parotid .................................................... KROTD • PROTD

**carpal** • car-pool .................................................. KPARL • KPAOL

**car-pool** • carpal .................................................. KPAOL • KPARL

**carriage** • miscarriage........................................... KAIRJ • SKAIRJ

**carrot**
    carat ............................................................ KRA*T
    caret ............................................................ KR*ET, KRA*ET
    carrot ........................................................... KAERT
    karat ............................................................ KA*ERT

**carry** • care ............................................................ KAER • KAIR

**carryover** • takeover ............................................. KROEVR • TOEVR

**cartilage** • collage, college ..................................... KLART • KLAJ, KLEJ

**cash** • cache .......................................................... KARB • KAERB

**castle** • calf ........................................................... KAFL • KAF

**casual** • causal ..................................................... KARBL • KAUFL

**cat** • CAT ............................................................... KAT • KATD

**catabolic** • impolitic ............................................... KBLO*K • KBLOK

**cat and mouse** • comes out .................................. KMOUZ • KMOUS

**catapult** • penultimate ........................................... PULT • P*ULT

**cater** • indicate ...................................................... KAET • KAIT

**caught** • cot .......................................................... KAUT • KOT

**caulk** • cock, coq .................................................. KAUK • KOK, KO*K

**causal** • casual ..................................................... KAUFL • KARBL

**cause** • because, just cause .................................. KAUZ • BAUZ, JAUZ

**cause** • caws ........................................................ KAUZ *or* KAUS • KA*US

**cause of action** • course of action ......................... KAUX • KORX

**cause of them** • accustom .................................... KAUFM • KA*UFM

**cauterization** • calling your attention..................... KA*URGS • KAURGS

**cave** • indicative .................................................... KAEV • KAIV

**caveat** • cavity ....................................................... KAEVT • KAVT

**cavity** • caveat ....................................................... KAVT • KAEVT

**caws** • cause ........................................................ KA*US • KAUS *or* KAUZ

**CD-ROM** • COM, ROM ........................................... DROM • KROM, ROM

**cease**
    assess .......................................................... SAES
    cease ............................................................ SAOES
    crease ........................................................... KRAOES

| | |
|---|---|
| decease | DAOES |
| seas | SA*ES, SAE/–S |
| sees | SAO*EZ, SAOE/–S |
| seize | SAOEZ |
| southeast | SAO*ES |

**cede** • creed, seed .......................... SAED • KRAOED, SAOED

**ceiling** • sealing .............................. KRAOELG • SAOELG

**celebrate** • inebriate ....................... SBRAIT • BRAIT

**celebrate** • intrastate ...................... SBRAIT • SPWRAET

**cell** • sell ....................................... KREL • SEL

**cellophane** • 79 .............................. SFAIN • SFAEN

**cell phones** • slowness ................... SLOENZ • SLOENS

**Celt** • kettle, seat belt ..................... K*ELT • KELT, KRELT

**cemetery** • symmetry ....................... KRAEMT • SMAOET

**censor** • sensor .............................. SNUR • SOERN

**census** • senses ............................. SKRENS • SENSZ

**cent** • scent, sent ............................ KRENT • SKRENT, SENT

**centerline** • center line, shrine .......... SLAOIN • SLOIN, SHRAO*IN

**cents** • scents, sense ....................... KRENTS • SKRENTS, SENS

**cereal** • serial ................................. KRAOERL • SAOERL

**certain**
| | |
|---|---|
| ascertain | SAERN |
| certain | SERN |
| uncertain | SNERN |

**certain** • surgeon ........................... SERN • SURN

**certainly** • uncertainly ..................... SERNL • SNERNL

**certainty** • uncertainty ..................... SERNT • SNERNT

**certifies** • suffice ............................ SFAOIS • FAOIS

**certiorari** • writ of certiorari .............. SHAIRB • WRAIRB

**cession** • session ............................ KREGS • SEGS

**chaining** • change ........................... KHA*ING • KHAING *or* KHAIJ

**chain of custody** • which you had ....... KH*UD • KHUD

**chains** • change .............................. KHAINS • KHAING *or* KHAIJ

**chairman** • Mr. Chairman .................. KHAIRM • MR–FP

**chance** • chants ............................. KHANS • KHANTSKHAIJ

**change** • chaining, chains ................. KHAIJ *or* KHAING • KHA*ING, KHAINS

**change** • exchange, interchange ........ KHAIJ • KPAIJ, SPWRAIJ

**chants** • chance ............................. KHANTS • KHANS

**chaos** • choose ............................... KAOS • KHAOS

**charge** • discharge, surcharge .......... KHARJ • DARJ, SKHARJ

| | |
|---|---|
| **charge the jury** • charge | KHAURJ • KHARJ |
| **charlatan** • Charlotte | SHARL • SHARLT |
| **chased** • chaste | KHAIFD • KHA*IS |
| **chasm** • capitalism | KHAFM • KAFM |
| **chaste** • chased | KHA*IS • KHAIFD |
| **cheap** • cheep | KHAEP • KHAOEP |
| **check** • Czech | KHEK • ZHEK |
| **cheep** • cheap | KHAOEP • KHAEP |
| **cheese** • Chinese | KHAOES • KHAOEZ |
| **chemical weapon** • weapon | KWEP • WEP |
| **chemical weapons** • quadriceps | KWEPZ • KWEPS |
| **chews** • child abuse, choose | KHAOUZ • KHAOUS, KHAOS *or* KHAOZ |
| **chic** • chick, sheik | SHAO*EK • KHIK, SHAOEK |
| **chickenpox** • alcoholics | KHOKZ • KHOX |
| **chickenpox** • smallpox | KHOKZ • SMAUX |
| **Chief Justice** • interest of justice | KH–J • TR–J |
| **child abuse** • chews, choose | KHAOUS • KHAOUZ, KHAOS *or* KHAOZ |
| **childish** • which I shall | KHAOIRB • KHIRB |
| **child molestation** • molestation | KHOELGS • MOELGS |
| **childproof** • proof | KHAOF • PRAOF |
| **Chinese** • cheese | KHAOEZ • KHAOES |
| **chiropractor** • Cairo | KAOIR • KRO |
| **choir** • acquire | KWOIR • KWAOIR |
| **choose** • chaos | KHAOS • KAOS |
| **choose** • chews, child abuse | KHAOS *or* KHAOZ • KHAOUZ, KHAOUS |
| **chord** • cord, cored, corridor | KHORD • KORD, KO*ERD, KOERD |
| **choreographer** • cinematographer | KRAURG • SMAURG |
| **choreography** • cinematography | KRAUG • SMAUG |
| **Christmas** • incriminate, incriminates | KROIM • KRIMT, KRIMS |
| **chute** • shoot | SHAOUT • SHAOT |
| **cigarette** • signature | SGRET *or* S–G • SIG |
| **cinematographer** • choreographer | SMAURG • KRAURG |
| **cinematography** • choreography | SMAUG • KRAUG |
| **cinnamon** • assassin, summon | SNON • SNIN, SMON |
| **circulate** • insulate, slate | SL– • SLAIT, SLAET |
| **circumstantial evidence** • $67 | SKEVD • SKEFD |

| | |
|---|---|
| **cite** • sight, site | KRAOIT • SAOIT, SAO*IT |
| **City Attorney's office** • office | STOFS • OFS |
| **civil law** • criminal law, federal law | SLA • KRA, FLA |
| **claim** • acclaim | KLAIM • KLAEM |
| **claim or** • claymore | KLAIM/OR • KLAI/MOER |
| **clairvoyance** • colonies | KLOINS • KLOINZ |
| **clamber** • clamor | KLAEB • KLARM |
| **clamor** • clamber | KLARM • KLAEB |
| **claps** • collapse | KLAPZ • KLAPS |
| **class action lawsuit** • lawsuit | KLAUT • LAUT |
| **classroom** • room | KLAOM • RAOM |
| **clause** • claws | KLAUZ • KLAUS |
| **claws** • clause | KLAUS • KLAUZ |
| **claymore** • claim or | KLAI/MOER • KLAIM/OR |
| **clench** • clinch | KLEFP • KLIFP |
| **clerk** • collector | KLERK • KLERKT |
| **click** • clique | KLIK • KL*IK |
| **clientele** • client tell | KLEL • KLAOI/TEL |
| **client tell** • clientele | KLAOI/TEL • KLEL |
| **climb** • clime | KLAOIM • KLOIM |
| **clinch** • clench | KLIFP • KLEFP |
| **clings** • inclination | KLINGZ • KLINGS |
| **clinic** • kiln | KLIN • KL*IN |
| **clinics** • Collins | KLINZ • KLINS |
| **clique** • click | KL*IK • KLIK |
| **close** • clothes, cloths | KLOES • KLO*ETS, KLO*TS |
| **closure** • cloture, enclosure | KLO*UR • KLOET, KLOERZ *or* KLOUR |
| **clot** • cloth | KLOT • KLO*T |
| **cloth** • clot | KLO*T • KLOT |
| **clothes** • close, cloths | KLO*ETS • KLOES, KLO*TS |
| **cloths** • clothes, clots | KLO*TS • KLO*ETS, KLOTS |
| **cloture** • closure, enclosure | KLOET • KLOERZ *or* KLO*UR, KLOUR |
| **clue** • collude, conclude | KLAO • KLAO*U, KLAOU |
| **coarse** • course | KORS • KOURS |
| **coax** • Cokes | KOEX • KOEKZ |
| **cock** • caulk, coq | KOK • KAUK, KO*K |
| **code** • co-ed | KOED • KO*ED |
| **co-ed** • code | KW*ED *or* KO*ED • KOED |

| | |
|---|---|
| **co-ed** • questioned | KW*ED *or* KO*ED • KWED |
| **coffer** • cougher | KAUFR • KOFR |
| **cog** • coming | KO*G • KOG |
| **coincidence** • convince | KWINZ • KWINS |
| **Coke** • coke | KOEK • KO*EK |
| **Cokes** • coax | KOEKZ • KOEX |
| **collaboration** • collation | KLAEX • KLA*IGS |
| **collaboration** • County of Los Angeles | KLAEX • KLAX |
| **collage** • cartilage, college | KLAJ • KLART, KLEJ |
| **collapse** • claps | KLAPS • KLAPZ |
| **collar** • caller | KLAR • KAURL |
| **collation** • calls for speculation | KLA*IGS • KLAIGS |
| **collation** • collaboration | KLA*IGS • KLAEX |
| **collector** • clerk | KLERKT • KLERK |
| **college** • collage | KLEJ • KLAJ |
| **Collins** • clinics | KLINS • KLINZ |
| **collude** • clue, conclude | KLAO*U • KLAO, KLAOU |
| **collusion** • conclusion | KLAO*UGS • KLAOUGS |
| **colonel** • kernel | KOL • KERNL |
| **colonies** • clairvoyance | KLOINZ • KLOINS |
| **color** • discolor | KLOR • SKLOR |
| **Colorado** • Cairo | KRO* • KRO |
| **coloration** • discoloration | KLORGS • SKLORGS |
| **COM** • CD-ROM, ROM | KROM • DROM, ROM |
| **coma** • comb, comma | KMO *or* KO*EM • KOEM, KMA |
| **comb** • coma | KOEM • KO*EM |
| **combative** • impassive | KBAV • KBIV |
| **comes out** • cat and mouse | KMOUS • KMOUZ |
| **comfort** • discomfort | K–FRT • SK–FRT |
| **comfortable** • uncomfortable | K–FRBL • N–FRBL |
| **coming** • cog | KOG • KO*G |
| **comma** • coma | KMA • KMO |
| **command** • demand | KMAN • DMAN *or* MAND |
| **commence** • comments | KMENS • KMENTS |
| **comments** • commence | KMENTS • KMENS |
| **committee** • subcommittee | KMAOET • SKMAOET |
| **common-law marriage** • marriage | KMAERJ • MAERJ |
| **communication** • miscommunication | KMUNGS • SKMUNGS |

**community property** • property, ............................ KPROT • PROT, SPROT
separate property

**companion** • company ............................................ KPAN • KPAEN

**company** • accompany ............................................ KPAEN • KPOIN

**company** • companion ............................................ KPAEN • KPAN

**compartment** • apartment ..................................... KPARMT • PARMT

**compel** • excel ....................................................... KMEL • KPEL

**compensatory damages** • punitive damages ...... K–DZ • P–DZ

**compile** • exile ...................................................... KPIL • KPAOIL

**complacence** • complains, complaisance ............. KPLAENZ • KPLAINS, KPLAENS

**complacent** • complaisant ..................................... KPLA*ENT • KPLAENT

**complainant** • complacent, complaisant ............... KPLAINT • KPLA*ENT, KPLAENT

**complainant** • complaint ....................................... KPLAINT • PLAINT

**complains** • complacence, complaisance ............. KPLAINS • KPLAENZ, KPLAENS

**complaint** • complainant ....................................... PLAINT • KPLAINT

**complaint** • planet .................................................. PLAINT • PLAENT

**complaisance** • complacence, complains ............ KPLAENS • KPLAENZ, KPLAINS

**complaisant** • complacent ..................................... KPLAENT • KPLA*ENT

**complement** • compliment ..................................... KPLEMT • KPLIMT

**complete** • plethora ................................................ PLET • PL*ET

**compliment** • complement ..................................... KPLIMT • KPLEMT

**composer** • composure .......................................... KPOER • KPOUR

**composure** • composer .......................................... KPOUR • KPOER

**compound interest** • conflict of interest, ............. KPINT • KINT, SFINT
self-interest

**comptroller** • controller .......................................... KROERL • KRORL

**compulsion** • expulsion ......................................... KPULGS • SPULGS

**compulsion** • exultation ......................................... KPULGS • KP*ULGS

**concept** • skeptic ................................................... SKEP • SKEPT

**concern** • discern .................................................. KERN • DERN

**concern** • kern ...................................................... KERN • K*ERN

**concierge** • serge, surge ....................................... SERJ • S*ERJ, SURJ

**conclude** • clue, collude ....................................... KLAOU • KLAO, KLAO*U

**conclusion** • collusion, inclusion .......................... KLAOUGS • KLAO*UGS, KLUGS

**concrete** • Crete .................................................... KRAOET • KRAO*ET

**concur** • conquer ................................................... KRUR • KWUR

**concussion** • cousin, cushion .............................. KUNGS • KUFN, KUGS

**conduct** • misconduct ........................................... KUK • SKUK

**conference**
| | |
|---|---|
| conference | K–FRNS |
| news conference | NAOUFRNS |
| press conference | PR–FRNS |
| teleconference | T–FRNS |

**conference** • inference ........................... K–FRNS • N–FRNS

**confidence** • self-confidence ................... K–FD • SK–FD

**confident** • self-confident ...................... K–FT • SK–FT

**conflict of interest** • compound interest, ............ KINT • KPINT, SFINT, DINT
self-interest, disinterest

**congress** • conk, conning ...................... KONG • KONK, K*NG

**congressional** • corral ........................... KRAL • KRA*L

**congressman** • cram ............................. KRAM • KRA*M

**congresswoman** • congresswomen ..................... KWAM • KWEM

**congresswomen** • congresswoman ..................... KWEM • KWAM

**conk** • congress, conning ...................... KONK • KONG, K*NG

**connect** • disconnect .............................. KEK • SKEK

**Connecticut** • contract ........................... KR*T • KR–T

**connection** • context ............................. KEX • K*EX

**connection** • disconnection ................... KEX • SKEX

**conning** • Congress, conk ...................... K*NG • KONG, KONK

**conquer** • concur ................................. KWUR • KRUR

**cons** • conscious ................................. KONZ • KONS

**conscience** • conscious ......................... K–RB • KONS

**conscientiousness** • consciousness ............ K–RBSZ • KONSZ

**conscious** • cons, conscience ............... KONS • KONZ, K–RB

**consciousness** • conscientiousness ........... KONSZ • K–RBSZ

**consequence** • sequence, sequins, ........... KWENS • SKW–NS, SKWINS,
subsequence          SKWENS

**consequently** • subsequently ............... KWENL • SKWENL

**conservation** • conversation ................ SKEFRBGS • K–FRGS

**conspire** • aspire, expire ...................... SKPAOIR • SPAOIR, KPAOIR

**constant**
| | |
|---|---|
| constant | SKANT |
| distant | SDANT |
| extant | STA*NT |
| instant | STANT |
| scant | SKA*NT |

**constantly** • scandal ........................... SKANL • SKANLD

**constituency** • suspends ...................... SWENS • SWENZ

**constitutional** • unconstitutional ......................... KAOLGS • NAOLGS

| | |
|---|---|
| **construction** • crux | KRUX • KR*UX |
| **consul** • council, counsel | SKWUL • KOUNS, KOUN |
| **consular** • councilor, counselor | SKWURL • KOUNLS, KOUNL |
| **contagious** • teenage | TAIJ • TAEJ |
| **contain** • obtain | TAIN • BAIN |
| **contends** • can he understand | KAENDZ *or* K*ENDZ • KENDZ |
| **context** • connection | K*EX • KEX |
| **continuation** • discontinuation | KONGS • SKONGS |
| **continue** • couldn't | KONT • KUNT |
| **continue** • discontinue | KONT • SKONT |
| **continuous** • cows | KOUS • KOUZ |
| **contract** • Connecticut | KR–T • KR*T |
| **contract** • subcontract | KR–T • SKR–T |
| **contraction** • cracks | KRAX • KRAKZ |
| **contractor** • subcontractor | KR–RT • SKR–RT |
| **contradiction** • contribution | KRIX • KRAOUGS |
| **contribution** • contradiction | KRAOUGS • KRIX |
| **contributory negligence** • incrimination | KRIJ • KRIJS |
| **controller** • comptroller | KRORL • KROERL |
| **controvert** • atrocity | TROVT • TROFT |
| **controvert** • extrovert, introvert | TROVT • KPROVT, SPWROVT |
| **convene** • queen | KWAO*EN • KWAOEN |
| **convenes** • queens | KWAOENZ • KWAOENS |
| **conversation** • conservation | K–FRGS • SKEFRBGS |

**conversation**

| | |
|---|---|
| conversation | K–FRGS |
| phone conversation | F–FRGS |
| telephone conversation | T–FRGS |

| | |
|---|---|
| **convince** • coincidence | KWINS • KWINZ |
| **coo** • coup | KAO • KAOUP |
| **coolie** • coolly | KLAO*L • KLAOL |
| **coolly** • coolie | KLAOL • KLAO*L |

**coop**

| | |
|---|---|
| coop | KAOP |
| co-op | KWOP |
| co-opt | KWOPT |
| could you please | KOUP |
| coup | KAOUP |
| coupe | KO*UP |

| | |
|---|---|
| **co-op** • co-opt | KWOP • KWOPT |
| **cooperation** • corporation | KAOPGS • KORPGS |

---

         

**coordinate**
 chord ................................................................ KHORD
 coordinate ...................................................... KAORD
 cord ................................................................... KORD
 cored ............................................................... KO*ERD
 corridor ............................................................ KOERD

**copper** • Corp. ....................................... KRORP • KORP

**coq** • caulk, cock ................................. KO*K • KAUK, KOK

**coral** • correlate .................................... KOERL • KORL

**cord** • chord, cored ............................... KORD • KHORD, KO*ERD

**core** • corps ........................................... KOER • KOERP

**cored** • chord, cord ............................... KO*ERD • KHORD, KORD

**corner** • coroner ................................... KRORN *or* KROERN • KR–RN

**corns** • correspondence ....................... KORNZ • KORNS

**coroner** • corner ................................... KR–RN • KRORN *or* KROERN

**coroner's office** • office ....................... KR–FS • OFS

**Corp.** • corporate, incorporate ............. KORP • KORPT, NORP

**corporate** • Corp., incorporate ............. KORPT • KORP, NORP

**corporation** • cooperation .................... KORPGS • KAOPGS

**corporation** • incorporation ................. KORPGS • NORPGS

**corps** • core ........................................... KOERP • KOER

**corps** • corpse ...................................... KOERP • KORPS

**corral** • congressional ......................... KRA*L • KRAL

**correlate**
 coral ................................................. KOERL
 corral ............................................... KRA*L
 correlate .......................................... KORL
 cortical ............................................. KOERLT
 court of law ...................................... KORLT

**correlation** • relation ............................ KORLGS • RELGS

**correspondence** • corns ...................... KORNS • KORNZ

**correspondence** • correspondents ...... KORNS • KORNTS

**correspondents** • correspondence ...... KORNTS • KORNS

**corridor** • cord, cored .......................... KOERD • KORD, KO*ERD

**cortical** • correlate, court of law ........... KOERLT • KORL, KORLT

**cosign** • cosine .................................... KAOIN • KAO*IN

**cosine** • cosign .................................... KAO*IN • KAOIN

**cosine** • sine ........................................ KAO*IN • SAO*IN

**costume** • custom ................................ KOFM • KUFM

**cot** • caught ......................................... KOT • KAUT

**cougher** • coffer ................................... KOFR • KAUFR

**couldn't** • continue ................................................. KUNT • KONT

**could you please** • coup, coupe ......................... KOUP • KAOUP, KO\*UP

**council**
    council ............................................................ KOUNS
    councilor ......................................................... KOUNLS
    counsel ............................................................ KOUN
    counselor ......................................................... KOUNL

**councilor** • counselor ........................................... KOUNLS • KOUNL

**counsel**
    council ............................................................ KOUNS
    councilor ......................................................... KOUNLS
    counsel ............................................................ KOUN
    counselor ......................................................... KOUNL

**counselor** • councilor ........................................... KOUNL • KOUNLS

**counsel table** • cable ............................................ KAEB *or* KAEBL • KAIBL

**countryside** • custodian ....................................... K\*UND • KUND

**County of Los Angeles** • collaboration ............... KLAX • KLAEX

**coup** • coo, coupe ................................................. KAOUP • KAO, KO\*UP

**coupe**
    coop ................................................................ KAOP
    co-op ............................................................... KWOP
    co-opt .............................................................. KWOPT
    could you please ............................................. KOUP
    coup ................................................................ KAOUP
    coupe ............................................................... KO\*UP

**coupe** • could you please ..................................... KO\*UP • KOUP

**courage**
    courage ............................................................ KOURJ, KURJ
    discourage ....................................................... SKOURJ
    encourage ........................................................ NURJ

**course** • coarse ..................................................... KOURS • KORS

**course** • discourse ................................................ KOURS • SKOURS

**course of action** • cause of action ...................... KORX • KAUX

**court**
    ask the Court ................................................... SKORT
    Circuit Court .................................................... SKOURT, SKRORT
    court ................................................................ KORT
    Court ................................................................ KOURT
    District Court ................................................... DRORT
    if it please the Court ........................................ FLOURT
    kangaroo court ................................................ GRAORT
    please the Court .............................................. PLOURT
    Superior Court ................................................. SYORT

**court of law**
    coral ................................................................ KOERL
    corral ............................................................... KRA\*L
    correlate .......................................................... KORL

| | |
|---|---|
| cortical | KOERLT |
| court of law | KORLT |
| **court of record** • courtyard | KROERD • KRORD |
| **courtroom** • room | KRAOM • RAOM |
| **courtyard** • court of record | KRORD • KROERD |
| **courtyard** • credit card | KRORD • KRARD |
| **cousin** • cushion | KUFN • KUGS |
| **coward** • cowered | KOURD • KO*URD |
| **cows** • continuous | KOUZ • KOUS |
| **cracks** • contraction | KRAKZ • KRAX |
| **cram** • congressman | KRA*M • KRAM |
| **crate** • caret | KRAET • KRA*ET |
| **crate** • incarcerate | KRAET • KRAIT |
| **creak** • creek | KRAEK • KRAOEK |
| **crease** • cease | KRAOES • SAOES |
| **credit** • discredit | KRED • SKRED |
| **credit card** • courtyard | KRARD • KRORD |
| **creditworthiness** • trustworthiness | KWORNS • TWORNS |
| **creditworthy** • trustworthy | KWO*RT • TWO*RT |
| **creek** • creak | KRAOEK • KRAEK |
| **Crete** • concrete | KRAO*ET • KRAOET |
| **crews** • cruise | KRAOUS • KRAOUZ |
| **crime** • scene of the crime | KRAOIM • SKRAOIM |
| **criminal law** • California | KRA • KRA* |
| **criminal law** • civil law, federal law | KRA • SLA, FLA |
| **cross** • across | KROSZ • KROS |
| **cruel** • accrual | KRAOUL • KRUL |
| **cruel and unusual punishment** • accruement | KRUMT • KR*UMT |
| **cruel and unusual punishment** • punishment | KRUMT • PUMT |
| **cruise** • crews | KRAOUZ • KRAOUS |
| **crunch** • scrunch | KRUN • SKRUN |
| **crux** • construction | KR*UX • KRUX |
| **cud** • custody | K*UD • KUD |
| **cue** • queue | KAOU • KWAOU |
| **cues** • accuse | KAOUZ • KAOUS |
| **cur** • occur | K*UR • KUR |
| **curd** • occurred | K*URD • KURD |
| **curl** • can you recall | K*URL • KURL |

**currant** • current ..................................................... KAURNT • KURNT

**current** • alternating current, direct current ........... KURNT • TURNT, DRURNT

**current** • currant ..................................................... KURNT • KAURNT

**currently** • kernel ..................................................... KURNL • KERNL

**curs** • curse, occurs ............................................... K*URS • KURS, KURZ

**curse** • curs, occurs ............................................... KURS • K*URS, KURZ

**cushion** • concussion .............................................. KUGS • KUNGS

**custodial** • stockholder ............................................ STOELD • STOLD

**custodian** • countryside ........................................... KUND • K*UND

**custody**
    chain of custody ............................................... KH*UD
    custody ............................................................. KUD
    in custody ......................................................... NUD
    protective custody ............................................ PRUVD

**custody** • cud ........................................................... KUD • K*UD

**custody** • in custody, into custody ......................... KUD • NUD, NOUD

**custom** • costume .................................................... KUFM • KOFM

**customer service** • answering service ................. KMEFRB • SNEFRB

**cut** • can you tell ...................................................... K*UT • KUT

**cyst** • assist ............................................................. KR*IS • S*IS

**Czech** • check ......................................................... ZHEK • KHEK

# D

**daily** • dale, detail ................................. DAIL • DA*EL, DAEL

**dairy**
    dairy .............................................. DA*IR
    dare .............................................. DAIR
    dear .............................................. DAER
    diary ............................................. DIR
    dire .............................................. DAOIR

**daisy** • dais, days, daze ....................... DAIZ • DAES, DAIS, DAEZ

**dale** • daily, detail ................................. DA*EL • DAIL, DAEL

**dam** • damn ........................................... DAM • DA*M

**dame** • democrat ................................... DAIM • DAEM

**damn** • dam ........................................... DA*M • DAM

**Dane** • detain ........................................ DAEN • DAIN

**danger** • endanger ................................ DAIRN • DAERN

**dangerous weapon** • deadly weapon .................. DWAP • DWEP

**D.A.'s office** • District Attorney's Office ................. DAFS • DAOFS

**dare** • dairy, dear .................................... DAIR • DA*IR, DAER

**date** • diet .............................................. DAIT • DAET

**dawn** • don, Don ................................... DAUN • DO*N, DON

**days** • dais, daisy, daze ....................... DAIS • DAES, DAIZ, DAEZ

**daytime** • dime ..................................... DAOIM • DAO*IM

**daze** • dais, daisy, days ....................... DAEZ • DAES, DAIZ, DAIS

**D.C.** • detective .................................... D*K • D–K

**dead** • did he do .................................. DAED *or* D*ED • DED

**deadlock** • gridlock, lock ...................... DLOK • GLOK, LOK

**deadly weapon** • adept, did he want .................... DWEP • DWEPT, DEPT

**deadly weapon** • assault with a deadly weapon ... DWEP • SDWEP *or* SWEP

**deadly weapon** • dangerous weapon .................. DWEP • DWAP

**deaf** • did he have ................................. DAEF • DEF

**deaf and hard of hearing** • .................... DHARD • DHORD
deaf or hard of hearing

**deafens** • deafness ............................... DAEFNZ • DAEFNS

**dear** • dare, deer .................................. DAER • DAIR, DAOER

**debar** • disbar ....................................... DBAR • SBAR

**debit** • debt .......................................... D–BT • DEBT

**debride** • debris .................................... DBR–D • DBRI

**debris** • debride .................................... DBRI • DBR–D

**debt** • did he tell ................................... DEBT • DET

**decease** • cease ..................................................... DAOES • SAOES

**decedent**
    decedent ......................................................... DAOENT
    decent .............................................................. SDAOENT
    descendant ...................................................... SDAENT
    descent ............................................................ SDENT
    dissent ............................................................. SD–N

**decent** • decedent, descent ................................... SDAOENT • DAOENT, SDENT

**decided** • acid ....................................................... SDID • SD*ID

**decidedly** • distilled ............................................... SDILD • SD*ILD

**decks** • dex, Dexedrine ......................................... DEKZ • D*EX, DEX

**declination** • inclination ......................................... DLINGS • KLINGS

**decline** • line ........................................................ DLAOIN • LAOIN

**decrease** • crease ................................................. DRAOES • KRAOES

**decree** • degree .................................................... KRE • DRE

**deduction** • ducks ................................................. DUX • DUKZ

**deer** • dear .......................................................... DAOER • DAER

**defense** • self-defense .......................................... D–FS • SD–FS

**deference** • difference ........................................... DEFRNS • DIFRNS

**deferential** • differential ........................................ DEFRNL • DIFRNL

**define** • divine ...................................................... DWAOIN • DWAO*IN

**definite** • definitive, indefinite ............................... DAF • DAV, SDA*F *or* SD–FT

**definitive** • definite .............................................. DAV • DAF

**degree** • decree .................................................... DRE • KRE

**Delaware** • de~ *(prefix)*, did he ........................... DWE *or* D*EL • DE, D*E

**delimit** • duly licensed to practice medicine .......... DLIMT *or* DL*IM • DLIM

**deltoid** • deployed ................................................. DELTD *or* DLOITD • DLO*ID

**delusion**
    delusion .......................................................... DLAOUGS
    disillusion ........................................................ DLU
    dissolution ...................................................... SDLAOUGS
    solution ........................................................... SLAOUGS

**demand** • command ............................................... MAND • KMAN

**demand** • remand ................................................. MAND • RAMD

**democrat** • dame, demonstrate ............................. DAEM • DAIM, DEM

**demonstrate** • democrat ....................................... DEM • DAEM

**denial** • dental ..................................................... D–NL • DENL

**dens** • dense, dents ............................................. DENZ • DENS, DENTS

**dense** • dens, dents ............................................. DENS • DENZ, DENTS

**dental** • denial ..................................................... DENL • D–NL

**dents** • dens, dense ............................................. DENTS • DENZ, DENS

**department**
      department ...................................................... D–PT
      justice department ........................................... J–PT
      State Department ............................................. SD–PT

**department** • did he want ...................................... D–PT • DEPT

**depend** • descend ................................................ DEND • SDEND

**dependence** • dependents .................................... DAENS • DAENTS

**dependents** • dependence .................................... DAENTS • DAENS

**depends** • did he understand .............................. D*ENDZ • DENDZ

**deplore** • implore .................................................. PLOER • KBLOER

**deploy** • employ .................................................. DLOI • PLOI

**deployed** • deltoid ................................................ DLO*ID • DLOITD *or* DELTD

**depo** • depot ......................................................... DPO • DPOT

**deposited** • posted .............................................. POFTD • POEFTD

**deposition** • disposition ........................................ DEPGS • SPOGS

**depot** • depo ......................................................... DPOT • DPO

**deprecation** • duration .......................................... DRAIX • DRAIGS

**depreciate** • appreciate ........................................ DRAOERB • PRAOERB

**depreciation** • appreciation ................................... DRAOERBGS • PRAOERBGS

**depth** • did he want .............................................. D*EPT • DEPT

**derange** • arrange, disarrange .............................. DARNG • ARNG, SARNG

**derive** • drive ........................................................ DRAOIV • DRI

**dermatologist** • dolt .............................................. DOLT • DOELT

**descend** • depend ................................................ SDEND • DEND

**descent** • accident ............................................... SDENT • SDEN

**descent** • descendant ........................................... SDENT • SDAENT

**desert** • dessert .................................................... SDERT • DERT

**deserve** • serve .................................................... SDEFRB • SEFRB

**desperate** • separate ............................................ SPRAET • SPRAIT

**desperation** • separation ...................................... SPRAEGS • SPRAIGS

**dessert** • desert .................................................... DERT • SDERT

**destroyed** • steroid ............................................... STROID • STERD

**detach** • attach ..................................................... DAFP • TAFP

**detachment** • attachment ...................................... DAFMT • TAFMT

**detail** • daily, dale ................................................. DAEL • DAIL, DA*EL

**detain** • Dane ....................................................... DAIN • DAEN

**detain** • disdain .................................................... DAIN • SDAIN

**detective** • D.C. .................................................... D–K • D*K

---

**detract**
    detract ........................................... DRAK
    distract .......................................... SDRAK
    extract ........................................... STRAK
    subtract ......................................... STRAKT

**detraction**
    detraction ...................................... DRAX
    distraction ..................................... SDRAX
    extraction ...................................... STRAX
    subtraction .................................... STRAEX

**devaluation** • valuation ......................... DWALGS • VALGS

**devalue** • value ...................................... DWAL • VAL

**deviance** • deviants ................................ DWAOENS • DWAOENTS

**deviants** • deviance ............................... DWAOENTS • DWAOENS

**device** • devise ...................................... DWAOIS • DWAOIZ

**devil** • did he feel .................................. DEVL • DEFL

**devise** • device ...................................... DWAOIZ • DWAOIS

**dew** • do, due ....................................... DAO*U • DO, DAOU

**Dexedrine** • decks, dex ......................... DEX • DEKZ, D*EX

**diary**
    dairy .............................................. DA*IR
    dare ............................................... DAIR
    dear ............................................... DAER
    diary .............................................. DIR
    dire ................................................ DAOIR

**dice** • dies ........................................... DAOIS • DAOIZ

**did he** • de~ *(prefix)*, Delaware ........... D*E • DE, D*EL *or* DWE

**did he do** • dead .................................. DED • D*ED *or* DAED

**did he feel** • devil ................................ DEFL • DEVL

**did he have** • deaf ............................... DEF • DAEF

**did he have** • did he live ....................... DEF • DEV

**did he tell** • debt .................................. DET • DEBT

**did he understand** • depends ............... DENDZ • D*ENDZ

**did he want**
    adept ............................................. DWEPT
    deadly weapon .............................. DWEP
    department ..................................... D–PT
    depth ............................................. D*EPT
    did he want ................................... DEPT

**did I ever** • differ .................................. DIVR • DIFR

**did you believe** • double, do you believe ............. DUBL • DOUBL, DAOUBL

**did you go** • dug .................................. DUG • D*UG

**did you know** • done, dun ..................... DUN • DOEN, D*UN

---

**did you say** • dust ......................................... D*US • DUFT

**die** • dye ............................................................ DAOI • DAO*I

**dies** • dice ....................................................... DAOIZ • DAOIS

**diesel** • deal, does he feel ...................... SDAOEL • DAOEL, DAOEFL

**diet** • date ...................................................... DAET • DAIT

**diet** • indict .................................................... DAET • DAOIT

**dieter** • dietary ........................................... DAERT • DA*ERT

**differ** • did I ever ....................................... DIFR • DIVR

**difference** • deference ........................... DIFRNS • DEFRNS

**different** • indifferent .............................. DIFT • SPWIFT

**differential** • deferential ......................... DIFRNL • DEFRNL

**digest** • DJ .................................................... D–J • D*J

**dike** • dyke .................................................... DAOIK • DAO*IK

**dilate** • late ................................................... DLAIT • LAIT

**dime** • daytime, do I mean ..................... DAO*IM • DAOIM, DOIM

**din** • incident.............................................. D*IN • DIN

**ding** • distinct, extinct, indistinct ........... D*ING • DING, KPING, NING

**dings** • distinction ..................................... DINGZ • DINGS

**dire** • diary, dyer ...................................... DAOIR • DIR, DAO*IR

**direct** • director, directory ...................... DREK • DRERK, DREKT

**direct** • indirect ......................................... DREK • SPWREK

**direct current** • alternating current, current .......... DRURNT • TURNT, KURNT

**direct evidence** • indirect evidence ...................... DREVD • SDREVD

**directly** • indirectly ................................... DREL • SPWREL

**director** • direct, directory ...................... DRERK • DREK, DREKT

**directory** • direct, director ...................... DREKT • DREK, DRERK

**direct your attention** • directing your attention .... DURT • DURGS

**disability** • ability ...................................... DAIBLT • AIBLT

**disable** • able ............................................. DAIBL • AIBL

**disagree** • agree ...................................... SGRE • GRE

**disagreeable** • agreeable ...................... SGREBL • GREBL

**disagreement** • agreement..................... SGREMT • GREMT

**disallow** • allow ......................................... DLOU • LOU

**disappear** • appear ................................... SPAER • PAER

**disappear** • spear ..................................... SPAER • SPAOER

**disappearance** • appearance ............... SPAERNS • PAERNS

**disappoint** • appoint ................................. SPOIN • POIN

**disappointment** • appointment ............... SPOIMT • POIMT

**disapproval** • approval ............................................ SPROVL • PROVL

**disapprove** • approve, prove ................................. SPRAOV • PRAOV, PROV

**disapprove** • disprove ........................................... SPRAOV • SPROV

**disarm** • arm ........................................................ DARM • ARM

**disarrange** • arrange, derange .............................. SARNG • ARNG, DARNG

**disassociate** • associate, dissociate .................... SDOERBT • SOERB, SDOERB

**disassociation** • association, dissociation ........... SDORBGS • SOERBGS, SDOERBGS

**disbar** • debar ..................................................... SBAR • DBAR

**disbelief** • belief .................................................. SBLAOEF • BLAOEF

**disbelieve** • believe ............................................. SBLAOEV • BLAOEV

**disburse** • disperse .............................................. SDBURS • SPERS

**disc** • disk ........................................................... D*IFK • DIFK

**discern** • concern ................................................ DERN • KERN

**discharge** • charge, surcharge ............................. DARJ • KHARJ, SKHARJ

**disclaim** • exclaim ............................................... SKLAIM • SKLAEM

**disclose** • sclerosis .............................................. SKLOES • SKLOEZ

**discolor** • color .................................................... SKLOR • KLOR

**discoloration** • coloration .................................... SKLORGS • KLORGS

**discomfit** • discomfort ......................................... SKOMT • SK–FRT

**discomfort** • comfort............................................ SK–FRT • K–FRT

**discomfort** • discomfit ......................................... SK–FRT • SKOMT

**disconnect** • connect............................................ SKEK • KEK

**disconnection** • connection ................................. SKEX • KEX

**discontinuation** • continuation ............................ SKONGS • KONGS

**discontinue** • continue ........................................ SKONT • KONT

**discount** • count................................................... SKOUNT • KOUNT

**discourage** • courage, scourge ............................ SKOURJ • KOURJ, SKURJ

**discourse** • course ............................................... SKOURS • KOURS

**discover** • cover ................................................... SKOVR • KOVR

**discredit** • credit .................................................. SKRED • KRED

**discreet** • discrete, secrete .................................. SKRAOET • SKRAET, SKRAO*ET

**discrete** • discreet, secrete .................................. SKRAET • SKRAOET, SKRAO*ET

**discriminate** • incriminate ................................... SKRIM • KRIMT

**discriminate** • manuscript .................................... SKRIM • SKRIMT

**discriminate** • self-incriminate ............................ SKRIM • SK–RM *or* SKR–M

**discrimination** • self-incrimination ...................... SKRIMGS • SK–RMGS *or* SKR–MGS

**discussed** • disgust .............................................. SKUFD • SGUF

**disdain** • detain ................................................... SDAIN • DAIN

---

**disengage** • engage ............................................. DAEJ • GAEJ

**disfavor** • favor ...................................................... SFAIVR • FAIVR

**disfigure** • figure ................................................... SFIG • FIG

**disgrace** • grace .................................................... SGRAIS • GRAIS

**disgust** • discussed ............................................... SGUF • SKUFD

**dishearten** • sharpen, sharper than ..................... SHARN • SHAURN, SHAERN

**dishonest** • honest ............................................... SHONS • HONS

**dishonesty** • honesty ............................................ HO*NS • SHO*NS

**dishonor** • honor ................................................... SHON • HON

**dishonorable** • honorable ..................................... SHONL • HONL

**disillusion**
    delusion .......................................................... DLAOUGS
    disillusion ........................................................ DLU, DLUGS
    dissolution ....................................................... SDLAOUGS
    solution ............................................................ SLAOUGS

**disinformation** • information, misinformation ....... D–FGS • N–FGS, M–FGS

**disinherit** • inherit ................................................. SHERT • HERT

**disjoint** • joint ....................................................... DOINT • JOINT

**disk** • disc ............................................................. DIFK • D*IFK

**dislike** • like .......................................................... SLAOIK • LAOIK

**dislocate** • locate .................................................. SLOEK • LOEK

**dislocation** • location ............................................ SLOEX • LOEX

**dislodge** • lodge ................................................... DLOJ *or* SLOJ • LOJ

**disloyal** • loyal ...................................................... SLOIL • LOIL

**disloyalty** • loyalty ................................................. SLOILT • LOILT

**dismay** • may ........................................................ SMAI • MAI

**dismember** • member ............................................ SMEB • MEB

**dismount** • surmount ............................................ SMOUNT • SMOUN

**disobedience** • obedience ..................................... SBAOENS • BAOENS

**disobedient** • obedient .......................................... SBAOENT • BAOENT

**disobediently** • obediently ..................................... SBAOENL • BAOENL

**disorganization** • organization .............................. DORGS • ORGS

**disorganize** • organize .......................................... DORG • ORG

**disorient** • disorientate ......................................... DORN • DORNT

**disorient** • orient ................................................... DORN • OERNT

**disorientation** • orientation ................................... DORNGS • OERNGS

**disparate** • disparity .............................................. SPAERT • SPAIRT

**disparity** • disparate .............................................. SPAIRT • SPAERT

**dispatch** • patch ................................................... SPAFP • PAFP

**dispel** • spell ........................................................ SDPEL • SPEL

**disperse** • disburse ............................................... SPERS • SDBURS

**dispersion** • experimentation ............................... SP*ERGS • SPERGS

**displace**
    displace ........................................................ SPLAES
    displays ......................................................... SPLAIZ
    someplace ...................................................... SPLAIS
    splays ............................................................ SPLAEZ

**displeasure** • pleasure ......................................... SPLERB • PLERB

**dispose** • pose ..................................................... SDPOES • POES

**disposition** • deposition, position, supposition ..... SPOGS • DEPGS, POGS, SPOEGS

**disprove** • disapprove ........................................... SPROV • SPRAOV

**disqualification** • qualification ............................. SKW–FGS • KW–FGS

**disqualify** • qualify ............................................... SKW–F • KW–F

**disregard** • regard ................................................ DRAR • RAR

**disrespect** • respect, self-respect ....................... D–RP • R–P *or* –RP, S–RP

**disrupt** • interrupt ................................................. DRUP • TRUP

**disruption** • interruption........................................ DRUPGS • TRUPGS

**dissatisfaction** • satisfaction ............................... SDAFX • SAFX

**dissatisfactory** • satisfactory .............................. SDAEF • SAEF

**dissatisfy** • satisfy ............................................... SDAF • SAF

**disseminate** • dissimilar ....................................... SDIM • SD*IM

**dissent** • decent, descent .................................... SD–N • SDAOENT, SDENT

**disservice** • service ............................................. SD–VS • S–VS

**dissimilar** • disseminate ....................................... SD*IM • SDIM

**dissimilar** • similar ............................................... SD*IM • SIM

**dissimilarity** • similarity ........................................ SDIMT • SIMT

**dissolution**
    delusion ......................................................... DLAOUGS
    disillusion ....................................................... DLU, DLUGS
    dissolution...................................................... SDLAOUGS
    solution ......................................................... SLAOUGS

**dissociate** • associate, disassociate ................... SDOERB • SOERB, SDOERBT

**dissociation** • association, disassociation ........... SDOERBGS • SOERBGS, SDORBGS

**dissolve** • resolve ................................................ DOFL • ROFL

**distant**
    constant ......................................................... SKANT
    distant ........................................................... SDANT
    extant ............................................................ STA*NT
    instant ........................................................... STANT

**distilled** • decidedly .............................................. SD*ILD • SDILD

**distinct** • ding ...................................................... DINGT *or* DING • D*ING

---

| | |
|---|---|
| **distinct** • extinct, indistinct, instinct ........................ | DINGT *or* DING • KPINGT, NINGT, STINGT |
| **distinction** • dings, extinction ............................... | DINGS • DINGZ, KPINGS |
| **distinguish** • extinguish ......................................... | DWIRB • TWIRB |
| **distinguishable** • extinguishable ........................... | DWIRBL • TWIRBL |

**distract**

| | |
|---|---|
| detract .............................................................. | DRAK |
| distract ............................................................. | SDRAK |
| extract .............................................................. | STRAK |
| subtract ............................................................ | STRAKT |

**distraction**

| | |
|---|---|
| detraction .......................................................... | DRAX |
| distraction ......................................................... | SDRAX |
| extraction .......................................................... | STRAX |
| subtraction ........................................................ | STRAEX |

| | |
|---|---|
| **District Attorney** • District Attorney's Office ......... | DAO • DAOFS |
| **District Attorney's office** • D.A.'s office ............... | DAOFS • DAFS |
| **divers** • diverse ...................................... | DAOIVRS • DWERS |
| **diverse** • adverse, averse ..................................... | DWERS • DWERZ, WERS |
| **divide** • subdivide ...................................... | DWI • SDWI |
| **divine** • define ...................................... | DWAO*IN • DWAOIN |
| **division** • subdivision ............................................. | DWIGS • SDWIGS |
| **divorce** • widowers ............................................... | DWORS • DWORZ |
| **DJ** • digest ............................................... | D*J • D–J |
| **do** • dew, due ......................................................... | DO • DAO*U, DAOU |
| **do** • do *(music)* ............................................. | DO • DO |
| **do** *(music)* • doe, dough ......................................... | DO • DOE, DOEG |
| **doctor** • Dr. ............................................... | D–R • DR– |
| **doe** • do *(music)*, dough ......................................... | DOE • DO, DOEG |

**does**

| | |
|---|---|
| does *(verb - "do")* ............................................. | DUZ |
| does *(noun - "deer")* ......................................... | DO*ES |
| dose ............................................................... | DOES |
| doughs ........................................................... | DOEGS |
| doze ............................................................... | DOEZ |

| | |
|---|---|
| **does he feel** • diesel .............................................. | DAOEFL • SDAOEL |
| **dog** • doing, Guide Dog ......................................... | DAUG • DOG, GAUG |
| **doily** • dolly, Doyle .................................................. | DO*IL • DLOL, DOIL |
| **doing** • dog ............................................................ | DOG • DAUG |
| **dolly** • doily, Doyle ................................................. | DLOL • DO*IL, DOIL |
| **dolt** • dermatologist ............................................... | DOELT • DOLT |
| **Don** • dawn, don ..................................................... | DON • DAUN, DO*N |

---

**don** • done ............................................. DO*N • DOEN

**done** • did you know, dun ....................................... DOEN • DUN, D*UN

**done** • don ............................................. DOEN • DO*N

**dose**
      does ( *verb - "do"* ) ............................................. DUZ
      does ( *noun - "deer"* ) ........................................ DO*ES
      dose ............................................. DOES
      doughs ............................................. DOEGS
      doze ............................................. DOEZ

**double** • did you believe, do you believe .............. DOUBL • DUBL, DAOUBL

**dough** • do ( *music* ), doe ...................................... DOEG • DO, DOE

**dough** • do you ...................................... DOEG • DOU

**dour** • dower, detour ............................................. DAO*R • DO*UR, DOUR

**dower** • dour, detour ............................................. DO*UR • DAO*R, DOUR

**Doyle** • doily, dolly ...................................... DOIL • DO*IL, DLOL

**do you** • dough ...................................... DOU • DOEG

**do you believe** • did you believe, double .............. DAOUBL • DUBL, DOUBL

**do you do** • dude ...................................... DAOUD • DAO*UD

**do you know** • dune ............................................. DAOUN • DAO*UN *or* DAON

**doze**
      does ( *verb - "do"* ) ............................................. DUZ
      does ( *noun - "deer"* ) ........................................ DO*ES
      dose ............................................. DOES
      doughs ............................................. DOEGS
      doze ............................................. DOEZ

**Dr.** • doctor ............................................. DR– • D–R

**draw your attention** • drawing your attention ....... DRAURT • DRAURGS

**dress** • address, degrees ........................................ DRESZ • DRAES, DRES

**drier** • dryer ........................................... DRAOIR • DROIR

**drive** • derive ........................................... DRI • DRAOIV

**driver** • bus driver ............................................. DRIR • BRIR

**drive under the influence** • under the influence .. DRUFL • NUFL

**driveway** • roadway ............................................. DROI • ROI

**drug store** • grocery store ..................................... DROR • GROR

**drunkards** • redundancy ..................................... DRUNS • DRUNZ

**dryer** • drier ............................................. DROIR • DRAOIR

**dual** • duel ............................................. DWAOL • DWAOUL

**ducked** • duct ............................................. DUKD • DUKT

**ducks** • deduction ..................................... DUKZ • DUX

**duct** • ducked ......................................... DUKT • DUKD

**dude** • do you do ............................................. DAO*UD • DAOUD

---

| | |
|---|---|
| **due** • dew, do | DAOU • DAO*U, DO |
| **duel** • dual | DWAOUL • DWAOL |
| **dug** • did you go | D*UG • DUG |
| **D.U.I.** • D.W.I | DW– *or* DY– • DW*I |
| **duly** • dual, duel | DAOUL • DWAOL, DWAOUL |
| **duly** • duty | DAOUL • DAOUT |
| **duly licensed to practice medicine** • delimit | DLIM • DL*IM *or* DLIMT |
| **dune** • do you know | DAON *or* DAO*UN • DAOUN |
| **dune** • sand dune | DAON *or* DAO*UN • SDAON |
| **duration** • deprecation | DRAIGS • DRAIX |
| **dust** • did you say | DUFT • D*US |
| **D.W.I.** • D.U.I | DW*I • DW– *or* DY– |
| **dye** • die | DAO*I • DAOI |
| **dyer** • dire | DAO*IR • DAOIR |
| **dyke** • dike | DAO*IK • DAOIK |

# E

| | |
|---|---|
| **eagle** • spread-eagle | AOEG • SPRAOEG |
| **earl** • early | *ERL • ERL |
| **early** • earl | ERL • *ERL |
| **earn** • urn | ERN • *URN |
| **earned** • errand, errant | ERND • AERND, ERNT |
| **eave** • eve | AEV • AOEV |
| **edict** • addict | DAOEK • DIKT |
| **edition** • addition | YIGS • DIGS |
| **educate** • generate | JAET • JAIT |
| **education** • generation | JAEGS • JAIGS *or* JENGS |
| **educational** • jail | JAEL • JAIL |
| **effect** • affect | FEK • FAEK |
| **effectiveness** • ferventness | FEVRNS • FEVRNZ |
| **effectuation** • affection | EFX • AFX |
| **efficient** • fish | FIRB • F*IRB |
| **efficiently** • official | F*IRBL • FIRBL |
| **eight** • ate | AIT • AET |
| **eighty-two** • I wouldn't tell | YAO*T • YAOT |
| **either** • ether | ET • AO*ET |
| **either** • neither | ET • NE |
| **elaboration** • leaks | LAEBGS • LAEKZ |
| **electric** • reflect | LEKT • LEK |
| **element** • ailment | L–MT • AIMT |
| **elevate** • alleviate | VAIT • LAOEVT |
| **elevation** • vacation | VAEGS • VAIGS |
| **eleven** • lesson | LEVN • LEFN |
| **elicit** • illicit | LAOEFT • YLIF |
| **eligibility** • ineligibility, legibility | JEBLT • NEBLT, LEBLT |
| **eligible** • ineligible, legible | JEBL • NEBL, LEBL |

**emergency**

| | |
|---|---|
| emergency | M–RJ |
| in case of emergency | KERJ |
| in emergency | NERJ |
| state of emergency | STERJ |

| | |
|---|---|
| **emergency** • merge | M–RJ • MERJ |
| **emergency room** • operating room | ERM • OERM |
| **emigrate** • immigrate | KBRAET • KBRAIT |

**eminent** • immanent, imminent ............................. KB*EMT • KBAMT, KBIMT

**eminent** • impediment ............................................ KB*EMT • KBEMT

**emphasis** • cannabis ............................................. KBIS • KBIZ

**employ** • deploy, ploy ............................................ PLOI • DLOI, PLO*I

**employed** • self-employed ..................................... PLOID • SPLOID

**employee** • employ .............................................. PLOE • PLOI

**employment** • self-employment ........................... PLOIMT • SPLOIMT

**empower** • power .................................................. KBAUR • PAUR

**enable** • unable .................................................... NA*IBL • NAIBL

**enactment** • enlargement ..................................... NAMT • NARMT

**enclosure** • closure .............................................. KLOERZ *or* KLOUR • KLO*UR *or* KLOERZ

**encourage** • courage ............................................ NURJ • KURJ

**encourage** • discourage, scourge ........................ NURJ • SKOURJ, SKURJ

**encyclopedia** • scallop, scalp .............................. SKLOP • SKLAOP, SKAP

**endanger** • danger ............................................... DAERN • DAIRN

**enforcement** • No. ................................................ NO*FMT • NOFPLT

**engage** • disengage .............................................. GAEJ • DAEJ

**engage** • gage, gauge ........................................... GAEJ • GAIG, GAIJ

**engine** • New Jersey ............................................. N–J • N*J

**enjoy** • joy ............................................................. GOI • JOI

**enlarge** • large ...................................................... NARJ • LARJ

**enlargement** • enactment ..................................... NARMT • NAMT

**enormous** • norms ................................................ NORMS • NORMZ

**ensure**
    assure ............................................................. SHOUR, SHAO*UR
    ensure ............................................................. SNAOUR
    insure .............................................................. SHUR
    sure .................................................................. SHAOUR

**entitle** • title ......................................................... SPWAOILT • TAOILT

**entrance** • entrants .............................................. SPWRANS • SPWRANTS

**entrants** • entrance .............................................. SPWRANTS • SPWRANS

**entrench** • trench .................................................. NEFP • TREFP

**entrust** • interview ................................................ SPWRUFT *or* SPWRUF • SPWUF

**entwine** • intertwine ............................................. SPWAOIN • SPWRAOIN

**enumerate** • rate ................................................... RAET • RAIT

**envelope** • informal .............................................. N–VL • N–FL

**envy** • inform ........................................................ N–V • N–F

**equip** • quip .......................................................... KWIP • KW*IP

**equity** • inequity ..................................................... EKT • NEKT

**equivalence** • equivalents ...................................... KWIVS • KWIVZ

**equivalents** • equivalence ...................................... KWIVZ • KWIVS

**err** • air, heir ........................................................ *ER • AIR, HA*IR *or* HIR

**errand** • earned, errant .......................................... AERND • ERND, ERNT

**errant** • earned, errand .......................................... ERNT • ERND, AERND

**erroneous** • roan .................................................... ROEN • RO*EN

**especially** • specially ............................................ EPS *or* SPAOERBL • SPERBL

**estate** • state ......................................................... STAET • STAIT

**esteem** • self-esteem ............................................. STAOEM • SFAOEM

**esteem** • steam ..................................................... STAOEM • STAEM

**estrange** • strange ................................................. STRAEJ • STRAIJ

**eternal** • alternatively ............................................. TAOERNL • TERNL

**ether** • either ......................................................... AO*ET • ET

**ethic** • they can ..................................................... TH*EK • THEK

**eulogy** • you'll, Yule .............................................. YAOULG • *UL, YAOUL

**evaluation** • valuation ........................................... VAELGS • VALGS

**eve** • eave ............................................................. AOEV • AEV

**even** • 18 .............................................................. AOEN • AO*EN

**evening**
    evening ............................................... AOENG
    good evening ..................................... GAOENG
    in the evening .................................... NAOENG
    that evening ....................................... THAENG
    this evening ....................................... THAOENG
    tomorrow evening ............................. TWAOENG

**events** • fence ....................................................... FENZ • FENS

**every body** • everybody .......................................... EF/BOD • EFRB *or* EVRB

**everybody else** • everyone else, ........................... EFRBL • EFRNL, EFRLG
everything else

**everyday** • evidentiary ........................................... EFRD • EVRD

**every day** • everyday ............................................. EF/DAI • EFRD

**every one** • everyone ............................................. EF/WUN • EFRN *or* EVRN

**everyone else** • everybody else, ........................... EFRNL • EFRBL, EFRLG
everything else

**every thing** • everything ........................................ EF/THING • EFRG *or* EVRG

**everything else** • everybody else, ......................... EFRLG • EFRB, EFRNL
everyone else

**everywhere** • wherever .......................................... WREF • WREFR

**evidence**
    best evidence ................................... BEVD
    blood evidence .................................. BLEVD

| | |
|---|---|
| circumstantial evidence | SKEVD |
| credible evidence | KREVD |
| direct evidence | DREVD |
| evidence | EVD |
| exculpatory evidence | KPEVD |
| forensic evidence | FREVD |
| indirect evidence | SPWREVD |
| in evidence | NEVD |
| medical evidence | MEVD |
| no evidence | NOEVD |
| received in evidence | SNEVD |
| what evidence | WHAEVD |

**evidence** • everyday, evidentiary ............................ EVD • EFRD, EVRD

**Evidence Code Section** • ex~ ( *prefix* ) ................. *EX • EX

**evidentiary** • everyday, evidence ........................... EVRD • EFRD, EVD

**ewe** • you ..................................................................... YAOU • U

**exalt** • exult ................................................................ KPALT • KPULT

**exaltation** • exultation ............................................. KPALGS • KP*ULGS

**excel** • compel ........................................................... KPEL • KMEL

**excellence** • silence ................................................. KPLENS • SLENS

**excellent** • silent...................................................... KPLENT • SLENT

**except** • accept ........................................................ KPEP • SEP

**excess** • access, assess ......................................... KPESZ • KRES, SAES

**exchange** • change, interchange ........................... KPAING *or* KPAIJ • KHAING *or* KHAIJ, SPWAIJ

**exclaim** • disclaim .................................................... SKLAEM • SKLAIM

**exclude** • include...................................................... SKLU • KLU

**exclusion** • inclusion ............................................... SKLUGS • KLUGS

**exclusive** • inclusive ............................................... SKLUV • KLUV

**exclusively** • inclusively .......................................... SKLUVL • KLUVL

**exclusiveness** • inclusiveness ............................... SKLUVNS • KLUVNS

**exhilarate** • accelerate ............................................ ZIL • SLERT

**exhilaration** • acceleration...................................... ZILGS • SLERGS

**exhort** • export, extort ............................................. KPORT • KPOERT, STORT

**exile** • compile ......................................................... KPAOIL • KPIL

**expanse** • spans ...................................................... SPANS • SPANZ

**expansive** • expensive ............................................ SPAV • SPEV

**expeditious** • specious ............................................ SPAO*ERB • SPAOERB

**expend** • spend ........................................................ SKPEN • SPEN

**expends** • expense .................................................. SKPENS • SPENS

**expense** • expends, suspense ............................... SPENS • SKPENS, SPENZ

**expensive** • expansive ............................................ SPEV • SPAV

             

**experience** • inexperience ......................................... SPERNS • NERNS

**experienced** • inexperienced ................................ SPERND • NERND

**expert witness** • hostile witness ......................... SPWIN • HIN

**expiration** • perspiration ........................................ KPRAIGS • SPIRGS

**expiration** • separation ........................................... KPRAIGS • SPRAIGS

**expire** • aspire, conspire ......................................... KPAOIR • SPAOIR, SKPAOIR

**explicit** • implicit ...................................................... PLIFT • KBLIFT

**explode** • implode ................................................... SPLOED • KBLOED

**explore** • splendor .................................................. SPLOER • SPLOR

**explosion** • implosion ............................................. SPLOEGS • KBLOEGS

**exponent** • opponent .............................................. SPOENT • POENT

**export** • exhort, extort ............................................ KPOERT • KPORT, STORT

**expose** • exposé ..................................................... SKPOES • SKPAI

**expressway** • roadway ............................................ KPROI • ROI

**expulsion** • compulsion .......................................... SPULGS • KPULGS

**extant** • extent, instant ........................................... STA*NT • STENT, STANT

**extent** • extant, instant ........................................... STENT • STA*NT, STANT

**exterior**
    anterior ............................................................. AOR
    exterior .............................................................. KPAOR
    inferior .............................................................. FAOR
    interior .............................................................. NAOR
    posterior ........................................................... PAO*R
    superior ............................................................. SAOR

**external** • sternal .................................................... STERNL • ST*ERNL

**extinct** • distinct, indistinct ................................... KPING • DING, NING

**extinct** • distinct, indistinct, instinct ................... KPINGT • DINGT, NINGT, STINGT

**extinction** • distinction ........................................... KPINGS • DINGS

**extinguish** • distinguish .......................................... TWIRB • DWIRB

**extinguishable** • distinguishable .......................... TWIRBL • DWIRBL

**extort** • exhort, export ............................................ STORT • KPORT, KPOERT

**extra** • supra ........................................................... KPRA • SPRA

**extract**
    detract ............................................................... DRAK
    distract .............................................................. SDRAK
    extract ............................................................... STRAK
    subtract ............................................................. STRAKT

**extraction**
    detraction .......................................................... DRAX
    distraction .......................................................... SDRAX
    extraction .......................................................... STRAX
    subtraction ........................................................ STRAEX

**extrinsic** • intrinsic ................................................ KPRIN • SPWRIN

**extrinsically** • intrinsically ...................................... KPRINL • SPWRINL

**extrovert** • controvert, introvert .............................. KPROVT • TROVT, SPWROVT

**extrude** • intrude ..................................................... KPRAOUD • SPWRAOUD

**extrusion** • intrusion ............................................. KPRAOUGS • SPWRAOUGS

**exult** • exalt ............................................................ KPULT • KPALT

**exultation** • compulsion ......................................... KP*ULGS • KPULGS

**exultation** • exaltation ........................................... KP*ULGS • KPALGS

**eye** • aye, I ............................................................. AOI • AO*I, I

**eyed** • I'd ................................................................ AO*ID • AOID

**eyes** • ice ............................................................... AOIZ • AOIS

# F

| | |
|---|---|
| **face** • faze, phase | FAIS • FAES, FAIZ *or* FAEZ |
| **facet** • faucet | FAFT • FAUFT |
| **facility** • faculty | FAFLT • FULT |
| **faction** • facts, fax | FA*X • FAKZ, FAX |
| **facts** • faction, fax | FAKZ • FA*X, FAX |
| **faculty** • facility | FULT • FAFLT |
| **fail** • female | FAIL • FAEL |
| **fair** • fare | FAIR • FAER |
| **fair trial** • get a fair trial | FRAOIL • GRAOIL |
| **fame** • family | FAIM • FAEM |
| **familiar** • familiarity, family | FAM • FAMT, FAEM |
| **family** • fame, familiar | FAEM • FAIM, FAM |
| **family room** • family | FAERM • FAEM |
| **fancy** • fantasy | FAENS • FAENT |
| **fantasy** • fancy | FAENT • FAENS |
| **faraway** • far away | FWAR • FWAI |
| **fare** • fair | FAER • FAIR |
| **farther** • further | FA*RT • FURT |
| **fatal** • fetal | FAILT • FAOELT |
| **father** • stepfather | FA *or* FAU • SFA *or* SFAU |
| **faucet** • facet | FAUFT • FAFT |
| **fawned** • offhand | FA*UND • FAUND |
| **fax** • faction, facts | FAX • FA*X, FAKZ |
| **faze** • face, phase | FAES • FAIS, FAIZ *or* FAEZ |
| **FBI** • fib | FIB • F*IB |
| **fear** • fare | FAOER • FAER |
| **fears** • fierce | FAOERZ • FAOERS |
| **feat** • feet | FAET • FAOET |
| **feature** • safety feature | FAOEFP • SFAOEFP |
| **federalization** • federal regulation, federation | FRAELGS • FRALGS, FRAIGS |
| **federal law** • civil law, criminal law | FLA • SLA, KRA |
| **federal regulation** • federalization, federation | FRALGS • FRAELGS, FRAIGS |
| **federation** • federalization, federal regulation | FRAIGS • FRAELGS, FRALGS |
| **feedback** • Federal Bureau of Investigation | FAOEB • FAO*EB |
| **feet** • feat | FAOET • FAET |
| **felonies** • flamboyance | FLOINS • FLOINZ |
| **female** • fail | FAEL • FAIL |

| | |
|---|---|
| **fence** • events | FENS • FENZ |
| **ferventness** • effectiveness | FEVRNZ • FEVRNS |
| **fetal** • fatal | FAOELT • FAILT |
| **few** • if you | FAOU • FU |
| **fiance** • fiancee | FAE • FA*E |
| **fib** • FBI | F*IB • FIB |
| **fibula** • if I believe | FLIB • FIBL |
| **fiction** • fix | F*IX • FIX |
| **fierce** • fears | FAOERS • FAOERZ |
| **Fifth Amendment** • amendment, First Amendment | FAEMT • AEMT, FIRMT |
| **Fifth Amendment right** • First Amendment right | FAERMT • FRIRMT |
| **fifty-eight cents** • vases | VA*ISZ • VAISZ |
| **fifty-eights** • vase | VAIS • VAIZ |
| **fig** • figure | F*IG • FIG |
| **figment** • pigment | FIMT • PIMT |
| **figure** • fig | FIG • F*IG |
| **figures** • fission, physician | FIGS • F*IGS, F–GS |
| **fillings** • affiliation | F*ILGS • FILGS |
| **fin** • finish, Finn, Finnish | F*IN • FIN, FWIN, FWIRB |
| **finagler** • fraying | FRAIG • FRA*IG |
| **final** • finale, finally, finely | FAOINL • FAINL, FAENL, FOINL |
| **finally** • finale, finely | FAENL • FAINL, FOINL |
| **find** • fined | FAOIND • FAO*IND |
| **fined** • find | FAO*IND • FAOIND |
| **finely** • finale, finally | FOINL • FAINL, FAENL |
| **finish** • fin, Finn, Finnish | FIN • F*IN, FWIN, FWIRB |
| **Finnish** • fin, finish, Finn | FWIRB • F*IN, FIN, FWIN |
| **fir** • fur | FIR • F*UR |
| **fireman** • foreman | FRAN • FRAM |
| **First Amendment** • amendment, Fifth Amendment | FIRMT • AEMT, FAEMT |
| **First Amendment right** • Fifth Amendment right | FRIRMT • FAERMT |
| **first class** • second class | FLAS • SLAS |
| **firsthand** • hand | FRAND • HAND |
| **First Lady** • forelady | FLAED • FRAED |
| **fiscal** • physical | SKAL • F–L |

**fish** • efficient .......................................................... F*IRB • FIRB

**fisher** • fissure ....................................................... FRIRB • FIRZ

**fission** • figures, physician ..................................... F*IGS • FIGS, F–GS

**fissure** • fisher ...................................................... FIRZ • FRIRB

**fix** • fiction ............................................................... FIX • F*IX

**flack**
    flack ................................................................ FLA*KT
    flak ................................................................... FLAK
    flax ................................................................... FLAX
    prophylactic ...................................................... FLAKT
    prophylaxis ...................................................... FLAKZ

**flak** • flack, prophylactic .......................................... FLAK • FLA*KT, FLAKT

**flagrant** • fragrant .................................................. FLAEGT • FRAIGT

**flagrant** • inflating .................................................. FLAEGT • FLAIGT

**flair** • flare ............................................................... FLAIR • FLAER

**flamboyance** • felonies ............................................ FLOINZ • FLOINS

**flammable liquid** • liquid ......................................... FLID • KLID

**flare** • flair ............................................................... FLAER • FLAIR

**flax** • prophylactics, prophylaxis ............................. FLAX • FLAKTS, FLAKZ

**flea** • flee ................................................................ FLAE • FLAOE

**fleas** • fleece, flees ................................................. FLAES • FLAOES, FLAOEZ

**flecks** • flex, flexion ................................................ FLEKZ • FLEX, FL*EX

**flee** • flea ................................................................ FLAOE • FLAE

**fleece** • fleas, flees ................................................. FLAOES • FLAES, FLAOEZ

**flees** • fleas, fleece ................................................. FLAOEZ • FLAES, FLAOES

**flew** • flu, flue, influence ......................................... FLAOU • FL*U, FLAO*U, FLU

**flex** • flecks, flexion ................................................ FLEX • FLEKZ, FL*EX

**flexion** • flecks, flex ................................................ FL*EX • FLEKZ, FLEX

**flick** • inflict ............................................................. FLOIK *or* FL*IK • FLIK

**flicks** • infliction ...................................................... FLOIKS *or* FL*IKS • FLIX

**flier** • flyer .............................................................. FLOIR • FLAOIR

**flight simulator** • simulator ..................................... FLAIRT • SMAIRT

**flogged** • freeloading .............................................. FLOGD • FLO*GD

**flood** • influenced ................................................... FLAOD • FLUD

**floored** • freeloader ................................................ FLAORD • FLORD

**flounce** • flounders ................................................. FLOUNS • FLOUNZ

**flounder** • flown ...................................................... FLOUN • FLOEN

**flounders** • flounce ................................................. FLOUNZ • FLOUNS

**flour** • flower ........................................................... FLOUR • FLAUR

**flower** • flour ........................................................... FLAUR • FLOUR

        

**flown** • flounder ...................................................... FLOEN • FLOUN

**flu** • flew, flue, influence ......................................... FL*U • FLAOU, FLAO*U, FLU

**flue** • flew, flu, influence ......................................... FLAO*U • FLAOU, FL*U, FLU

**flux** • influx .............................................................. FLUX • NUX

**flyer** • flier .............................................................. FLAOIR • FLOIR

**foal** • focal ............................................................... FOEL • FOEFL

**focal** • foal .............................................................. FOEFL • FOEL

**~fold**
    centerfold ....................................................... SNOLD
    twofold ............................................................. TWOFLD
    threefold ........................................................... THREFLD
    fourfold ............................................................. FOUFRLD
    fivefold ............................................................. FAOIVLD
    sixfold .............................................................. SWIFLD
    sevenfold ......................................................... SEVLD

**follower** • fortunately ............................................. FO*RL • FORL

**footage** • square footage ....................................... FAOJ • SKWAOJ

**for** • fore, four ........................................................ FOR • FOER, FOUR

**fore** • for, four ........................................................ FOER • FOR, FOUR

**forelady** • afraid, frayed ......................................... FRAED • FRAID, FRA*ED

**forelady** • First Lady .............................................. FRAED • FLAED

**foreman** • fireman ................................................... FRAM • FRAN

**for identification** • marked for identification ......... FOID • MOID

**formally** • formerly ................................................. FAL • FOERL

**formerly** • formally ................................................. FOERL • FAL

**for probable cause** • probable cause ................... FRAUZ • PRAUZ

**fort** • forte ............................................................... FORT • FOERT

**forte** • fort .............................................................. FOERT • FORT

**forth** • fourth ........................................................... FO*RT • FO*URT

**fortunate** • unfortunate .......................................... FORNT • UFRN *or* UFRNT

**fortunately** • follower ............................................. FORL • FO*RL

**fortunately** • unfortunately .................................... FORL • UFRNL

**forty-eight cents** • phrases .................................... FRA*ISZ • FRAISZ

**forty-eights** • frays, phrase ................................... FRAIZ • FRAES, FRAIS

**forty-three cents** • freezes .................................... FRAO*ESZ • FRAOESZ

**forty-threes** • frees, freeze .................................... FRAO*ES • FRAOES, FRAOEZ

**foul** • fowl ............................................................... FOUL • FO*UL *or* FWOUL

**foundation**
    foundation ....................................................... FOUNGS
    lack of foundation ........................................... LOUNGS
    without foundation .......................................... WOUNGS

| | |
|---|---|
| **four** • for, fore | FOUR • FOR, FOER |
| **fourth** • forth | FO*URT • FO*RT |
| **fowl** • foul | FWOUL *or* FO*UL • FOUL |
| **fragrant** • flagrant | FRAIGT • FLAEGT |
| **fragrant** • perforating | FRAIGT • FRAEGT |
| **frayed** • afraid, forelady | FRA*ED • FRAID, FRAED |
| **fraying** • finagler, further reading | FRA*EG • FRAIG, FRAEG |
| **frays** • forty-eights, phrase | FRAES • FRAIZ, FRAIS |
| **freaks** • frequencies | FRAOEKZ • FRAOEKS |
| **freelancing** • phalanges | FLANGS • FLANGZ |
| **freeloader** • floored | FLORD • FLAORD |
| **freeloading** • flogged | FLO*GD • FLOGD |
| **freely** • frequently | FRAOEL • FREL |
| **frees** • freeze, frieze | FRES *or* FRAOES • FRAOEZ, FRAO*EZ |
| **freeway** • highway | FOI • HOI |
| **freeze** • frees, frieze | FRAOEZ • FRAOES *or* FRES, FRAO*EZ |
| **frequencies** • freaks | FRAOEKS • FRAOEKZ |
| **frequently** • freely | FREL • FRAOEL |
| **friar** • fryer | FRAR • FRAOIR |
| **fridge** • infringe | FR*IJ • FRIJ |
| **frieze** • frees, freeze | FRAO*EZ • FRES *or* FRAOES, FRAOEZ |
| **fryer** • friar | FRAOIR • FRAR |
| **fun** • if you know | F*UN • FUN |
| **fur** • fir, if you are | F*UR • FIR, FUR |
| **further** • farther | FURT • FA*RT |
| **furthermore** • if you remember | F*URM • FURM |
| **fuss** • fuzz, if you say, if you say so | F*USZ • FUZ, FUS, FUSZ |
| **fuzz** • fuss, if you say, if you say so | FUZ • F*USZ, FUS, FUSZ |

# G

| | | |
|---|---|---|
| **gage** • engage, gauge | GAIG • GAEJ, GAIJ | |
| **Gail** • gale | GAIL • GAEL | |
| **gait** • gate, investigate | GA*IT • GAET, GAIT | |
| **gale** • Gail | GAEL • GAIL | |
| **gamma globulin** • immunoglobulin | GLAUB • KBLAUB | |
| **ganglia** • gorilla | GLA* • GLA | |
| **garb** • gash | GAURB • GARB | |
| **gash** • garb | GARB • GAURB | |
| **gasoline** • glean | GLAEN • GLAOEN | |
| **gate** • gait, investigate | GAET • GA*IT, GAIT | |
| **gauge** • engage, gage | GAIJ • GAEJ, GAIG | |
| **gays** • gaze | GAIS • GAIZ | |
| **gaze** • gays | GAIZ • GAIS | |
| **gee** • apology, ghee | GAOE • JAOE, GAO*E | |
| **geese** • goodies | GAOES • GAOEZ | |
| **gel** • jell | GEL • JEL | |
| **gender** • agenda | JERND • JEND | |

**general**

| | |
|---|---|
| attorney general | TOERNG |
| consulate general | SKWULG |
| lieutenant general | LAOUNGT |
| State Attorney General | STOERNG |
| Surgeon General | SURNG |

**generate** • educate ............... JAIT • JAET

**generation** • education ............... JENGS *or* JAIGS • JAEGS

**genes**

| | |
|---|---|
| genes | GAOENS |
| genius | JAOENZ |
| genus | GAOENZ |
| jeans | JAOENS |

**genius** • genus ............... JAOENZ • GAOENZ

**genius** • jeans ............... JAOENZ • JAOENS

**genuine** • June ............... JAOUN • JUN

**genus** • genius ............... GAOENZ • JAOENZ

**germ**

| | |
|---|---|
| germ | JERM |
| German | JOIM |
| germane | JAIM |
| Germany | JOIRM |
| germinate | JERMT |

**German** • germane, Germany .............................. JOIM • JAIM, JOIRM

**germane** • German, germinate ............................ JAIM • JOIM, JERMT

**Germany** • German, germane ............................ JOIRM • JOIM, JAIM

**germinate** • germane ........................................ JERMT • JAIM

**get a fair trial** • fair trial ............................... GRAOIL • FRAOIL

**ghee** • gee ........................................................ GAO*E • GAOE

**gibberish** • jib ................................................... GIB • JIB

**gibe** • jibe ........................................................ GAOIB • JAOIB

**gigabit** • megabit ............................................. GIBT • MIBT

**gigabyte** • megabyte ........................................ GIGT • MEGT

**gigs** • ignition ................................................... GIGZ • GIGS

**gild** • gilled, guild ............................................ G*ILD • GLILD, GILD

**gilled** • gild, guild ............................................. GLILD • G*ILD, GILD

**girlfriend** • boyfriend ....................................... GOIF • BOIF

**glance** • glands, glans ..................................... GLANS • GLANDZ, GLANZ

**glands** • glance, glans ..................................... GLANDZ • GLANS, GLANZ

**glans** • glance, glands ..................................... GLANZ • GLANS, GLANDZ

**glean** • gasoline ............................................... GLAOEN • GLAEN

**globin** • globulin ............................................... GLUB • GLAOUB

**globulin** • globin ............................................... GLAOUB • GLUB

**gnat** • in that ..................................................... NA*T • NAT

**gofer** • gopher, governor .................................. GO*EFR • GOEFR, GOFR

**good afternoon** • afternoon ............................. GAFRN • AFRN

**good evening** • evening ................................... GAOENG • AOENG

**good faith** • bad faith ...................................... G–F • B–F

**goodies** • geese .............................................. GAOEZ • GAOES

**good morning** • morning .................................. GORNG • MORNG

**Good Samaritan** • Samaritan .......................... GAIRM • SMAIRN

**go out** • gout ................................................... GOUT • GO*UT

**gopher** • gofer, governor ................................. GOEFR • GO*EFR, GOFR

**gored** • gourd, ignored .................................... GOERD • GOURD, GORD

**gorgeous** • gorges .......................................... GORJS • GORJZ

**gorges** • gorgeous .......................................... GORJZ • GORJS

**gorilla** • ganglia, guerilla ................................. GORL • GLA*, GREL

**gourd** • gored, ignored .................................... GOURD • GOERD, GORD

**governor** • gofer, gopher ................................. GOFR • GO*EFR, GOEFR

**governor's office** • office ................................. GOFS • OFS

**grace**
     grace ......................................................... GRAIS

| | |
|---|---|
| grays | GRA*IS |
| graze | GRAIZ |
| grease | GRAES |
| Greece | GRAOES |
| greys | GRAEZ |

**grade** • grayed, greyed ....................... GRAID • GRA*ID, GRAED

**gradually** • great deal ......................... GRAOEL • GRAEL

**graft** • graphed ....................................... GRAFT • GRAFD

**gram** • grapple ....................................... GRAM • GRAP

**grand mal seizure** • petit mal seizure ................... G–MZ • P–MZ

**grandmother**

| | |
|---|---|
| grandmother | GROER |
| grocer | GROEFR |
| grocery store | GROR |
| grosser | GRORSZ |
| grower | GRO*ER, GROUR |

**graphed** • graft ....................................... GRAFD • GRAFT

**grapple** • gram ....................................... GRAP • GRAM

**grate** • great, integrate ......................... GRA*IT • GRAET, GRAIT

**gratification** • gravitation ....................................... GRAFGS • GRAVGS

**grave** • gravy ....................................... GRAIV • GRAEV

**gravitation** • gratification ....................................... GRAVGS • GRAFGS

**gravity** • graft ....................................... GRAVT • GRAFT

**gravy** • aggravate, grave ......................... GRAEV • GRAEVT, GRAIV

**gray** • grey ....................................... GRAI • GRAE

**grayed** • grade, greyed ......................... GRA*ID • GRAID, GRAED

**graying** • Greg, greying ......................... GRA*IG • GRAIG, GRAEG

**grays**

| | |
|---|---|
| grace | GRAIS |
| grays | GRA*IS |
| graze | GRAIZ |
| grease | GRAES |
| Greece | GRAOES |
| greys | GRAEZ |

**graze** • grace, grays, greys ......................... GRAIZ • GRAIS, GRA*IS, GRAEZ

**grease** • grace ....................................... GRAES • GRAIS

**grease** • Greece ....................................... GRAES • GRAOES

**great** • grate, integrate ......................... GRAET • GRA*IT, GRAIT

**great deal** • gradually ......................... GRAEL • GRAOEL

**great extent** • to a great extent ......................... GRAEX • TRAEX

**Greece** • grease ....................................... GRAOES • GRAES

**green light** • red light, yellow light ......................... GR–LT • R–LT, Y–LT

**Greg** • graying, greying ......................... GRAIG • GRA*IG, GRAEG

          © 2006 White-Boucke Publishing

| | |
|---|---|
| **grey** • gray | GRAE • GRAI |
| **greyed** • grade, grayed | GRAED • GRAID, GRA*ID |
| **greying** • graying, Greg | GRAEG • GRA*IG, GRAIG |
| **greys** • grays | GRAEZ • GRA*IS |
| **gridlock** • deadlock, lock | GLOK • DLOK, LOK |
| **grip** • grippe | GRIP • GREP |
| **grippe** • grip | GREP • GRIP |
| **grisly** • gristly, grizzly | GRILZ • GRIFL, GRIZ |
| **gristly** • grisly, grizzly | GRIFL • GRILZ, GRIZ |
| **grizzly** • grisly, gristly | GRIZ • GRILZ, GRIFL |
| **groan** • grown | GROEN • GROUN |
| **grocer** • grocery store, grosser | GROEFR • GROR, GRORSZ |
| **grocery store** • drugstore | GROR • DROR |
| **grocery store** • grandmother | GROR • GROER |
| **grosser** • grocer | GRORSZ • GROEFR |
| **grower** • grandmother | GROUR *or* GRO*ER • GROER |
| **grown** • groan | GROUN • GROEN |
| **guarantee** • guaranty | GARNT • GIRNT |

~guard

| | |
|---|---|
| bodyguard | BORGD, BAUGD |
| coast guard | KOEFGD |
| lifeguard | LAOIFGD |
| safeguard | SAIFGD |
| vanguard | VANGD |

| | |
|---|---|
| **guerilla** • gorilla | GREL • GORL |
| **guessed** • guest | GEFD • G*ES |
| **guest** • guessed | G*ES • GEFD |
| **guidance** • misguidance | GAOINS • SGAOINS |
| **guide** • misguide | GAOID • SGAOID |
| **Guide Dog** • dog | GAUG • DAUG |
| **guideline** • line | GLAOIN • LAOIN |
| **guild** • gild, gilled | GILD • G*ILD, GLILD |
| **guise** • guys | GAOIZ • GAOIS |
| **guys** • guise | GAOIS • GAOIZ |
| **gym** • Jim | GIM • JIM |

---

# H

| | |
|---|---|
| **habit** • inhabit | HABT • NABT |
| **hail** • hale, heal | HAIL • HA\*EL, HAEL |
| **hair** • hare | HAIR • HA\*ER |
| **hair** • heir | HAIR • HA\*IR *or* HIR |
| **hale** • hail | HA\*EL • HAIL |
| **hale** • heal | HA\*EL • HAEL |
| **half** • halve, hassle | HAF • HAVL, HAFL |
| **half of the** • one-half of the | HAFT • WAFT |
| **hall** • haul | HAL • HAUL |
| **halve** • half, hassle | HAVL • HAF, HAFL |
| **hammer** • harem | HAERM • HAIRM |
| **hand** • handy | HAND • HAEND |
| **handcuff** • huff | HUF • H\*UF |
| **handle** • mishandle | HANL • SHANL |
| **handwriting** • hanger | HARNG • HA\*RNG |
| **handy** • hand | HAEND • HAND |
| **hanger** • handwriting | HA\*RNG • HARNG |
| **happy** • heap | HAEP • HAOEP |
| **harassment** • sexual harassment | HARMT • SWARMT |
| **hardly** • Harley | HARL • HAERL |
| **hardware** • software | DWAER • SWAER |
| **hare** • hair | HA\*ER • HAIR |
| **hare** • hear | HA\*ER • HAER |
| **harem** • hammer | HAIRM • HAERM |
| **Harley** • hardly | HAERL • HARL |
| **harsh** • hash | HAURB • HARB |
| **Harvard** • hazard | HAVRD • HAFRD |
| **hash** • harsh | HARB • HAURB |
| **has he** • hay | HAE • HA\*E |
| **hassle** • half, halve | HAFL • HAF, HAVL |
| **hateful** • ahead of | HAIFL • HAIF |
| **haul** • hall | HAUL • HAL |
| **have the** • Vermont | V–T • V\*T |
| **Hawaii** • hi | H\*I • HI |
| **hay** • hey | HA\*E • HAI |
| **hazard** • Harvard | HAFRD • HAVRD |
| **head** • he'd, he had | HAED • H\*ED, HED |

| | |
|---|---|
| **headlight** • taillight | HAELT • TAILT |
| **heal** • heel, he'll | HAEL • HAOEL, H*EL |
| **health** • good health | H*ELT • G*ELT |
| **health** • wealth | H*ELT • W*ELT |
| **healthy** • wealthy | HA*ELT • WA*ELT |
| **heap** • happy | HAOEP • HAEP |
| **hear** • here | HAER • HAOER |
| **hearing aid** • hearing impaired | HIRD • HIRMD |
| **hearing impaired** • speech impaired | HIRMD • SPIRD |
| **hearing impairment** • speech impairment | HIRMT • SPIRMT |
| **hears** • hearse, hers | HAERS • HA*ERS, HERS |
| **hearse** • hears, hers | HA*ERS • HAERS, HERS |
| **head** • he had | HAED • HED |
| **heard** • herd, hurried | HAERD • HERD, HURD |
| **he'd** • heed | H*ED • HAOED |
| **he'd** • he had | H*ED • HED |
| **heed** • he'd | HAOED • H*ED |
| **heel** • heal, he'll | HAOEL • HAEL, H*EL |
| **he had** • head | HED • HAED |
| **he had** • he'd | HED • H*ED |
| **heir** • air, err | HIR *or* HA*IR • AIR, *ER |
| **heir** • hair | HIR *or* HA*IR • HAIR |
| **he is** • he's | HES • H*ES |
| **he'll** • heal, heel | H*EL • HAEL, HAOEL |
| **he'll** • hell | H*EL • HEL |
| **hell** • he'll | HEL • H*EL |
| **her** • hers, herself | HER • HERS, H*ERS *or* HERSZ |
| **herd** • heard, hurried | HERD • HAERD, HURD |
| **here** • hear | HAOER • HAER |
| **heroin** • heroine | HERN • H*ERN *or* HOIRN |
| **heroine** • heroin | HOIRN *or* H*ERN • HERN |
| **hers** • hearse, hears | HERS • HA*ERS, HAERS |
| **herself** • her, hers | H*ERS • HER, HERS |

**hertz**

| | |
|---|---|
| hers | HERS |
| herself | H*ERS, HERSZ |
| hertz | HERZ, H–RTS |
| Hertz | H*ERTS |
| hurts | HURTS |
| inherits | HERTS |

| | |
|---|---|
| **he's** • he is | H*ES • HES |
| **heterogeneous** • homogeneous | HAOENS • HAOEMS |
| **heterosexual** • homosexual | H–T • H–L |
| **heterosexuality** • homosexuality | HELT • H–LT |
| **hew** • hue, Hugh | HAO*U • HAOU, HAOUG |
| **hey** • hay, has he | HAI • HA*E, HAE |
| **hi** • Hawaii | HI • H*I |
| **hi** • high | HI • HAOI |
| **hibernated** • hybrid | HAO*IBD • HAOIBD |
| **hicks** • prohibition | HIKZ • HIX |
| **high** • hi | HAOI • HI |
| **higher** • hire | HAO*IR • HAOIR |
| **highway** • freeway | HOI • FOI |
| **him** • hymn | HIM • H*IM |
| **hire** • higher | HAOIR • HAO*IR |
| **His Honor** • your Honor | HIRN • URN |
| **hiss** • his | HISZ • HIS |
| **ho** • hoe | HO • HOE |
| **hoar** • abhor, whore | HAOR • HOER, WHOER |
| **hoard** • horde | HAORD • HORD |
| **hoarse** • horse | HAORS • HORS |
| **hoe** • ho | HOE • HO |
| **hoes** • hose | HOES • HOEZ |
| **hold** • holed, how old | HOLD • HO*ELD, HOELD |
| **hold** • hollow | HOLD *or* HOL • HO*L |
| **hole** • whole | HOEL • WHOEL |
| **holed** • hold, how old | HO*ELD • HOLD, HOELD |
| **holey** • holy, wholly | HO*EL • HO*IL, WHOIL |
| **hollow** • hold | HO*L • HOL *or* HOLD |
| **holy** • holey, wholly | HO*IL • HO*EL, WHOIL |
| **home** • at home, hometown | HOEM • THOEM, HOEMT |
| **homogeneous** • heterogeneous | HAOEMS • HAOENS |
| **homogeneous** • homogenous | HAOEMS • HOJZ *or* MOJZ |
| **homogenous** • homogeneous | MOJZ *or* HOJZ • HAOEMS |
| **homosexual** • heterosexual | H–L • H–T |
| **homosexuality** • heterosexuality | H–LT • HELT |
| **honest** • dishonest | HONS • SHONS |
| **honesty** • dishonesty | HO*NS • SHO*NS |

| | |
|---|---|
| **honor** • dishonor | HON • SHON |
| **honorable** • dishonorable | HONL • SHONL |
| **hoop** • whoop | HAOP • WHAOP |
| **horde** • abhorred, hoard | HORD • HOERD, HAORD |
| **horizontal** • horizontally, zonal | ZONL • ZOENL, ZAUNL |
| **horse** • abhors, hoarse | HORS • HOERS, HAORS |
| **hose** • hoes | HOEZ • HOES |
| **hospitable** • hospital | HIBL • HOPT |
| **hospital** • hospitable | HOPT • HIBL |
| **hostile witness** • expert witness | HIN • SPWIN |
| **hotel** • motel | HOELT • MOELT |
| **hour** • how're, our | HOUR • HO*UR, OUR |
| **hours** • ours | HOURS • OURS |
| **house** • how is, how's | HOUS • HOUZ, HO*US |
| **how is** • house, how's | HOUZ • HOUS, HO*US |
| **how late** • about how late | HOULT • BOULT |
| **howled** • how would | HO*ULD • HOULD |
| **how old** • hold, holed | HOELD • HOLD, HO*ELD |
| **how're** • hour | HO*UR • HOUR |
| **how's** • how is, house | HO*US • HOUZ, HOUS |
| **how shall** • how should | HOURB • HOURBD |
| **how should** • how shall | HOURBD • HOURB |
| **how would** • howled | HOULD • HO*ULD |
| **hue** • hew, Hugh | HAOU • HAO*U, HAOUG |
| **huff** • handcuff | H*UF • HUF |
| **Hugh** • hew, hue | HAOUG • HAO*U, HAOU |
| **Hughes** • hues | HAOUZ • HAOUS |
| **huh** • uh | HU • H*U |
| **human** • humanity | HAOUM • HAOUMT |
| **human** • subhuman | HAOUM • SHAOUM |
| **humerus** • humorous | HURMZ • HAOURMZ |
| **humor** • sense of humor | HAOURM • SHAOURM |
| **humorous** • humerus | HAOURMZ • HURMZ |
| **Hungarian** • Hungary, hungry | HAIRN • HAUNG, HURNG |
| **Hungary** • Hungarian, hungry | HAUNG • HAIRN, HURNG |
| **hunger** • Hungary, hungry | H–NG • HAUNG, HURNG |
| **hungry** • Hungary | HURNG • HAUNG |
| **hurdle** • hurled | H*URLD • HURLD |

**hurled** • hurdle, hurtled ......................................... HURLD • H*URLD, HURLTD

**hurried** • heard, herd ............................................ HURD • HAERD, HERD

**hurt** • inherit .......................................................... HURT • HERT

**hurtled** • hurled ..................................................... HURLTD • HURLD

**hurts**
    hers ............................................................... HERS
    herself .......................................................... H*ERS, HERSZ
    hertz ............................................................. HERZ, H–RTS
    Hertz ............................................................. H*ERTS
    hurts .............................................................. HURTS
    inherits .......................................................... HERTS

**hymn** • him ......................................................... H*IM • HIM

# I

| | |
|---|---|
| I • aye, eye | I • AO*I, AOI |
| I am • I'm | IM • AOIM |
| ice • eyes | AOIS • AOIZ |
| I'd • eyed | AOID • AO*ID |
| I.D. • Idaho, I had | *ID • *ID/*ID *or* DHOE, ID |
| Idaho • I.D., I had | *ID/*ID *or* DHOE • *ID, ID |

**identification**

| | |
|---|---|
| People's 1 for identification | PUND |
| People's 2 for identification | PAOD |
| People's 3 for identification | PAOED |
| People's 4 for identification | POERD |
| People's 5 for identification | PAOIVD |
| People's 6 for identification | POIKD |
| People's 7 for identification | PEVD |

**idle**

| | |
|---|---|
| I'd | AOID |
| idle | AOILD |
| idled | AO*ILD |
| idol | DOLD |
| idyll | DYIL, DY–L |
| I would | ILD |

| | |
|---|---|
| idol • idle, idled, idyll | DOLD • AOILD, AO*ILD, DYIL *or* DY–L |
| idyll • idle, idled, idol | DYIL *or* DY–L • AOILD, AO*ILD, DOLD |
| if I believe • fibula | FIBL • FLIB |
| if you • few | FU • FAOU |
| if you are • fur | FUR • F*UR |
| if you know • fun | FUN • F*UN |
| if you remember • furthermore | FURM • F*URM |
| if you say • fuss, fuzz | FUS • F*USZ, FUZ |
| if you say so • fuss, fuzz | FUSZ • F*USZ, FUZ |
| ignition • gigs | GIGS • GIGZ |
| ignored • gored, gourd | GORD • GOERD, GOURD |
| I had • I.D., Idaho | ID • *ID, *ID/*ID *or* DHOE |
| ill • Illinois | IL • *IL |
| I'll • aisle, isle | AOIL • AOIFL, YAOIL |
| illicit • elicit | YLIF • LAOEFT |
| Illinois • ill, I'll | *IL • IL, AOIL |
| illustrate • straight, strait | STRAET • STRAIT, STRA*IT |
| I'm • I am | AOIM • IM |
| imaginary • major | MAEJ • MAIJ |

immanent • eminent, imminent ............ KBAMT • KB*EMT, KBIMT

immature • empower ........... KBA*UR • KBAUR

immerse • submerse ........... KBERS • SMERB

immersion • imperfection ........... KBERGS • KBEFRGS

immersion • submersion ........... KBERGS • SMERGS

immigrate • emigrate ........... KBRAIT • KBRAET

imminent • eminent, immanent ........... KBIMT • KB*EMT, KBAMT

immunization • munition ........... MAO*UNGS • MAOUNGS

immunity • impunity ........... MAOUNT • KBAOUNT

immunoglobulin • gamma globulin ........... KBLAUB • GLAUB

impassive • combative ........... KBIV • KBAV

impatience • inpatients ........... KBAIRBS • NAIRBS

impatience • patience ........... KBAIRBS • PAIRBS

impediment • eminent ........... KBEMT • KB*EMT

imperfection • immersion ........... KBEFRGS • KBERGS

impervious • pervious ........... KBEFRB • PEFRB

implicit • explicit ........... KBLIFT • PLIFT

implode • explode ........... KBLOED • SPLOED

implore • deplore ........... KBLOER • PLOER

implosion • explosion ........... KBLOEGS • SPLOEGS

impolitic • catabolic ........... KBLOK • KBLO*K

impossibility • possibility ........... KBOBLT • POBLT

impossible • possible ........... KBOBL • POBL

impossibly • possibly ........... KBOEBL • POEBL

impregnation • impression ........... KBRAEGS • KBREGS

impression • impregnation ........... KBREGS • KBRAEGS

imprison • prison ........... KBRIZ • PRIZ

imprisonment • false imprisonment ........... KBRIMT *or* PRIFMT • FIFMT

improbability • probability ........... KBROBLT • PROBLT

improbable • probable ........... KBROBL • PROBL

improbably • probably ........... KBROEBL • PROEBL

improper • proper ........... KBROR • PROR

improperly • properly ........... KBRORL • PRORL

impropriety • propriety ........... KBRAOIT • PRAOIT

improve • prove ........... KBROV • PROV

improvise • embryo ........... KBRO • KBROE

impunity • immunity ........... KBAOUNT • MAOUNT

in • in~ ( *prefix* ), inn ........... N– • IN, *IN

---

| | |
|---|---|
| **inaccurate** • accurate | NAEK • KRAT |
| **in addition** • addition | NIGS • DIGS |
| **inadmissibility** • admissibility | NIFLT • MIFLT |
| **inadmissible** • admissible | NIFL • MIFL |
| **in any event** • in that event, in this event | NINT • NAFT, NIFT |
| **in any way, shape or form** • way, shape or form | NOFM • WOFM |
| **inapt** • inept | NAPT • NEPT |
| **inaudible** • audible | NAUBL • AUBL |
| **Inc.** • ink, I think | *ING • INK, ING |
| **incarcerate** • crate | KRAIT • KRAET |

**in case of emergency**

| | |
|---|---|
| emergency | M–RJ |
| in case of emergency | KERJ |
| in emergency | NERJ |
| state of emergency | STERJ |

| | |
|---|---|
| **incidence** • incidents | DINZ • DINS |
| **incident** • din | DIN • D*IN |
| **incidents** • incidence | DINS • DINZ |
| **incision** • insignificance | SNIGS • SNIGZ |
| **incite** • inside the, insight | SNAO*IT • SNAOIT, SNOIT |
| **inclination** • clings | KLINGS • KLINGZ |
| **inclination** • declination | KLINGS • DLINGS |
| **incline** • line | KLAOIN • LAOIN |
| **include** • exclude | KLU • SKLU |
| **inclusion** • conclusion, exclusion | KLUGS • KLAOUGS, SKLUGS |
| **inclusive** • exclusive | KLUV • SKLUV |
| **inclusively** • exclusively | KLUVL • SKLUVL |
| **inclusiveness** • exclusiveness | KLUVNS • SKLUVNS |
| **income** • North Carolina | N–K • N*K |
| **incomes** • index | N–KZ • N–X |
| **incorporate** • Corp., corporate | NORP • KORP, KORPT |
| **incorporation** • corporation | NORPGS • KORPGS |
| **incriminate** • Christmas, incriminates | KRIMT • KROIM, KRIMS |
| **incriminate** • discriminate | KRIMT • SKRIM |
| **incrimination** • contributory negligence | KRIJS • KRIJ |
| **incurs** • reimburse | KBURZ • KBURS |
| **in custody** • custody | NUD • KUD |
| **in custody** • into custody | NUD • NOUD |
| **indeed** • North Dakota | N–D • N*D |

**indefinite** • definite ................................. SD–FT *or* SDA\*F • DAF

**index** • incomes ...................................... N–X • N–KZ

**Indiana** • in, inn ....................... DWIN *or* \*IN/\*IN • N–, \*IN

**indicate** • cater ...................................... KAIT • KAET

**indication** • occasion ............................. KAIGS • KAIRB

**indicative** • cave .................................... KAIV • KAEV

**indifferent** • different ............................. SPWIFT • DIFT

**in different** • indifferent ........................ N–/DIFT • SPWIFT

**indigence** • gins, indigents .................... JINS • JINZ, JINTS

**indigents** • indigence ............................ JINTS • JINS

**indirect** • direct...................................... SPWREK • DREK

**in direct** • indirect.................................. N–/DREK • SPWREK

**indirect evidence** • direct evidence ..................... SDREVD • DREVD

**indirectly** • directly ................................ SPWREL • DREL

**indoctrinate** • intoxicate ....................... SPWOKT • SPWOK

**indoctrination** • intoxication ................. SPWOGS *or* SPWO\*X • SPWOX

**inebriation** • abrasion ........................... BRAIGS • BRAEGS

**ineligibility** • eligibility, legibility ........................... NEBLT • JEBLT, LEBLT

**ineligible** • eligible, legible .................... NEBL • JEBL, LEBL

**ineligible** • nebulous ............................. NEBL • NEB

**inept** • inapt ......................................... NEPT • NAPT

**inequity** • equity .................................. NEKT • EKT

**inequity** • iniquity ................................. NEKT • NOIKT

**inert** • unearth ...................................... NERT • N\*ERT

**inexperience** • experience .................... NERNS • SPERNS

**inexperienced** • experienced .............. NERND • SPERND

**inference** • conference ......................... N–FRNS • K–FRNS

**inference** • in reference ....................... N–FRNS • NREFRNS

**inference** • nervousness ...................... N–FRNS • NEFRNS

**inferior**
    anterior ........................................ AOR
    exterior ......................................... KPAOR
    inferior .......................................... FAOR
    interior .......................................... NAOR
    posterior ....................................... PAO\*R
    superior ........................................ SAOR

**inflict** • flick ......................................... FLIK • FL\*IK *or* FLOIK

**infliction** • flicks .................................. FLIX • FL\*IKS *or* FLOIKS

**influence** • flu ...................................... FLU • FL\*U

**influenced** • flood ................................ FLUD • FLAOD

**influx** • flux ............. NUX • FLUX

**informal** • envelope ............. N–FL • N–VL

**information** • disinformation, misinformation ........ N–FGS • D–FGS, M–FGS

**information** • inversion ............. N–FRGS • N–VRGS

**infringe** • fridge, refrigerator ............. FRIJ • FR*IJ, FRIR

**inhabit** • habit ............. NABT • HABT

**inhale** • nail, naturally ............. NA*EL • NAIL, NAEL

**inherit** • disinherit ............. HERT • SHERT

**inherit** • hurt ............. HERT • HURT

**inherits** • hertz, Hertz ............. HERTS • HERZ *or* H–RTS, H*ERTS

**inhibit** • anybody ............. NIBT • NIB

**inhibit** • prohibit ............. NIBT • HIBT *or* HIB

**iniquity** • inequity ............. NOIKT • NEKT

**initiation** • nicks, nix ............. NIRBGS • NIRKZ, NIX

**injunction** • junction, temporary injunction .......... NUNGS • JUNGS, TRUNGS

**injustice** • justice, unjust ............. NUS • JUS, N*US

**ink** • Inc., I think ............. INK • *ING, ING

**in liminie motion** • motion in liminie ............. NAOEMGS • MAOEMGS

**in my opinion** • my opinion ............. NAOIP • MAOIP

**inn** • in, Indiana ............. *IN • N–, *IN/*IN *or* DWIN

**inner** • under ............. N*R • N–R

**innocence** • innocents ............. N–NS • N–NTS

**inorganic** • organic ............. NANK • GANK

**inpatient** • outpatient, patient ............. NAIRB • TAIRB, PAIRB

**inpatients** • impatience ............. NAIRBS • KBAIRB

**in reference** • inference ............. NREFRNS • N–FRNS

**in reference** • reference, with reference ............. NREFRNS • REFRNS, WREFRNS

**in respect** • nonresponsive ............. NR–P • N–RP

**in respect** • respect ............. NR–P • R–P

**insane** • sane ............. SNAIN • SAIN

**insanity** • sanity ............. SNANT • SANT

**inside** • snide ............. SNAOI • SNAOID

**inside the** • incite, insight ............. SNAOIT • SNAO*IT, SNOIT

**insight** • incite, inside the ............. SNOIT • SNAO*IT, SNAOIT

**in sight** • insight ............. N–/SAOIT • SNOIT

**insignificance** • incision ............. SNIGZ • SNIGS

**insoluble** • soluble ............. SNOBL • SOBL

**inspect** • speck, spec ............. SPEK • SP*EK, SP–K

**inspection** • specks, specs ..................................... SPEX • SP*EKS, SP–KS

**instance** • instants ................................................. SNANS • STANTS

**instant**
    constant ........................................................... SKANT
    distant ............................................................. SDANT
    extant ............................................................. STA*NT
    instant ............................................................. STANT

**instantaneous** • attendance ................................... TAENS • TAENZ

**instantaneous** • spontaneous .............................. TAENS • SPAEN

**instantaneously** • spontaneously ........................ TAENL • SPAENL

**instants** • instance ................................................. STANTS • SNANS

**instead** • stead ........................................................ STED • STAED

**instigate** • segregate ............................................. SGAIT • SGRAIT

**instigation** • segregation ....................................... SGAIGS • SGRAIGS

**instinct**
    distinct ............................................................. DINGT
    extinct ............................................................. KPINGT
    indistinct .......................................................... NINGT
    instinct ............................................................. STINGT

**institutionalized** • attitudinal ................................. TAOUFLD *or* TAO*ULD • TAOULD

**insufficient** • insufficient proof ............................. SNUF • SNAOF

**insufficient** • snuff ................................................. SNUF • SN*UF

**insufficient** • sufficient .......................................... SNUF • SUF

**insufficient evidence** • received in evidence ....... SNUVD • SNEVD

**insufficient proof** • proof ....................................... SNAOF • PRAOF

**insulate** • circulate, slate ...................................... SLAIT • SL–, SLAET

**insurance** • assurance, sureness .......................... SHURNS • SHAOURNZ, SHAOURNS

**insure**
    assure ............................................................. SHOUR, SHAO*UR
    ensure ............................................................. SNAOUR
    insure .............................................................. SHUR
    sure ................................................................. SHAOUR

**integrate** • grate, great ......................................... GRAIT • GRA*ET, GRAET

**integrate** • segregate ............................................ GRAIT • SGRAIT

**integration** • segregation ...................................... GRAIGS • SGRAIGS

**intense** • intents ................................................... SPWENS • SPWENTS

**intents** • intense .................................................... SPWENTS • SPWENS

**in tents** • intents .................................................... N–/TENTS • SPWENTS

**intercepts** • synapse ............................................. SNEPS • SNEPZ

**interchange** • change, exchange .......................... SPWRAIJ • KHAIJ, KPAIJ

**interest**
    compound interest ........................................... KPINT

---

                 

conflict of interest ........................................... KINT
self-interest ...................................................... SFINT

**interest of justice** • Chief Justice ......................... TR–J • KH–J

**interfere** • intervene ................................................ SPW–FR • SPW–VN

**interior**
    anterior ............................................... AOR
    exterior ................................................ KPAOR
    inferior ................................................ FAOR
    interior ................................................ NAOR
    posterior ............................................. PAO*R
    superior .............................................. SAOR

**internship** • interpret ............................................ SPWERP • TERP

**interpret** • internship ............................................ TERP • SPWERP

**interpret** • interpreter, misinterpret ..................... TERP • TRERP, MERP

**interpretation** • misinterpretation ......................... TERPGS • MERPGS

**interrelate** • relate ................................................ SPWERLT • RELT

**interrogative** • interrogatory ................................ TROG • ROG

**interrogatory** • interrogative ................................ ROG • TROG

**interrupt** • disrupt ................................................ TRUP • DRUP

**interruption** • disruption ...................................... TRUPGS • DRUPGS

**intersection** • intersects ...................................... SPW–X • SPWEKS

**intersection** • section ........................................... SPW–X • S–X

**intersects** • intersection ...................................... SPWEKS • SPW–X

**interstate** • intestate, intrastate ............................ SPWAIT • SPWEFT, SPWRAET

**intertwine** • entwine ............................................. SPWRAOIN • SPWAOIN

**intervene** • interfere ............................................. SPW–VN • SPW–FR

**interview** • entrust ............................................... SPWUF • SPWRUF *or* SPWRUFT

**intestate** • interstate ........................................... SPWEFT • SPWAIT

**intestate** • testate ............................................... SPWEFT • TWEFT

**in that** • gnat ....................................................... NAT • NA*T

**in that event** • in any event, in this event ............. NAFT • NINT, NIFT

**in the afternoon** • afternoon ................................. NAFRN • AFRN

**in the evening** • evening ....................................... NAOENG • AOENG

**in their** • in there ................................................. N*ER • NER

**in the morning** • morning ..................................... NORNG • MORNG

**in there** • in their ................................................. NER • N*ER

**in this case** • nick, Nick, 96 ................................. NIK • NIRK, N*IRK, N*IK

**in this event** • in any event, in that event ............. NIFT • NINT, NAFT

**intimate** • intimidate ............................................. SPWEM • SPWIM

**intimidate** • intimate ............................................. SPWIM • SPWEM

**in to** • into ................................................................ N–/TO • NAO

**into custody** • in custody ....................................... NOUD • NUD

**intolerance** • stubbornness, subordinates ............ SPWORNS • STORNS, SBORNZ

**intolerant** • stubborn, subordinate ......................... SPWORNT • STORN, SBORN

**intoxicate** • indoctrinate .......................................... SPWOK • SPWOKT

**intoxication** • indoctrination ................................... SPWOX • SPWO*X

**intrastate** • interstate ............................................. SPWRAET • SPWAIT

**intrinsic** • extrinsic ................................................. SPWRIN • KPRIN

**intrinsically** • extrinsically ...................................... SPWRINL • KPRINL

**introvert** • controvert, extrovert ............................. SPWROVT • TROVT, KPROVT

**intrude** • extrude .................................................... SPWRAOUD • KPRAOUD

**intrusion** • extrusion .............................................. SPWRAOUGS • KPRAOUGS

**intuition** • tuition .................................................... SPWAOUGS • TWAOUGS

**invader** • verified ................................................... VA*ERD • VAERD

**invention** • veneration ............................................ VENGS • VERNGS

**inversion** • information ............................................ N–VRGS • N–FRGS

**investigate** • gait, gate .......................................... GAIT • GA*IT, GAET

**invisible** • visible .................................................... NIFBL • VIFBL

**invoices** • voice ..................................................... VOIZ • VOIS

**Iranian** • rein ......................................................... RA*EN • RAEN

**iris** • IRS ................................................................ AOIRZ • AOIRS

**irrelevance** • irreverence, IRS .............................. *IRS • IVS *or* IVRS, IRS

**irrelevant** • irreverent ............................................ IR • IVRT

**irresponsibility** • responsibility ............................ RONT • SPOBT *or* SP–BLT

**IRS** • iris ................................................................ AOIRS • AOIRZ

**isle** • aisle, I'll ....................................................... YAOIL • AOIFL, AOIL

**isn't it right** • isn't that right .................................. SNIRT • SNART

**it**

      it .................................................................... IT

      it'd .................................................................. ITD

      it'll .................................................................. *ILT

      its .................................................................. ITS

      it's .................................................................. *ITS

      itself ............................................................... ISZ

**I think** • Inc., ink ................................................... ING • *ING, INK

# J

jack • Jack ............................................................... JAK • JA*K

jail • county jail ...................................................... JAIL • KAIL

jail • educational ................................................... JAIL • JAEL

jam • jamb, pajama ............................................... JAM • JA*M, JAUM

January • Jan ........................................................ JAN • JA*N

jar • jugular ........................................................... JAR • JARL

jaws • just cause .................................................. JAUS • JAUZ

jeans
    genes ............................................................ GAOENS
    genius ........................................................... JAOENZ
    genus ........................................................... GAOENZ
    jeans ............................................................ JAOENS

jell • gel ................................................................ JEL • GEL

Jesus • apologies ................................................. JAOEZ • JAOES

jewel • joule, jowl ................................................. JAOUL • JAO*UL, JOUL

Jews • juice .......................................................... JAOUZ • JAOUS

jib • gibberish ....................................................... JIB • GIB

jibe • gibe ............................................................. JAOIB • GAOIB

jilt • legitimately ................................................... J*ILT • JILT

Jim • gym ............................................................. JIM • GIM

John • john ........................................................... JON • JO*N

joinder • joined ..................................................... JO*IND • JOIND

joule • jewel, jowl ................................................. JAO*UL • JAOUL, JOUL

journalist • jury trial .............................................. JOURT • JURT

joust • just ............................................................ JO*US • J*US

joy • enjoy ............................................................ JOI • GOI

Jr. • junior ............................................................. J*R • J–R

juggle • jugular ..................................................... JULG • JARL *or* JAUR

jugular • juggle, juggler ........................................ JARL • JULG, JURLG

juice • Jews .......................................................... JAOUS • JAOUZ

junction • injunction, temporary injunction ........... JUNGS • NUNGS, TRUNGS

June • genuine ..................................................... JUN • JAOUN

junior • Jr. ............................................................. J–R • J*R

jurist • jury trial .................................................... JIRT • JURT

jury
    charge the jury ............................................. KHAURJ
    court and jury ............................................... KORJ
    Court instructs the jury .................................. K–J
    gentlemen of the jury .................................... JERJ

grand jury ....................................................... GR–J
hung jury ........................................................ HURJ
instruct the jury ............................................. STRUJ
ladies and gentlemen of the jury ................... LAIRJ
members of the jury ..................................... MEJ

**jury nullification** • nullification ............................ JULGS • NULGS

**jury trial** • journalist, jurist ................................... JURT • JOURT, JIRT

**just** • joust ............................................................ J*US • JO*US

**just** • unjust .......................................................... J*US • N*US

**just a second** • reject ........................................... JEK • JEKT

**just cause** • cause, jaws ...................................... JAUZ • KAUZ, JAUS

**justice** • injustice, unjust ...................................... JUS • NUS, N*US

**justice department** • department ........................ J–PT • D–PT

# K

**karat**

| | |
|---|---|
| carat | KRA*T |
| caret | KR*ET, KRA*ET |
| carrot | KAERT |
| karat | KA*ERT |

**kern** • concern .................................................. K*ERN • KERN

**kernel** • colonel, currently ....................................... KERNL • KOL, KURNL

**kettle** • Celt, seat belt .............................................. KELT • K*ELT, KRELT

**key** • quay ............................................................ KAOE • KWAE

**kill** • kiln ............................................................... KIL • KL*IN

**killer** • can I recall ................................................ KIRL • K*IRL

**kiln** • clinic ........................................................... KL*IN • KLIN

**kiln** • kill .............................................................. KL*IN • KIL

**kilos** • close, clothes ............................................. KLOEZ • KLOES, KLO*ETS

**knave** • navy ........................................................ NAEV • NAIV

**knead** • kneed, need ............................................. NAED • N*ED, NAOED

**kneed** • knead, need ............................................. N*ED • NAED, NAOED

**kneeing** • Negro ................................................... NAOEG • NAO*EG

**knees** • niece ...................................................... NAOEZ • NAOES

**knelt** • the Netherlands ......................................... NELT • N*ELT

**knew** • new ......................................................... NAOU • NU

**knight** • night ....................................................... NAO*IT • NAOIT

**knit** • anytime ...................................................... N*IT • NIT

**knob** • nob, nobody .............................................. NOB • NO*B, NOEB

**knoll** • noel, normal .............................................. NOEL • NO*EL, NOL

**knot** • naught, not ................................................ NO*T • NAUGT, NOT

**knotty** • naughty .................................................. NO*IT *or* NOT/TI • NAUT

**know** • no ........................................................... NOE • NO

**knowledge**

| | |
|---|---|
| acknowledge | NAOJ |
| best of my knowledge | BEJ |
| best of your knowledge | BURJ |
| knowledge | NOJ |
| to the best of my knowledge | TAOIJ |
| to the best of your knowledge | TURJ |
| to your knowledge | TOURJ |
| with my knowledge | WAOIJ |
| with your knowledge | WOURJ |

**knows** • nose ...................................................... NOES • NOEZ

---

# L

| | |
|---|---|
| **L.A.** • Louisiana | LA • LA* |
| **laboratory** • lavatory | LABT • LAVT |
| **lace** • lays, laze | LAIS • LA*IS, LAEZ |
| **laches** • lashes, latches | LAFPS • LARBS, LAFPZ |

**lack of foundation**

| | |
|---|---|
| foundation | FOUNGS |
| lack of foundation | LOUNGS |
| without foundation | WOUNGS |

| | |
|---|---|
| **lacks** • lax, LAX | LAKZ • LAX, LA*X |
| **lade** • lady, laid, lead ( *metal* ) | LA*ID • LAED, LAID, L*ED |

**lady**

| | |
|---|---|
| First Lady | FLAED |
| forelady | FRAED |
| lady | LAED |
| saleslady | SLAED |

| | |
|---|---|
| **lady** • lade, laid, lead ( *metal* ) | LAED • LA*ID, LAID, L*ED |
| **laid** • lade, lady, lead ( *metal* ) | LAID • LA*ID, LAED, L*ED |
| **lain** • lane | LAIN • LAEN |
| **lair** • layer | LA*IR • LAIR |
| **lake** • leak | LAIK • LAEK |
| **lam** • lamb | LA*M • LAM |
| **lane** • lain | LAEN • LAIN |

**lane**

| | |
|---|---|
| left-hand lane | L–NL |
| left lane | L–L |
| right-hand lane | R–NLD, –RNL |
| right lane | R–L, –RL |

| | |
|---|---|
| **laps** • lapse | LAPZ • LAPS |
| **lashes** • laches, latches | LARBS • LAFPS, LAPFZ |
| **latches** • laches, lashes | LAFPZ • LAFPS, LARBS |
| **later** • latter | LAIRT • LART |
| **lath** • lathe | LA*T • LA*IT |
| **latter** • later | LART • LAIRT |
| **laud** • lord | LAUD • LORD |
| **lavatory** • laboratory | LAVT • LABT |
| **law enforcement officer** • law officer | LAIFR • LAUFR |
| **law officer** • law enforcement officer | LAUFR • LAIFR |
| **law schools** • loosely | LAOLZ • LAOLS |
| **lawsuit** • class action lawsuit | LAUT • KLAUT |
| **lax** • lacks, LAX | LAX • LAKZ, LA*X |

**lay** • lei ................................................................. LAI • LA*I

**layer** • lair ............................................................ LAIR • LA*IR

**lays**
    lace .................................................................. LAIS
    lays .................................................................. LA*IS
    laze .................................................................. LAEZ
    lazy .................................................................. LAIZ
    leis .................................................................. LA*IZ
    relays ............................................................... LAES

**laze** • lazy ......................................................... LAEZ • LAIZ

**lazy** • laze ......................................................... LAIZ • LAEZ

**leach** • leech, Long Beach ..................................... LA*EFP • LAOEFP, LAEFP

**lead** ( *metal* ) • lady, led .......................................... L*ED • LAED, LED

**lead** ( *guide* ) • mislead ......................................... LAOED • SLAOED

**leader** • liter ...................................................... LERD • LAOERT

**leading and suggestive**
    leading and suggestive ................................... LUG
    lug ................................................................... L*UG
    luggage ............................................................. LAUG
    lunge ................................................................ LUJ

**leaf** • leave .......................................................... LAOEF • LAOEV

**leak** • lake .......................................................... LAEK • LAIK

**leak** • leek .......................................................... LAEK • LAOEK

**leaks** • elaboration ................................................ LAEKZ • LAEBGS

**lean** • lien .......................................................... LAOEN • LAO*EN

**lease** • sublease ..................................................... LAOES • SLAOES

**leased** • least ........................................................ LAOEFD • LAO*ES

**least** • leased ........................................................ LAO*ES • LAOEFD

**leave** • leaf .......................................................... LAOEV • LAOEF

**led** • lead ( *metal* ) ................................................ LED • L*ED

**leech** • leach, Long Beach ...................................... LAOEFP • LA*EFP, LAEFP

**leek** • leak .......................................................... LAOEK • LAEK

**left-hand lane** • left lane ........................................ L–NL • L–L

**legalize** • likewise ................................................... LOIZ • LOIS

**legibility** • eligibility, ineligibility ........................... LEBLT • JEBLT, NEBLT

**legible** • eligible, ineligible ..................................... LEBL • JEBL, NEBL

**legion**
    allegiance ........................................................ LAOEJ
    leagues ............................................................ LAOEGZ
    legion ............................................................... LAO*EJ
    lesion ............................................................... LAOEGS

**legislation** • legs .................................................. LAEGS • LEGS

**legislator** • legislature ............................................. LOR • LUR

**legislature** • legislator ............................................. LUR • LOR

**legitimately** • jilt ...................................................... JILT • J*ILT

**legs** • legislation ...................................................... LEGS • LAEGS

**lei** • lay ...................................................................... LA*I • LAI

**leis**
    lace ............................................................. LAIS
    lays ............................................................. LA*IS
    laze ............................................................. LAEZ
    lazy ............................................................. LAIZ
    leis ............................................................. LA*IZ
    relays ............................................................. LAES

**lends** • lens ............................................................. LENDZ • LENS

**lens** • lends ............................................................. LENS • LENDZ

**lentil** • linoleum, lintel ........................................... LENL • LINL, LINLT

**lesion**
    alliegance ....................................................... LAOEJ
    leagues ......................................................... LAOEGZ
    legion ........................................................... LAO*EJ
    lesion ........................................................... LAOEGS

**lessen** • lesson, less than ...................................... L*EN • LEFN, LEN

**lesson** • eleven, lessen ........................................... LEFN • LEVN, L*EN

**less than** • lessen .................................................. LEN • L*EN

**let me ask you that** • let me ask you this ............. SKLAT • SKLIS

**lets** • let's ............................................................. LETS • L*ETS

**let's** • lets ............................................................. L*ETS • LETS

**let the record show** • may the record show ......... LORS • MORS

**lettuce** • let us ....................................................... TUS *or* LET/TUS • LET/US

**let us** • lettuce ....................................................... LET/US • LET/TUS *or* TUS

**liability** • reliability ................................................. LAOIBLT • RAOIBLT

**liable** • reliable ....................................................... LAOIBL • RAOIBL

**liar** • lyre ............................................................... LAOIR • LAO*IR

**libel** • liable ............................................................. LAOIB • LAOIBL

**lice** • lies ............................................................... LAOIS • LAOIZ

**lie** • lye ................................................................... LAOI • LAO*I

**lien** • lean ............................................................... LAO*EN • LAOEN

**lies** • lice ............................................................... LAOIZ • LAOIS

**lieu** • allow, loo, Lou ............................................... LAOU • LOU, LAO, LO*U

**light**
    amber light ..................................................... BERLT
    approach light ................................................. PROEFPLT
    brake light ....................................................... BRAILT

| | |
|---|---|
| candlelight | KANLT, KAENLT |
| daylight | DAILT |
| desk light | DEFLT |
| flashlight | FLARBLT |
| floodlight | FLAOLT |
| fluorescent light | FLORLT |
| green light | GR–LT |
| headlight | HAELT |
| highlight | HAOILT |
| incandescent light | NANLT |
| moonlight | MAONLT |
| neon light | NAOENLT |
| night-light | NAOILT |
| pilot light | PAOILT |
| red light | R–LT |
| runway light | RUNLT |
| searchlight | SEFPLT |
| skylight | SKAOILT |
| spotlight | SPOLT |
| starlight | STARLT |
| stop light | ST–LT |
| street light | STR–LT |
| strobe light | STROEBLT |
| sunlight | SUNLT |
| taillight | TAILT |
| traffic light | TR–LT |
| twilight | TWAOILT |
| yellow light | Y–LT |

**lightening • lightning** ............................... LAOINGT • LOINGT

**likewise • legalize** ..................................... LOIS • LOIZ

**line**

| | |
|---|---|
| bottom line | BLAO*IN |
| centerline | SLAOIN |
| center line | SLOIN |
| deadline | DLOIN |
| guideline | GLAOIN |
| line | LAOIN |
| outline | TLAOIN |
| sideline | SDLAOIN |
| straight line | STLAOIN |
| yellow line | YAOIN |

**lines • alliance** ....................................... LAOINS • LAOINZ

**linguists • lynx** ...................................... LINGS • L*INGS

**lining**

| | |
|---|---|
| lightening | LAOINGT |
| lighting | LAOIGT |
| lightning | LOINGT |
| lining | LAOING |

**links • lynx** ......................................... LINKS • L*INKS *or* L*INGS

**linoleum • lentil, lintel** ........................... LINL • LENL, LINLT

| | |
|---|---|
| **lintel** • lentil, linoleum | LINLT • LENL, LINL |
| **lipid** • lipoid, poisoned | PID • PO*ID, POID |
| **lipoid** • lipid, poisoned | PO*ID • PID, POID |
| **liqueur** • liquor | LIRK • LIR |
| **liquid** • flammable liquid | KLID • FLID |
| **liquor** • liqueur | LIR • LIRK |
| **liter** • leader, litter | LAOERT • LERD, LIRT |
| **litter** • leader, liter | LIRT • LERD, LAOERT |
| **little** • belittle | LIL • BLIL |
| **lo** • low | LO • LOE |
| **load** • lode, lowed | LOED • LO*ED, LOE/–D |
| **loan** • lone | LOEN • LO*EN |
| **loath** • loathe | LO*T • LO*ET |
| **loathe** • loath | LO*ET • LO*T |
| **local** • locale, locally | LOL • LO*L, LOEL |
| **locate** • dislocate | LOEK • SLOEK |
| **locates** • location | LOEKTS *or* LOEKZ • LOEX |
| **location** • dislocation | LOEX • SLOEX |
| **lock** • deadlock, gridlock | LOK • DLOK, GLOK |
| **locks** • lox | LOX • LO*X *or* LAUX |
| **locus** • locust | LOKZ • LOKT |
| **locust** • locus | LOKT • LOKZ |
| **lode** • load, lowed | LO*ED • LOED, LOE/–D |
| **lodge** • dislodge | LOJ • DLOJ *or* SLOJ |
| **logs** • Los Angeles | LOGZ *or* LO*GS • LOGS |
| **lone** • alone | LO*EN • LAON |
| **lone** • loan | LO*EN • LOEN |
| **Long Beach** • leach, leech | LAEFP • LA*EFP, LAOEFP |
| **loo** • lieu, Lou | LAO • LAOU, LO*U |
| **loon** • alone | LAO*N • LAON |
| **loose** • lose | LAOS • LAOZ |
| **loosely** • law schools | LAOLS • LAOLZ |
| **lord** • laud | LORD • LAUD |
| **lore** • lower | LO*ER • LOER |
| **Los Angeles** • logs | LOGS • LO*GS *or* LOGZ |
| **lose** • loose | LAOZ • LAOS |
| **Lou** • allow, lieu, loo | LO*U • LOU, LAOU, LAO |
| **loud** • allowed | LOUD • LO*UD *or* LOU/–D |

---

**Louisiana** • L.A. ...................................................... LA* • LA

**low** • lo ...................................................................... LOE • LO

**lowed** • load, lode .................................................. LOE/–D • LOED, LO*ED

**lower** • lore ............................................................. LOER • LO*ER

**lox** • locks .............................................................. LAUX *or* LO*X • LOX

**loyal** • disloyal ........................................................ LOIL • SLOIL

**loyalty** • disloyalty ................................................. LOILT • SLOILT

**lug** • leading and suggestive .................................. L*UG • LUG

**luggage**
    leading and suggestive .................................. LUG
    lug ................................................................... L*UG
    luggage ............................................................ LAUG
    lunge ............................................................... LUJ

**lumbar** • aluminum ................................................. L*UM • LUM

**lumbar** • will you be ............................................... L*UB • LUB

**lunacy** • translucence ............................................ LAOUNZ • LAOUNS

**lunge** • luggage ...................................................... LUJ • LAUG

**lye** • lie .................................................................... LAO*I • LAOI

**lynx** • linguists ........................................................ L*INKS *or* L*INGS • LINGS

**lynx** • links .............................................................. L*INGS *or* L*INKS • LINKS

**lyre** • liar ................................................................. LAO*IR • LAOIR

# M

**ma'am** • no, ma'am; yes, ma'am ............................ MAM • NAM, YEM

mace
    amaze .............................................................. MAES
    mace ................................................................ MA*IS
    maize ............................................................... MA*IZ
    may say ........................................................... MAIS
    may see ........................................................... MAIZ
    maze ................................................................ MAEZ

**made** • maid ........................................................... MAED • MAID

**maid** • made ........................................................... MAID • MAED

**mail** • male ............................................................ MAIL • MAEL

**maim** • mayhem ...................................................... MAIM • MAEM

main
    main .................................................................. MAIN
    Maine ............................................................... M*E
    maintain ........................................................... MAEN
    mane ................................................................ MA*EN

**Maine** • main, mane .............................................. M*E • MAIN, MA*EN

**Maine** • me ............................................................ M*E • ME

**mainly** • manually .................................................. MAINL • MAENL

**maintain** • mane, may not ...................................... MAEN • MA*EN, MAINT

**maintenance** • mandate, may not ......................... MAENT • MA*ENT, MAINT

**maize** • mace, maze .............................................. MA*IZ • MA*IS, MAEZ

**major** • imaginary, marriage .................................. MAIJ • MAEJ, MAERJ

**make** • mistake ...................................................... MAIK • MAEK

**maladjusted** • adjusted, readjusted ...................... MAUFD • JAUFD, RAUFD

**male** • mail ............................................................. MAEL • MAIL

malfeasance
    malfeasance ..................................................... MAFZ
    misfeasance ..................................................... MIFZ
    nonfeasance ..................................................... NOFZ

**mall** • maul ............................................................ MAL • MAUL

**malt** • manslaughter .............................................. MAULT • MALT

**mandate** • maintenance ........................................ MA*ENT • MAENT

**mandatory** • mannered ......................................... MARND • MA*RND

**mane** • main, Maine .............................................. MA*EN • MAIN, M*E

**mane** • maintain .................................................... MA*EN • MAEN

**maneuver** • outmaneuver ...................................... MAOUVR • NAOUVR

**manner** • manor .................................................... MARN • MAORN

**mannered** • mandatory ......................................... MA*RND • MARND

**manor**
    manner ............................................................ MARN
    manor ............................................................... MAORN
    man or .............................................................. MAN/OR
    man nor ............................................................ MAN/NOR

**manor** • manner ...................................................... MAORN • MARN

**manslaughter** • malt ............................................. MALT • MAULT

**manually** • mainly .................................................. MAENL • MAINL

**manuscript** • script ............................................... SKRIMT • SKRIPT

**mar** • march, March ............................................... MA*R • MAUFP, MAR

**march** • March ........................................................ MAUFP • MAR

**mare**
    mare ................................................................. MA*ER
    marry ................................................................ MAER
    may or .............................................................. MAI/OR
    mayor .............................................................. MAIR
    Mayor .............................................................. MA*IR

**marital** • marshal, martial ...................................... MAERT • MAURBL, MARL

**marked for identification** • for identification ........ MOID • FOID

**marked for identification** • miffed ........................ MOID • MOIFD

**market** • stock market ........................................... MAERK • SMAERK

**marking** • marring ................................................. MARG • MA*RG

**marriage** • common-law marriage ......................... MAERJ • KMAERJ

**marriage** • major, mirage ....................................... MAIRJ • MAIJ, MIRJ

**marring** • marking .................................................. MA*RG • MARG

**marry** • mare, mayor, Mayor .................................. MAER • MA*ER, MAIR, MA*IR

**marshal** • marital, martial ...................................... MAURBL • MAERT, MARL

**martial** • marital, marshal ...................................... MARL • MAERT, MAURBL

**martial law** • maturely ........................................... MA*URL • MAURL

**Maryland** • M.D. .................................................... M*D • M–D

**Massachusetts** • ma .............................................. MA* • MA

**master bedroom** • bathroom, bedroom, ............... MARM • BARM, BERM, MERM
midterm

**mate** • meat ........................................................... MAIT • MAET

**material** • terminal ................................................. TERL • TAERL

**mathematical** • manslaughter, malt ...................... MA*LT • MALT, MAULT

**mature** • premature ............................................... MAUR • PRAUR

**maturely** • martial law ........................................... MAURL • MA*URL

**maturely** • prematurely .......................................... MAURL • PRAURL

**matureness** • prematureness .............................. MAURNS • PRAURNS

**maturity** • prematurity ........................................... MAURT • PRAURT

| | |
|---|---|
| **maul** • mall | MAUL • MAL |
| **maximum** • Max | MAX • MA*X |
| **may** • May | MAI • MA*I |
| **may be** • maybe | MAI/B– • MAIB |
| **mayhem** • maim | MAEM • MAIM |
| **may or** • mayor, Mayor | MAI/OR • MAIR, MA*IR |

**mayor**

| | |
|---|---|
| mare | MA*ER |
| marry | MAER |
| may or | MAI/OR |
| mayor | MAIR |
| Mayor | MA*IR |

| | |
|---|---|
| **may the record reflect** • mortgage | MORT • MO*RT |
| **may the record show** • let the record show | MORS • LORS |
| **may the record show** • mores | MORS • MORZ |

**maze**

| | |
|---|---|
| amaze | MAES |
| mace | MA*IS |
| maize | MA*IZ |
| may say | MAIS |
| may see | MAIZ |
| maze | MAEZ |

| | |
|---|---|
| **M.D.** • Maryland | M–D • M*D |
| **meager** • you may proceed | MAOERG • MAOEG |
| **mean** • mesne, mien | MAOEN • MAOENZ, MAO*EN |
| **meanwhile** • in the meantime | MAOENL • MAOENT |
| **meanwhile** • mentally | MAOENL • MOINL |
| **meat** • mate | MAET • MAIT |
| **meat** • meet, mete | MAET • MAOET, MAO*ET |
| **medal** • meddle | MAELD • MELD |
| **medal** • metal | MAELD • MAELT |
| **medal** • model | MAELD • MOELD |
| **meddle** • medal, meld | MELD • MAELD, M*ELD |
| **medical malpractice** • millimeter | M*M • M–M |
| **meet** • meat, mete | MAOET • MAET, MAO*ET |
| **megabit** • gigabit | MIBT • GIBT |
| **megabyte** • gigabyte | MEGT • GIGT |
| **melt** • mental health, mettle | MELT • M*ELT, M*LT |
| **member** • dismember | MEB • SMEB |

**memo**

| | |
|---|---|
| memento | MEMT |
| memo | MOE |

memoranda ..................................................... MEMD
memorandum ................................................. MUM
memory ........................................................... MEM

**memo** • mow ..................................................... MOE • MOU

**memorandum** • mum ..................................... MUM • M*UM

**mentally** • meanwhile .................................... MOINL • MAOENL

**mere** • mirror ..................................................... MAOER • M*IR *or* MOIR

**merge** • submerge ........................................... MERJ • SMERJ

**metal** • medal ................................................... MAELT • MAELD

**metal** • melt, mettle ........................................ MAELT • MELT, MET/–L

**mete** • meat, meet ........................................... MAO*ET • MAET, MAOET

**mettle** • melt, metal ........................................ M*LT • MELT, MAELT

**mews** • amuse, muse ...................................... MAO*US • MAOUS, MAOUZ

**Miami** • yam ...................................................... YAM • YA*M

**mice** • myself .................................................... MAOIS • MAOIZ

**Michigan** • my ................................................... M*I • MI

**midst** • missed, mist ....................................... M*ID *or* M*IDZ • MAOIFD, M*IS

**midterm** • term .................................................. MERM • TERM

**mien** • mean, mesne ....................................... MAO*EN • MAOEN, MAOENZ

**miffed** • marked for identification ........................ MOIFD • MOID

**miffed** • might have had, missed .......................... MOIFD • MIFD, MAOIFD

**might** • mite ...................................................... MAOIT • MAO*IT

**might have** • administrative .................................... MIF • MIV

**might have had** • miffed, missed .......................... MIFD • MOIFD, MAOIFD

**mike** • Mike ...................................................... MAOIK • MAO*IK

**mile-an-hour** • mile-per-hour ................................ MIR • MIRP

**mile-an-hour** • mirror ............................................ MIR • M*IR *or* MOIR

**mile-per-hour** • mile-an-hour ................................ MIRP • MIR

**millimeter** • medical malpractice .......................... M–M • M*M

**million** • billion, trillion .......................................... M–L • B–L, TR–L

**mince** • mints, minutes ......................................... MINZ • MINTS, MINS

**mind** • minded, mined ........................................... MAOIND • MAO*IND *or* DMAOIND, MO*IND

**mined** • mind ........................................................ MO*IND • MAOIND

**mine or**
     mine nor ........................................................... MAOIN/NOR
     mine or .............................................................. MAOIN/OR
     miner ................................................................. MAOIRN
     minor ................................................................. MOIRN

**miner** • minor .................................................. MAOIRN • MOIRN

| | |
|---|---|
| **minor** • miner | MOIRN • MAOIRN |
| **mints** • mince, minutes | MINTS • MINZ, MINS |
| **minutes** • mince, mints | MINS • MINZ, MINTS |
| **mirage** • marriage | MIRJ • MAIRJ |
| **mirror** • mere | MOIR *or* M*IR • MAOER |
| **mirror** • mile-an-hour | MOIR *or* M*IR • MIR |
| **misappropriate** • appropriate | MOEPT • PROEPT |
| **misappropriation** • appropriation | MOEPGS • PROEPGS |
| **miscarriage** • carriage | SKAIRJ • KAIRJ |
| **miscommunication** • communication | SKMUNGS • KMUNGS |
| **misconduct** • conduct | SKUK • KUK |

**misfeasance**

| | |
|---|---|
| malfeasance | MAFZ |
| misfeasance | MIFZ |
| nonfeasance | NOFZ |

| | |
|---|---|
| **misguidance** • guidance | SGAOINS • GAOINS |
| **misguide** • guide | SGAOID • GAOID |
| **mishandle** • handle | SHANL • HANL |
| **misinformation** • disinformation, information | M–FGS • D–FGS, N–FGS |
| **misinterpret** • interpret | MERP • TERP |
| **misinterpretation** • interpretation | MERPGS • TERPGS |
| **mislead** • lead | SLAOED • LAOED |
| **misquotation** • quotation | SKWOEGS • KWOEGS |
| **misquote** • quote | SKWOET • KWOET |
| **misrepresent** • membership | M*EP • MEP |
| **misrepresent** • represent | M*EP • REP |
| **misrepresentation** • representation | MEPGS • REPGS |
| **miss** • Miss | MISZ • M–S |
| **Miss** • Mississippi | M–S • M*S |
| **Miss** • Ms. | M–S • M–Z |
| **missed** • midst, mist | MAOIFD • M*ID *or* M*IDZ, M*IS |
| **Mississippi** • Miss | M*S • M–S |
| **Missouri** • month | MO* • MO |
| **mist** • midst, missed | M*IS • M*ID *or* M*IDZ, MAOIFD |
| **mistake** • make | MAEK • MAIK |
| **mistrial** • trial | STRAOIL • TRAOIL |
| **mite** • might | MAO*IT • MAOIT |
| **mitt** • admit, myth | MOIT • MIT, M*IT |
| **moan** • mown | MOEN • MOUN |

| | |
|---|---|
| **moat** • moot | MAO*T • MAOT |
| **moat** • mote, motor | MAO*T • MO*ET, MOET |
| **mode** • mowed | MOED • MOUD |
| **model** • mold | MOELD • MOLD |
| **modern** • more than | MOERND • MOERN |
| **mold** • model | MOLD • MOELD |
| **mole** • mostly | MOEL • MOL |
| **molestation** • child molestation | MOELGS • KHOELGS |
| **molt** • motel, ophthalmologist | MOULT *or* MO*LT • MOELT, MOLT |
| **moment** • momentum | MOEMT • MOEM |
| **moment** • wait a moment | MOMT • WOMT |
| **monaural** • aural, binaural | MAURNL • AURL, BAURL *or* AURNL |
| **money** • month | MON *or* MUN • MO |
| **Montana** • mountain | M*T • M–T |
| **month** • Missouri | MO • MO* |
| **month** • money | MO • MON *or* MUN |
| **mooch** • mutual | MAOFP • MAOUFP |
| **mood** • mooed | MAOD • MAO*D |
| **mooed** • mood | MAO*D • MAOD |
| **moor** • Moor, more, mother | MAOR • MAO*R, MOR, MOER |
| **moored** • motherhood | MAORD • MOERD |
| **moos** • moose | MAOZ • MAOS |
| **moose** • moos | MAOS • MAOZ |
| **moot** • mute | MAOT • MAOUT |
| **moral** • morale | MORL • MAORL |
| **moral** • mother-in-law | MORL • MOERL |
| **morality** • mortality | MORLT • MO*RLT |
| **more** • moor, Moor, mother | MOR • MAOR, MAO*R, MOER |
| **more** • some more | MOR • SMOR |
| **more or less** • morals, mothers-in-law | MORLS • MORLZ, MOERLS |
| **mores** • may the record show | MORZ • MORS |
| **more than** • modern | MOERN • MOERND |
| **morn** • mourn | MORN • MOURN |
| **morning** | |
|     good morning | GORNG |
|     in the morning | NORNG |
|     morning | MORNG |
|     that morning | THAORNG |
|     this morning | THORNG |

tomorrow morning ......................................... TWORNG
yesterday morning ........................................ YORNG

**morning** • mourning ............................................. MORNG • MOURNG

**mortality** • morality ............................................. MO\*RLT • MORLT

**mortgage** • may the record reflect ........................ MO\*RT • MORT

**most** • at the very most, very most ........................ MO\*S • TO\*S, VO\*S

**mostly** • mole ....................................................... MOL • MOEL

**mostly** • moll ........................................................ MOL • MO\*L

**most of** • motive .................................................... MOEF • MOEV

**mote** • moat, motor ............................................... MO\*ET • MAO\*T, MOET

**motel** • hotel ......................................................... MOELT • HOELT

**motel** • molt, ophthalmologist ............................... MOELT • MOULT *or* MO\*LT, MOLT

**mother** • moor, more ............................................. MOER • MAOR, MOR

**mother** • stepmother ............................................. MOER • SMOER

**motherhood** • moored ........................................... MOERD • MAORD

**mother-in-law** • moral, morale ............................. MOERL • MORL, MAORL

**mothers-in-law** • morals, more or less ................. MOERLS • MORLZ, MORLS

**motif** • motive ....................................................... TAOEF • MOEV

**motion in liminie** • in liminie motion .................... MAOEMGS • NAOEMGS

**motive** • most of, motif ......................................... MOEV • MOEF, TAOEF

**motor** • moat, mote ............................................... MOET • MAO\*T, MO\*ET

**mountain** • Montana ............................................. M–T • M\*T

**mourn** • morn ....................................................... MOURN • MORN

**mourning** • morning .............................................. MOURNG • MORNG

**mow** • memo ......................................................... MOU • MOE

**mowed** • mode ...................................................... MOUD • MOED

**mown** • moan ........................................................ MOUN • MOEN

**Mr.**
    Mr. ................................................................. MR–, MR–FPLT
    Mr. and Mrs. ................................................... MR–RS
    Mr. Chairman ................................................. MR–FP
    Mr. or Mrs. ..................................................... MR\*RS
    Mr. President .................................................. MR–PT
    Mr. Secretary ................................................. MRAEK
    Mr. Speaker ................................................... MR–K
    Mr. Vice President ......................................... MR–VP

**Ms.** • Miss ............................................................ M–Z • M–S

**muffle** • muscle .................................................... M\*UFL • MUFL

**mum** • memorandum ............................................. M\*UM • MUM

**munition** • immunization, remuneration ............... MAOUNGS • MAO\*UNGS, MAOUMGS

**mural** • must recall ............................................... MAOURL • MURL muscle • muffle ........................................................ MUFL • M*UFL

muscle • mussel, muzzle ......................................... MUFL • M–FL, MUZ

muscle • must feel .................................................. MUFL • M*US/FAOEL

muse • amuse, mews .............................................. MAOUZ • MAOUS, MAO*US

musician • ammunition ............................................ MAOUGS • NAOUGS

mussed • must, must have had ............................. M*UFD • M*US, MUFD

mussel • muscle, muzzle ......................................... M–FL • MUFL, MUZ

must • mussed, must have had ............................. M*US • M*UFD, MUFD

must feel • muscle .................................................. M*US/FAOEL • MUFL

mute • moot ............................................................. MAOUT • MAOT

mutual • mooch ....................................................... MAOUFP • MAOFP

muzzle • muscle, mussel ......................................... MUZ • MUFL, M–FL

my • Michigan .......................................................... MI • M*I

my opinion • in my opinion ..................................... MAOIP • NAOIP

myself • mice .......................................................... MAOIZ • MAOIS

myth • admit, mitt .................................................... M*IT • MIT, MOIT

# N

**nail** • inhale, naturally .......................................... NAIL • NA*EL, NAEL

**name** • namely ..................................................... NAIM • NAEM

**name and occupation** • occupation ..................... NOUPGS • OUPGS

**name**
    brand name ................................................. BRAIM
    Christian name ............................................. KRA*IM, KRA*EM
    domain name ............................................... DMAIM
    first name .................................................... FRA*IM, FRA*EM
    full name .................................................... FA*IM, FA*EM
    last name .................................................... LA*IM, LA*EM
    middle name ............................................... MA*EM
    nickname .................................................... NA*IM, NA*EM
    surname ...................................................... SA*IM, SA*EM
    trade name ................................................. TRA*IM, TRA*EM
    your name ................................................... YAOURM

**namely** • name ..................................................... NAEM • NAIM

**nap** • nappe .......................................................... NAP • NA*P

**nape** • anyplace .................................................... NAEP • NAIP

**nappe** • nap .......................................................... NA*P • NAP

**nation** • negates, negation ................................... NAIGS • NAIGZ, NEGS

**native** • knave, navy .............................................. NAIF • NAEV, NAIV

**naturally** • inhale, nail .......................................... NAEL • NA*EL, NAIL

**naught** • naughty, not ........................................... NAUGT • NAUT, NOT

**naughty** • knotty, naught ...................................... NAUT • NOT/TI, NAUGT

**naval** • navel ......................................................... NAIVL • NAEVL

**nave** • knave, navy ............................................... NAEF • NAEV, NAIV

**navel** • naval ......................................................... NAEVL • NAIVL

**navy**
    knave .......................................................... NAEV
    native .......................................................... NAIF
    nave ............................................................ NAEF
    navy ............................................................ NAIV

**nay**
    anyway ........................................................ NAI
    nay .............................................................. NAE
    nee .............................................................. NA*E
    neigh ........................................................... NAEG
    98 ............................................................... NA*I

**nearly** • northeasterly ........................................... NAERL • NAOERL

**Nebraska** • neither ............................................... N*E • NE

**nebulous** • ineligible ............................................. NEB • NEBL

**necks** • next ......................................................... NEKZ • NEX

**nee** • nay ............................................................. NA*E • NAE

**need** • knead, kneed, $93 ........................................ NAOED • NAED, N*ED, NYAO*ED

**negate** • negative, neigh ......................................... NAIG • NEG, NAEG

**negates** • negation ................................................ NAIGZ • NEGS

**negation** • nation, negates ..................................... NEGS • NAIGS, NAIGZ

**negative** • negate, neigh ......................................... NEG • NAIG, NAEG

**Negro** • kneeing ..................................................... NAO*EG • NAOEG

**neigh**

      anyway ............................................................ NAI
      nay ................................................................... NAE
      nee ................................................................... NA*E
      neigh ................................................................ NAEG
      98 ..................................................................... NA*I

**neither** • either ...................................................... NE • ET

**neither** • Nebraska ................................................. NE • N*E

**nervousness** • inference ......................................... NEFRNS • N–FRNS

**nest** • northwest ..................................................... NEFT • N*ES

**Netherlands** • knelt, the Netherlands .................... NELTS • NELT, N*ELT

**new** • knew ............................................................. NU • NAOU

**New Jersey** • engine .............................................. N*J • N–J

**New Mexico** • independently ................................. N*M • N–PL

**news** • noose ......................................................... NAOUS • NAOS

**news conference** • conference ............................... NAOUFRNS • K–FRNS

**news conference** • inference .................................. NAOUFRNS • N–FRNS

**New York City** • no, ................................................ NO*RKS • NORBGS

**next** • necks ........................................................... NEX • NEKZ

**nib** • anybody ........................................................ N*IB • NIB

**nibble** • anybody else ............................................. N*IBL • NIBL

**nice** • Nobel Prize .................................................. NAOIS • NAOIZ

**nick** • in this case, Nick, 96 ................................... NIRK • NIK, N*IRK, N*IK

**nicks** • initiation, nix .............................................. NIRKZ • NIRBGS, NIX

**niece** • knees ......................................................... NAOES • NAOEZ

**night** • knight ......................................................... NAOIT • NAO*IT

**night** • tomorrow night ........................................... NAOIT • TWAOIT

**Nile** • annihilate ..................................................... NAO*IL • NAOIL

**nineties** • nice, Nobel Prize .................................... NAO*IS • NAOIS, NAOIZ

**ninety-eights** • in any case .................................... NAIZ • NAIS

**ninety-sixes** • nix .................................................. NIKZ • NIX

**nix** • initiation, nicks .............................................. NIX • NIRBGS, NIRKZ

**no** • know .............................................................. NO • NOE

**No.** • enforcement ................................................. NOFPLT • NO*FMT

**no,** • New York City ............................................... NORBGS • NO*RKS

**no audible response** • audible, inaudible ............. NAUBLS • AUBL, NAUBL

**nob** • knob, nobody ............................................... NO*B • NOB, NOEB

**Nobel Prize** • nice ............................................... NAOIZ • NAOIS

**noble** • nobody else ............................................. NOEBL • NOBL

**no body** • nobody ................................................. NO/BOD • NOEB

**nobody else** • noble ............................................. NOBL • NOEBL

**noel** • knoll, normal ............................................. NO*EL • NOEL, NOL

**no evidence** • evidence ....................................... NOEVD • EVD

**no idea** • annoyed ............................................... NOID • NO*ID

**noise** • annoys ..................................................... NOIS • NOIZ

**no, ma'am** • ma'am; yes, ma'am ......................... NAM • MAM, YEM

**no more** • anymore ............................................... NOM • NIM

**none** • no one ....................................................... NUN • NO/WUN

**none** • nun, 91 ..................................................... NUN • NAUN, N*UN

**none of your business** • unusual ......................... NURBS • NURB

**nonfeasance**
    malfeasance ................................................. MAFZ
    misfeasance ................................................. MIFZ
    nonfeasance ................................................. NOFZ

**nonresponsive** • in respect, not responsive ......... N–RP • NR–P, N*RP

**non sui juris** • sui juris ......................................... NAOEJ • SWAOEJ

**no objection** • objection ....................................... NOEX • OX

**no one** • none ....................................................... NO/WUN • NUN

**noose** • news ....................................................... NAOS • NAOUS

**normal** • knoll ....................................................... NOL • NOEL

**norms** • enormous ............................................... NORMZ • NORMS

**North Carolina** • income ...................................... N*K • N–K

**North Dakota** • indeed ......................................... N*D • N–D

**northeasterly** • nearly ........................................... NAOERL • NAERL

**northwest** • nest ................................................... N*ES • NEFT

**nose** • knows ....................................................... NOEZ • NOES

**no, sir** • yes, sir ................................................... NORS • YER

**no such** • such ..................................................... NOUFP • SUFP

**not** • knot, naught ................................................. NOT • NO*T, NAUGT

**nothing further** • anything further ......................... NORT • NIRT

**not relevant** • 97 ................................................. NEV • NEF

**not responsive** • nonresponsive ........................... N*RP • N–RP

**nouns** • announce ................................................. NOUNZ • NOUNS

**novel** • nozzle .......................................................... NOVL • NOFL

**now** • anyhow ......................................................... NOU • NO*U

**no, your Honor** • your Honor ................................ NURN • URN

**nozzle** • novel .......................................................... NOFL • NOVL

**nuance** • nuisance ................................................. NAOUNS • NAOUNZ

**nuances** • nuisances ............................................. NAOUNSZ • NAOUNZ/–S

**nub** • number ........................................................... N*UB • NUB

**nuisance** • nuance ................................................. NAOUNZ • NAOUNS

**null** • annul ............................................................. NUL • N*UL

**nullification** • jury nullification ............................. NULGS • JULGS

**number** • nub ......................................................... NUB • N*UB

**nun** • none, 91 ....................................................... NAUN • NUN, N*UN

# O

| | |
|---|---|
| **oar** • anterior | AO*R • AOR |
| **oar** • or, ore, 84 | AO*R • OR, YO*ER, YOER |
| **obedience** • disobedience | BAOENS • SBAOENS |
| **obedient** • disobedient | BAOENT • SBAOENT |
| **obediently** • disobediently | BAOENL • SBAOENL |
| **objection** • no objection | OX • NOEX |
| **objection** • ox | OX • O*X |
| **objection overruled** • overruled | KPOEVRLD • OEVRLD |
| **objections** • oxen | OXZ • O*XZ |
| **objection, your Honor** • your Honor | ORN • URN |
| **oblique** • bleak | BLAOEK • BLAEK |
| **obscure** • secure | SKAOUR • SKUR |
| **obscurity** • security | SKAOURT • SKURT |
| **obtain** • bane | BAIN • BAEN |
| **obtain** • contain | BAIN • TAIN |
| **occasion** • indication | KAIRB • KAIGS |
| **Occident** • accident | SDON • SDEN |
| **Occidental** • accidental | SDONL • SDENL |
| **occupation** • name and occupation, preoccupation | OUPGS • NOUPGS, PROUPGS |
| **occupy** • preoccupy | OUP • PROUP |
| **occurred** • curd | KURD • K*URD |
| **occurrence** • currency | KURNS • KURNZ |
| **occurs** • curs, curse | KURZ • K*URS, KURS |
| **ocean** • on the grounds | OEGS • OGS |
| **odd** • awed | O*D • A*UD |
| **odder** • otter | O*RD • OT |
| **ode** • owed | YOED *or* O*ED • OED |
| **offer** • officer | AUFR • SAUFR |
| **offer** • proffer | AUFR • PRAUFR |
| **offer of proof** • proof | FRAOF • PRAOF |
| **offhand** • fawned | FAUND • FA*UND |

**office**

| | |
|---|---|
| City Attorney's Office | STOFS |
| coroner's office | KR–FS |
| D.A.'s office | DAFS |
| District Attorney's Office | DAOFS |
| governor's office | GOFS |
| office | OFS |

| | |
|---|---|
| post office | POFS |
| registrar's office | STROFS |
| sheriff's office | SHOFS |

**officer**
| | |
|---|---|
| Chief Executive Officer | KHOFR |
| investigating officer | GAIFR |
| law enforcement officer | LAIFR |
| law officer | LAUFR |
| officer | SAUFR |
| peace officer | PEFR |
| police officer | PLOFR |
| probation officer | PRAIFR |

| | |
|---|---|
| **official** • efficiently | FIRBL • F*IRBL |
| **oh** • owe | O*E • OE |
| **Ohio** • ho | HO* • HO |
| **OK** • okay, Oklahoma | O*K • OK, O*K/O*K or KLOEM |
| **okay** • OK, Oklahoma | OK • O*K, O*K/O*K or KLOEM |
| **Oklahoma** • OK, okay | KLOEM or O*K/O*K • O*K, OK |
| **one** • won | WUN • WON |
| **one-and-a-quarter** • and a quarter | NAERT • NART |
| **one-half of the** • half of the | WAFT • HAFT |
| **one quarter** • one-quarter | WUN/KWAERT • WAERT |
| **one-third** • third, two-thirds | WIRD • THIRD, TWIRDZ |
| **one time** • wasn't | WAOIM • WUNT |
| **on one hand** • on the one hand | WHAND • TWAND |
| **on the grounds** • ocean | OGS • OEGS |
| **on the other hand** • oriented | OERND • OERNTD |
| **on to** • onto | ON/TO • AONT |
| **operating room** • emergency room | OERM • ERM |
| **ophthalmologist** • molt, motel | MOLT • MOULT or MO*LT, MOELT |
| **opponent** • exponent | POENT • SPOENT |
| **or** • Oregon | OR • O*R |
| **oral** • aural | ORL • AURL |
| **order** • ordinary | OD • ORD |
| **ordinance** • ordnance | ORNS • AORNS |
| **ordinary** • order | ORD • OD |
| **ore** • oar, or, 84 | YO*ER • AO*R, OR, YOER |
| **Oregon** • or | O*R • OR |
| **organic** • inorganic | GANK • NANK |
| **organism** • orgasm | GIFM • GAFM |
| **organization** • disorganization | ORGS • DORGS |

**organize** • disorganize .......................................... ORG • DORG

**orgasm** • organism ................................................ GAFM • GIFM

**orient** • disorient .................................................... OERNT • DORN

**orient** • disorientate ............................................. OERNT • DORNT

**orient** • orientate, ornament ................................ OERNT • TOERNT, ORNT

**orientate** • torrent ................................................. TOERNT • TORNT

**orientating** • attorney general ............................. TOERNGT • TOERNG

**orientation** • disorientation ................................. OERNGS • DORNGS

**oriented** • on the other hand ............................... OERNTD • OERND

**origin** • original ..................................................... AURJ • ORJ

**original** • origin ..................................................... ORJ • AURJ

**ornament** • orient ................................................. ORNT • OERNT

**otter** • odder ......................................................... OT • O*RD

**ought** • auto ......................................................... AUT • AOUT

**our**
    our .................................................................. OUR
    ours ............................................................... OURS
    ourself ........................................................... OURZ
    ourselves ...................................................... OURSZ, O*URS

**ours** • hours .......................................................... OURS • HOURS

**outer** • outright ..................................................... OURT • TR–T

**outlet** • outline ..................................................... OLT • OULT

**outmaneuver** • maneuver ..................................... NAOUVR • MAOUVR

**outpatient** • inpatient, patient ............................. TAIRB • NAIRB, PAIRB

**outreach** • teacher ............................................... TRAEFP • TRAOEFP

**outright** • out right ................................................ TR–T • OUT/–RT

**outright** • the right ................................................ TR–T • T–RT

**outside** • other side .............................................. OUD • OID

**over all** • overall .................................................. OEVR/AUL • OUVRL

**overhauled** • vaudevillian ..................................... VA*ULD • VAULD

**overly** • overrule ................................................... OVRL • OEVRL

**overrule** • overly ................................................... OEVRL • OVRL

**overruled** • objection overruled ........................... OEVRLD • KPOEVRLD

**owe** • oh; oh, ........................................................ OE • O*E, OERBGS

**owed** • ode ........................................................... OED • O*ED

**ox** • objection ....................................................... O*X • OX

**oxen** • objections .................................................. O*XZ • OXZ

# P

pa • paw ................................................................. PA • PAU

pa • Pennsylvania ............................................. PA • PA*

pace • pays, peace ........................................... PAIS • PAIZ, PAES

paced • paste .................................................... PAIFD • PA*IS

pacifism • part of them ............................... POIFM *or* PA*FM • PAFM

package • passage .......................................... PAJ • PAUJ

packet • pact .................................................... PAEKT • PAKT

pact • packed, packet .................................... PAKT • PAKD, PAEKT

pail • pale ......................................................... PAIL • PA*IL

pain • pane ....................................................... PAIN • PAEN

painful • peaceful .......................................... PAIF • PAEF

painfully • peacefully .................................... PAIFL • PAEFL

pair
    appear ............................................................. PAER
    pair ................................................................... PAIR
    pare .................................................................. PA*IR
    pear .................................................................. PA*ER

pajama • jam, jamb ....................................... JAUM • JAM, JA*M

pal • appall, pall, Paul ................................... PAL • PAUL, PA*L, PA*UL

palate • palette, pallet .................................. PLA • PLELT, PALT

pale
    appeal .............................................................. PAEL
    pail ................................................................... PAIL
    pale .................................................................. PA*IL
    peal .................................................................. PA*EL

pallet • palate, palette .................................. PALT • PLA, PLELT

pane • pain ....................................................... PAEN • PAIN

parade • persuade, prayed, preyed .......... PRAID • PRAED, PRA*ID, PRA*ED

paralegal
    paralegal .......................................................... PLAEL
    parallel ............................................................. PAERL
    paraphernalia ................................................... PAIRL
    particle ............................................................ PARL
    peril .................................................................. PIRL

parallel • paraphernalia, particle ............. PAERL • PAIRL, PARL

parameter • perimeter ................................... PRAMT • PRIRMT

parameter • prior inconsistent statement ............ PRAMT • PRIMT

paraphernalia • parallel, particle, peril ......... PAIRL • PAERL, PARL, PIRL

pardon • partner ............................................. PARD • PARN

pare • pair, pear ............................................. PA*IR • PAIR, PA*ER

**parole** • patrol ......................................................... PROEL • PROL

**parotid** • carotid ..................................................... PROTD • KROTD

**parotid** • property .................................................. PROTD • PROT

**part**

      apart ................................................... PAURT

      counterpart ..................................... KPART

      depart ............................................... DPART

      ex parte ........................................... KPAERT

      impart............................................... KBART

      part ................................................... PART

      partly ............................................... PARLT

      party ............................................... PAERT

      spare part ...................................... SPAURT

**particle** • parallel, paraphernalia ........................... PARL • PAERL, PAIRL

**particular** • spectacular ...................................... PLAR • SPLAR

**part of them** • pacifism ...................................... PAFM • PA*FM *or* POIFM

**party** • ex parte, part ........................................... PAERT • KPAERT, PART

**passage** • package ............................................. PAUJ • PAJ

**passed** • past ....................................................... PAFD • PA*S

**past** • passed ....................................................... PA*S • PAFD

**paste** • paced ....................................................... PA*ES • PAIFD

**patent** • pattern .................................................... PAENT • PAERN

**paternal** • apparently ........................................... PARNL • PAERNL

**patience** • impatience .......................................... PAIRBS • KBAIRBS

**patience** • patients .............................................. PAIRBS • PAIRBZ

**patient** • inpatient, outpatient ............................... PAIRB • NAIRB, TAIRB

**patients** • patience .............................................. PAIRBZ • PAIRBS

**patrol** • parole ...................................................... PROL • PROEL

**patrol** • petroleum ................................................ TROL • TROEL

**pattern** • patent .................................................... PAERN • PAENT

**patterns** • appearance ......................................... PAERNZ • PAERNS

**pauper** • poplar, popular ....................................... PAUP • PLAP, PLARP

**pause** • paws ....................................................... PAUS • PAUZ

**paw** • pa .............................................................. PAU • PA

**pawn** • upon ........................................................ PAUN • PON

**paws** • pause ....................................................... PAUZ • PAUS

**pays** • pace.......................................................... PAIZ • PAIS

**pea** • pee, People's 3 ........................................... PAE • PAO*E, PAOE

**peace** • appease, peas, piece ............................... PAES • PAOEZ, PAEZ, PAOES

**peace** • pace ....................................................... PAES • PAIS

**peaceful** • painful ................................................ PAEF • PAIF

| | |
|---|---|
| **peacefully** • painfully | PAEFL • PAIFL |
| **peak** • peek, pique | PAEK • PAOEK, PAO*EK |
| **peal** • appeal, peel | PA*EL • PAEL, PAOEL |
| **pear** • appear | PA*ER • PAER |
| **pear** • pair, pare | PA*ER • PAIR, PA*IR |
| **pearl** • peril, purl | PERL • PIRL, PURL |
| **peas** • appease, peace, piece | PAEZ • PAOEZ, PAES, PAOES |
| **peat** • Pete | PAET • PAOET |
| **peck** • peculiar | P*EK • PEK |
| **pecks** • People's exhibit | PEKZ • PEX |
| **peculiar** • peck, pecuniary | PEK • P*EK, PUK |
| **pecuniary** • peculiar | PUK • PEK |
| **pedestrian** • ped | PED • P*ED |
| **pee** • pea, People's 3 | PAO*E • PAE, PAOE |
| **peed** • People's 3 for identification | PAO*ED • PAOED |
| **peek** • peak, pique | PAOEK • PAEK, PAO*EK |
| **peel** • appeal, peal | PAOEL • PAEL, PA*EL |
| **peer** • pier | PAOER • PAO*ER |
| **peers** • appears, pierce | PAOERZ • PAERS, PAOERS |
| **pegs** • possession | PEGZ • PEGS |
| **penal** • penalize | PAOENL • PENL |
| **Penal Code Section** • plaintiff's exhibit | P*X • P–X |
| **penalty of perjury** • pop | POP • PO*P |
| **pend** • penned | P*END • PEND |
| **penned** • pend | PEND • P*END |
| **Pennsylvania** • pa | PA* • PA |
| **penultimate** • catapult | P*ULT • PULT |
| **People's exhibit** • pecks | PEX • PEKZ |
| **People's 3** • pea, pee | PAOE • PAE, PAO*E |
| **People's 3 for identification** • peed | PAOED • PAO*ED |
| **per** • purr | PER • PUR |
| **percipient** • percipient witness | SPIP • SWIP |
| **perfect** • prefect | P–F • PREFK |
| **peril** • pearl, purl | PIRL • PERL, PURL |
| **perimeter** • parameter | PRIRMT • PRAMT |
| **perimeter** • prior inconsistent statement | PRIRMT • PRIMT |
| **perjure** • PJ | P–J • P*J |
| **perm** • permanent | P*ERM • PERM *or* PAMT |

| | |
|---|---|
| **permanent** • perm | PAMT *or* PERM • P*ERM |
| **permission** • pigs | PIGS • PIGZ |
| **perpendicular** • perpetrate | PERP • PERPT |
| **perpendicular** • purpose | PERP • PURP |
| **perpetrate** • perpendicular, perpetuate | PERPT • PERP, PEFPT |
| **perpetration** • perpetuation | PERPGS • PEFPGS |
| **perpetuate** • perpetrate | PEFPT • PERPT |
| **perpetuation** • perpetration | PEFPGS • PERPGS |
| **persecute** • prosecute | SKWAOT • PR– |
| **personal** • personnel | PERNL • SNEL |
| **personnel** • personal | SNEL • PERNL |
| **perspective** • prospective | SPEVT • PR–VP |
| **perspiration** • expiration | SPIRGS • KPRAIGS |
| **persuade** • parade, prayed, preyed | PRAED • PRAID, PRA*ID, PRA*ED |
| **persuasion** • pregnancies | PRAEGS • PRAEGZ |
| **pertinent** • pursuant | PERNT • PURNT |
| **pervious** • impervious | PEFRB • KBEFRB |
| **Pete** • peat | PAOET • PAET |
| **petit mal seizure** • grand mal seizure, PMS | P–MZ • G–MZ, P–MS |
| **petroleum** • patrol | TROEL • TROL |
| **pew** • repudiate | PAO*U • PAOU |
| **phalanges** • freelancing | FLANGZ • FLANGS |
| **phase** • face, faze | FAIZ *or* FAEZ • FAIS, FAES |
| **photograph** • stenograph | FRAF • SGRAF |
| **photographer** • stenographer | FRAFR • SGRAFR |
| **photographic** • stenographic | FRAFK • SGRAFK |
| **photographically** • stenographically | FRAEFK • SGRAEFK |
| **photography** • stenography | FRAEF • SGRAEF |
| **phrase** • forty-eights, frays | FRAIS • FRAIZ, FRAES |
| **physical** • fiscal | F–L • SKAL |
| **physical therapist** • therapist | FAERPT • THAERPT |
| **physical therapy** • therapy | FAERP • THAERP |
| **physician** • figures, fission | F–GS • FIGS, F*IGS |
| **pi** • pie | PI • PAOI |
| **pick up** • pup | PUP • P*UP |
| **picture** • pitcher | PIR • PRIFP |
| **pidgin** • pigeon | PIJD • PIJ |
| **pie** • pi | PAOI • PI |

**piece** • appease, peace, peas ............................. PAOES • PAOEZ, PAES, PAEZ

**piece**
    centerpiece ...................................... SNAOERP, SN*ERP
    two-piece .......................................... TWOP
    three-piece ........................................ THREP
    four-piece .......................................... FOURP
    five-piece .......................................... FAOIVP
    six-piece ........................................... SW*IP
    seven-piece ....................................... SEVP

**pier** • peer ................................................ PAO*ER • PAOER

**pierce** • appears, peers ........................................... PAOERS • PAERS, PAOERZ

**pigeon** • pidgin ....................................... PIJ • PIJD

**pigment** • figment .................................... PIMT • FIMT

**pigs** • permission ..................................... PIGZ • PIGS

**pique** • peak, peek .................................. PAO*EK • PAEK, PAOEK

**pitcher** • picture ..................................... PRIFP • PIR

**PJ** • perjure .............................................. P*J • P–J

**place** • plaice, plays ............................... PLAIS • PLA*IS, PLAIZ

**plague** • playing ..................................... PLAEG *or* PLA*IG • PLAIG

**plagues** • pleadings ................................ PLAEGZ • PLAEGS

**plaice** • place, plays ............................... PLA*IS • PLAIS, PLAIZ

**plaid** • played, plead ............................. PLAD • PLAID, PLAED

**plain** • plane ......................................... PLAIN • PLAEN

**plaintiff** • plaintive .................................... PL–F • PLAIV

**plaintiff's exhibit** • Penal Code Section ............... P–X • P*X

**plaintive** • plaintiff ................................. PLAIV • PL–F

**plait** • plate ............................................ PLAIT • PLAET

**plane** • plain ........................................... PLAEN • PLAIN

**planet** • complaint .................................. PLAENT • PLAINT

**plantar** • planter ..................................... PLA*RNT • PLARNT

**planter** • plantar ..................................... PLARNT • PLA*RNT

**plastic surgeon** • surgeon ..................................... PLURN • SURN

**plastic surgery** • surgery ...................................... PLURG • SURG

**plate** • plait ............................................ PLAET • PLAIT

**play** • plea.............................................. PLAI • PLAE

**played** • plaid, plead............................... PLAID • PLAD, PLAED

**playing** • plague ..................................... PLAIG • PLA*IG *or* PLAEG

**plays** • place, plaice ............................... PLAIZ • PLAIS, PLA*IS

**plea** • appellee...................................... PLAE • PLAOE

**plea** • play ............................................. PLAE • PLAI

---

         

| | |
|---|---|
| **plead** • played | PLAED • PLAID |
| **pleading** • plagued | PLAEGD • PLA*EGD |
| **pleadings** • plagues | PLAEGS • PLAEGZ |
| **pleas** • please | PLAES • PLAOES |
| **please** • pleas, police | PLAOES • PLAES, PLIS |
| **pleasure** • displeasure | PLERB • SPLERB |
| **pledge of allegiance** • allegiance | PLAOEJS • LAOEJ |
| **plethora** • complete | PL*ET • PLET |
| **pleural** • plural | PLERL • PLURL |
| **plied** • applied | PLAO*ID • PLAOID |
| **plight** • polite | PLAOIT • PLOIT |
| **ploy** • employ | PLO*I • PLOI |
| **plum** • plumb | PL*UM • PLUM |
| **plumber** • plus or minus | PLOIRM • PLURM |
| **plural** • pleural | PLURL • PLERL |
| **plus or minus** • plumber | PLURM • PLOIRM |
| **ply** • apply, reply | PLAO*I • PLAOI, PLI |
| **p.m.** • a.m. | PM *or* P*M • A*M |
| **PMS** • petit mal seizure | P–MS • P–MZ |
| **point** • appoint | POINT • POIN |
| **poisoned** • lipoid | POID • PO*ID |
| **poisoning** • blood poisoning | POIG • BLOIG |
| **pole** • poll | POEL • POL |
| **police** • pleas, please | PLIS • PLAES, PLAOES |
| **police** • replies | PLIS • PLIZ |
| **polite** • plight | PLOIT • PLAOIT |
| **politician** • application | POLGS • PLIGS |
| **poll** • pole | POL • POEL |
| **poor** • pore, pour | PAOR • POER, POUR |
| **poor** • posterior | PAOR • PAO*R |
| **poorly** • posteriorly | PAORL • PAO*RL |
| **pop** | |
|     pauper | PAUP |
|     penalty of perjury | POP |
|     pop | PO*P |
|     poplar | PLAP |
|     popular | PLARP |
| **poplar** • popular | PLAP • PLARP |
| **popular** • poplar | PLARP • PLAP |
| **popular** • popularity | PLARP • PLARPT |

| | | |
|---|---|---|
| **popularity** • popular | PLARPT • PLARP |
| **pore** • poor, pour | POER • PAOR, POUR |
| **portable** • potable | PORBL • POEBT |
| **portion** • apportion, proportion | PORGS • PAORGS, PRORGS |
| **position** • disposition, supposition | POGS • SPOGS, SPOEGS |
| **possession** • pegs | PEGS • PEGZ |
| **possibility** • impossibility | POBLT • KBOBLT |
| **possible** • impossible | POBL • KBOBL |
| **possibly** • impossibly | POEBL • KBOEBL |
| **posted** • deposited | POEFTD • POFTD |

**posterior**

| | |
|---|---|
| anterior | AOR |
| exterior | KPAOR |
| inferior | FAOR |
| interior | NAOR |
| posterior | PAO*R |
| superior | SAOR |

| | |
|---|---|
| **post office** • office | POFS • OFS |
| **potable** • portable | POEBT • PORBL |
| **pounce** • pounds | POUNS • POUNDZ |
| **pounce** • ups and downs | POUNS • POUNZ |
| **pounds** • pounce | POUNDZ • POUNS |
| **pour** • poor, pore | POUR • PAOR, POER |
| **power** • empower | PAUR • KBAUR |
| **power** • pour | PAUR • POUR |
| **PR** • Puerto Rico | P–R • P*R |
| **pram** • program | PRA*M • PRAM |
| **pray** • prey | PRAI • PRAE |
| **prayed** • parade, persuade, preyed | PRA*ID • PRAID, PRAED, PRA*ED |
| **precede** • proceed | PROID • PRAOED |
| **precedence** • precedents, presidents | PR–NS • PR–NTS, P–TS |
| **precedent** • president | PR–NT • P–T |
| **precedents** • precedence, presidents | PR–NTS • PR–NS, P–TS |
| **precipitation** • prescription | PR*IPGS • PRIPGS |
| **prediction** • predicts, pricks | PRIX • PRIKTS, PRIKZ |
| **preempt** • premeditate | PREMT • PRAEMT |
| **prefect** • perfect | PREFK • P–F |
| **preference** • sexual preference | PREFRNS • SWEFRNS |
| **pregnancies** • persuasion | PRAEGZ • PRAEGS |
| **pregnancy** • preying | PRAEG • PRA*EG |

---

| | |
|---|---|
| **pregnancy** • tubal pregnancy | PRAEG • TRAEG |
| **prelim** • preliminary | PL*IM • PLIM |
| **preliminary** • prelim | PLIM • PL*IM |
| **premature** • mature | PRAUR • MAUR |
| **prematurely** • maturely | PRAURL • MAURL |
| **prematureness** • matureness | PRAURNS • MAURNS |
| **prematurity** • maturity | PRAURT • MAURT |
| **premeditate** • preempt | PRAEMT • PREMT |
| **premier** • premiere, premium | PRAOERM • PRERM, PRAOEM |
| **premise** • promise | PR–M *or* PREMS • PROM |
| **preoccupation** • name and occupation, occupation | PROUPGS • NOUPGS, OUPGS |
| **preoccupy** • occupy | PROUP • OUP |
| **preschool** • private school, public school | PRAOL • VAOL, PLAOL |
| **prescription** • precipitation | PRIPGS • PR*IPGS |
| **prescription** • subscription | PRIPGS • SKRIGS |
| **presence** • presents | PRENS • PRENTS |
| **presents** • presence | PRENTS • PRENS |
| **preserve** • serve | PREFRB • SEFRB |
| **president** • Mr. President, the president | P–T • MR–PT, T–PT |
| **president** • precedent | P–T • PR–NT |
| **presidents** • precedence | P–TS • PR–NS |

**press conference**

| | |
|---|---|
| conference | K–FRNS |
| news conference | NAOUFRNS |
| press conference | PR–FRNS |
| teleconference | T–FRNS |

| | |
|---|---|
| **press conference** • preference | PR–FRNS • PREFRNS |
| **presumed innocent** • prudent | PRAOUNT • PRUNT |

**pretrial**

| | |
|---|---|
| mistrial | STRAOIL |
| pretrial | PRAOIL |
| speedy trial | SPRAOIL |
| trial | TRAOIL |

| | |
|---|---|
| **prey** • pray | PRAE • PRAI |
| **preyed** • parade, persuade, prayed | PRA*ED • PRAID, PRAED, PRA*ID |
| **preying** • pregnancy | PRA*EG • PRAEG |
| **preys** • appraise | PRAEZ • PRAES |
| **Prez** • princess | PREZ • PRES |
| **price** • pries, prize | PRAOIS • PRAO*IS, PRAOIZ |
| **pricks** • prediction, predicts | PRIKZ • PRIX, PRIKTS |

| | |
|---|---|
| **pride** • pried | PRAOID • PRAO*ID |
| **pried** • pride | PRAO*ID • PRAOID |
| **pries** • price, prize | PRAO*IS • PRAOIS, PRAOIZ |
| **primary** • primer | PROIRM • PRAOIRM |
| **primer** • primary | PRAOIRM • PROIRM |
| **prince** • prints | PRINS • PRINTS |
| **princes** • princess | PRINSZ • PRES |
| **princess** • Prez, princes | PRES • PREZ, PRINSZ |
| **principal** • principle | PRAL • PREL |
| **prints** • prince | PRINTS • PRINS |
| **prior** • priority, prior to | PRAOIR • PROIRT, PRAOIRT |
| **prior inconsistent statement** • perimeter | PRIMT • PRIRMT |
| **prioritize** • priority | PROIR • PROIRT |
| **priority** • prioritize | PROIRT • PROIR |
| **prior to** • prior, priority | PRAOIRT • PRAOIR, PROIRT |
| **prison** • imprison | PRIZ • KBRIZ |
| **prison** • state prison | PRIN • STIN |
| **private school** • preschool, pubic school | VAOL • PRAOL, PLAOL |
| **prize** • price, pries | PRAOIZ • PRAOIS, PRAO*IS |
| **probability** • improbability | PROBLT • KBROBLT |
| **probable** • improbable | PROBL • KBROBL |
| **probable cause** • for probable cause, proximate cause | PRAUZ • FRAUZ, PRAUS |
| **probably** • improbably | PROEBL • KBROEBL |
| **proceed** • precede | PRAOED • PROID |
| **process** • pros, prose | PROS • PROZ, PROEZ |
| **procure** • producer | PRAOUR • PRUR |
| **producer** • procure | PRUR • PRAOUR |
| **profession** • provocation | PROFGS • PROVGS |
| **professor** • proffer | PROFR • PRAUFR |
| **proffer** • offer | PRAUFR • AUFR |
| **proffer** • professor | PRAUFR • PROFR |
| **profit** • prophet | PROFT • PROEFT |
| **program** • pram | PRAM • PRA*M |
| **prohibit** • inhibit | HIB *or* HIBT • NIBT |
| **prohibition** • hicks | HIX • HIKZ |
| **prom** • promise | PRAUM *or* PRO*M • PROM |
| **promise** • premise | PROM • PR–M *or* PREMS |

**promise** • prom ...................................................... PROM • PRAUM *or* PRO*M

**proof**
    bulletproof ...................................................... BLAOF
    burden of proof .............................................. BRAOF
    childproof ........................................................ KHAOF
    foolproof ......................................................... FLAOF
    insufficient proof ........................................... SNAOF
    offer of proof ................................................. FRAOF
    proof ............................................................... PRAOF
    soundproof ...................................................... SPRAOF
    sufficient proof .............................................. SAOF
    waterproof ...................................................... WRAOF

**proper** • improper ............................................... PROR • KBROR

**properly** • improperly ............................................ PRORL • KBRORL

**property** • community property, ......................... PROT • KPROT, SPROT
separate property

**property** • parotid .................................................. PROT • PROTD

**prophet** • profit ...................................................... PROEFT • PROFT

**prophylactic** • flack, flak .................................... FLAKT • FLA*KT, FLAK

**prophylaxis** • flax, prophylactics ......................... FLAKZ • FLAX, FLAKTS

**proportion** • apportion, portion ............................ PRORGS • PAORGS, PORGS

**propose** • appropriate .......................................... PROEP • PROEPT

**propose** • prototype ............................................. PROEP • PRAOIP

**proposition** • appropriation ................................. PROPGS • PROEPGS

**proprietary** • proprietor, propriety ........................ PR–T • PR–RT, PRAOIT

**proprietor** • proprietary, propriety ........................ PR–RT • PR–T, PRAOIT

**propriety** • impropriety ......................................... PRAOIT • KBRAOIT

**propriety** • proprietary, proprietor ........................ PRAOIT • PR–T, PR–RT

**pros** • process, prose ........................................... PROZ • PROS, PROES *or* PROEZ

**prose** • process, pros ........................................... PROEZ *or* PROES • PROS, PROZ

**prosecute** • persecute ......................................... PR– • SKWAOT

**prospective** • perspective .................................... PR–VP • SPEVT

**protective custody** • custody ............................... PRUVD • KUD

**prototype** • propose ............................................. PRAOIP • PROEP

**proudly** • prowled ................................................. PROULD • PRO*ULD

**prove**
    approve ........................................................... PRAOV
    disapprove ...................................................... SPRAOV
    disprove .......................................................... SPROV
    improve ............................................................ KBROV
    prove ............................................................... PROV

**provocation** • profession ...................................... PROVGS • PROFGS

**prowled** • proudly ................................................. PRO*ULD • PROULD

| | |
|---|---|
| **proximate** • approximate | PR–KT • P– |
| **proximate cause** • probable cause | PRAUS • PRAUZ |
| **proxy** • approximation | PRO*X • PROX |
| **prudent** • presumed innocent, pursuant, pursue | PRUNT • PRAOUNT, PURNT, PRAOU |
| **psychic** • 66 | SK*IK • SKIK |
| **psychoses** • skis | SKAOEZ • SKAOES |
| **pub** • public | P*UB • PUB |
| **public** • pub | PUB • P*UB |
| **public relations** • relation | PRELGS • RELGS |
| **public school** • preschool, private school | PLAOL • PRAOL, VAOL |
| **Puerto Rico** • PR | P*R • P–R |
| **pulls** • pulse | PULZ • PULS |
| **pulse** • pulls | PULS • PULZ |

**punishment**

| | |
|---|---|
| capital punishment | KPUMT |
| cruel and unusual punishment | KRUMT |
| punishment | PUMT |

| | |
|---|---|
| **punitive** • putative | PAOUV • PAOUVT |
| **punitive damages** • compensatory damages | P–DZ • K–DZ |
| **pup** • pick up | P*UP • PUP |
| **purl** • pearl, peril | PURL • PERL, PIRL |
| **purple** • purpose | PURPL • PURP |
| **purpose** • perpendicular | PURP • PERP |
| **purpose** • purple | PURP • PURPL |
| **purpose** • sense of purpose | PURP • SPURP |
| **purr** • per | PUR • PER |
| **purrs** • purse | PURZ • PURS |
| **purse** • purrs | PURS • PURZ |
| **pursuant** • pertinent | PURNT • PERNT |
| **pursuant** • prudent, pursue | PURNT • PRUNT, PRAOU |
| **pursue** • prudent, pursuant | PRAOU • PRUNT, PURNT |
| **put** • putt | PUT • P*UT |
| **putative** • punitive | PAOUVT • PAOUV |
| **putt** • put | P*UT • PUT |

---

# Q

quadriceps • chemical weapons .......................... KWEPS • KWEPZ

quadriplegia • pledge of allegiance .................... PLAOEJ • PLAOEJS

qualification • disqualification ............................. KW–FGS • SKW–FGS

qualify • disqualify ............................................... KW–F • SKW–F

**quarter**
    and a quarter ................................................. NART
    one-and-a-quarter ......................................... WA\*RT
    one-quarter .................................................... WAERT
    quarter ........................................................... KWAERT
    quarterly ........................................................ KWAERL, KWAERLT

quarts • quartz .................................................... KWARTS • KWA\*RTS *or* KWARZ

quartz • quarts .................................................... KWA\*RTS *or* KWARZ • KWARTS

quay • key ............................................................ KWAE • KAOE

queen • convene .................................................. KWAOEN • KWAO\*EN

queens • convenes .............................................. KWAOENS • KWAOENZ

queue • cue .......................................................... KWAOU • KAOU

quiet • quite ......................................................... KWAET • KWAOIT

quip • equip ......................................................... KW\*IP • KWIP

quite • quiet ......................................................... KWAOIT • KWAET

quota • quote ....................................................... KWA • KWOET

quotation • misquotation ..................................... KWOEGS • SKWOEGS

quotation • quotient ............................................. KWOEGS • KWOERB

quote • misquote ................................................. KWOET • SKWOET

quote • quota ....................................................... KWOET • KWA

quotient • quotation ............................................. KWOERB • KWOEGS

# R

race • raise ....................................................... RAIS • RAIZ

racist • rapist .................................................. RAIFT • RAIPT

rack • wrack .................................................... RAK • WRAK

racket • react ................................................. RAEKT • RAKT

racks • reaction ............................................. RAKZ • RAX

rags • ration ................................................... RAGZ • RAGS

rail • rale, real .............................................. RAIL • RA*EL, RAEL

rain • reign, rein ........................................... RAIN • RA*IN, RAEN

raise • rays, Ray's, raze ............................. RAIZ • RA*IZ, RA*IS, RAEZ

raiser • razer, razor ...................................... RAIRZ • RAERZ, RAZ

rale • rail, real .............................................. RA*EL • RAIL, RAEL

ram • RAM ...................................................... RAM • RA*M

rammed • remand ......................................... RA*MD • RAMD

rap • wrap ...................................................... RAP • WRAP

rape • relationshp ........................................ RAIP • RAEP

rapist • racist ................................................ RAIPT • RAIFT

rapped • rapt, wrapped .............................. RAPD • RAPT, WRAPD

rapport • report ............................................ RARP • RORT

rapt • rapped, wrapped .............................. RAPT • RAPD, WRAPD

rare • rear, repair ......................................... RAER • RAOER, RAIR

rate • enumerate ........................................... RAIT • RAET

rather than • ravine ..................................... RAFN • RAVN

rating • regularity, regulate ...................... RAIGT • REGT, RAIG

ration • rags .................................................. RAGS • RAGZ

rational • rationale ....................................... RAL • RA*L

raven • ravine ............................................... RAIVN • RAVN

ravenous • ravines ....................................... RAVNS • RAVNZ

ravine • rather than, raven ......................... RAVN • RAFN, RAIVN

ravines • ravenous ....................................... RAVNZ • RAVNS

ray • Ray, re .................................................. RAI • RA*I, RAOE

rays • Ray's ................................................... RA*IZ • RA*IS

raze

    race ............................................................ RAIS

    raise ........................................................... RAIZ

    rays ............................................................ RA*IZ

    Ray's ........................................................... RA*IS

    raze ............................................................ RAEZ

razer • raiser, razor ..................................... RAERZ • RAIRZ, RAZ

**razor** • raiser, razer ................................................. RAZ • RAIRZ, RAERZ

**re** • ray, Ray ............................................................ RAOE • RAI, RA*I

**re~** ( *prefix* ) • re ................................................... RE • RAOE

**react** • racket ........................................................ RAKT • RAEKT

**reaction** • racks .................................................... RAX • RAKZ

**read** • red ............................................................... RAED • RED

**read** • reed ............................................................. RAED • RAOED

**readjusted** • adjusted, maladjusted ..................... RAUFD • JAUFD, MAUFD

**ready** • reasonable doubt ...................................... R–D • –RD

**real** • rail, rale ........................................................ RAEL • RAIL, RA*EL

**real** • reel .............................................................. RAEL • RAOEL

**reality** • realty ........................................................ RAELT • RAOELT

**realtime captioning** • caption ............................. RAPGS • KAPGS

**realty** • reality ........................................................ RAOELT • RAELT

**rear** • rare, repair .................................................. RAOER • RAER, RAIR

**rears** • arrears ....................................................... RAOERS • RAOERZ

**reasonable doubt**
    beyond all reasonable doubt .......................... Y–RLD
    beyond any reasonable doubt ....................... YIRD
    beyond a reasonable doubt ........................... Y–RD
    beyond every reasonable doubt ................... YERD
    beyond reasonable doubt .............................. YORD
    reasonable doubt ........................................... –RD

**reasonable doubt** • ready ..................................... –RD • R–D

**receipt** • rhetoric .................................................. RET • WRET

**received in evidence** • insufficient evidence ........ SNEVD • SNUVD

**recent** • resent ...................................................... RAOENT • RAOEFNT

**recently** • rental, reprehensible ............................ RAOENL • R*ENL, RENL

**reck** • recognize, wreck ......................................... R*EK • REK, WREK

**recognize**
    reck ............................................................... R*EK
    recognize ....................................................... REK
    recollect ........................................................ R–K
    wreck ............................................................ WREK

**recognizes** • recollection ..................................... REKZ • REX

**recollect** • recommend ......................................... R–K • R–M

**recollection** • recognizes ..................................... REX • REKZ

**recommend** • recollect ......................................... R–M • R–K

**recommend** • remember ...................................... R–M • REM

**recorder** • tape recorder ...................................... ROERD • TROERD

**recount** • count .................................................... ROUNT • KOUNT

| | |
|---|---|
| **recover** • cover | ROVR • KOVR |
| **recruitment** • accruement | KRAOUMT • KRAO*UMT |
| **red** • read | RED • RAED |
| **red light** • green light, yellow light | R–LT • GR–LT, Y–LT |
| **redundancy** • drunkenness | DRUNZ • DRUNS |
| **reed** • read | RAOED • RAED |
| **reek** • wreak | RAOEK • WRAOEK |
| **reel** • real | RAOEL • RAEL |
| **reference** • in reference, with reference | REFRNS • NREFRNS, WREFRNS |
| **reference** • reverence | REFRNS • REVRNS |
| **reflect** • electric | LEK • LEKT |
| **reflection** • reflects, reflex | LEX • LEKZ, L*EX |
| **reflects** • reflection, reflex | LEKZ • LEX, L*EX |
| **reflex** • reflection, reflects | L*EX • LEX, LEKZ |
| **refrigerate** • refrigerator | FRAIJ • FRIR |
| **refrigerator** • infringe | FRIR • FRIJ |
| **refrigerator** • refrigerate | FRIR • FRAIJ |
| **refuge** • rouge | RAOUJ • ROUJ |
| **refund** • fund | RUND • FUND |
| **regard** • disregard | RAR • DRAR |
| **register** • registrar | REJ • STRAR |
| **registrar** • register | STRAR • REJ |
| **registrar's office** • office | STROFS • OFS |
| **regularity** • rating, regulate | REGT • RAIGT, RAIG |
| **regulate** • rating, regularity | RAIG • RAIGT, REGT |
| **reign** • rain, rein | RA*IN • RAIN, RAEN |
| **reimburse** • incurs | KBURS • KBURZ |
| **rein** • rain, reign | RAEN • RAIN, RA*IN |
| **reiterates** • ritz, writs | RITS • RITSZ, WRITS |
| **reiteration** • rigs | RIGS • RIGZ |
| **reject** • just a second | JEKT • JEK |
| **relate** • interrelate | RELT • SPWERLT |
| **relation** • public relations, relationship | RELGS • PRELGS, HRELGS |
| **relationship** • rape | RAEP • RAIP |
| **relays** • lace, lays, laze, lazy | LAES • LAIS, LA*IS, LAEZ, LAIZ |
| **reliability** • liability | RAOIBLT • LAOIBLT |
| **reliable** • liable | RAOIBL • LAOIBL |
| **remand** • demand | RAMD • MAND |

**remand** • rammed ................................... RAMD • RA*MD *or* RAM/–D

**remember** • recommend ........................ REM • R–M

**renal** • recently, reprehensible .............. RAENL • RAOENL, RENL

**rental**
    recently ........................................... RAOENL
    renal ................................................ RAENL
    rental ............................................... R*ENL
    reprehensible .................................. RENL

**rep** • represent ...................................... R*EP • REP

**repair** • rare, rear ................................... RAIR • RAER, RAOER

**repertoire** • repertory ............................ TWAR • TWOIR

**repertory** • repertoire ............................ TWOIR • TWAR

**replies** • police ...................................... PLIZ • PLIS

**reply** • apply, ply .................................... PLI • PLAOI, PLAO*I

**report** • rapport ..................................... RORT • RARP

**represent** • misrepresent, rep .............. REP • M*EP, R*EP

**representation** • misrepresentation ...... REPGS • MEPGS

**representation** • reputation .................. REPGS • R–PGS

**representative** • retch ........................... REVP • WR*EFP

**republic** • Dominican Republic ............ REB • DREB

**repudiate** • pew ..................................... PAOU • PAO*U

**repulse** • rule ........................................ RUL • RAOUL

**reputation** • representation ................... R–PGS • REPGS

**research** • retch, wretch ....................... REFP • WR*EFP, WREFP

**research** • search .................................. REFP • SEFP

**resent** • recent ...................................... RAOEFNT • RAOENT

**residence** • residents ........................... –RZ • RESZ *or* R–SZ

**residents** • residence ........................... RESZ *or* R–SZ • –RZ

**resolve** • revolve .................................. ROFL • ROVL

**resource** • source ................................ SRORS • SORS

**respect**
    disrespect ...................................... D–RP
    in respect ....................................... NR–P
    respect ........................................... R–P, –RP
    self-respect .................................... S–RP
    with respect .................................... WR–P

**rest** • wrest .......................................... R*ES • WR*ES

**restraining order** • temporary restraining order ... RO *or* STRO • TRO

**retail** • trail ........................................... TRAEL • TRAIL

**retailer** • temporarily ............................ TROIL *or* TROIRL • TRAERL

**retch** • representative, wretch .............. WR*EFP • REVP, WREFP

| | |
|---|---|
| **retch** • research | WR*EFP • REFP |
| **retina** • detached retina | RAENT • DRAENT |
| **retouch** • touch | RUFP • TUFP |
| **retreat** • at any rate, trait | TRA*ET • TRAET, TRAIT |
| **Reuters** • riots | ROIRZ • ROITS |
| **revenge** • vengeance | RENG • VAENG |
| **reverence** • reference, reverends | REVRNS • REFRNS, REVRNDZ |
| **reverence** • revolutionaries | REVRNS • REVNZ |
| **reverend** • reverent | REVRND • REVRNT |
| **reverends** • reverence | REVRNDZ • REVRNS |
| **reverent** • reverend | REVRNT • REVRND |
| **revolutionaries** • reverence | REVNZ • REVRNS |
| **revolve** • resolve | ROVL • ROFL |
| **reward** • award | RAUR • WAURD |
| **rhetoric** • receipt | WRET • RET |
| **rhyme** • rime | RAOIM • RO*IM |
| **rice** • rise, ryes | RAOIS • RAOIZ, RAO*IZ |
| **riddle** • ridiculous | RILD • RIL |
| **ridged** • rigid | R*IJD • RIJD |
| **ridicule** • ridiculous | KAOUL • RIL |
| **ridiculous** • riddle | RIL • RILD |

**rifle**

| | |
|---|---|
| arrival | RAOIVL |
| riffle | RIFL |
| rifle | RAOIFL |
| rival | R–VL |

| | |
|---|---|
| **rigid** • ridged | RIJD • R*IJD |
| **right** • riot, rite, Wright, write | –RT • ROIT, RAOIT, WRAOIT, WRI |
| **rigs** • reiteration | RIGZ • RIGS |
| **rime** • rhyme | RO*IM • RAOIM |
| **ring** • wring, where I think | RING • WRING, WR*ING |
| **riot** • rite | ROIT • RAOIT |
| **riots** • Reuters | ROITS • ROIRZ |
| **rise** • rice, ryes | RAOIZ • RAOIS, RAO*IZ |
| **rite** • right, riot, Wright, write | RAOIT • –RT, ROIT, WRAOIT, WRI |
| **ritz** • reiterates, writs | RITSZ • RITS, WRITS |

**rival**

| | |
|---|---|
| arrival | RAOIVL |
| riffle | RIFL |
| rifle | RAOIFL |
| rival | R–VL |

**road** • rode, rowed .................................................. ROED • RO*ED, ROUD

**roadway** • driveway, expressway ........................... ROI • DROI, KPROI

**roam** • Rome .......................................................... ROEM • RO*EM

**roan** • erroneous ................................................... RO*EN • ROEN

**rode** • road, rowed ................................................. RO*ED • ROED, ROUD

**rodent** • rotten ....................................................... ROEND • ROENT

**role** • roll ............................................................... ROEL • ROL

**roll** • role ............................................................... ROL • ROEL

**Rome** • roam .......................................................... RO*EM • ROEM

**room**
      boardroom ..................................................... BAORM
      checkroom ..................................................... KHAOM
      classroom ...................................................... KLAOM
      courtroom ...................................................... KRAOM
      dressing room ................................................ DRAOM
      emergency room ............................................ MAOM
      examination room .......................................... KPAOM
      front room ...................................................... FRAOM
      jury room ....................................................... JAOM
      mushroom ...................................................... SHRAOM
      press room ..................................................... PRAOM
      rest room ....................................................... STRAOM

**room**
      barroom ......................................................... BR–RM
      bathroom ....................................................... BARM
      bedroom ......................................................... BERM
      boiler room ..................................................... BOIRM
      dining room ..................................................... D–RM
      emergency room ............................................ ERM, M–RM
      family room ..................................................... FAERM
      front room ...................................................... FR–RM
      jury room ....................................................... JURM
      locker room .................................................... LORM
      lunchroom ...................................................... LURM
      master bedroom ............................................. MARM
      operating room .............................................. OERM
      recovery room ............................................... R–RM

**root** • rout, route ................................................... RAOT • ROUT, RAOUT

**rose** • rows ........................................................... ROEZ • ROES

**rot** • wrought ......................................................... ROT • WRAUT

**rote** • wrote .......................................................... ROET • WRO

**rotten** • rodent ...................................................... ROENT • ROEND

**rouge** • refuge ...................................................... ROUJ • RAOUJ

**roughly** • ruffle ...................................................... RUFL • ROIFL

**rout** • root, route ................................................... ROUT • RAOT, RAOUT

**route** • root, rout ................................................... RAOUT • RAOT, ROUT

| | |
|---|---|
| **rowed** • road, rode | ROUD • ROED, RO*ED |
| **rows** • rose | ROES • ROEZ |
| **rubble** • ruble | RUBL • RAOUBL |
| **ruble** • rubble | RAOUBL • RUBL |
| **ruffle** • roughly | ROIFL • RUFL |
| **rugs** • Russian | RUGZ • RUGS |
| **rule** • repulse | RAOUL • RUL |
| **rung** • running | R*UNG • RUNG |
| **rung** • wrung | R*UNG • WR*UNG |
| **Russian** • rugs | RUGS • RUGZ |
| **rye** • wry | RAOI • WRAOI |
| **ryes** • rice, rise | RAO*IZ • RAOIS, RAOIZ |

# S

| | | |
|---|---|---|
| **sac** • sack | SKRA • | SAK |
| **sack** • sac | SAK • | SKRA |
| **sacks** • sacs, sax | SAKZ • | SKRAS, SAX |
| **sacrum** • sake | SKRUM • | SAIK |
| **sacs** • sacks, sax | SKRAS • | SAKZ, SAX |
| **saddle** • salaried | SALD • | SA*LD |
| **safe** • unsafe | SAIF • | SNAIF |
| **safe-deposit box** • safety-deposit box | SD–B • | SDEB |
| **sail** • sale | SAIL • | SAEL |
| **sake** • sacrum | SAIK • | SKRUM |
| **sake** • secretary | SAIK • | SAEK |
| **salaried** • saddle | SA*LD • | SALD |
| **sale** • sail | SAEL • | SAIL |
| **saleswoman** • saleswomen | SWOM • | SWEM |
| **salon** • saloon | SLON • | SLAON |
| **saloon** • salon | SLAON • | SLON |
| **salute** • absolute | SLAOUT • | SLU |
| **salute** • sleuth | SLAOUT • | SLAO*UT |
| **salvage** • savage | SWAJ • | SAVJ |
| **Samaritan** • Good Samaritan | SMAIRN • | GAIRM |

**same**

| | |
|---|---|
| at the same time | TAIMT |
| at the same time as | TAIMTS |
| same as | SAIMS |
| same day | SAIMD |
| same objection | SAIMGS |
| same time | SAIMT |
| same time as | SAIMTS |

| | | |
|---|---|---|
| **sand dune** • dune | SDAON • | DAON |
| **sane** • insane | SAIN • | SNAIN |
| **sane** • scene | SAIN • | SAEN |
| **sanity** • insanity | SANT • | SNANT |
| **sarcastic** • so marked | SARKT • | SARK |
| **sarcoma** • carcinoma, scrotum, so marked | SKOEM • | SKROEM, SKROET, SARK |
| **satisfaction** • dissatisfaction | SAFX • | SDAFX |
| **satisfactory** • dissatisfactory | SAEF • | SDAEF |
| **satisfactory** • unsatisfactory | SAEF • | SNAF |
| **satisfy** • dissatisfy | SAF • | SDAF |

**savage** • salvage ..................................... SAVJ • SWAJ

**saver** • savior, savor ............................... SAIVR • SYOER, SWAOR

**savior** • saver, savor .............................. SYOER • SAIVR, SWAOR

**savor** • saver, savior .............................. SWAOR • SAIVR, SYOER

**sax** • sacs, sacks ..................................... SAX • SKRAS, SAKZ

**scallop** • encyclopedia, scalp ............................. SKLAOP • SKLOP, SKAP

**scalp** • encyclopedia, scallop ............................. SKAP • SKLOP, SKLAOP

**scalp** • scapula ..................................... SKAP • SKLAP

**scandal** • constantly .............................. SKANLD • SKANL

**Scandinavia** • asked and answered, scanned ...... SKAIV • SKARND, SKAND

**scanned** • asked and answered, Scandinavia ...... SKAND • SKARND, SKAIV

**scant** • constant ..................................... SKA*NT *or* SKRANT • SKANT

**scapula** • scalp ..................................... SKLAP • SKAP

**scarce** • scares ..................................... SKAIRS • SKAIRZ

**scarcity** • skaters ................................. SKAIRTS • SKA*IRTS

**scares** • scarce ..................................... SKAIRZ • SKAIRS

**scene** • sane ....................................... SAEN • SAIN

**scene** • seen ....................................... SAEN • SAOEN

**scene of the crime** • crime ................... SKRAOIM • KRAOIM

**scent** • cent, sent ................................. SKRENT • KRENT, SENT

**scents** • cents, sense ............................ SKRENTS • KRENTS, SENS

**school**
|  |  |
|---|---|
| Bible school .................................... | BAOL |
| boarding school ............................... | BRAOL |
| court reporting school ..................... | KRAOL |
| dental school .................................. | DAOL |
| flight school ................................... | FLAOL |
| graduate school .............................. | GRAOL |
| high school ..................................... | HAOL |
| junior high school ........................... | JAOL |
| law school ...................................... | LAOL |
| medical school ................................ | MAOL |
| night school .................................... | NAOL |
| preschool ....................................... | PRAOL |
| private school .................................. | VAOL |
| public school ................................... | PLAOL |
| school ............................................ | SKAOL |
| summer school ................................ | SAOL |
| Sunday school ................................. | SDAOL |
| trade school .................................... | TRAOL |

**school district** • district ......................... SDRIK • DRIK

**school teacher** • teacher ....................... STRAOEFP • TRAOEFP

**science** • signs ..................................... SAOINS • SAOINZ

**sclerosis** • disclose ............... SKLOEZ • SKLOES

**scope** • beyond the scope ................... SKOEP • YOEP

**score** • 64 ............... SKOER • SKO*ER

**scores** • sixty-fours ............... SKOERZ • SKOERS

**scotch** • Scots ............... SKOFP • SKOTS

**Scots** • scotch ............... SKOTS • SKOFP

**scourge** • discourage ............... SKURJ • SKOURJ

**script** • manuscript ............... SKRIPT • SKRIMT

**scrotum** • carcinoma, sarcoma ............... SKROET • SKROEM, SKOEM

**scrunch** • crunch ............... SKRUN • KRUN

**scull** • skull ............... SKRUL • SKUL

**sculpt** • sculptor, sculpture ............... SKUPLT • SKUPT, SKUP

**sculptor** • sculpt, sculpture ............... SKUPT • SKUPLT, SKUP

**sculpture** • sculpt, sculptor ............... SKUP • SKUPLT, SKUPT

**scythe** • cite, sight ............... SYAO*IT • KRAOIT, SAOIT

**sea** • see ............... SAE • SAOE

**sealing** • ceiling ............... SAOELG • KRAOELG

**seam** • seem ............... SAEM • SAOEM

**sear** • seer ............... SAER • SAOER

**search** • research ............... SEFP • REFP

**seas**
    assess ............... SAES
    cease ............... SAOES
    crease ............... KRAOES
    decease ............... DAOES
    seas ............... SA*ES, SAE/–S
    sees ............... SAO*EZ, SAOE/–S
    seize ............... SAOEZ
    southeast ............... SAO*ES

**seat belt** • Celt, kettle ............... KRELT • K*ELT, KELT

**second class** • first class ............... SLAS • FLAS

**second degree** • South Dakota ............... S–D • S*D

**second-degree burn**
    first-degree burn ............... F–BD
    second-degree burn ............... S–BD
    third-degree burn ............... TH–BD, THR–BD

**seconds** • sex ............... SEKZ • SEX

**secret** • secrete ............... SKRET • SKRAO*ET

**secretary** • sake ............... SAEK • SAIK

**secrete** • discrete ............... SKRAO*ET • SKRAOET

**secrete** • secret ............... SKRAO*ET • SKRET

**section**
| | |
|---|---|
| code section | K*X |
| Evidence Code Section | *EX |
| intersection | SPW–X |
| Penal Code Section | P*X |
| section | S–X |
| Vehicle Code Section | V–X |
| violation of section | VIX |

**section** • session, sex ........................................... S–X • SEGS, SEX

**sects** • sex ........................................... SEKTS • SEX

**secure** • obscure ........................................... SKUR • SKAOUR

**security** • obscurity ........................................... SKURT • SKAOURT

**see** • sea ........................................... SAOE • SAE

**seed** • cede ........................................... SAOED • SAED

**seem** • seam ........................................... SAOEM • SAEM

**seen** • scene ........................................... SAOEN • SAEN

**seer** • sear ........................................... SAOER • SAER

**sees**
| | |
|---|---|
| assess | SAES |
| cease | SAOES |
| crease | KRAOES |
| decease | DAOES |
| seas | SA*ES, SAE/–S |
| sees | SAO*EZ, SAOE/–S |
| seize | SAOEZ |
| southeast | SAO*ES |

**segment** • assessment ........................................... SAEMT • SAEFMT

**segregate**
| | |
|---|---|
| grate | GRA*IT |
| great | GRAET |
| instigate | SGAIT |
| integrate | GRAIT |
| segregate | SGRAIT |

**segregation** • instigation ........................................... SGRAIGS • SGAIGS

**segregation** • integration ........................................... SGRAIGS • GRAIGS

**seize**
| | |
|---|---|
| assess | SAES |
| cease | SAOES |
| crease | KRAOES |
| decease | DAOES |
| seas | SA*ES, SAE/–S |
| sees | SAO*EZ, SAOE/–S |
| seize | SAOEZ |
| southeast | SAO*ES |

**self**
| | |
|---|---|
| herself | H*ERS, HERSZ |
| himself | HOIM, HOIMS, HIMS |

| | |
|---|---|
| itself .............................................. | ISZ |
| myself ........................................... | MAOIZ |
| ourself ........................................... | OURZ |
| yourself ......................................... | URZ, *URS |

**self-confidence** • confidence .............................. SK–FD • K–FD

**self-confident** • confident ................................... SK–FT • K–FT

**self-defense** • defense ........................................ SD–FS • D–FS

**self-employed** • employed ................................... SPLOID • PLOID

**self-employment** • employment .......................... SPLOIMT • PLOIMT

**self-esteem** • esteem ........................................... SFAOEM • STAOEM

**self-incriminate** • discriminate ............................. SK–RM *or* SKR–M • SKRIM

**self-incrimination** • discriminate ......................... SK–RMGS *or* SKR–MGS • SKRIMGS

**self-interest** • compound interest, ...................... SFINT • KPINT, KINT, DINT
conflict of interest, disinterest

**self-respect** • disrespect ..................................... S–RP • D–RP

**sell** • cell ................................................................ SEL • KREL

**senator** • snore ..................................................... SNOR • SNOER

**senior** • Sr. ............................................................ S–R • S*R

**senior** • superior ................................................... S–R • SYOR *or* SAOR

**sense** • cents, scents ........................................... SENS • KRENTS, SKRENTS

**sense of purpose** • purpose ................................ SPURP • PURP

**senses** • census ................................................... SENSZ • SKRENS

**sensor** • censor .................................................... SOERN • SNUR

**sent** • cent, scent ................................................. SENT • KRENT, SKRENT

**sentiment** • meant, settlement ............................. SMENT • MENT, ST–MT

**separate property** • community property, ............. SPROT • KPROT, PROT
property

**separation** • expiration ......................................... SPRAIGS • KPRAIGS

**sequence** • consequence, sequins, ..................... SKW–NS • KWENS, SKWINS,
subsequence　　　　　　　　　　　　　　　　　　SKWENS

**sequentially** • subsequently ................................. SKWAOENL • SKWENL

**sequins** • consequence, sequence, ..................... SKWINS • KWENS, SKW–NS,
subsequence　　　　　　　　　　　　　　　　　　SKWENS

**serf** • surf .............................................................. SWEF • SWUF

**serge** • concierge, surge ...................................... S*ERJ • SERJ, SURJ

**serial** • cereal ....................................................... SAOERL • KRAOERL

**series** • serious .................................................... SERZ • SERS

**serious** • series .................................................... SERS • SERZ

**sermon** • summon ................................................ SERM • SMON

**serve** • deserve, preserve .................................... SEFRB • SDEFRB, PREFRB

| | |
|---|---|
| **service** • disservice | S–VS • SD–VS |
| **session** • cession | SEGS • KREGS |
| **session** • section, sex | SEGS • S–X, SEX |
| **settlement** • sentiment | ST–MT • SMENT |
| **seventy-sixes** • suffix | SF*IKS • SFIX |
| **sever** • zephyr | SEVR • ZFER |
| **severity** • subvert, sweater | SWAOERT • SWERT, SWAERT |
| **sew** • so, sow | SOE • SO, SO*U |
| **sewer** • superior | SAOUR • SAOR |
| **sewn** • sound, sown | SAOUN • SOUN, SOEN |

**sex**

| | |
|---|---|
| seconds | SEKZ |
| section | S–X |
| sects | SEKTS |
| session | SEGS |
| sex | SEX |
| successes | S–KZ |

| | |
|---|---|
| **sexual harassment** • harassment | SWARMT • HARMT |
| **sexually** • surveil, swale | SWAEL • SWAIL, SWA*EL |
| **sexual relation** • relation | SWRELGS • RELGS |
| **sharpen** • dishearten | SHAURN • SHARN |
| **sharper than** • dishearten | SHAERN • SHARN |
| **shear** • sheer | SHAER • SHAOER |
| **shed** • she'd | SHED • SH*ED |
| **she'd** • shed | SH*ED • SHED |
| **sheer** • shear | SHAOER • SHAER |
| **she feel** • shelf | SHAOEFL • SHEFL |
| **sheik** • chic | SHAOEK • SHAO*EK |
| **she is** • she's | SHES • SH*ES |
| **shelf** • she feel | SHEFL • SHAOEFL |
| **shelf** • shelve | SHEFL • SHEVL |
| **shell** • she'll | SHEL • SH*EL |
| **she'll** • shell | SH*EL • SHEL |
| **shelve** • shelf | SHEVL • SHEFL |
| **sheriff's office** • office | SHOFS • OFS |
| **she's** • she is | SH*ES • SHES |

**~ship**

| | |
|---|---|
| apprenticeship | PRAEP |
| authorship | THORP, THAORP |
| bipartisanship | BARP, BAURP |
| censorship | SNURP |

conservatorship ............................................. SKEFRP
consulship ...................................................... SKWIP
dealership ...................................................... DLERP
distributorship ............................................... DRIRP
fellowship ...................................................... FLEP
friendship ...................................................... FRIP
governorship .................................................. GORP
guardianship .................................................. GARP
hardship ........................................................ H–RP
internship ...................................................... SPWERP
leadership ..................................................... LERP
lordship ......................................................... LORP
membership ................................................... MEP
ownership ...................................................... OERP
partnership .................................................... PIP
proprietorship ................................................ PRORP
relationship ................................................... RAEP
scholarship .................................................... SKLARP
sole proprietorship ......................................... SPRIP
sportsmanship ............................................... SPORP
township ........................................................ TWIP
trusteeship .................................................... TRUFP
worship ......................................................... WORP

**shoe** • shoo ...................................................... SHAOU • SHAO

**shone** • shown ...................................................... SHOEN • SHOUN

**shoo** • shoe ...................................................... SHAO • SHAOU

**shoot** • chute ...................................................... SHAOT • SHAOUT

**shorthand** • hand ...................................................... SHAND • HAND

**shortwave** • wave ...................................................... SWAEV • WAEV

**should** • shudder ...................................................... SHUD • SH*UD

**show cause** • order to show cause ...................... SHOEK • SHOERK

**shower** • assure ...................................................... SHAUR • SHOUR

**shown** • shone ...................................................... SHOUN • SHOEN

**shred** • sled ...................................................... SHRED • SL*ED

**shriek** • sleek ...................................................... SHRAO*EK • SLAOEK

**shrine** • centerline ...................................................... SHRAO*IN • SLAOIN

**shrink** • slink ...................................................... SHRINK • SLAOENK

**shrug** • slug ...................................................... SH–R *or* SHR*UG • SLUG

**shudder** • insured, should ...................................... SH*UD • SHURD, SHUD

**sic** • sick ...................................................... SWIK • SIK

**sick** • sic ...................................................... SIK • SWIK

**side** • sighed ...................................................... SAOID • SAO*ID

**sides of** • sizes ...................................................... SAOIFS • SAOIFZ

**sidewalk** • walk ...................................................... SWAUK • WAUK

**sidewall** • wall ...................................................... SWAUL • WAUL

| | |
|---|---|
| **sighed** • side | SAO*ID • SAOID |
| **sighs** • size | SAOIS • SAOIZ |
| **sight** • cite, site | SAOIT • KRAOIT, SAO*IT |
| **sight** • scythe | SAOIT • SYAO*IT |
| **sign** • assign, sine | SAOIN • SOIN, SAO*IN |
| **signature** • cigarette | SIG • SGRET *or* S–G |
| **signs** • science | SAOINZ • SAOINS |
| **silence** • excellence | SLENS • KPLENS |
| **silent** • excellent | SLENT • KPLENT |
| **similar** • dissimilar | SIM • SD*IM |
| **similarity** • dissimilarity | SIMT • SDIMT |
| **simulator** • flight simulator | SMAIRT • FLAIRT |
| **since** • sins | SINS • SINZ |
| **sine** • assign, sign | SAO*IN • SOIN, SAOIN |
| **sine** • cosine | SAO*IN • KAO*IN |
| **sing** • zing | SING • ZING |
| **sink** • sync, zinc | SINK • SY–NK, ZINK |
| **sins** • since | SINZ • SINS |
| **Sioux** • sue, Sue | SWAOU • SAOU, SAO*U |
| **sister-in-law** • brother-in-law | SOINL • BROINL |
| **site** • cite, sight | SAO*IT • KRAOIT, SAOIT |
| **sixties** • skis | SKIS • SKAOES |
| **sixty-fours** • scores | SKOERS • SKOERZ |
| **sixty-threes** • psychoses, skis | SKAO*ES • SKAOEZ, SKAOES |
| **size** • sighs | SAOIZ • SAOIS |
| **sizes** • sides of | SAOIFZ • SAOIFS |
| **skaters** • scarcity | SKA*IRTS • SKAIRTS |
| **skeptic** • concept | SKEPT • SKEP |
| **skis** • psychoses, sixties | SKAOES • SKAOEZ, SKIS |
| **skull** • scull | SKUL • SKRUL |
| **slate** • circulate, insulate | SLAET • SL–, SLAIT |
| **slay** • sleigh | SLAI • SLAE |
| **sleaze** • sublease | SLAOEZ • SLAOES |
| **sled** • shred | SL*ED • SHRED |
| **sleek** • shriek | SLAOEK • SHRAO*EK |
| **sleigh** • slay | SLAE • SLAI |
| **sleight** • slight | SLAO*IT • SLAOIT |
| **slew** • shrew, slough | SLAOU • SHRAO, SLOUG |

| | |
|---|---|
| **sliced** • socialized | SLAOIFD • SLOIFD |
| **slight** • sleight | SLAOIT • SLAO*IT |
| **slightly** • slyly | SLAOIL • SLAO*IL |
| **sling** • shrink, slink | SLING • SHRINK, SLAOENK |
| **slink** • shrink | SLAOENK • SHRINK |
| **slough** • slew | SLOUG • SLAOU |
| **slow motion** • motion | SLOEGS • MOEGS |
| **slowness** • cell phones | SLOENS • SLOENZ |
| **slug** • shrug | SLUG • SHR*UG *or* SH–R |
| **slyly** • slightly | SLAO*IL • SLAOIL |
| **smallpox** • chickenpox | SMAUX • KHAUX |
| **snide** • inside | SNAOID • SNAOI |
| **sniffle** • snivel | SNIFL • SNIVL |
| **snivel** • sniffle | SNIVL • SNIFL |
| **snore** • senator | SNOER • SNOR |
| **snowstorm** • storm, thunderstorm | SNORM • STORM, THORM |
| **snuff** • insufficient | SN*UF • SNUF |
| **so** • sew, sow | SO ⸱ SOE, SO*U |
| **soar** • sore, superior | SO*ER • SOER, SAOR |
| **socialized** • sliced | SLOIFD • SLAOIFD |
| **software** • hardware | SWAER • DWAER *or* WHAER |
| **sold** • soled, so he would | SOLD • SO*ELD, SOELD |
| **sole** • soul | SOEL • SOUL |
| **soled** • sold, so he would | SO*ELD • SOLD, SOELD |
| **solemnly swear** • swear | SLAER • SWER |
| **soluble** • insoluble | SOBL • SNOBL |
| **soluble** • solvable | SOBL • SOVBL |
| **solution** • delusion, dissolution | SLAOUGS • DLAOUGS, SDLAOUGS |
| **solvable** • soluble | SOVBL • SOBL |
| **so marked** • sarcastic | SARK • SARKT |
| **some** • sum | SOM • SUM |
| **~some** | |
|     twosome | TWOM |
|     threesome | THREM |
|     foursome | FOURM |
| **some body** • somebody | SOM/BOD • SM–B |
| **somebody like this** • somebody's | SM–BS • SM–BZ |
| **somebody's** • somebody like this | SM–BZ • SM–BS |
| **some more** • more | SMOR • MOR |

**some more** • stepmother ........................................ SMOR • SMOER

**some one** • someone ............................................. SOM/WUN • SWUN

**someone like this** • someone's .......................... SWUNS • SWUNZ

**someone's** • someone like this ............................. SWUNZ • SWUNS

**someplace**
    displace ........................................................... SPLAES
    displays ............................................................. SPLAIZ
    someplace ........................................................ SPLAIS
    splays ................................................................ SPLAEZ

**something like that** • sign language interpreter ... SL–T • S–LT

**some time** • sometime ........................................... SOM/TAOIM • STAOIM

**son** • sun .................................................................. SON • SUN

**so order** • sword .................................................... SORD • SWORD

**soot** • suit ............................................................... SAOT • SAOUT

**sore** • soar .............................................................. SOER • SO*ER

**soul** • sole .............................................................. SOUL • SOEL

**sound** • sewn, sown ............................................... SOUN • SAOUN, SOEN

**soundproof** • bulletproof, waterproof .................... SPRAOF • BLAOF, WRAOF

**source** • resource .................................................. SORS *or* SOURS • SRORS

**source** • sours ....................................................... SORS *or* SOURS • SOURZ

**sours** • source ........................................................ SOURZ • SOURS *or* SORS

**South Carolina** • success ..................................... S*K • S–K

**South Dakota** • second degree ............................. S*D • S–D

**southeast** • sees .................................................... SAO*ES • SAO*EZ *or* SAOE/–S

**sow** • sew, so .......................................................... SO*U • SOE, SO

**sow** • so you ........................................................... SO*U • SOU

**so waive** • waive .................................................... SWAIV • WAIV

**sown** • sewn, sound ................................................ SOEN • SAOUN, SOUN

**sown** • zone ............................................................. SOEN • ZOEN

**so you** • sow ........................................................... SOU • SO*U

**space** • spays ......................................................... SPAIS • SPAIZ

**spacious** • Spanish, spatial .................................... SPAIRB • SPARB, SPAL

**spaciously** • spacious, spatial ............................... SPAIRBL • SPAIRB, SPAL

**spade** • spayed ....................................................... SPAID • SPA*ID

**Spain** • spontaneous .............................................. SPAIN • SPAEN

**Spanish** • spacious, suspicious ............................. SPARB • SPAIRB, SPIRB

**spans** • expanse .................................................... SPANZ • SPANS

**sparkles** • sparsely ................................................ SPARLZ • SPARLS

**spars** • sparse ....................................................... SPARZ • SPARS

---

**sparsely** • sparkles ................................................ SPARLS • SPARLZ

**spatial** • spacious, spaciously ............................. SPAL • SPAIRB, SPAIRBL

**spayed** • spade ..................................................... SPA*ID • SPAID

**spays** • space ........................................................ SPAIZ • SPAIS

**speak about** • speedboat ..................................... SPEB • SPAOEB

**speak about them** • specimen ............................ SPEFM • SPEM

**spear** • disappear ................................................. SPAOER • SPAER

**spec** • inspect, speck ........................................... SP–K • SPEK, SP*EK

**special**
    especially ...................................................... SPAOERBL, EPS
    special .......................................................... SPERB
    specialist....................................................... SPERBT
    speciality....................................................... SPERBLT
    specially........................................................ SPERBL

**specially** • especially ........................................... SPERBL • SPAOERBL *or* EPS

**specimen** • speak about them ............................ SPEM • SPEFM

**specious** • expeditious ........................................ SPAOERB • SPAO*ERB

**speck** • inspect, spec ........................................... SP*EK • SPEK, SP–K

**speckle** • spectacle .............................................. SPEKL • SPAEKT

**specks** • inspection, specs .................................. SP*EKS • SPEX, SP–KS

**spectacle**
    inspect .......................................................... SPEK
    spec .............................................................. SP–K
    speck ............................................................ SPAEK
    speckle ......................................................... SPEKL
    spectacle ...................................................... SPAEKT
    spectacular ................................................... SPLAR

**spectacular** • particular ....................................... SPLAR • PLAR

**speech impaired** • hearing impaired ................... SPIRD • HIRMD

**speech impairment** • hearing impairment ........... SPIRMT • HIRMT

**speech impairment** • speech impediment........... SPIRMT • SPEFMT

**speedboat** • speak about...................................... SPAOEB • SPEB

**speed limit** • limit .................................................. SPLIMT • LIMT

**speedy trial** • trial ................................................. SPRAOIL • TRAOIL

**spell your last name** • spell your name ............... SPLAIM • SPAIM

**spell your name** • spell your last name ............... SPAIM • SPLAIM

**sphere** • atmosphere ............................................ SFAOER • SFAER

**sphincters** • sphinx ............................................... SFINGSZ • SFINGS

**sphinx** • sphincters ............................................... SFINGS • SFINGSZ

**spinal cord** • cord ................................................. SKORD • KORD

**splay** • displace .................................................... SPLAE • SPLAES

**splays**
    displace ........................................ SPLAES
    displays ........................................ SPLAIZ
    someplace ...................................... SPLAIS
    splays ........................................... SPLAEZ

**splendidly** • supplemental ..................... SPLENLD • SPLENL

**splendor** • explore ................................. SPLOR • SPLOER

**spontaneous** • instantaneous ............................ SPAEN • TAENS

**spontaneous** • Spain ................................ SPAEN • SPAIN

**spontaneously** • instantaneously ........................ SPAENL • TAENL

**sporadically** • supportable ..................... SPOERL • SPORL

**spore** • sport, support ........................... SPOER • SPORT, SPOR

**sport** • spore, support .......................... SPORT • SPOER, SPOR

**square footage** • footage ...................... SKWAOJ • FAOJ

**Sr.** • senior .............................................. S*R • S–R

**staid** • stayed........................................ STA*ID • STAID

**stain** • sustain...................................... STAIN • STAEN

**stair** • stare ........................................ STAIR • STAER

**stake** • steak........................................ STAIK • STAEK

**stalactite** • stalagmite ......................... STLAK • STLAM

**stalagmite** • stalactite ........................... STLAM • STLAK

**stale** • steal.......................................... STAIL • STAEL

**stare** • stair ........................................ STAER • STAIR

**starlight** • startle .................................. STARLT • STARL

**starling** • startling ............................. STAURLG • STARLG

**startle** • starlight................................... STARL • STARLT

**startling** • starling ................................. STARLG • STAURLG

**stat** • statistic ................................... STA*T • STAT

**state** • estate ....................................... STAIT • STAET

**state constitution** • restitution ............................ STAO*GS • STAOGS

**State Department** • department ......................... SD–PT • D–PT

**statement of rights** • state of the art ................... STAIRTS • STAIRT

**state of emergency**
    emergency ...................................... M–RJ
    in case of emergency ...................................... KERJ
    in emergency .................................... NERJ
    state of emergency ........................................ STERJ

**state your business** • what is your business ........ STURBS • WHAURBS

**state your full name** • state your name ............... STUFRN • STURN

**state your name** • state your full name ................. STURN • STUFRN

**stationary** • stationery ......................... STAIRN • STAERN

| | |
|---|---|
| **stationery** • stationary | STAERN • STAIRN |
| **statistic** • stat | STAT • STA*T |
| **statue** • stature, statute | STAOUFP • STAUR, STAFP |
| **stature** • statue, statute | STAUR • STAOUFP, STAFP |
| **statute** • statue, stature, statutory | STAFP • STAOUFP, STAUR, STRAFP |
| **statutory** • statute | STRAFP • STAFP |
| **stayed** • staid | STAID • STA*ID |
| **stead** • instead | STAED • STED |
| **steak** • stake | STAEK • STAIK |
| **steal** • stale | STAEL • STAIL |
| **steal** • steel | STAEL • STAOEL |
| **steam** • esteem | STAEM • STAOEM |
| **steel** • steal | STAOEL • STAEL |
| **stenograph** • photograph | SGRAF • FRAF |
| **stenographer** • photographer | SGRAFR • FRAFR |
| **stenographic** • photographic | SGRAFK • FRAFK |
| **stenographically** • photographically | SGRAEFK • FRAEFK |
| **stenography** • photography | SGRAEF • FRAEF |
| **step** • steppe | STEP • ST*EP |
| **stepfather** • father | SFA *or* SFAU • FA *or* FAU |
| **stepfather** • stepmother | STEFR • SMEFR *or* SMOER |
| **stepmother** • mother | SMEFR *or* SMOER • MOER |
| **steppe** • step | ST*EP • STEP |
| **stereo** • stereotype | STER • STERP |
| **stereo** • steroid | STER • STERD |
| **sternal** • external | ST*ERNL • STERNL |
| **steroid** • destroyed | STERD • STROID |
| **steroid** • stereo | STERD • STER |
| **sticker** • stickler | STIRK • STLIK |
| **stickler** • sticker | STLIK • STIRK |
| **stickler** • systolic | STLIK • STLOK |
| **stockholder** • custodial | STOLD • STOELD |
| **stoop** • stupid | STAOP • STAOUP *or* STAOUPD |
| **stooped** • stupid | STAOPD • STAOUPD *or* STAOUP |
| **stop light** • street light, traffic light | ST–LT • STR–LT, TR–LT |
| **store** • story | STOER • STROER |
| **storm** | |
| brainstorm | BRORM |
| snowstorm | SNORM |

| | |
|---|---|
| storm | STORM |
| thunderstorm | THORM |

**story** • store .......... STROER • STOER

**straight** • illustrate, strait .......... STRAIT • STRAET, STRA*IT

**strait** • illustrate, straight .......... STRA*IT • STRAET, STRAIT

**strange** • estrange .......... STRAIJ • STRAEJ

**street light** • stop light, traffic light .......... STR–LT • ST–LT, TR–LT

**stress and trauma** • trauma .......... STRAUM • TRAUM

**stubborn** • subordinate .......... STORN • SBORN

**stubbornness** • intolerance, subordinates .......... STORNS • SPWORNS, SBORNZ

**stupid** • stoop, stooped .......... STAOUPD *or* STAOUP • STAOP, STAOPD

**subcommittee** • committee .......... SKMAOET • KMAOET

**subcontract** • contract .......... SKR–T • KR–T

**subcontractor** • contractor .......... SKR–RT • KR–RT

**subdivide** • divide .......... SDWI • DWI

**subdivision** • division .......... SDWIGS • DWIGS

**subgroup** • group .......... SGRAOUP • GRAOUP

**subhuman** • human .......... SHAOUM • HAOUM

**sublease** • lease .......... SLAOES • LAOES

**sublease** • sleaze .......... SLAOES • SLAOEZ

**sublet** • let .......... SLET • LET

**submerge** • merge .......... SMERJ • MERJ

**submerse** • immerse .......... SMERB • KBERS

**subordinate** • intolerant, stubborn .......... SBORN • SPWORNT, STORN

**subordinates** • intolerance, stubbornness .......... SBORNZ • SPWORNS, STORNS

**subscription** • prescription .......... SKRIGS • PRIPGS

**subsequence** • consequence, sequence, .......... SKWENS • KWENS, SKW–NS,
sequins          SKWINS

**subsequently** • consequently, sequentially .......... SKWENL • KWENL, SKWAOENL

**substantially** • sustain .......... STAENL • STAEN

**subtitle** • title .......... STAOILT • TAOILT

**subtract**

| | |
|---|---|
| detract | DRAK |
| distract | SDRAK |
| extract | STRAK |
| subtract | STRAKT |

**subtraction**

| | |
|---|---|
| detraction | DRAX |
| distraction | SDRAX |
| extraction | STRAX |

| | |
|---|---|
| subtraction | STRAEX |
| **suburb** • superb | SBURB *or* SB–B • SPR–B |
| **subversion** • aversion | SWERGS • WERGS |
| **subvert** • avert | SWERT • WERT |
| **subvert** • severity, sweater | SWERT • SWAOERT, SWAERT |
| **success** • South Carolina | S–K • S*K |
| **successes** • sex | S–KZ • SEX |
| **succor** • sucker | SKROR • SURK |
| **such** • no such | SUFP • NOUFP |
| **sucker** • succor | SURK • SKROR |
| **suddenness** • suns | SUNS • SUNZ |
| **sue** • Sioux, Sue | SAOU • SWAOU, SAO*U |
| **suede** • swayed | SWED • SWAID |
| **suffer** • sulfur | SUFR • SUFRL |
| **suffice** • certifies | FAOIS • SFAOIS |
| **sufficient** • insufficient | SUF • SNUF |
| **sufficiently** • sulfur | SUFL • SUFRL |
| **sufficient proof** • insufficient proof, proof | SAOF • SNAOF, PRAOF |
| **sugar** • suggest | SHUG • SUG |
| **suggest** • sugar | SUG • SHUG |
| **sui juris** • non sui juris | SWAOEJ • NAOEJ |
| **sui juris** • sui generis | SWAOEJ • SWAOEG |
| **suit** • soot, suite | SAOUT • SAOT, SWAET |
| **suite** • soot, suit | SWAET • SAOT, SAOUT |
| **suite** • sweat, sweet | SWAET • SWET, SWAOET |
| **sulfur** • suffer, sufficiently | SUFRL • SUFR, SUFL |
| **sullenness** • absoluteness | SLUNZ • SLUNS |
| **sum** • some, summon | SUM • SOM, SMON |
| **summary** • summery | SMAIR • SMRER |
| **summery** • summary | SMRER • SMAIR |
| **summon** • cinnamon | SMON • SNON |
| **summon** • sermon, sum | SMON • SERM, SUM |
| **sun** • son | SUN • SON |
| **sundae** • Sunday | SDAE • SUND |
| **Sunday** • sundae | SUND • SDAE |
| **suns** • suddenness | SUNZ • SUNS |
| **superb** • suburb | SPR–B • SBURB *or* SB–B |

**superior**
    anterior .......................................... AOR
    exterior .......................................... KPAOR
    inferior ........................................... FAOR
    interior ........................................... NAOR
    posterior ........................................ PAO*R
    superior ......................................... SAOR

**superior** • senior .................................... SYOR *or* SAOR • S–R

**superior** • Superior Court ..................... SYOR • SYORT

**supplemental** • splendidly .................... SPLENL • SPLENLD

**support** • spore, sport ........................... SPOR • SPOER, SPORT

**supportable** • sporadically ................... SPORL • SPOERL

**supposition** • disposition ..................... SPOEGS • SPOGS

**supra** • extra .......................................... SPRA • KPRA

**surcharge** • charge, discharge ............. SKHARJ • KHARJ, DARJ

**sure**
    assure .......................................... SHOUR, SHAO*UR
    ensure .......................................... SNAOUR
    insure ........................................... SHUR
    sure .............................................. SHAOUR

**surely** • surly ....................................... SHAOURL • SAOURL

**sureness** • assurance, insurance ......... SHAOURNS • SHAOURNZ, SHURNS

**surf** • serf .............................................. SWUF • SWEF

**surge** • concierge, serge ....................... SURJ • SERJ, S*ERJ

**surgeon** • certain .................................. SURN • SERN

**surgeon** • plastic surgeon, Surgeon General ........ SURN • PLURN, SURNG

**Surgeon General** • plastic surgeon, surgeon ....... SURNG • PLURN, SURN

**surgery** • plastic surgery ...................... SURG • PLURG

**surmount** • dismount ............................. SMOUN • SMOUNT

**surname** • name .................................... SA*IM *or* SA*EM • NAIM

**surprised** • absurd, surrender ............... SPRAOIFD *or* SURPD • S*URD, SURD

**surrender** • absurd, surprised .............. SURD • S*URD, SUR/–D

**surround** • around ................................. SROUN • ARND

**surveil**
    assail ........................................... SW–L
    sexually ........................................ SWAEL
    surveil .......................................... SWAIL
    swale ........................................... SWA*EL

**survey** • sway ....................................... SWAE • SWAI

**surveyed** • suede, swayed .................... SWAED • SWED, SWAID

**suspends**
    constituency ................................. SWENS
    expense ........................................ SPENS

suspends ......................................................... SWENZ
suspense ........................................................ SPENZ

**suspense** • expense .............................................. SPENZ • SPENS

**suspicious** • spacious, Spanish ............................ SPIRB • SPAIRB, SPARB

**sustain** • stain ......................................................... STAEN • STAIN

**swale**
    assail ............................................................ SW–L
    sexually .......................................................... SWAEL
    surveil ............................................................ SWAIL
    swale .............................................................. SWA*EL

**sway** • survey ......................................................... SWAI • SWAE

**swayed** • suede, surveyed .................................... SWAID • SWED, SWAED

**swear** • solemnly swear ......................................... SWER • SLAER

**sweater** • severity, subvert ..................................... SWAERT • SWAOERT, SWERT

**Sweden** • sweeten ................................................ SWAOE • SWAOEN

**sweet** • suite ........................................................... SWAOET • SWAET

**sweeten** • Sweden ................................................. SWAOEN • SWAOE

**sweetheart** • heart ................................................. SWHART • HART

**swells** • as well as ................................................. SWELZ • SWELS

**swimming pool** • pool ........................................... SMAOL *or* SWAO*L • PAOL

**switch on** • turn on ............................................... SWON • TWON

**sword** • so order .................................................... SWORD • SORD

**symmetry** • cemetery ............................................. SMAOET • KRAEMT

**synapse** • intercepts .............................................. SNEPZ • SNEPS

**sync** • sink, zinc .................................................... SY–NK • SINK, ZINK

**systolic** • stickler ................................................... STLOK • STLIK

# T

| | |
|---|---|
| **tacked** • tact | TAKD • TAKT |
| **tacks** • tax | TAKZ • TAX |
| **tact** • tacked | TAKT • TAKD |
| **tail** • tale | TAIL • TAEL |
| **taillight** • headlight | TAILT • HAELT |
| **take-off** • write off | TAUF • WRAUF |
| **takeover** • carryover | TOEVR • KROEVR |
| **takes** • taxi | TAIKS • TAEX |
| **tale** • tail | TAEL • TAIL |
| **talents** • talons | TAELTS • TLAONS |
| **talk** • talks, toxin | TAUK • TAUKS, TOX |
| **talons** • talents | TLAONS • TAELTS |
| **tame** • team | TAIM • TAEM |
| **tape recorder** • recorder | TROERD • ROERD |
| **tare** • taxpayer, tear *( rip )* | TA*IR • TAIR, TAER |
| **taser** • taxpayers | TAIRZ • TAIRS |
| **taught** • taut, tot | TAUT • TA*UT, TO*T |
| **taut** • taught, tot | TA*UT • TAUT, TO*T |
| **tax** • tacks | TAX • TAKZ |
| **taxi** • takes | TAEX • TAIKS |
| **taxpayer** • tare, tear *( rip )* | TAIR • TA*ER, TAER |
| **taxpayers** • taser | TAIRS • TAIRZ |
| **TDD** • TTY | TAOED • TWAOI |
| **tea** • tee | TAE • TAOE |
| **teacher** • outreach | TRAOEFP • TRAEFP |
| **teacher** • school teacher | TRAOEFP • STRAOEFP |
| **teak** • technique | TAEK • TAOEK *or* NAOEK |
| **team** • tame, teem | TAEM • TAIM, TAOEM |
| **tear** *( rip )* • tare, taxpayer | TAER • TA*IR, TAIR |
| **tear** *( cry )* • tier | TAER • TAOER |
| **teas** • tease, tees | TAES • TAOEZ, TAOES |
| **tech** • technical | TEFP *or* T*EK • TEK |
| **technical** • tech | TEK • T*EK *or* TEFP |
| **technique** • teak | TAOEK *or* NAOEK • TAEK |
| **tee** • tea | TAOE • TAE |
| **teem** • team | TAOEM • TAEM |
| **teenage** • contagious | TAEJ • TAIJ |

**tees** • teas, tease ................................................... TAOES • TAES, TAOEZ

**Telecommunications Device for the Deaf** • ........ TAOEDZ • TAOED
TDD

**teleconference**
    conference ...................................................... K–FRNS
    news conference ............................................ NAOUFRNS
    press conference ............................................ PR–FRNS
    teleconference ................................................ T–FRNS

**teletypewriter** • TTY ............................................. TWOI • TWAOI

**televise** • twice ..................................................... TWAOIZ • TWAOIS

**television** • intuition, tuition .................................... TWIGS • SPWAOUGS, TWAOUGS

**television** • twigs .................................................... TWIGS • TWIGZ

**television set** • TV set .......................................... TWET • TWEVT

**television station** • TV station ............................. TWAIGS • T–VGS

**temp** • temperature ............................................... TEMP *or* T*EM • TEM

**temperature** • temp .............................................. TEM • T*EM *or* TEMP

**temporarily** • retailer, trailer .................................. TRAERL • TROIL *or* TROIRL, TRAIRL

**temporary injunction** • injunction, junction .......... TRUNGS • NUNGS, JUNGS

**temporary restraining order** • restraining order .. TRO • RO *or* STRO

**tempt** • attempt...................................................... TEMT • TAEMT

**tenant** • attendant.................................................. TANT • TAENT

**tends** • tens, tense, tents ...................................... TENDZ • TENZ, TENS, TENTS

**tens** • tends, tense, tents ....................................... TENZ • TENDZ, TENS, TENTS

**tense** • tends, tens, tents ....................................... TENS • TENDZ, TENZ, TENTS

**tension** • attention ................................................. TENGS • TAENGS

**terminal** • material ................................................. TAERL • TERL

**tern** • alternative, turn ........................................... T*ERN • TERN, TURN

**terrain** • train ......................................................... TRAEN • TRAIN

**terrorize** • tries ...................................................... TRAOIZ • TRAOIS

**testate** • intestate .................................................. TWEFT • SPWEFT

**Thai** • thigh, thy ..................................................... THAO*I • THAOI, THOI

**than** • then ............................................................. THAN • THEN

**thankful** • that feel................................................. THAFL • THA*FL

**thank you, your Honor** • your Honor ................... THAURN • URN

**that afternoon** • afternoon ................................... THAFRN • AFRN

**that evening** • evening .......................................... THAENG • AOENG

**that feel** • thankful ................................................ THA*FL • THAFL

**that is correct** • that's correct .............................. THARK • THAERK

**that is right** • that's right ...................................... THART • THA*RT *or* THAERT

**that morning** • morning ........................................ THAORNG • MORNG

| | |
|---|---|
| **that's correct** • that is correct | THAERK • THARK |
| **that's right** • that is right | THAERT *or* THA*RT • THART |
| **the** • they | T– • THE |
| **theatrical** • theatrics | THAOERK • THAOERKS |
| **theatrical** • theoretical | THAOERK • THAOERLT |
| **theatrics** • theatrical | THAOERKS • THAOERK |
| **the first time** • the last time, the whole time | T–FRT • T–LT, T–WT |
| **their** • there, they're | THAIR • THR–, TH*ER |
| **theirs** • there's | THAIRS • THR*S |
| **the last time** • the first time, the whole time | T–LT • T–FRT, T–WT |
| **then** • than | THEN • THAN |
| **the only** • tonal | TONL • TOENL |
| **theoretical** • theatrical | THAOERLT • THAOERK |
| **therapist** • physical therapist | THAERPT • FAERPT |
| **therapy** • physical therapy | THAERP • FAERP |
| **there** • their, they're | THR– • THAIR, TH*ER |
| **there are** • they're | THR–R • TH*ER |
| **there be** • thereby | THR–B • THR*B |
| **thereby** • there be | THR*B • THR–B |
| **there ever** • therefor, therefore | THREVR • THREFR, THR–FR |
| **therefor** • there ever, therefore | THREFR • THREVR, THR–FR |
| **therefore** • there ever, therefor | THR–FR • THREVR, THREFR |
| **there's** • theirs | THR*S • THAIRS |
| **the right** • outright | T–RT • TR–T |
| **these** • thesis | THEZ • THAOEZ |
| **thesis** • these | THAOEZ • THEZ |
| **the whole time** • the first time, the last time | TW–T • T–FRT, T–LT |
| **they** • the | THE • T– |
| **they are** • they're | THER • TH*ER |
| **they'd** • they had | TH*ED • THED |
| **they had** • they'd | THED • TH*ED |
| **they're** • their, there | TH*ER • THAIR, THR– |
| **they're** • there are | TH*ER • THR–R |
| **they're** • they are | TH*ER • THER |
| **thigh** • Thai, thy | THAOI • THAO*I, THOI |
| **thinness** • thins | THINS • THINZ |
| **thins** • thinness | THINZ • THINS |
| **third** • one-third, two-thirds | THIRD • WIRD, TWIRDZ |

**third-degree burn**
first-degree burn ........................................... F–BD
second-degree burn ...................................... S–BD
third-degree burn ......................................... TH–BD, THR–BD

**this afternoon** • afternoon ................................. TH–FRN • AFRN

**this evening** • evening ...................................... THAOENG • AOENG

**this morning** • morning ..................................... THORNG • MORNG

**threw** • through ..................................... THRAOU • THRU

**thrive** • 35 .............................................. THRAOIV • THRAOIF

**throe** • throw ......................................... THRO*E • THROE

**throne** • thrown ..................................... THROEN • THROUN

**through** • threw ..................................... THRU • THRAOU

**throw** • throe ......................................... THROE • THRO*E

**thrown** • throne ..................................... THROUN • THROEN

**thunderstorm** • storm ............................... THORM • STORM

**thy** • Thai, thigh ...................................... THOI • THAO*I, THAOI

**thyme** • thymus ...................................... TAO*IM *or* THAO*IM • THAOIM

**thyme** • time ........................................... TAO*IM *or* THAO*IM • TAOIM

**thymus** • thyme ..................................... THAOIM • TAO*IM *or* THAO*IM

**tic** • tick ................................................ T*IK • TIK

**tick** • tic ................................................ TIK • T*IK

**tidal** • tiled, titled ................................... TAO*ILD *or* TALD • TAOILD, TAOILTD

**tide** • tidy, tied ....................................... TAOID • TOID, TAO*ID

**tidy** • tide, tied ....................................... TOID • TAOID, TAO*ID

**tied** • tide .............................................. TAO*ID • TAOID

**tier** • tear ( *cry* ) ..................................... TAOER • TAER

**tiled** • tidal, titled ................................... TAOILD • TAO*ILD *or* TALD, TAOILTD

**time** • thyme .......................................... TAOIM • TAO*IM *or* THAO*IM

**title** • entitle, subtitle .............................. TAOILT • SPWAOILT, STAOILT

**titled** • tidal, tiled ................................... TAOILTD • TAO*ILD, TAOILD

**to** • too, two .......................................... TO • TAO, TWO

**to a certain extent** • great extent, ........... TAERX • GRAEX, TRAEX
to a great extent

**toad** • toed, towed .................................. TOED • TO*ED, TOUD

**to a great extent** • great extent, .............. TRAEX • GRAEX, TAERX
to a certain extent

**today** • day ........................................... TAI • DAI

**toe** • tow .............................................. TOE • TOU

**toed** • toad, towed .................................. TO*ED • TOED, TOUD

| | |
|---|---|
| **told** • tolled | TOLD • TOELD |
| **tolled** • told | TOELD • TOLD |
| **tomorrow** • to remember | TW– • TORM |
| **tonal** • the only | TOENL • TONL |
| **tonight** • at no time | TONT • TOENT |
| **too** • to, two | TAO • TO, TWO |
| **to remember** • tomorrow | TORM • TW– |
| **torrent** • orientate | TORNT • TOERNT |
| **tot** • taught, taut | TO*T • TAUT, TA*UT |
| **tot** • to the | TO*T • TOT |
| **to the** • tot | TOT • TO*T |
| **to the best of my knowledge** • <br> to the best of your knowledge | TAOIJ • TURJ |
| **to the best of my knowledge** • <br> with my knowledge | TAOIJ • WAOIJ |
| **to the best of your knowledge** • <br> to the best of my knowledge | TURJ • TAOIJ |
| **to the best of your recollection** • Turks | TURKS • TURKZ |
| **tour** • tower | TOUR • TAUR |
| **tow** • toe | TOU • TOE |
| **towed** • toad, toed | TOUD • TOED, TO*ED |
| **tower** • tour | TAUR • TOUR |
| **township** • ship | TWIP • SHIP |
| **toxic** • toxin | TOK • TOX |
| **toxin** • talk, talks | TOX • TAUK, TAUKS |
| **trace** • trays | TRAIS • TRAIZ |
| **track** • tract | TRAK • TRAKT |
| **tracked** • tract | TRAKD • TRAKT |
| **tracker** • tractor | TRARK • TRAOK |
| **tracks** • traction, tracts | TRAKZ • TRAX, TRAKTS |
| **tract** • track, tracked | TRAKT • TRAK, TRAKD |
| **traction** • tracks, tracts | TRAX • TRAKZ, TRAKTS |
| **tractor** • tracker | TRAOK • TRARK |
| **tracts** • tracks, traction | TRAKTS • TRAKZ, TRAX |
| **trademark** • tracker | TRAIRK • TRARK |
| **trade union** • union | TROIN • YOIN |
| **traffic light** • stop light | TR–LT • ST–LT |
| **tragedy** • tragic | TRAJ • TRIJ |
| **tragic** • tragedy | TRIJ • TRAJ |

**trail** • retail .............................................................. TRAIL • TRAEL

**trailer** • temporarily ............................................ TRAIRL • TRAERL

**train** • terrain ...................................................... TRAIN • TRAEN

**trait** • at any rate, retreat ...................................... TRAIT • TRAET, TRA*ET

**trance**
    terrains .......................................................... TRA*ENS, TRAEN/–S
    trains ............................................................... TRAINS
    trance .............................................................. TRAENS
    trans~ ( *prefix* )............................................... TRANS
    transience ....................................................... TRAENZ
    translates ....................................................... TRANZ

**transcribe** • tribute ............................................... TRIB • TRAOUT

**transcript** • script ................................................. TRIPT • SKRIPT

**transfusion** • blood transfusion ........................... TRAOUFGS • BLAOUFGS

**transience** • transients ......................................... TRAENZ • TRAENTS

**transients** • transience ......................................... TRAENTS • TRAENZ

**translates** • trance .............................................. TRANZ • TRAENS

**translucence** • lunacy........................................... LAOUNS • LAOUNZ

**trauma** • stress and trauma ................................. TRAUM • STRAUM

**travel** • attractively................................................ TRAFL • TRAVL

**trays** • trace ........................................................ TRAIZ • TRAIS

**treachery** • trench, outreach ................................ TRAFP • TREFP, TRAEFP

**treatable** • treble .................................................. TRAOEBL • TREBL

**treble** • treatable ................................................. TREBL • TRAOEBL

**trembler** • temblor, tremor..................................... TREB • TEB, TRER

**tremor** • temblor, trembler .................................... TRER • TEB, TREB

**trench** • entrench ................................................. TREFP • NEFP

**trespasses** • triceps ............................................. TREPS • TREPZ

**trial**
    during the course of the trial ........................ DRAOIL
    fair trial .......................................................... FRAOIL
    get a fair trial ................................................ GRAOIL
    mistrial .......................................................... STRAOIL
    pretrial ........................................................... PRAOIL
    speedy trial ................................................... SPRAOIL
    trial ............................................................... TRAOIL

**tribute** • transcribe ............................................... TRAOUT • TRIB

**triceps** • trespasses ............................................ TREPZ • TREPS

**tries** • terrorize.................................................... TRAOIS • TRAOIZ

**trillion** • billion, million .......................................... TR–L • B–L, M–L

**trim** • triple ......................................................... TRIM • TR*IPL

**triple** • trim ......................................................... TR*IPL • TRIM

**troop** • troupe ........................ TRAOP • TRAOUP

**troupe** • troop ........................ TRAOUP • TRAOP

**trustworthiness** • creditworthiness ........................ TWORNS • KWORNS

**trustworthy** • creditworthy ........................ TWO*RT • KWO*RT

**TTY** • TDD ........................ TWAOI • TAOED

**TTY** • teletypewriter ........................ TWAOI • TWOI

**TTY** • typewriter ........................ TWAOI • TWAOIR

**tubal pregnancy** • pregnancy ........................ TRAEG • PRAEG

**tucks** • tux ........................ TUKZ • TUX

**tuition** • intuition ........................ TWAOUGS • SPWAOUGS

**tumor** • brain tumor ........................ TAOURM • BRAOURM

**Turks** • to the best of your recollection ........................ TURKZ • TURKS

**turn** • alternative, tern ........................ TURN • TERN, T*ERN

**turn**
    turn around ........................ TWARN
    turn down ........................ TWOUN
    turn off ........................ TWAUF
    turn on ........................ TWON
    turn out ........................ TWOUT
    turnover ........................ TWOEVR
    turn over ........................ TWOVR

**turn on** • switch on ........................ TWON • SWON

**tux** • tucks, tuxedo ........................ TUX • TUKZ, TWUX

**tuxedo** • tucks, tux ........................ TWUX • TUKZ, TUX

**TV set** • television set ........................ TWEVT • TWET

**TV station** • television station ........................ T–VGS • TWAIGS

**twain** • attain ........................ TWA*IN • TWAIN

**tweeze** • twenty-threes ........................ TWAOEZ • TWAOES

**twenty-threes** • tweeze ........................ TWAOES • TWAOEZ

**twice** • televise ........................ TWAOIS • TWAOIZ

**twit** • at which time, therewith ........................ TWOIT • TWIT, TW*IT

**two** • to, too ........................ TWO • TO, TAO

**two-thirds** • one-third, third ........................ TWIRDZ • WIRD, THIRD

**typewriter** • TTY ........................ TWAOIR • TWAOI

# U

**UCLA** • yuck ............................................................. YUK • Y*UK

**uh** • huh ............................................................ H*U • HU

**uh-huh** ( *yes* ) • uh-uh ( *no* ) ................................... HUP • H*UP

**uh-uh** ( *no* ) • uh-huh ( *yes* ) .................................. H*UP • HUP

**umbrella** • bridle ................................................. BREL • BRELD

**unable**
    able ................................................................. AIBL
    be able ............................................................. BAIBL
    disable ............................................................ DAIBL, SDAIBL
    enable .......................................................... NA*IBL, NABL
    unable ............................................................. NAIBL

**unacceptability** • acceptability ............................ SNEBLT • SEBLT

**unacceptable** • acceptable ................................. SNEBL • SEBL

**unarmed** • armed ................................................. NARMD • ARMD

**unbelievable** • believable ..................................... NEFBL • BLEFBL

**uncertain** • certain ................................................ SNERN • SERN

**uncertainly** • certainly .......................................... SNERNL • SERNL

**uncertainty** • certainty .......................................... SNERNT • SERNT

**uncomfortable** • comfortable .............................. N–FRBL • K–FRBL

**unconstitutional** • constitutional .......................... NAOLGS • KAOLGS

**under** • inner ....................................................... N–R • N*R

**under the** • underwent .......................................... N–RT • NR–T

**under the influence** • drive under the influence ... NUFL • DRUFL

**underwent** • under the .......................................... NR–T • N–RT

**unearth** • inert ...................................................... N*ERT • NERT

**unfortunate** • fortunate ........................................ UFRN • FORNT

**unfortunately** • fortunately ................................... UFRNL • FORNL

**unify** • union, unite ................................................ YAOI • YOIN, YAOUN

**union** • trade union ............................................... YOIN • TROIN

**union** • unify, unite ............................................... YOIN • YAOI, YAOUN

**unite** • unify, union ............................................... YAOUN • YAOI, YOIN

**United States** • U.S., USA .................................... USZ • *US, UZ

**university** • you haven't ........................................ UVRT • UVT

**unjust** • justice, injustice ....................................... N*US • JUS, NUS

**unlawful** • lawful ................................................... NAUFL • LAUF

**unsafe** • safe ....................................................... SNAIF • SAIF

**unsatisfactory** • satisfactory ................................ SNAF • SAEF

**unstable** • stable .................................................. SNAIBL • STAIBL

---

**unusual** • anything unusual ................................. NURB • THURB

**unusual** • none of your business ........................ NURB • NURBS

**unusual** • usual ....................................... NURB • URB

**unusually** • usually ................................. NURBL • URBL

**unwarranted** • warranted ........................ NARNTD • WARNTD

**unwilling** • willing .................................... N–LG • L–G

**update** • date ........................................ PAIT • DAIT

**update** • peat ........................................ PAIT • PAET

**upon** • pawn ........................................... PON • PAUN

**ups and downs** • pounce ................................... POUNZ • POUNS

**urn** • earn, your Honor ........................... *URN • ERN, URN

**us** • U.S., USA ........................................ US • *US, UZ

**USA** • U.S. ........................................... UZ • *US

**use** • Uzi ............................ AOUS *or* AOUZ • AO*UZ

**usual** • unusual ..................................... URB • NURB

**usually** • unusually .................................. URBL • NURBL

**Utah** • U-turn ........................................ *UT • UT

**U-turn** • Utah ........................................ UT • *UT

**Uzi** • use ............................. AO*UZ • AOUS *or* AOUZ

# V

| | |
|---|---|
| **vacation** • elevation | VAIGS • VAEGS |
| **vacation** • vaccination | VAIGS • VAGS |
| **vaccination** • vacation | VAGS • VAIGS |
| **vail** • vale, valley, veil | VA*IL • VA*EL, VAEL, VAIL |
| **vain** • vane, vein, 59 | VAIN • VA*EN, VA*IN, VAEN |
| **vale** • vail, valley, veil | VA*EL • VA*IL, VAEL, VAIL |
| **valley** • vale | VAEL • VA*EL |
| **valuation** • devaluation | VALGS • DWALGS |
| **valuation** • evaluation | VALGS • VAELGS |
| **value** • devalue | VAL • DWAL |
| **vandal** • vandalize | VANL • V–NL |
| **vandalize** • vandal | V–NL • VANL |
| **vane** • vain, vein, 59 | VA*EN • VAIN, VA*IN, VAEN |
| **vans** • advance | VANZ • VANS |
| **variance** • veterinarians | VAIRNS • VAIRNZ |
| **variation** • various | VAIRGS • VAIRB |
| **various** • variation | VAIRB • VAIRGS |
| **various** • vary | VAIRB • VAIR |
| **vary** • various | VAIR • VAIRB |
| **vary** • verify, very | VAIR • VAER, V–R |
| **vase** • fifty-eights | VAIZ • VAIS |
| **VCR** • Vietnamese | VAOES • VAOEZ |
| **vehicles** • vex | VAOEKS • VEX |
| **veil** • vail, vale, valley | VAIL • VA*IL, VA*EL, VAEL |
| **vein** • vain, vane, 59 | VA*IN • VAIN, VA*EN, VAEN |
| **veneration** • invention | VERNGS • VENGS |
| **vengeance** • revenge | VAENG • RENG |
| **ventured** • overburden | VUR/–D *or* V*URD • VURD |
| **verge** • virgin | VERJ • VIRJ |
| **verified** • invader | VAERD • VA*ERD |
| **verify** • vary, very | VAER • VAIR, V–R |
| **Vermont** • have the | V*T • V–T |
| **verse** • versus | VERS • VERZ *or* V–RS |
| **verses** • versus | VERSZ • VERZ *or* V–RS |
| **versus** • verse, verses | VERZ • VERS, VERSZ |
| **versus** • vs. | VERZ *or* V–RS • V–S |

| | |
|---|---|
| **vertebra** • Virginia | VA • VA* |
| **vertical** • veteran | VERL • VERT |
| **very** • vary, verify | V–R • VAIR, VAER |
| **very good** • video game | VAOG • VAOGD |
| **very most** • at the very most, most | VO*S • TO*S, MO*S |
| **very well** • well | VEL • WEL |
| **very young** • young | VUNG • YUNG |
| **veteran** • vertical | VERT • VERL |
| **veteran** • veterinarian | VERT • VAIRN |
| **veterinarian** • veteran | VAIRN • VERT |
| **veterinarians** • variance | VAIRNZ • VAIRNS |
| **vex** • vehicles | VEX • VAOEKS |
| **via** • 53 | VAOEV • VAOE |
| **vial** • vile | VAOIL • VAO*IL |
| **vice** • vise | VAOIS • VAOIZ |
| **vice president** • Mr. Vice President | V–PT • MR–VP |
| **victim** • vim | VIM • V*IM |
| **video game** • very good | VAOGD • VAOG |
| **Vietnamese** • VCR | VAOEZ • VAOES |
| **vigilant** • vigilante | VIJ • VIJT |
| **vigilante** • vigilant | VIJT • VIJ |
| **vile** • vial | VAO*IL • VAOIL |
| **vilification** • violation | VIFLGS • VILGS |
| **vilification** • visualization | VIFLGS • VIRBLGS |
| **vim** • victim | V*IM • VIM |
| **violation** • vilification | VILGS • VIFLGS |
| **viral** • virile | VAOIRL • VIRL |
| **virgin** • verge | VIRJ • VERJ |
| **Virginia** • vertebra | VA* • VA |
| **virile** • viral | VIRL • VAOIRL |
| **vise** • vice | VAOIZ • VAOIS |
| **visibility** • invisibility | VIFBLT • NIFBLT |
| **visible** • invisible | VIFBL • NIFBL |
| **visualization** • vilification | VIRBLGS • VIFLGS |
| **vocalization** • volition | VOELGS • VOLGS |
| **vocalize** • vole | VOEL • VO*EL |
| **vogue** • volunteering | VOEG • VO*EG |
| **voice** • invoices | VOIS • VOIZ |

| | |
|---|---|
| **voile** • volatile | VO\*IL • VOIL |
| **voir dire** • voyeur | V–RD *or* VOIRD • VOIR |
| **volatile** • voile | VOIL • VO\*IL |
| **vole** • vocalize | VO\*EL • VOEL |
| **volition** • vocalization | VOLGS • VOELGS |
| **Volkswagen** • advocates, advocation | VO\*EX • VOEKZ, VOEX |
| **volt-ampere** • ampere | VAEMP • AEMP |
| **voluntary** • volunteer | VO • VOE |
| **voluntary manslaughter** • involuntary manslaughter | VOM • VOIM |
| **volunteer** • voluntary | VOE • VO |
| **volunteering** • vogue | VO\*EG • VOEG |
| **voyeur** • voir dire | VOIR • VOIRD *or* V–RD |
| **vs.** • versus | V–S • V–RS *or* VERZ |

# W

| | |
|---|---|
| **wade** • weighed | WAID • WAED |
| **wag** • wagon | WAG • WHAG |
| **wagon** • wag | WHAG • WAG |

**wail**
| | |
|---|---|
| wail | WAIL |
| whale | WHA*EL |
| what he will | WHAEL |
| what I will | WHAIL |
| wholesale | WAEL |

| | |
|---|---|
| **wails** • Wales, whales | WAILS • WAELS, WHA*ELS |
| **waist** • waste | WA*IS • WA*ES |
| **wait** • weight | WAIT • WAET |
| **waive** • so waive | WAIV • SWAIV |
| **waive** • wave | WAIV • WAEV |
| **waiver** • waver | WAIVR • WAEVR |
| **wake** • weak | WAIK • WAEK |
| **Wales** • wails, whales | WAELS • WAILS, WHA*ELS |
| **walk** • wok | WAUK • WOK |
| **wallet** • Walt | WALT • WAULT |
| **Walt** • wallet | WAULT • WALT |
| **wand** • witness stand | WAUND • WAND |
| **wane** • awaken, Wayne | WAIN • WAEN, WA*IN |
| **want** • wasn't, wont | WANT • WUNT, WAUNT |
| **wanted** • unwanted | WANTD • NANTD |
| **war** • wore | WAR • WOER |
| **ward** • award | WARD • WAURD |
| **ware** • aware, wear, where | WA*ER • WAIR, WAER, WR– |

**warrant**
| | |
|---|---|
| arrest warrant | A*RNT |
| bench warrant | BARNT |
| death warrant | DWARNT |
| search warrant | SWARNT, SW– |
| traffic warrant | TWARNT |
| warrant | WARNT |

| | |
|---|---|
| **warranted** • unwarranted | WARNTD • NARNTD |
| **wart** • water | WAURT • WART |
| **Washington** • away | WA* • WA |
| **wasn't** • want | WUNT • WANT |
| **waste** • waist | WA*ES • WA*IS |
| **water** • one-and-a-quarter, wart | WART • WA*RT, WAURT |

---

| | |
|---|---|
| **waterproof** • bulletproof, soundproof | WRAOF • BLAOF, SPRAOF |
| **wave** • shortwave | WAEV • SWAEV |
| **wave** • waive | WAEV • WAIV |
| **waver** • waiver | WAEVR • WAIVR |
| **wax** • whacks | WAX • WHAKS |
| **way** • away | WAI • WA |
| **way** • weigh, whey | WAI • WAE, WHA*I |
| **Wayne** • awaken, wane | WA*IN • WAEN, WAIN |
| **way, shape or form** • in any way, shape or form | WOFM • NOFM |
| **we** • wee, whee | WE • WAOE, WHAOE |
| **weak** • wake | WAEK • WAIK |
| **weak** • week | WAEK • WAOEK |
| **weaken** • awaken | WAOEN • WAEN |
| **weaken** • wean | WAOEN • WAO*EN |
| **weakened** • weekend | WAOEND • WEND |
| **weal** • we'll, wheel | WAOEL • W*EL, WHAOEL |
| **we also** • wells | WELS • W*ELS |
| **wean** • awaken, weaken | WAO*EN • WAEN, WAOEN |
| **weaned** • weakened | WAO*END • WAOEND |

**weapon**

| | |
|---|---|
| chemical weapon | KWEP |
| dangerous weapon | DWAP |
| deadly weapon | DWEP |
| weapon | WEP |

| | |
|---|---|
| **wear** • ware, where | WAER • WA*ER, WR– |
| **we are** • were, we're | WER • W–R, W*ER |
| **weather** • whether | W*ET • WHR– |
| **weave** • we've | WAOEV • WEV |
| **wed** • we'd | WED • W*ED |
| **we'd** • wed | W*ED • WED |
| **we'd** • weed | W*ED • WAOED |
| **wee** • we, whee | WAOE • WE, WHAOE |
| **weed** • we'd | WAOED • W*ED |
| **weekend** • weakened | WEND • WAOEND |
| **we have** • we've | WEF • WEV |
| **weigh** • way, whey | WAE • WAI, WHA*I |
| **weighed** • wade | WAED • WAID |
| **weight** • wait | WAET • WAIT |
| **weld** • welled, we would | WELD • W–LD, W*ELD |

| | |
|---|---|
| **well** • as well as | WEL • SWELS |
| **well** • very well | WEL • VEL |
| **well** • we'll | WEL • W*EL |
| **we'll** • weal, wheel | W*EL • WAOEL, WHAOEL |
| **we'll** • well | W*EL • WEL |
| **welled** • weld, we would | W–LD • WELD, W*ELD |
| **wells** • we also, Welsh | W*ELS • WELS, WELZ |
| **Welsh** • we also, wells | WELZ • WELS, W*ELS |
| **welt** • wilt | WELT • WILT |
| **wept** • we want | W*EPT • WEPT |
| **were** • we are, we're | W–R • WER, W*ER |
| **we're** • we are, were | W*ER • WER, W–R |
| **wet** • whet | WET • WHET |
| **we've** • weave | WEV • WAOEV |
| **we would** • weld, welled | W*ELD • WELD, W–LD |
| **whacks** • wax | WHAKS • WAX |
| **whale** • wail, wholesale | WHA*EL • WAIL, WAEL |
| **whale** • what he will | WHA*EL • WHAEL |
| **whales** • wails, Wales | WHA*ELS • WAILS, WAELS |
| **whales** • what else | WHA*ELS • WHAELS |
| **what else** • whales | WHAELS • WHA*ELS |
| **what he will** • whale | WHAEL • WHA*EL |
| **what I am** • what time | WHAIM • WHAOIM |
| **what I will** • whale, wholesale | WHAIL • WHA*EL, WAEL |
| **what kind** • whined | WHAOIND • WHAO*IND |
| **what time** • what I am | WHAOIM • WHAIM |
| **whee** • we, wee | WHAOE • WE, WAOE |
| **wheel** • weal, we'll | WHAOEL • WAOEL, W*EL |
| **wheeled** • wield | WHAOELD • WAOELD |
| **when I recalled** • whirled, world | WHIRLD • WH*IRLD, WORLD |
| **where I** • write | WR*I • WRI |
| **wherein** • wren, written | WRIN • WR*EN, WREN |
| **where you think** • wrung | WRUNG • WR*UNG |
| **whet** • wet | WHET • WET |
| **whether** • weather | WHR– • W*ET |
| **whey** • way, weigh | WHA*I • WAI, WAE |
| **which** • Wisconsin | WI • W*I |
| **which** • witch | WI • WIFP |

| | |
|---|---|
| **Whig** • when I go | WH*IG • WHIG |
| **Whig** • wig | WH*IG • WIG |
| **while** • wile | WHAOIL • WAOIL |
| **whine** • wine | WHAOIN • WAOIN |

**whined**

| | |
|---|---|
| what kind | WHAOIND |
| whined | WHAO*IND |
| wind ( *turn* ) | WAOIND |
| wined | WAO*IND |

| | |
|---|---|
| **whirled** • when I recalled, world | WH*IRLD • WHIRLD, WORLD |
| **whistle** • when I feel | WH*IFL • WHIFL |
| **whit** • wit | WHIT • WIT |
| **whither** • wither | WHIRT • WIRT |

**who**

| | |
|---|---|
| who | WHO |
| who is | WHOS |
| who's | WHO*S |
| whose | WHOZ |

| | |
|---|---|
| **whoa** • who he, woe | WHAO • WHOE, WOE |
| **who ever** • whoever | WHO/EVR • WHOEVR |
| **who he** • whoa, woe | WHOE • WHAO, WOE |
| **whole** • hole | WHOEL • HOEL |
| **wholesale** • wail, whale | WAEL • WAIL, WHA*EL |
| **wholly** • holey, holy | WHOIL • HO*EL, HO*IL |
| **whoop** • hoop | WHAOP • HAOP |
| **whore** • abhor, hoar | WHOER • HOER, HAOR |
| **whorled** • who recalled, world | WHO*RLD • WHORLD, WORLD |
| **whose** • who is, who's | WHOZ • WHOS, WHO*S |
| **why** • Wyoming | WAOI • WAO*I |
| **whys** • wise | WAOIS • WAOIZ |
| **widowers** • divorce | DWORZ • DWORS |
| **wield** • wheeled | WAOELD • WHAOELD |
| **wig** • Whig | WIG • WH*IG |
| **wild** • wiled | WAOILD • WAO*ILD |
| **wile** • while | WAOIL • WHAOIL |
| **wiled** • wild | WAO*ILD • WAOILD |
| **willing** • unwilling | L–G • N–LG |
| **will you be** • lumbar | LUB • L*UB |
| **wilt** • welt | WILT • WELT |
| **wince** • wins | WINS • WINZ |

---

wind ( *turn* ) • whined, wined ................................. WAOIND • WHAO*IND, WAO*IND

wine • whine ......................................................... WAOIN • WHAOIN

wined • whined, wind ( *turn* ) ................................... WAO*IND • WHAO*IND, WAOIND

wins • wince ......................................................... WINZ • WINS

Wisconsin • which .................................................. W*I • WI

wise • whys .......................................................... WAOIZ • WAOIS

wit • whit ............................................................. WIT • WHIT

witch • which ........................................................ WIFP • WI

withdraw • draw .................................................... WRAU • DRAU

wither • whither .................................................... WIRT • WHIRT

with my knowledge • ............................................. WAOIJ • TAOIJ
to the best of my knowledge

without foundation
    foundation ....................................................... FOUNGS
    lack of foundation ........................................... LOUNGS
    without foundation .......................................... WOUNGS

with reference • in reference, reference ............... WREFRNS • NREFRNS, REFRNS

witness stand • stand ........................................... WAND • STAND

witness stand • wand ........................................... WAND • WAUND

woe • whoa .......................................................... WOE • WHAO

wok • walk ........................................................... WOK • WAUK

wolf • woof .......................................................... WOFL • WAOF

wolf • would feel .................................................. WOFL • WOUFL

woman • black woman, businesswoman ............... WOM • BLOM, BO*M

woman • women .................................................... WOM • WIM

women • black women, businesswomen .............. WIM • BLIM, B*IM

won • one ............................................................ WON • WUN

wont • want .......................................................... WAUNT • WANT

won't • wont, wouldn't ........................................... WOENT • WAUNT, WONT

wood • would ....................................................... WAOD • WO *or* WOULD

woof • wolf ........................................................... WAOF • WOFL

wore • war, whore ................................................ WOER • WAR, WHOER

workout • out........................................................ WROUT • OUT

world • who recalled, whorled .............................. WORLD • WHORLD, WHO*RLD

worse • averse ..................................................... WORS • WERS

worth less • worthless .......................................... WO*RT/LESZ • WORLS

would • wood........................................................ WO *or* WOULD • WAOD

would feel • wolf .................................................. WOUFL • WOFL

wouldn't • wont, won't .......................................... WONT • WAUNT, WOENT

| | |
|---|---|
| **wrack** • rack | WRAK • RAK |
| **wrap** • rap | WRAP • RAP |
| **wrapped** • rapped, rapt | WRAPD • RAPD, RAPT |
| **wreak** • reek | WRAOEK • RAOEK |
| **wreck** • reck, recognize | WREK • R*EK, REK |
| **wren** • wherein, written | WR*EN • WRIN, WREN |
| **wrest** • rest | WR*ES • R*ES |
| **wretch** • research, retch | WREFP • REFP, WR*EFP |
| **Wright** • write | WRAOIT • WRI |
| **wring** • ring, where I think | WRING • RING, WR*ING |
| **write** • right, rite, Wright | WRI • –RT, RAOIT, WRAOIT |
| **write** • where I | WRI • WR*I |
| **write off** • take-off | WRAUF • TAUF |
| **writ of certiorari** • certiorari | WRAIRB • SHAIRB |
| **writs** • reiterates, ritz | WRITS • RITS, RITSZ |
| **written** • wherein, wren | WREN • WRIN, WR*EN |
| **wrongdoing** • wronged | WROND • WRONGD |
| **wrote** • rote | WRO • ROET |
| **wrought** • rot | WRAUT • ROT |
| **wrung** • rung, running | WR*UNG • R*UNG, RUNG |
| **wrung** • where you think | WR*UNG • WRUNG |
| **wry** • rye | WRAOI • RAOI |
| **Wyoming** • why | WAO*I • WAOI |

# Y

| | | |
|---|---|---|
| **y'all** • yowl, yawl | ..................................................... | YAL • YOUL, YAUL |
| **yam** • Miami | ............................................................ | YA*M • YAM |

**yard**

| | | |
|---|---|---|
| backyard | .......................................................... | BARD |
| barnyard | .......................................................... | BRARD |
| courtyard | ......................................................... | KRORD |
| front yard | .......................................................... | FRARD |
| graveyard | .......................................................... | GRARD |
| square yard | ...................................................... | SKWARD |

| | | |
|---|---|---|
| **yawl** • y'all, yowl | ..................................................... | YAUL • YAL, YOUL |
| **yeah** • yes | .............................................................. | YAE • YE |
| **yearn** • yes, your Honor | ..................................... | YAERN • YERN |
| **yellow light** • green light, red light | ........................ | Y–LT • GR–LT, R–LT |
| **yellow line** • line | ................................................... | YAOIN • LAOIN |
| **yellow zone** • zone | ............................................... | YOEN • ZOEN |
| **yen** • yes, your Honor | .......................................... | Y*EN • YEN *or* YERN |
| **yes, ma'am** • ma'am; no, ma'am | ......................... | YEM • MAM, NAM |
| **yes, ma'am** • yes, sir | .......................................... | YEM • YER |
| **yes, sir** • no, sir | ................................................... | YER • NORS |
| **yesterday afternoon** • afternoon | .......................... | YAFRN • AFRN |
| **yesterday morning** • morning | .............................. | YORNG • MORNG |
| **yes, your Honor** • yen | ......................................... | YEN *or* YERN • Y*EN |
| **yoke** • yolk | ............................................................ | YO*EK • YOEK |
| **yolk** • yoke | ........................................................... | YOEK • YO*EK |
| **you** • ewe | ............................................................. | U • YAOU |
| **you'd** • you had | ..................................................... | *UD • UD |
| **you had** • you'd | ..................................................... | UD • *UD |
| **you'll** • you will | ..................................................... | *UL • UL |
| **you'll** • Yule, yule | ................................................ | *UL • YAOUL, YAO*UL |

**your**

| | | |
|---|---|---|
| your | ................................................................. | UR |
| you're | .............................................................. | *UR |
| yours | ............................................................... | URS |
| yourself | .......................................................... | URZ, *URS |
| yourselves | ...................................................... | URSZ, *URSZ |

| | | |
|---|---|---|
| **your Honor** • his Honor | ......................................... | URN • HIRN |

**your Honor**

| | | |
|---|---|---|
| no, your Honor | ................................................. | NURN |
| objection, your Honor | ...................................... | ORN |
| urn | ................................................................... | *URN |
| yes, your Honor | .............................................. | YEN, YERN |

| | |
|---|---|
| your Honor | URN |
| **yours** • yourself | URS • *URS *or* URSZ |
| **yourself** • yours | URZ *or* *URS • URS |
| **yourself** • yourselves | URZ *or* *URS • URSZ *or* *URSZ |
| **yourselves** • yourself | URSZ *or* *URSZ • URZ *or* *URS |
| **you will** • you'll | UL • *UL |
| **yowl** • y'all, yawl | YOUL • YAL, YAUL |
| **yuck** • UCLA | Y*UK • YUK |
| **Yule** • eulogy, you'll | YAOUL • YAOULG, *UL |

# Z

| | |
|---|---|
| **Zambia** • sample | ZAMP • SAMP |
| **Zambia** • Zimbabwe | ZAMP • ZIMP |
| **zephyr** • sever | ZFER • SEVR |
| **Zimbabwe** • simple | ZIMP • SIMP |
| **Zimbabwe** • Zambia | ZIMP • ZAMP |
| **zinc** • sink, sync | ZINK • SINK, SY–NK |
| **zing** • sing | ZING • SING |
| **zonal** • horizontal, horizontally | ZAUNL • ZONL, ZOENL |
| **zone** • sown | ZOEN • SOEN |
| **zone** • yellow zone | ZOEN • YOEN |

# NUMBERS

| | | |
|---|---|---|
| **9.** • anoint | .......... | NO*INT • NOINT |
| **18** • even | .......... | AO*EN • AOEN |
| **35** • thrive | .......... | THRAOIF • THRAOIV |
| **53** • via | .......... | VAOE • VAOEV |
| **59** • vain, vane, vein | .......... | VAEN • VAIN, VA*EN, VA*IN |
| **60** • ski | .......... | SKI • SKAO*E |
| **63** • ski | .......... | SKAOE • SKAO*E |
| **64** • score | .......... | SKO*ER • SKOER |
| **66** • psychic | .......... | SKIK • SK*IK |
| **69** • skein | .......... | SKAEN • SKAIN |
| **79** • cellophane | .......... | SFAEN • SFAIN |
| **80** • I didn't | .......... | Y*I • YI |
| **82** • I wouldn't | .......... | YAO* • YAO |
| **84** • ore | .......... | YOER • YO*ER |
| **90** • nigh | .......... | NAOI • NAO*I |
| **91** • none, nun | .......... | N*UN • NUN, NAUN |
| **92** • into, knew, new | .......... | NAO* • NAO, NAOU, NU |
| **93** • knee | .......... | NAO*E • NAOE |
| **96** • in this case, nick, Nick | .......... | N*IK • NIK, NIRK, N*IRK |
| **97** • not relevant | .......... | NEF • NEV |
| **98** • anyway, nay, negate, neigh | .......... | NA*I • NAI, NAE, NAIG, NAEG |

| | | |
|---|---|---|
| **$3** • thread | .......... | THR*ED • THRED |
| **$6** • sicked | .......... | SIKD • S*IKD |
| **$10** • tend | .......... | T*END • TEND |
| **$15** • fiend | .......... | FAO*END • FAOEND |
| **$18** • evened | .......... | AO*END • AOEND |
| **$23** • tweed | .......... | TWAO*ED • TWAOED |
| **$35** • thrived | .......... | THRAOIFD • THRAOIVD |
| **$40** • Friday | .......... | FR*ID • FRID |
| **$43** • freed | .......... | FRAO*ED • FRAOED |
| **$48** • afraid, forelady, frayed | .......... | FRA*ID • FRAID, FRAED, FRA*ED |
| **$50** • individual | .......... | V*ID • VID |
| **$51** • have you understood | .......... | V*UND • VUND |
| **$52** • video | .......... | VAO*D • VAOD |
| **$58** • evade | .......... | VA*ID • VAID |

**$60** • skid ............................................................... SK*ID • SKID

**$63** • concede, skied .................................................. SKAO*ED • SKAOED, SKAOE/–D *or* SK*D

**$64** • scored ............................................................ SKO*ERD • SKOERD

**$67** • circumstantial evidence .............................. SKEFD • SKEVD

**$80** • I didn't do ..................................................... Y*ID • YID

**$82** • I wouldn't do ................................................. YAO*D • YAOD

**$93** • knead, kneed, need .......................................... NYAO*ED • NAED, N*ED, NAOED

**$96** • nicked ........................................................... NIKD • NIRKD

**$97** • in evidence ................................................. NEFD • NEVD

# OTHER REALTIME REFERENCE BOOKS

---

## *Brief Encounters (4 ed.)*

The essential reference dictionary for all court reporters, captionists and students. Now contains over 64,000 conflict-free, general-vocabulary steno briefs.

*principal parts of verbs, irregular steno plurals, irregular English plurals, irregular verbs, speaker identification arbitraries, numbers, punctuation, homonyms, special characters*

*BRIEF ENCOUNTERS* ................................. $58.00

---

## *Medical Briefs (2 ed.)*

The definitive medical reference for court reporters and medical transcribers, based on *Stedman's, Dorland's* and *Taber's*, with one-stroke and/or two-stroke conflict-free briefs. Includes a companion volume of prefixes and suffixes listed by both English and steno. Unique and indispensable for complex medical jobs. Now includes 62,000 steno briefs.

*MEDICAL BRIEFS (2-volume set)* ............................... $75.00

---

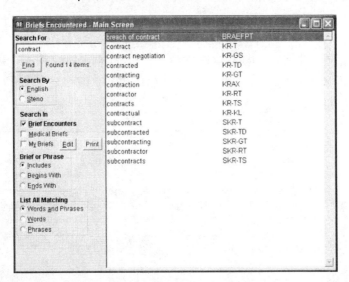